Nutritional Physiology of the Horse

Nutritional Physiology of the Horse

Andrea D Ellis and Julian Hill

NOTTINGHAM
University Press

First published by Nottingham University Press

This reissued original edition published 2023 by 5m Books Ltd www.5mbooks.com

Copyright © AD Ellis and J Hill 2023

All rights reserved. No part of this publication may be reproduced in any material form (including photocopying or storing in any medium by electronic means and whether or not transiently or incidentally to some other use of this publication) without the written permission of the copyright holder except in accordance with the provisions of the Copyright, Designs and Patents Act 1988. Applications for the copyright holder's written permission to reproduce any part of this publication should be addressed to the publishers.

British Library Cataloguing in Publication Data
Nutritional Physiology of the Horse
I Ellis, A.D. II Hill, J.

ISBN   9781789182958

Disclaimer

Every reasonable effort has been made to ensure that the material in this book is true, correct, complete and appropriate at the time of writing. Nevertheless, the publishers and authors do not accept responsibility for any omission or error, or for any injury, damage, loss or financial consequences arising from the use of the book.

Typeset by Nottingham University Press, Nottingham

EU GPSR Authorised Representative
LOGOS EUROPE, 9 rue Nicolas Poussin, 17000, LA ROCHELLE, France
E-mail: Contact@logoseurope.eu

Contents

Introduction		ix
1	**Biological status of horse**	**1**
	Taxonomy and evolutionary status	1
	Biological status	3
2	**Digestive physiology of the horse**	**7**
	Anatomy of the digestive tract	7
	The head tract	9
	Salivary glands	14
	Dental architecture	18
	The oesophagus and stomach	29
	The small intestine	34
	The large intestine	37
	Small colon and rectum	41
3	**Feed chemistry and digestive processes**	**43**
	Carbohydrate and dietary fibre	44
	Non-structural carbohydrates	45
	The processes of digestion and absorption of non-structural carbohydrate	47
	Structural carbohydrate and lignin	52
	Degradation and fermentation of structural polysaccharides and lignin	55
	Protein and other nitrogen compounds in feed	61
	The processes of digestion of proteins and absorption of amino acids and non- protein nitrogen	61
	Fats and oils (lipids)	64
	Digestion and utilisation of fat	65
	Physico-chemical properties of feeds	66
4	**Feed and feed evaluation *in vivo***	**69**
	Feed classification and the feed industry	69
	Hay and silage	70
	Concentrate feeds	74
	Feed characterisation	75
	Characterisation of structural and non-structural carbohydrate in feeds	78
	Characterisation of the nitrogen content of feeds	80
	Characterisation of fats, oils and related compounds	81
	Feed evaluation *in vivo*	82

Table of contents

	Diet presentation and composition	87
	Digesta flow, particle dynamics and degradation	89
	Associative effects	96

5 Energy from feed — **101**

Introduction — 101
Predicting energy value of feed — 101
Which predictors for energy? — 104
Predicting GE and DE — 105
Predicting metabolisable energy — 110
Prediction of Net Energy — 114

6 Energy metabolism — **119**

Maintenance requirements of the horse — 119
Correction for metabolic bodyweight — 120
Requirements for maintenance estimated by the DE and NE systems — 121
Requirement for maintenance predicted *in vivo* — 123
Assessing ME requirements for maintenance — 126
Assessing NE requirements for maintenance — 128
Energy requirements for work — 130
Protein — 139
Carbohydrates and fat — 140
Measuring energy expenditure during work *in vivo* — 146
Comparing recommendations — 156

7 Protein metabolism — **159**

Nitrogen metabolism — 159
Dietary protein — 160
Requirements for maintenance — 172
Requirements for work — 175
Protein requirements for growth — 177

8 Mineral nutrition — **179**

Calcium and phosphorus — 180
Magnesium — 194
Sodium, potassium and chloride — 198
Sulphur — 205
Trace elements — 209
Copper — 210
Zinc — 218

Manganese	224
Molybdenum	226
Iron	227
Iodine	231
Fluorine	234
Selenium	235
Cobalt	238
Chromium	239
9 Vitamins	**241**
Fat-soluble vitamins	241
Water-soluble vitamins	246
10 Feeding practice in relation to health and welfare	**253**
Feeding in practice	253
Welfare and health	255
References	259
Index	357

Introduction

The estimated global population of domesticated horses is 58.2 million (FAOSTAT Database, 2001). A further 13.5m mules and 42.8m asses are also reported, suggesting 114.5m domesticated *Equus*. In the United Kingdom it was estimated that 900,000 horses and ponies are owned by approximately 2% of households (BETA National Equestrian Survey, 1999). The professional sector of the equine industry in the UK is about 120,000 horses. At least £1.3bn is spent each year on horse management (an average of £1500 per horse per annum) of which feeding costs are approximately 20%. The nutrition sector may represent £ 260m per annum of the equine industry. A good grasp of basic and advanced nutrition is therefore essential for the owner of the horse, the veterinarian and the feed manufacturer.

Nutrition is an essential part of the daily management of the horse. It affects the health, welfare and performance of the animal. The horse has evolved as a "plant eating fibre digestion machine" that spends up to 60% to 80% of time foraging. The digestive system reflects this behavioural process. Xenophon, the ancient Greek military horseman wrote "If you wish to have a horse that is excitable, a measure of oats per day will help". The advances in equine nutrition have improved our knowledge of how to optimise the feeding of the animal under different physiological challenges, but we must not lose sight of the interaction between nutrition and behaviour.

Any text on the nutrition of the horse has to address the dynamic interaction between the physiology of the animal and the mechanisms of supply of nutrients. We acknowledge that there is a balance that needs to be maintained between feeds available to the animal, the biology of digestion and feed conversion, and the requirements of the horse. It is therefore our intention to examine these three areas in considerable depth, drawing on a biological approach to solving problems associated with nutrition as well as an applied approach for the equine industry. The book aims to "blend" theoretical knowledge and practical feed management by creating an understanding of the physiological processes which form the basis for practical rationing.

Andrea D Ellis
Julian Hill
May 2005

1
Biological status of horse

Taxonomy and evolutionary status

The horse is classified in the Order Perissodactyla (odd-toed ungulates) and thus related taxonomically to tapirs and rhinoceros. Groves and Ryder (2000) outlined a classification of the Perissodactyla (Table 1.1) suggesting the family Equidae comprised at least 14 stem genera of which *Equus* being the only genus to include all living equids.

In contrast, the Artiodactyla (ungulates) are divided into four families comprising about 155 species. There is still considerable debate over the issue of membership of the genus *Equus*. The controversy is based on the argument that the genus either includes all living species (Bennett, 1980; Groves and Mazák, 1967), or a further subdivision is necessary. Recently, it has been suggested that the genus is subdivided into three subgenera (Groves and Ryder, 2000; George and Ryder, 1986). The analysis reported by Groves and Ryder (2000) provides greater clarity to the debate. The analysis of anatomical morphology (supported by studies of mitochondrial DNA) of all living representatives of the genus *Equus* separated the current classification to three subgenera (subgenus *Equus* – horses; *Asinus* – ass, onager and kiang; *Hippotigris* – zebras).

The subgenus *Equus* is distinct morphologically from the subgenus *Asinus*. The anatomical features that lead to the separation are the presence of 'cranial broadening complex', the degree of cranial flexion (a reduction), the relationships of the mastoid, paramastoid and mastoid temporal, and the orientation of the post-orbital bar in relation to the horizontal plane (Bennett, 1980). This separation, however, is not able to separate horses from zebra and further subdivision between the horse and zebra is necessary. The characteristics suggested by Groves and Ryder (2000) were the state of the frontal doming of the skull, hypostylid on the third deciduous molar and the length of the muzzle (greater than 50% of palate length in the zebra).

Table 1.1 Classification of the Perissodactyla.

Order Perissodactyla	
Suborder Titanotheriomorpha – brontheres	
Suborder Hippomorpha	
Superfamily	Pachynolophoidea
Superfamily	Equioidea
Family	Palaeotheriidae
Family	Equidae
Genus	*Cymbalophus*
	Orohippus
	Epihippus
	Mesohippus
	Miohippus
Subfamily Anchitheriinae	
Subfamily Equinae	
Genus	*Kalobatippus*
	Archaeohippus
	Parahippus
Tribe	Protohippini
Tribe	Hipparionini
Tribe	Equini
Genus	*Dinohippus*
	Hippidion
	Onohippidion
	Astrohippus
	Pliohippus
	Equus
Suborder Moropomorpha	
Parvorder	Ancylopoda – chalicotheres
Parvorder	Ceratomorpha – tapirs and rhinoceros

It is not the aim in this text to discuss in any depth the subgenus *Equus* and the reader is directed to specific reviews, for instance, Boyd and Houpt (1993), Prothero and Schoch (1989), Meadow and Uerpmann (1986). It is, however, important to consider the similarities and differences in digestive physiology, evolutionary adaptation of ethology and their influences on domestication between the Perissodactyla and the Artiodactyla (especially the Bovidae).

Biological status

Herbivores have been classified either according to their preferences during feeding or according to their ability to ingest and process feeds containing varying levels of cellulose and dietary fibre (Hoffman, 1989; Langer, 1988; van Soest, 1994; Table 1.2).

Table 1.2 Classification of herbivores according to feeding strategy (after van Soest, 1994).

Class	Ruminants	Non ruminants
Concentrate selectors		
Fruits and foliage selectors	Duikers and Sunis	Rabbits
Tree and shrub browsers	Deer, Giraffes and Kudus	Sumatran and Black Rhinoceros
Intermediate feeders		
Prefer forbs or browsing	Moose, Goats and Elands	
Prefer grass	Sheep and Impalas	
Bulk and roughage eaters		
Fresh grass grazers	Buffaloes, Cattle, Gnus, Kobs and Oribis	Hippopotamus
Roughage grazers	Hartebeests and Topis	Horses, Elephants, White Rhinoceros, Indian Rhinoceros and Zebra
Dry region grazers	Oryxes, Camels, Roan and Sables antelopes	Kangaroos

Horses are classified as 'bulk and roughage eaters' feeding predominately on leaves, buds, plant stems and considerable amounts of grass (Hubbard and Hanson, 1976; Salter and Hudson, 1979; Waring, 1983; Janis and Ehrhardt, 1988; Hoffman, 1989). Starch rich components of plants play only a minor role in the nutrition of wild Equidae. The classification was modified to consider grazing and the horse is therefore considered as a non-ruminant 'roughage grazer'. However within the genus *Equus*, the Zebra (*Hippotigris*) shows a degree of variation in its method of acquisition of feed, being more selective in its process of feeding than the horse. These classifications are however relatively ill-defined and an animal represented in one class may well have attributes during feeding which would allow its inclusion into another class. A classic example would be the horse when it is housed and fed rations that contain very high levels of concentrate feed – e.g. racehorses during training could be included in an "intermediate" feeding class (Halnan and Garner, 1953; Morrison, 1950).

The possible sequence of herbivore evolution played an important role in the development of strategies for feed acquisition by horses and related species. The appearance of the ruminants and tylopods (camels) in the Eocene represented a specialisation in the Artiodactyla. The ruminants were thought to possess the competitive advantage of pre-gastric fermentation compared to the Perissodactyla (Duncan et al., 1990; van Wieren, 1996). This adaptation in the ruminants was probably a mechanism to detoxicify secondary plant compounds (Janis, 1989; Stebbins, 1981; Hofmann, 1973). The Perissodactyla, even though they are competitive grazers, had a lower digestive capacity. This potential lack of competitiveness in digestive physiology, forced the Perissodactyla to develop unique processes in grazing behaviour independent to the ruminants (Langer, 1988; Voorhies and Thomasson, 1979). These strategies allowed the Perissodactyla to achieve dominance in the Eocene and Oligocene, but declined in the Pleistocene, being replaced by the ruminants (Cifelli, 1981). It is therefore understandable why the Perissodactyla are represented by a few taxa. Arguably the only major successful genus in the Perissodactyla is *Equus*. The remainder of the genera still extant are relatively rare. Concurrently with the development of behavioural strategies to maintain intake of grazed forage, the elaboration of the hind-gut fermentation system in Equinae is important.

The sequence of digestion in the Equinae has to be considered in relation to the utilisation of dietary fibre. Dietary fibre sources must be degraded by gut microorganisms in the gastrointestinal tract before utilisation of nutrients as the animal does not possess cellulases or hemicellulases. The post gastric location of the main centre of fermentation in the horse means that available, soluble carbohydrate and protein can be absorbed by the animal, without potential loss of substrates associated with microbial processes (Leek, 1993; Frape, 1998; Vulink et al., 2001). In relation to ruminants, the horses have evolved to utilise forages of lower nutrient content (Foose, 1982; Prins and Beekman, 1989; Duncan et al., 1990). The gastrointestinal tract must not be viewed as a series of "bags" linked together with "pipes". Many areas of the gastrointestinal tract are sacculated. Sacculation may act to slow digesta flow, leading to a more efficient extraction of nutrients. Moir (1968) and Langer (1988) suggested the stomach of the horse is relatively simple in its anatomical form. However, recent observations on the complexity of the stomach of the horse (Morris *et al.*, 2003), from a digestion point of view, may mean these earlier observations have to be reviewed. The role of pre-gastric fermentation without rumination is well understood in many non-ruminant herbivores (for instance kangaroos (Hume, 1982); hippopotamus (Moir, 1968) and several species of monkey (Stevens, 1988; Bauchop and Martucci, 1968).

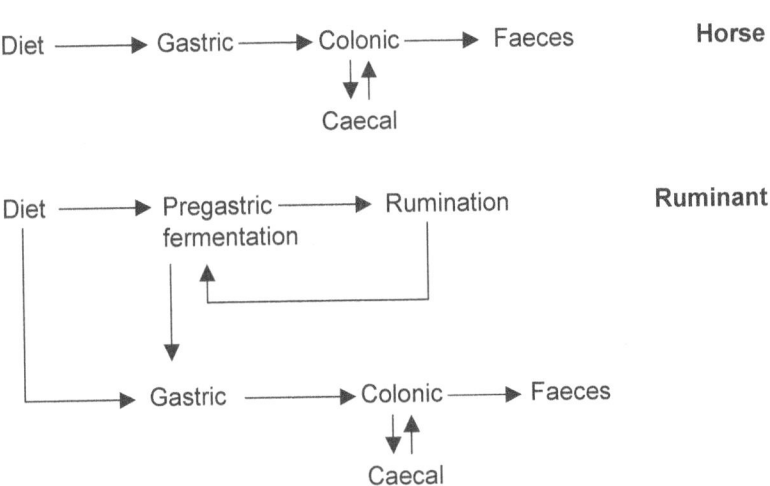

Figure 1.1 Sequence of digestion in horses and ruminants (after van Soest, 1995).

The sequence of digestion in the horse has traditionally focussed on the colon and caecum as the main sites of fermentation. Much of the detail of microbial physiology and ecology of the hind-gut system of the horse has been drawn from rumen microbial studies. In light of recent advances in our understanding of the equine hind gut, the use of ruminant based studies for modelling the functionality of the microbial processes has to be re-appraised.

Horses are social, non-territorial nomadic animals, which live generally in hierarchical groups. They are prey animals and flight is their primary reaction to danger. Horses are selective grazers and socially synchronised grazing behaviour occurs both during the day and at night. Wild horses spend an average of 12 to 16 hours each day grazing in bouts of 2 to 3 hours, interspersed with resting behaviour and social interaction (Ralston, 1984). Generally periods of fasting can last for approximately 3 to 4 hours consecutively, with the longest periods recorded between 0100 hours and 0600 hours. When water is close at hand, horses will drink regularly during the day and night, depending on environmental factors. Despite domestication, there is little effect on cognitive or motivational ethology of the animal.

Domestication of the horse has, however, reduced the feeding time of the animal to about 6 to 10 hours each day when it is managed in the stable environment. Furthermore, the exploitation of the horse for leisure and work purposes has lead to the introduction of potentially high levels of starch and protein to the diet (Tinker *et al.*, 1997). These diets may lead to the development of stereotypic behaviour (crib-biting (Nicol *et al.*, 2002), weaving, wind-sucking (McGreevy *et al.*, 1995) and coprophagy) and compromised welfare (Kennedy and Hill, 2000). It is therefore important that animal behaviour is studied alongside digestive physiology (Davidson and Harris, 2002). Survival of a species is partially facilitated through adaptation of senses, cognitive processes, physiological capability and species-specific behaviour to environmental factors. Cognitive, emotional and motivational processes are behavioural and/or physiological strategies in response to stressful or changing situations within an environment enhancing the chances of survival of the animal. As a non-ruminant herbivore with a reduced capacity for extraction of nutrients from the diet, the horse has a high voluntary feed intake. This makes the horse more suited to environments with low nutrient forages. It is not the task of this book to assess in detail the ethological evolution of the horse, but it will consider behavioural aspects related to perception of feed, choice of feed and voluntary feed intake.

2

Digestive physiology of the horse

This chapter describes the anatomy of the digestive tract of the horse. Many text books have been written on the subject. However, we attempt to incorporate information relevant on anatomy as well as digestive physiology. The reason for the inclusion of the chapter is to reiterate the point that animal nutrition is a dynamic study that requires a reasonably detailed understanding of the gastrointestinal tract as well as the ability to apply this knowledge for practical formulation of rations optimised for animal performance. It is also essential to understand that the process of eating of a feed by any animal cannot be described purely on the basis of digestive and metabolic characteristics.

Anatomy of the digestive tract

The digestive tract of the horse is multi-compartmental. The "fore gut" including the stomach and small intestines (duodenum, jejunum, ileum) is relatively small in volume and its main functions are the processing and transport of soluble or easily degradable nutrients, for example, carbohydrates (stomach and small intestine), fatty acids (small intestine) and amino acids, to sites of uptake and hence entry to metabolism. The large intestine ("hind gut" including the caecum and colon) accounts for the majority of the volume of the gut and is the major site of microbial fermentation and absorption of products of fermentation (Table 2.1 and Figure 2.1).

Compartmentation of the "fore-gut" is relatively simple being based on differentiation of tissue type between sites of enzyme secretion and sites of nutrient absorption. The physical compartmentation is limited. However, the compartmentation in the hind gut is more complex. Unlike the physical separation of sites of fermentation in ruminants, the large

Nutritional Physiology of the Horse

intestine of the horse demonstrates both physical and temporal compartmentation. A temporal compartment is one where digesta can remain for a period of time longer than expected but is not separated physically from the rest of the digestive tract.

Table 2.1 Volume in litres and proportion of total digestive tract length (%) for pigs, horses and cattle.

	Total digestive tract Volume	Stomach Volume	%	Small intestine Volume	%	Caecum Volume	%	Colon and rectum Volume	%
Pig	30	9	30	10	33	2	7	9	30
Horse	230	15	7	70	30	30	13	115	50
Cattle	330	230	70	65	20	10	3	25	7

(*after* Wolter, 1984)

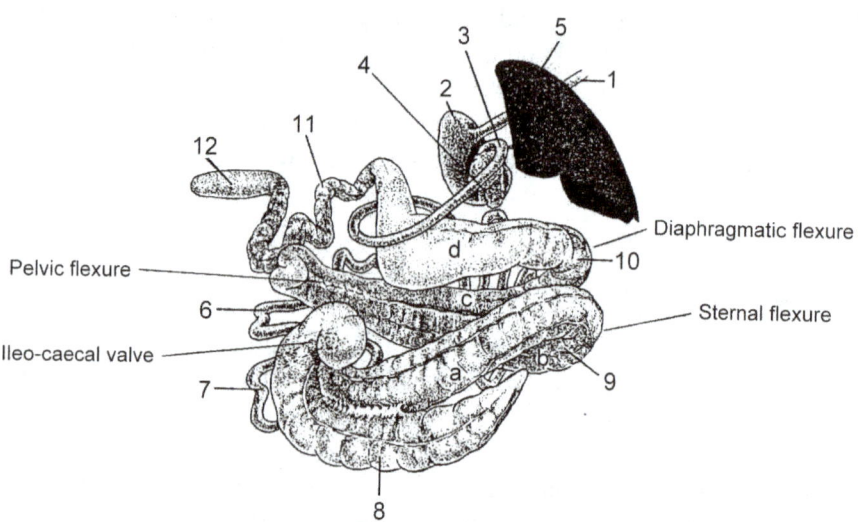

Figure 2.1 Digestive tract of the horse.
1 - Oesophagus, 2 - Stomach, 3 - Pancreas, 5 - Liver, 6 - Jejunum, 7 - Ileum, 8 - Caecum, 9 - Ventral Colon (a) right, (b) left, 10 - Dorsal Colon (c) left, (d) right, 11 - Small Colon, 12 - Rectum (adapted from Bo Furugren in Palmgren Karlsson, 2001 and Frape, 1998).

For instance, the caecum could be classified from an anatomical point of view as a physical compartment, similar to that observed in the ruminant digestive tract. However, in the large colon there are temporal compartments (sacculation). Within each compartment, muscular contractions of the wall of the gastrointestinal tract aid the mixing of

Digestive physiology of the horse

digesta and the different compartments are separated partially by a series of "valves" or "tight passages" along the curvature of the large intestine. For instance, the caecal-ventral colonic valve prevents retrograde flow of digesta in the large right ventral colon; a tight pelvic flexure separates the ventral colon from the left dorsal colon thus altering digesta flow. The wider diaphragmatic flexure into the right dorsal colon terminates into the narrow tube of the small colon leading to the rectum, limiting the rate of flow of digesta (Table 2.2).

Table 2.2 Digesta weight (kg), moisture content (g/kg), partial digestibility coefficients (g/kg) of pelleted (P) and extruded (E) concentrate feeds offered to horses (after Wolter and Caarbouni, 1979).

Section	Feed form	Weight (kg)[+]	Moisture content (g/kg)	Partial digestibility of DM (g/kg)	Partial digestibility of CP (g/kg)	pH	Lactate (g/l)
Stomach	P	2.400	694.5	104	473	5.21	2.02
	E		692.9	118	429	5.03	2.87
1st section of jejeno-ileum	P	0.131	891.3	-163	561	6.72	2.02
	E		867.4	-56	819	6.63	1.72
2nd section of jejeno-ileum	P	0.567	907.3	-30	806	6.87	1.29
	E		914.5	-3	879	6.79	1.89
3rd section of jejeno-ileum	P	0.826	919.1	-12	898	7.02	1.16
	E		909.0	3	882	6.94	0
Caecum	P	1.526	913.1	214	951	6.44	0
	E		884.3	193	930	6.50	0
Colon – ventral	P	2.296	851.0	360	965	6.38	0
	E		838.3	287	951	6.58	0
Colon – dorsal	P	2.272	814.4	382	965	6.23	0
	E		812.4	378	954	6.40	0
Faecal	P		706.4	485	970		0
	E		700.2	469	953		0

[+] digesta weight only recorded as mean weight of all animals offered pelleted and extruded diets.

The head tract

The inclusion of the mouth cavity and gullet within the description of the digestive tract ("head-tract" or Kopfdarm) is necessary to understand the processes of orosensory selection of feeds, voluntary intake and comminution of food. The inclusion of the nasal cavity is also necessary in the discussion when considering the important role of olfaction (distance chemo-reception) in the acquisition of forage during grazing. For a feed to be eaten it has to be recognised as edible and therefore the roles of touch, taste, sight and smell have to be considered when studying feeding behaviour of horses and ruminants.

The differences in the anatomy of the lips, teeth and nasal cavities of the ruminants and equids have led to distinct differences in the processes of acquiring feed dry matter (DM). In general, ruminants and equids use their lips and/or tongue to take food into the mouth. Horses however, unlike ruminants, have upper incisors that are used to cut the feed when being taken into the mouth. The mouth is divided into two parts; the *vestibulum oris* and the *cavum oris proprium*. The *vestibulum oris* is the space external to the teeth and alveolar processes and enclosed by the lips and cheeks. The volume of the *vestibulum oris* is small when the animal is at rest. However, expansion of the space external to the *cavum oris proprium* occurs when the animal is feeding. Even at full expansion during feeding, the *cavum oris* of the horse is still considerably smaller in volume than that of the cow.

The lips (*labia oris*) are muscular with external surfaces covered with skin and long tactile hairs in addition to ordinary fine hairs. The lips are relatively large but mobile and assist the horse to pick up and separate very small objects (e.g. concentrate pellets; Harris, 1997). Many genera of the Artiodactyla have thin lips that possess a greater or lesser degree of prehensile activity, while the cow has thick lips that are relatively immobile. The long tactile hairs on the muzzle of the horse may be important in the process of grazing (Naujeck *et al.*, 2005), especially the ability of the horse to graze to short sward heights (below 5 cm). The *cavum oris proprium* is surrounded by the hard and soft palates, the dental architecture, the tongue (*lingua*) and the floor of the mouth. The length of the soft palate and its contact with the epiglottis leads to an absence of mouth breathing under normal conditions. Similarly, the process of oesophageal backflow due to extreme pressure in the stomach leads to the ingesta escaping through the nasal cavity and not directly via the buccal cavity.

Digestive physiology of the horse

The tongue of the horse is supported by a 'sling' formed by the mylo-hyoid muscles and is attached to the hyoid bone, soft palate and pharynx. Four types of papillae are found on the tongue surface; filiform, fungiform, vallate and foliate. Taste buds are located on all types of papillae with the exception of the filiform type. Three lingual muscle groups are located in the tongue and mouth cavity to allow protrusion (*genio-glossus*), retraction of the tongue (*genio-glossus, stylo-glossus and hyo-glossus*), movement of the tongue side to side (*stylo-glossus*) and depression of the tongue (*hyo-glossus*). The associated musculature of the tongue is important in the manipulation of feed in the mouth cavity but there are no modified papillae on the surface of the tongue that assist the gathering or manipulation of herbage during grazing. The role of the tongue in the process of eating is therefore relatively minor in the horse. However, it is the major organ of prehension in the cow but not in the sheep. The tongue of the cow has many horny filiform and conical papillae that possess sharp points directed backwards into the mouth. These modified papillae are numerous at the tip of the tongue leading to a "rasp" like surface that is extremely efficient in manipulating herbage during grazing. The incidence of modified papillae on the end of the tongue of the sheep is low and therefore there is a clear anatomical difference leading to a difference in prehension between the two species of ruminant. During eating, the horse grinds the feed with teeth and a bolus is formed towards the back of the mouth. The bolus migrates along the surface of the tongue to the soft palate and is then swallowed. The high hypsodonty index (crown depth) and high muzzle width index in horses has been suggested by several authors to lead to a greater efficiency in chewing of feeds compared with ruminants (Janis and Ehrhardt, 1988; van Soest, 1994; Frape 1998).

The nasal cavity (*cavum nasi*) of the horse extends through the upper part of the face. The floor of the cavity is the palate bones and the soft palate. The site of Jacobson's organ, the vomeronasal organ, is in the anterior part of the nasal cavity in the furrows either side of the medial groove locating the cartilage septum. The vomeronasal organ is thought to supplement the olfactory system, for instance in horses it may play a part in oestrus seeking. The gross anatomy of the vomeronasal organ of the ruminants is similar to that of horses.

The role of taste (oral chemoreception) during the process of ingestion of feeds by horses has been investigated by several authors (for example Cairns et al., 2002; Hill, 2002; Randall et al., 1978). Equids can be very sensitive to the inclusion of novel feeds in the diet. The sensitivity to the novel feed or compound may be a taste-aversion response or a neophobic response (Launchbaugh, 1995). Compounds with acidic or bitter tastes (for example acetic acid or quinine) were rejected by horses as solutions but when added to solid food, higher concentrations of the compounds were tolerated (Randall *et al.*, 1978). Similar observations have been made in ruminants offered various adulterants to diets (e.g. sheep; Provenza *et al.*, 1998 and cattle, Strojan and Phillips, 2002). Furthermore, Cairns *et al.* (2002) demonstrated that horses can associate differences in flavour (garlic and mint flavours) and texture in relation to nutrient (digestible energy) density. Limited studies have been conducted to investigate the impact of texture on the processes of intake. For instance, the rate of intake by horses offered soaked hay declines by 17% compared to dry hay suggesting that the process of soaking the hay has modified its fracture properties (Hill, *unpublished data*).

The processes of palatability are poorly understood in horses. The sensory perception of a feed by an animal and the acceptability of a new feedstuff can only be expressed in terms of 'apparent palatability' due to the subjectivity of such an assessment (Greenhalgh, 1982). Palatability can be summarised as the overall sensory perception of a feed by the animal (appearance, taste, smell, temperature, texture and consistency). However, this definition has been altered by many authors to reflect stimulation of selective response by the animal (Church, 1979), preference for feeds (Matthews, 1983) and the interaction between the animals' physiological and metabolic state, and a feed (Forbes, 1988).

Palatability can also be measured as those characteristics of a feed which invoke a sensory response in the animal (Greenhalgh and Reid, 1971; Baumont, 1996). These pre-gastric factors, together with previous experience of a feed, are the first and most direct regulator of food intake and chewing behaviour in horses (Ralston, 1984). In foals, a strong "cultural" transmission of food preferences from the mother has been established and social facilitation also plays an important role in total voluntary intake (Houpt, 1990).

Lawrence (1990) summarises the stages in food ingestion by ruminants as: 'food recognition' (vision and smell), 'orientation' (vision, proprioception, equilibrium) and 'grasping, mandibulation and swallowing' (or mechanoreception, thermoreception, chemoreception, proprioreception, noiception). The most detailed study relating to voluntary intake of horses was conducted by the French Institute for Agricultural Research (INRA) between 1980 and 1995. A total of 37 forages were offered *ad libitum* during digestibility trials. Voluntary intakes of forages were measured in both horses and sheep (Dulphy *et al.*, 1997a and 1997b). For conserved forages, a linear relationship between horses and sheep was established with the voluntary intake (corrected for bodyweight) of fresh forages being lower in horses than in sheep. There was, however, no relationship between voluntary intake and physicochemical properties (e.g. structural carbohydrate) of forages. Furthermore no effect of season was noted in horses but was apparent with sheep. The authors concluded that physical appetite-regulating mechanisms are not apparent in horses and suggested organoleptic (sensory) processes controlled voluntary intake of horses (Dulphy *et al.*, 1997a). These observations were supported by other studies that demonstrated that ponies failed to regulate their intake according to energy requirements over a period of 4 weeks (Ralston, 1992; Cuddeford and Hyslop, 1996).

An alternative approach to assessing taste preferences and palatability of feed, is to conduct choice tests (also known as cafeteria tests), when two or more feeds are offered simultaneously (Rodgers, 1988; Van Soest, 1994). Short-term choice tests allow a comprehensive assessment of palatability of different feedstuffs in horses by measuring preference indices, short term intake rates and intake behaviour. The measurements taken then can be used to compare "palatability" between feeds and between animals under different physiological conditions.

A limited number of choice-preference tests have been performed with horses with distillers' dried grains and silages (Pagan and Jackson, 1991; Hawkes *et al.*, 1985). In one short-term choice test, horses were offered two concentrate feeds of known amounts, with one feed containing an added component of distillers' dried grains for a period of 5 minutes (Pagan and Jackson, 1991). The amount of each feed ingested at a given time was recorded. At low inclusion rates distillers' grains (20% of dry matter offered) were more readily eaten than the basal concentrate diet.

Unfortunately order of eating (rank of choice) and intake behaviour were not recorded and analysed. Rates of eating may change, reflecting the physical properties of a feed (moisture, fracture properties). Randall (1978) offered foals sweet (sucrose), sour (acetic acid), salty (NaCl) and bitter (quinine) solutions at various concentrations. Preference for a sweet solution, containing between 1.25 and 10 g sucrose per litre was clearly established, while concentrations above or below this were treated indifferently. Higher concentrations of the other solutions were rejected. Distillery by-products have also been offered to horses at varying levels of inclusion (0, 0.25, 0.50, 0.75 and 1.00) to assess palatability, showing a decline in rate of eating proportional to increasing rate of inclusion (Hill and Braithwaite, 1999; Hill, 2002).

Salivary glands

Lubrication of the mouth and gullet in the horse is provided by the release of saliva from three pairs of large glands situated on the sides of the face and adjacent areas of the neck. The ducts of each gland drain to the mouth cavity (Stick *et al.*, 1981; Schumacher and Schumacher, 1995). The parotid glands (*glandula parotis*) are the largest salivary glands in the horse. In the adult horse they are approximately 20 to 25 cm in length and 2 cm in width. The average weight of each gland is approximately 200 to 225 g. This is substantially larger than the similar gland in the cow (approximately 115 g). The duct enters the mouth in the cheek opposite to the third upper cheek tooth. The mandibular or submaxillary gland (*glandula mandiularis*) is smaller (about 20 cm by 1 cm, weighing 45 to 60 g) than the parotid gland and drains to the region of the cheek opposite to the canine. The mandibular gland in the cow is substantially larger than that of the horse, weighing about 140 g. The sublingual gland (*glandula sublingualis*) of the horse has multiple ducts (approximately 30) opening into the sub-lingual fold (base of the tongue). The gland is considerably smaller than the parotid being 12 to 15 cm in length and weighing about 15 g). There are also a series of minor salivary glands (scattered lobules of salivary tissue on the dorsal and ventral borders of the buccinator muscle, the lips, the tongue and soft palate; Schumacher and Schumacher, 1995) ducting to the buccal cavity of the horse. These glands individually do not produce copious amounts of saliva but collectively their contribution is considerable (Dyce *et al.*, 1996).

Saliva has four main functions in animals. During chewing, both horses and ruminants secrete copious amounts of saliva to the ingesta to assist swallowing. The volume of saliva produced may be related to physiological control of voluntary intake (especially the control of rate of eating) and is important in determining the buffering capacity of the feed-saliva mixture (see Bailey, 1958; Bauman *et al.*, 1971 for ruminant studies). In horses, this may be an important consideration in the survival of epiphytic microflora associated with feeds in the *saccus caecus* (first point of entry to the stomach of the horse; Morris *et al.*, 2003) and to maintain an environment which may prevent the development of ulcers (Nieto *et al.*, 2001; Nadau *et al.*, 1998; Pagan, 1997; Table 2.3). Finally saliva production is necessary for the formation of the fluid seal necessary for suckling in neonate foals.

Table 2.3 Chemical composition of equine and ruminant parotid saliva (meq/l).

Element	Equine [b]	Bovine [c]	Ovine [d]
Na^+	55	163-168	193
Cl^-	50	16-34	10
K^+	15	6-14	11
Ca^{2+}	13	nd	1.2
pH			8.6
Bicarbonate (HCO_3^-)	50[a]	88-94	91-125

nd: not determined
(*Sources:* (a) Meyer (1995), (b) Alexander and Hickson (1970), (c) Kay, 1960; (d) Welch and Hooper (1988))

In ruminants, saliva helps to maintain pH in the rumen within the range of 6.5 to 6.8 allowing optimal conditions for fermentation of feeds by ruminal microflora. Saliva also buffers the production of volatile fatty acids (VFA). The situation in the horse is different. Little is known about pre-gastric digestion in the horse. However the rate of fermentation of feeds by microflora is low and yields mainly lactic acid (Alexander and Davies, 1963; Kern *et al.*, 1973 and 1974; Morris *et al.*, 2003). Alexander (1966) suggested that the buffering capacity of equine parotid saliva was considerably lower than that of ruminant parotid saliva and therefore its activity in buffering lactic acid being produced in the stomach is limited. Therefore, the roles of saliva in maintaining correct physiological environment for microbial activity in the stomach of the horse are still open to conjecture and have not been elucidated.

Secretion of saliva by the parotid gland in ruminants is continuous and isotonic compared to an intermittent flow of hypotonic saliva flow by horses (Alexander and Hickson, 1970). Salivation is a reflex response controlled by sympathetic and parasympathetic nerve stimulation. Parasympathetic stimulation of the salivary tissue leads to the release of high volumes of dilute secretion which act to keep the mucous membranes moist and lubricate the tongue during movement. Sympathetic stimulation leads to small quantities of viscous mucoid saliva being released. In horses there is no psychological stimulation therefore food must be present in the mouth for saliva flow (Frandson, 1986). The principal stimulus for saliva flow in horses is mastication and reflex secretion following stimulation inside the mouth cavity (presumably the tongue surface). However, the secretion of saliva is a function of the presence of food in the mouth and the moisture content of the feed ingested (Alexander, 1966). When dry feeds are ingested copious amounts of watery saliva is produced. However, if the feed is moist, only sufficient mucus rich saliva is produced to assist swallowing (Schumacher and Schumacher, 1995).

Saliva production is a two stage process. First, there is the development of an osmotic gradient across the acini and secondly, the active re-absorption of sodium and chloride ions and secretion of potassium ions (Young and van Lennep, 1979). This leads to the production of hypotonic saliva compared to the plasma. The parotid gland secretes thin watery saliva that contains variable concentrations of mineral ions. Mandibular and sublingual salivary glands however produce thicker saliva (containing copious amounts of mucus). Saliva produced by the mandibular gland may contain enzymes, but no enzymes are found in saliva produced by the sublingual glands (Eckersall *et al.*, 1995). Ruminant saliva contains a limited range and concentration of enzymes (for example, lipases are present but there is no amylolytic activity). It is currently thought that equine saliva does not contain any enzyme activity (Frape, 1998; Meyer 1995). Recent studies by Hill and Courtnell (*unpublished data*) confirmed the observations of Frandson (1986) by demonstrating that equine saliva does not contain amylolytic activity however the microflora present in the mouth can degrade starch (amylose). It is, however, unlikely that the process of starch degradation in the mouth has a major overall effect on the utilisation of starch by the horse but microflora that can degrade simple carbohydrate polymers may be important in the development of dental caries or periodontal disease. Schumacher and Schumacher (1995) have suggested that equine saliva also contains limited levels of lactoperoxidase activity and immunoglobulin A (IgA). Production of lactoperoxidase and IgA would confer antibacterial properties to the saliva. It has been suggested that parotid saliva is an important factor in controlling the chemical environment in the stomach. High fibre diets may lead to a higher yield of bicarbonate in the stomach reflecting the greater insalivation of the diet during chewing (Alexander and Hickson, 1970).

Digestive physiology of the horse

There is a degree of contention over how much saliva per day a horse will secrete. In ruminants, the typically quoted figures for saliva production per day are 150 *l* for cattle and 10 *l* for sheep (McDonald *et al.*, 1995). Alexander and Hickson (1970) reported the rate of production of saliva by the parotid gland in horses during chewing of up to 50 ml/min. This rate of production has been used to calculate the often quoted 10 to 12 litres of saliva produced by the horse per day if fed 'normally' (Frape, 1988). However, in the original publication by Alexander (1966), volumes of saliva secreted were recorded as ranging from 4.9 to 6.4 *l* per day (n = 15 and 17 respectively). Furthermore, the definition of "normal" feeding is not clear and individual animal variation has to be considered carefully. Meyer (1995) suggested that a horse will produce between 3 and 5 litres of saliva per 100 kg body-weight per day, thus a 500 kg horse may produce up to 25 litres of saliva per day if fed on roughage only. The considerable lack of information concerning the variation in production and composition of saliva by the horse may lead to difficulties in evaluating the role of saliva in the maintenance of the mineral balance of the animal, especially when under moderate to severe exercise. Eckersall *et al.* (1995) examined the chemical composition of equine saliva to establish the natural variation in constituents (Table 2.4).

Table 2.4 Variation in chemical composition of equine saliva (Eckersall *et al.*, 1995).

	Mean	Range	Overall s.d.	Overall % CV	Variation explained by horse[1]	Variation explained by time[2]	Unaccounted variation[3]
Sodium	8.86	2-21	5.26	59	0.162	0.643	0.194
Potassium	17.47	2.8-27.1	5.68	33	0.383	0.379	0.238
Calcium	6.24	1.38-9.84	1.86	30	0.157	0.466	0.377
Magnesium	1.57	0.32-2.27	0.48	30	0.164	0.326	0.510
Chloride	11.86	3-25	5.75	48	0.204	0.383	0.413
Phosphate	0.89	0.19-2.15	0.49	55	0.164	0.311	0.525
Urea	1.09	0.2-2.2	0.47	43	0.211	0.415	0.374
Protein	0.657	0.2-1.5	0.16	25	0.245	0.201	0.554
pH	6.83	3.86-9.16	1.47	22	0.603	0.155	0.242

[1] Six pony mares offered *ad libitum* hay and pony cubes (amount not stipulated)
[2] Experimental period of 5 weeks – saliva collected twice weekly between 0900 and 1000 hrs.
[3] residual variation (proportion of total sum of squares not associated with horse or time.

The composition of whole saliva is likely to be more variable than plasma, cerebrospinal fluid, urine or individual gland output. However, the variation in pH, sodium and chloride are noteworthy. The range in pH of whole saliva is great and over 60% of the variation is associated with individual horse factors. The concentrations of sodium and chloride are low in comparison with the findings of Stick *et al.* (1981). This observation may reflect the nature of the saliva collected (whole *vs.* individual gland) and the flow rate of saliva from parotid glands (Alexander, 1966). The variation noted in Table 2.4 is not ideal from an animal management point of view. Therefore, before saliva could be used as a management tool to monitor the influence of exercise or drug metabolism further studies have to be performed to consider the impact of natural and animal inherent variation.

Dental architecture

The differences in feeding behaviour of ruminants and non-ruminants are partly related to the anatomical adaptations of mouth parts and teeth. The most common comparative approach to investigate the impact of dentition in relation to the type of vegetation eaten and the digestive strategy is the muzzle width index and the hypsodonty index (van Soest, 1994). The muzzle width index (MWI) is the ratio of the muzzle width to the palatal width at the 5th molar and the hypsodonty index is calculated as the height of the 3rd lower molar divided by the length of the 2nd lower molar (Janis and Ehrhardt, 1988). Janis and Ehrhardt (1988) suggested that the high hypsodonty index (HI) and high muzzle width index (MWI) in horses compared to the majority of ruminants was related to the need to chew forages efficiently on the first pass through the mouth as the high HI is thought to reflect the ability to masticate forage with a high fibre content. This observation would suggest the equid to have a more robust dentition whilst still retaining the ability to sort or select components of feeds. Sheep however, have a lower hypsodonty index while still retaining a relatively high muzzle width ratio, a characteristic of a 'concentrate selector'. The mean HI:MWI ratio for horses and sheep are approximately 2.5 and 1.7: 1 respectively (Janis and Ehrhardt, 1988). The difference in efficiencies of chewing in sheep compared to horses may also be due to the architecture of the ovine dental apparatus, composition of foodstuffs selected and to size of animals. Ovine molars (except the third molars) of the upper and lower jaw fit into each other perfectly forming a solid row between which

Digestive physiology of the horse

food is ground. The animals' life-span is partially dependent upon the sustainability of this grinding apparatus, which eventually gets worn down completely.

The surface morphology, shape of crown of tooth, and contact of occlusal surfaces are important factors in the physical disruption of feeds (Murphy and Kennedy, 1993). The physical disruption of the feed and the addition of saliva in the oral cavity start the processes of digestion. For efficient utilisation of feeds, effective mastication of the food must take place. The dental architecture of the horse differs from that of the ruminant in that the horse has upper and lower incisor teeth implanted in the premaxilla and the mandible. The dental (permanent) formula of the horse is:

$$2 (I\ ^3/_3\ C\ ^1/_1\ P\ ^{3\ or\ 4}/_3\ M\ ^3/_3) = 40\ or\ 42$$

whereas the formula for sheep or cow is:

$$2 (I\ ^0/_4\ C\ ^0/_0\ P\ ^3/_3\ M\ ^3/_3) = 32$$

The incisor teeth (*dentes incisivi*; 12 in number) of horses are unique in their structure in having a deep invagination or *infundibulum* that becomes partially filled with dental cement. The incisors of mammals are normally constructed with a simple cap of enamel on the crown. As the tooth wears, in addition to the peripheral enamel, the masticatory surface (or table) has a central ring of enamel surrounding the infundibulum. Debris of partially chewed feed can deposit in the masticatory surface leading to the "cup" or "mark". The position and degree of development of the "table", "cup" and "mark" changes and has been used to estimate the age of the horse (Richardson *et al.*, 1995). The cheek teeth (pre-molars and molars) have well developed grinding surfaces. Upper cheek teeth or maxillary teeth form a continuous row arranged with slight convexity to the cheek. The mandibular or lower cheek teeth also form a continuous row but they are straight in their orientation to the cheek.

From about the age of 4 to 5 years horses are pre-disposed to an uneven wear of dental surfaces as a result of the anatomical structure of the upper and lower jaw and the arrangement of the maxillary and mandibular teeth in relation to each other. The equine mandibule (lower jaw) is approximately one third narrower than the maxillary jaw causing a discrepancy in occlusal contact of molars. This leads to the formation of sharp rostral apexes on the teeth to the buccal side (outside) of the upper molars and the lingual side (inside) of the lower molars. Furthermore, in some horses, particularly those of malformed jaws such as parrot mouth, the mandibular row of cheek teeth (both molars and pre-molars) may be set slightly behind those of the maxillary. This may create further uneven wear along the first pre-molars and last molars. Sharp edges may cause discomfort during eating and result in a possible reduction in grinding efficiency, loss of concentrate feed from the mouth during eating and eventually may lead to lacerations and ulceration of the soft oral tissues, gums, cheeks and tongue (Lewis, 1995; Baker, 1998; Easley, 1997). Other abnormalities that can be removed by corrective dentistry are broken or missing teeth, shear-mouth and mouth wave (Brigham and Duncanson, 2000; Lane, 1994). The so-called "dental hooks" forming on the pre-molars and molars as a result of misaligned occlusal surfaces are removed with hand rasps of various sizes or automatic grinders (Stanback, 1997, Scoggins, 1998; Dixon, 2000). The awareness of uneven tooth wear has been highlighted recently in a number of equine veterinary journals (Scoggins, 1998; Dixon, 2000) and corrective dentistry has become a routine procedure in horse management. There has also been considerable interest in routine dentistry compared with the more aggressive performance float techniques that smooth and round the dental arcade (Scrutchfield *et al.*, 1996; Lane, 1994; Wilewski and Rubin, 1999; Ralston *et al.*, 2001).

The primary function of the teeth is the mastication and communition of feed, the chewing process. This can be measured by the observation of the process itself and by the effect the process has on particle fragmentation (reflected in faecal particle size). Short term intake rates (STIR) (chews kg^{-1} DM, chews min^{-1}) and bites min^{-1}) are used to empirically to assess intake behaviour and change in processes controlling intake rate (Hodgson, 1985). Automatic recording equipment has been developed for measurement of ingestive behaviour of ruminants (Meyer *et al.*, 1975; Chambers *et al.*, 1981; Rutter, 2000) but has had limited use in horses. Meyer *et al.* (1975) investigated chewing frequency in riding horses (450-550kg) at two study sites in Germany. Measurements were taken using a telemetric heat sensor with electrodes attached to the upper jaw, below the medial eye corner at the lower edge of the mandibulum. For hays a range of 3000-3500 chews kg^{-1} DM were observed. The mean value for straw was 3645 chews kg^{-1} DM and for concentrates a range in chews per kg were more variable ranging from 832 chews kg^{-1} DM (oats) to 1383 chews kg^{-1} DM (mixed concentrates). Grinding oats led to an increase in chews per kg and

Digestive physiology of the horse

pelleting seemed to have no influence on eating time, however in a later report, pelleting of mixed feed decreased intake times from a mean of 18.6 min kg^{-1} (mixed concentrates) to around 8.31 min kg^{-1} (8 mm cubes) (Meyer, 1980b). These observations were confirmed by Ellis (2003a; Figure 2.3).

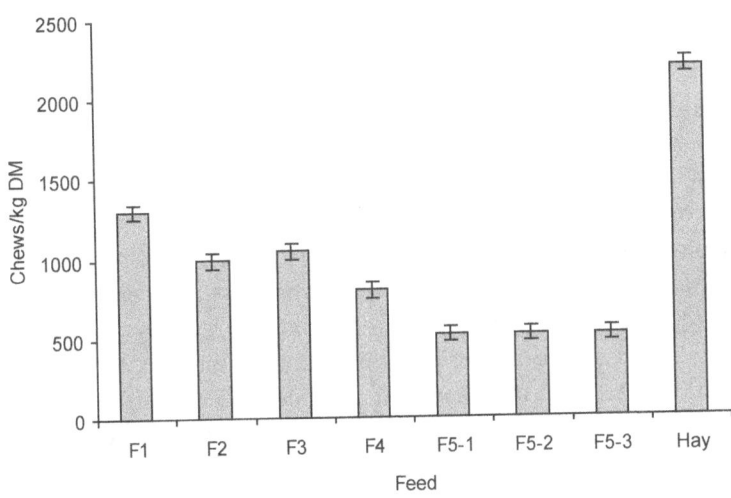

Figure 2.3 Chews/kg DM for various feedstuffs (Source: Ellis, 2003a) (F1 = dried chopped lucerne; F2 = hay pellets; F3 = whole barley; F4 = micronised barley; F5 = various combinations of mixed feed (F1-F4) plus wet sugar beet pulp at a wet matter ratio of 2:1)

In the study by Ellis (2003a), all feeds were chewed at a rate of approximately 60 to 75 chews per minute. There was some evidence that the horse changed its intake rate according to feed properties but maintained the rhythm and rate of chewing.

A number of authors have suggested that chews per minute are directly related to type (ponies *vs.* horses) and size of animals. Meyer *et al.* (1975) reported for ponies an increase in chewing rate (by about 50% for roughages and 150% for concentrate feeds) to approximately 100 chews per minute with a concurrent increase in chewing time kg^{-1} DM. It was suggested that a reduction in dental chewing surface of the molars and smaller buccal capacity of ponies was responsible for these differences. Large molar hooks may, therefore, have a similar effect, if the horse adjusts its' intake and chews for longer periods. If this is the case, increased production of saliva may occur. On the other hand, if no adjustment to poor dental condition occurs a negative effect on particle size reduction may be expected, possibly leading to a greater energy cost of chewing during ingestion and a reduction in net energy available for maintenance (Ellis, 2003a; Vernet *et al.*, 1995).

Although widely reported in the popular literature, the effects of dental condition on eating behaviour have not been measured accurately. The majority of the literature concerned with voluntary intake and rate of eating of forages and concentrates do not refer to the condition of teeth (for instance, Dulphy *et al.*, 1997a; 1997b; Meyer *et al.*, 1975; Hill 2002). However, the few reports concerning eating behaviour and digestibility assessment which refer to dental condition of animals vary in their approach to assessment of the pre-molars and molars (Ellis and Hill, 2001; Ralston *et al.*, 2001). Various methods of assessment of dental condition have been developed to examine the role of dental condition on eating behaviour (e.g. Ellis *et al.*, 2000; Ellis and Hill, 2001; Ralston *et al.*, 2001). The two approaches are either descriptive in nature (routine *vs.* performance float correction) or based on a numerical scale. The numerical tooth scoring method devised by Ellis *et al.* (2000) recorded the degree of sharpness of edges of the upper and lower molars as well as the development of hooks. A score of one indicates a flat molar table, unlikely to occur in natural conditions in the horse over 3 years old and score five represents the other extreme, which is likely to develop naturally (Table 2.5 and Figure 2.4).

Table 2.5 Description of dental scores.

Score		
1		Flat molar table
2		Protrusion but smooth
3		Large protrusion, no hook
3.5		Large protrusion, no edge sharp edge
4		Large protrusion, hook
4.5		Large sharp hook, no damage to soft tissue
5		Large sharp hook, damage to soft tissue

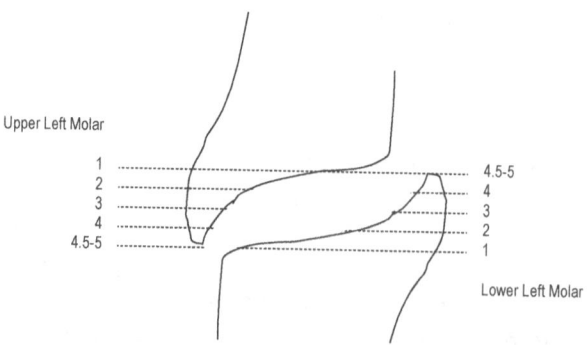

Figure 2.4 Dental scoring system.

The half-score of 4.5 was used in the scoring system when the molar edges were sharp and a large hook was observed, however no visible damage to the gums (buccal) or the tongue (lingual) tissue has occurred. The impact of poor dental architecture (scores of up to 4) was limited to changes in eating behaviour to compensate for a reduced efficiency of chewing (Ellis *et al.*, 2000). Horses compensated poor dental condition and subsequent reduced chewing efficiency by a reduced intake rate (g min^{-1}) leading to a greater number of chews kg^{-1} DM (Table 2.6).

Table 2.6 Mean intake rates on medium cut mixture hay before and after dental treatment (number of horses = 16; Ellis, 2003a).

	Before treatment	s.e.	After treatment	s.e.
Intake (g DM min^{-1})	28.0	0.09	33.1	0.20
Intake time for 8 kg DM hay (hours)	4.8	0.01	4.0	0.02
Chews kg^{-1} DM	2581	78	2199	69
Chewing rate (chews min^{-1})	69	0.9	71	1.2

No changes in digestibility, rate of passage of digesta or faecal particle index were observed after dental correction of seven horses with scores between 3.5 and 4. However, a slight but insignificant trend towards a reduced digestibility at the highest molar hook score was noticed (Figure 2.5). Ralston *et al.* (2001) also found no changes in digestibility for 8 horses before and after dental treatment. Both authors concluded that molar hooks which have caused damage to the inside of the mouth (Ellis – score 4.5-5) are likely to lead to a reduction in digestibility of nutrients. Ellis (2003a) hypothesized that this is most likely due to a reduction in chews kg DM or at best failure to adjust intake behaviour, due to pain.

The faecal particle index for sheep and horses is an important but controversial measurement in assessment of dental architecture (Uden and van Soest, 1982). Faecal particle indices of horses have been reported in a contradictory manner in the literature (Frape, 1998; Cuddeford; 1999; Ruckebusch, 1984). Frape (1998) suggested that sound teeth generally reduce hay and grass particles to less than 1.6 mm in length and two thirds of hay particles in the horse's stomach are less than 1 mm across. Cuddeford (1999) also suggested that one kilogram of hay requires about 3500 to 4500 chews to reduce it to lengths of less than 1.6 mm. It was, however, not indicated whether the chews per kg are based on dry matter or fresh matter.

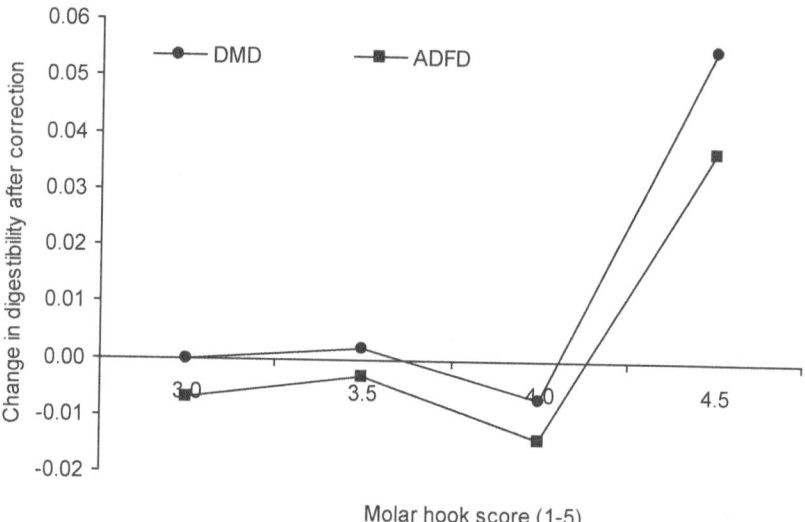

Figure 2.5 Effect of dental correction on digestibility of DM and ADF in horses (Ellis, 2003a).

Other authors have demonstrated that this degree of reduction of feed particles during chewing is unlikely (Grenet *et al.*, 1984; Meyer, 1987; Uden and Van Soest, 1982; Ellis *et al.*, 2000a). The controversy over faecal particle size data arises from the original paper by Meyer *et al.* (1975). Meyer concluded that forage is minced in the equine oral cavity to a particle size of less than 1.6 mm, but this was later refuted by the same author (Meyer *et al.*, 1985). In a later experiment, the particle size distribution of sieved boluses (collected via oesophageal fistulas) contained over 30% of particles above 1.5 mm and lengths of up to 12 mm were described (Meyer *et al.*, 1985). The method of sieving in the paper of 1975 was not described, but a 'drying of stomach contents' is mentioned, suggesting a dry sieving method was applied leading to the "unrealistic" results. Dry sieving has been criticised by many authors (for instance Ulyatt, 1986; Murphy and Kennedy, 1993) as allowing particles to pass through the sieve in a vertical direction and also to lead to fracture and fragmentation of dry fibre.

The distributions of size of particles for different forage offered to horses and sheep were assessed by Ellis (2003a). Substantial differences in the mean particle size and distribution of particles were observed between feeds and species (Figure 2.6).

Digestive physiology of the horse

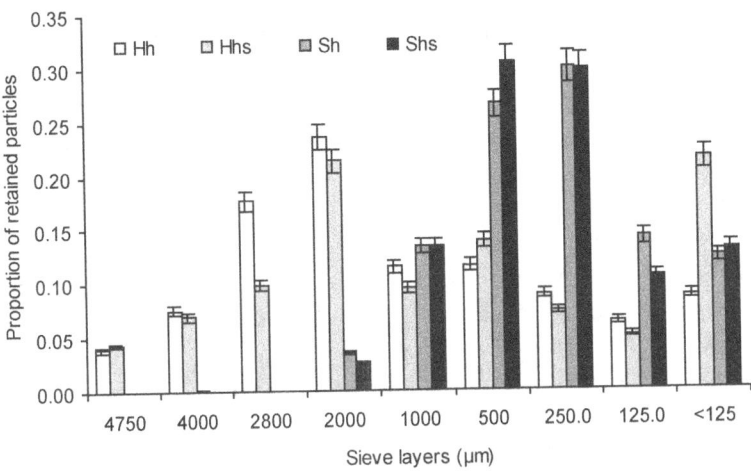

Figure 2.6 Faecal particle distributions from horses (H) and sheep (S) on a hay (h) or high dry matter silage (hs) diet (Ellis, 2003a).

The differences between forages may reflect differences in physical and chemical composition. Silages seem to fragment more easily than hay. This observation may reflect the lower physical resilience to mastication of silage as a result of the processes of fermentation (Vincent, 1990). Furthermore, slower rates of ingestion of silage as a result of the ensiling process may have lead to a longer period of time the feed is in the mouth and therefore the greater proportion of smaller particles excreted by the horse (Figure 2.7).

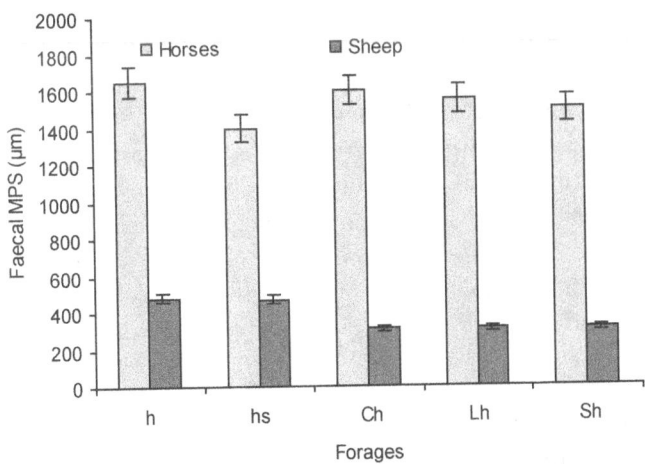

Figure 2.7 Mean particle sizes (MPS) for horses and sheep on various forage diets. (h = medium quality hay; hs = high dry matter silage (58% DM); Ch = chopped hay <3cm; Lh = long late cut hay; Sh = soft early cut hay) (Ellis, 2003a).

Welch and Hooper (1988) defined the processes of chewing in ruminants as the 'regurgitation, re-insalivation, re-mastication and re-swallowing of rumen ingesta'. Feed particles are therefore disrupted to a greater extent than during the initial chewing of the feed with the primary function of ensuring clearance of digested particles from the reticulo-rumen (Murphy and Kennedy, 1993). In general, the more fibrous the feed-material is, the greater the rumination time. However, this relationship is open to criticism as being too simplistic as differences in chemical and anatomical features of forages as well as the brittleness of the forage lead to differences in particle size in the rumen (Kennedy, 1985; Akin, 1989; Wilson et al., 1989 a and b). Rumination does however lead to a greater breakdown in particle size, an increase in surface area for rumen microflora to colonise, and an increase in specific gravity of particles (Murphy and Kennedy, 1993). These processes are not available to the horse and this has lead to the suggestion that the ruminant has a competitive advantage compared to herbivores relying on hind gut fermentation (van Soest, 1994; Janis and Ehrhardt, 1988; Hoffman, 1989).

Olfactory processes and chemoreception play an important role in the processes of eating. The slower rates of ingestion of ensiled feeds can lead to a lower intake of dry matter (and fresh matter) per chew, increased saliva production to buffer the fermented feed and more efficient particle breakdown (e.g. more chews per kg DM; Alexander and Hickson, 1970). The full effect on overall tract digestibility is difficult to ascertain, but increased surface area of feed could lead to an increased microbial colonisation and thus a greater rate of degradation (van Soest, 1995). Eating behaviour has also been demonstrated to affect the rate of flow of particles through the small intestine. Kienzle and co-workers (1992), when assessing the digestibility of feeds containing whole maize demonstrated that horses with very high short-term intake rates (STIR) had 49% of particles in jejunal chyme of greater than 1.4 mm and very low apparent digestibility of starch ($\sim$ 1%). However animals with low STIR had a considerably lower proportion of particles greater than 1.4 mm (27%) and a considerably greater apparent digestibility of starch (49.8%).

The lower total fermentative capacity observed in non-ruminants compared to ruminants does not limit their potential as competitors to ruminants (Foose, 1982; Vulink, 2002). The horse does not have an elaborate mechanism of retention and recycling of ingesta (no rumination or tract restrictions; van Soest, 1995) and therefore maintain their nutrient uptake by having a high sustained voluntary intake (Stebbins, 1981; van Wieren, 1996). The differences between ruminants and horses in particle sizes excreted in the faeces may also reflect the lesser ability of non-ruminant herbivores to disrupt particles (Uden and van Soest, 1982; Table 2.7). However, the inability of ruminants to allow the transit of large particles to the small intestine and hind gut, owing to the selective retention of larger particles in the reticulo-rumen for re-mastication (van Soest, 1994; Murphy and Kennedy, 1993), is apparent and therefore the process of re-chewing of ingesta (rumination) will lead to a lower faecal particle index.

Table 2.7 Comparison of fibre particle size index (μm) of intestinal tract content and faeces (Source: Uden and van Soest, 1982).

Species	n	Rumen-reticulum (μm)	Caecum (μm)	Faeces (μm)
Large Heifer	3	2290		830
Goats	3	1470	520	460
Sheep	3	1290	490	460
Ponies	4			1600
Horses	3			1630
Rabbits	2		339	443

Uden and van Soest (1982) concluded that passage rates of digesta in ruminants were likely to be affected to a greater extent by particle size compared to equines, as larger particles are retained in the rumen-reticulum until they are fragmented by rumination. However, the rate of passage in horses (and rabbits) also may be affected by particle size but in the opposite manner. Larger particles seem to increase the passage rate through the small intestines and caecum (Drogoul et al., 1996) – a protective mechanism to presumably avoid excess gas production and acidosis in the lower digestive tract.

The processes of mastication of different feeds in ruminants has been examined by many authors (for example, Baumont et al., 2000; Hutchings and Gordon, 2001; Unger, 1996). However, the number of studies concerning processes of mastication of feeds by the horse is limited. Chewing rates per minute for horses and sheep offered unchopped hay range from 73 to 92 and 73 to 115 respectively (Ellis, 2003a). However, the amount of hay ingested per chew and the ingestion rate per kilogram of metabolic body weight (kg $BW^{0.75}$) is three to four times higher in ruminants than in horses and ponies (Frape, 1998). These comparisons are mainly based on separate short-term intake rate (STIR) studies conducted with either horses or sheep.

Feed manufacturers sell short chopped dried grasses, hays and dried legumes, indicating that added value of the product lies within a prolonged intake time, keeping horses busy for longer. Cuddeford (1994) reported the intake rate of ponies offered short chopped hay (4 cm mean particle length) was 820 g per hour, whereas if the same hay was offered in an unchopped form (33 cm mean particle length) the intake rate was greater being 1360 g per hour. These observations confirm the observations of Meyer et al. (1975), who noted an increased time for ingesting known quantities of chopped (5 – 15 mm) and unchopped hay (1140 g per hour and 1540 g per hour respectively). Meyer et al. (1975) also noted that chews per kg of hay DM were not changed and time taken for eating was increased in response to a longer period of prehension (handling time increased; Unger and Noy-Meir, 1996) and the greater disruption in pattern of eating (Ralston, 1984). In contrast, Cuddeford (1997) observed a significant increase in chews per kg DM for the chopped hay compared with hay which had not been processed (increased from 3351 chews per kg DM for unchopped hay to 5326 chews per kg DM for chopped hay). Ellis (2003) offered a hay diet to horses that was either chopped (3.5 cm mean particle size) or left unchopped (>20 cm mean particle size). No differences in mean intake rate (approximately 20 g/min) or chews per kg DM (on average 3900) were observed between the two treatments. However, the mean faecal particle size excreted from horses offered chopped hay was greater than that observed for unchopped hay. Following a series of intake behaviour experiments, it was noted, that horses did need a considerable acclimatisation period to forages presented in a novel manner, before settling into a repeatable 'rhythm of intake' (Ellis, 2003). Therefore, length of adaptation periods before taking intake behaviour measurements may influence results.

The voluntary intake of horses is greater than ruminants when offered the same forage (Haenlein et al., 1966; Duncan et al., 1990; Dulphy et al., 1997a; Fleurence and Duncan, 2001). This process of bulk feeding is thought to compensate for the lower digestibility of feeds offered (Janis, 1989; Stebbins, 1981; Hofmann, 1973). However, the control of the processes concerned with voluntary intake is poorly understood. Furthermore, it is not known if the processes of control are similar in ponies and horses (Cuddeford, 2000). Studies examining the regulation of voluntary intake in horses are relatively scarce, however the majority conclude that non-working horses will consume excess energy in relation to their requirements, leading to obesity (Ralston, 1992; Gibbs and Smith, 1978; Ralston and Baile, 1982a, 1982b and 1983). Changes in post-absorptive state have been reflected in the work by Ralston and Baile (1983). Intra-gastric loading of corn-oil after a period of 4 hours fasting did not affect the voluntary intake of a concentrate meal, but did alter the inter-meal interval (tripled the normal interval). However, intra-gastric loading with glucose and cellulose did reduce voluntary intake (10 to 15 minutes and 4 to 6 hours respectively). It was concluded that elevated concentration of glucose and insulin in the plasma did not generate the cues for satiety. Intra-gastric infusions of short-chain volatile fatty acids (acetate and propionate) increase voluntary intake by reducing the first inter-meal interval. Gut-fill has been demonstrated as an important mechanism in regulating voluntary intake in farm animals (Forbes, 1988). Localised gastric response to gut fill has not been demonstrated as an important mechanism in regulating voluntary intake of horses (Aiken et al., 1989 and Frape et al., 1982). For instance, intra-gastric infusions of kaolin or removal of approximately 20% of caecal contents did not impact on intake or feeding behaviour of ponies (Ralston and Baile, 1982b). This is not surprising as the anatomy of the hind-gut does not have physical barriers limiting particle movement in the same way the reticulorumen – omasal orifice regulates flow in the fore-stomach of the ruminant. Further, apparent digestibility of NDF or concentrations of NDF in the feed are not reliable predictors of voluntary DM intake (Cymbaluk, 1990).

The oesophagus and stomach

The oesophagus of the horse is a musculo-membranous tube about 120 to 150 cm in length. The oesophagus extends from the pharynx to the stomach. The structure of the wall reflects its function. The wall is composed of four layers, a fibrous protective sheath (*tunica adventitia*), the muscular coat (a layer of circular and spirally arranged striated muscle), a sub-mucous layer and the mucous membrane. The mucous membrane is characterised by a covering of stratified epithelia cells. The entry of the oesophagus to the stomach (*ventriculus*) is limited at the cardiac orifice by the cardiac sphincter. Closure of the cardiac sphincter prevents gastric reflux to the mouth and eructation of gases. In contrast, the oesophagus of the cow is much shorter (on average 90 to 105 cm), wider and more dilatable than that of the horse.

The stomach of the horse and the rumen of the cow have little in common except as the first digestive surface in the gastrointestinal tract. In the horse, the stomach represents approximately 10% (about 15 litres) of the volume of the digestive tract while the rumen of the cow accounts for 67% of the total tract volume (Frape, 1998; Meyer, 1995; Pond *et al.*, 1995). The ruminant fore-gut is a complex quadrolocular fermentation vat. The four compartments are divided into the reticulum, the rumen, the omasum and the abomasum (also called the 'true stomach'). The abomasum has been suggested to be similar to the stomach of the horse, however there are quite distinct differences at both anatomical and functional level (Frape, 1998; Morris *et al.*, 2003).

The stomach of the horse is a sharply curved, J-shaped sac lying between the oesophagus and the small intestine. Its function has been poorly understood and to a certain extent ignored. The degree of curvature of the stomach partly explains the development of different areas of acidity within the digesta and the physical characteristics of the digesta (particle size distribution). The great curvature of the stomach is responsible for the development of the main sac whereas the lesser curvature is very short, extending from the entry point of the oesophagus to the exit via the pylorus. The degree of curvature results in the *extremitas sinistra* (to the extreme left ventral to the left crus of the diaphragm) being known as the *saccus caecus* or oesophageal region. The area to the right (*extremitas dextra*) is the pyloric extremity draining the digesta into the anterior small intestine. The region between the pyloric extremity and the *saccus caecus* is the fundic region.

The structure of the wall of the stomach is constructed of four layers; the serous coat (*tunica serosa*), the muscular coat (*tunica muscularis*), a submucosal layer (*tela submucosa*) and the mucosa (*tunica mucosa*). The latter is clearly divided into two regions, an area lining the *saccus caecus* devoid of mucous glands and the lining of the fundic and pyloric area. The thick squamous epithelia of the *saccus caecus* are terminated by the *margo plicatus*. The area adjacent to the *margo plicatus* is characterised by being glandular and producing copious amounts of mucus. The glandular part of the lining of the stomach is differentiated into two distinct regions; an area of short tubular cardiac glands yellowish-grey in colour and the more extensive area of reddish-brown fundus glands (two distinct cell types). The remainder of the stomach epithelia comprises pyloric glands of a single cell type. The fundic and pyloric regions are similar in their tissue type to areas within the stomach

Digestive physiology of the horse

of the dog. The passage of the digesta from the stomach is regulated via the pyloric sphincter.

The differences in the chemical composition of the digesta in the stomach are a result of how long the feed resides in each distinct region and the degree of mixing with secretions produced by the gastric mucosa. The *saccus caecus* receives ingesta in the form of a feed bolus containing a variable level of saliva. The pH is generally high as a result of buffering of feed components (e.g. volatile fatty acids in ensiled feeds) by saliva. Recent work by Morris *et al.* (2003) has identified a substantial and diverse microbial community within the *saccus caecus*. The communities of micro-organisms residing in the *saccus caecus* are likely to be dominated by epiphytic microflora associated with the feed. Limited microbial utilisation of soluble carbohydrate in the feed is also likely to occur in the *saccus caecus* (Hintz *et al.*, 1971; Hill *et al.*, 2001; Morris *et al.*, 2003; de Fombelle *et al.*, 2003). The region between the non-glandular area of the *saccus caecus* and the fundic gland region is the cardiac gland region, adjacent to the *margo plicatus*. The cardiac glands secrete mucus and bicarbonate (HCO_3^-) by exchange of chloride ions (Singer, 1998).

The microbial activity within the fundic region of the stomach is also quite extensive, yielding moderate concentrations of volatile fatty acids and lactic acid (pH 5 to 5.5, Kern *et al.*, 1974; Murray and Schusser, 1993; Morris *et al.*, 2003; de Fombelle *et al.*, 2003). de Fombelle *et al.* (2003) isolated relatively low numbers of cellulolytic bacteria from the stomach (1.0 to 1.4 $\log_{10}$ MPN/ml), however relatively extensive populations of lactobacilli, streptococci and lactate-utilising bacteria were present. The products of fermentation and the microbial community structure are likely to reflect the utilisation of soluble components of the feed (e.g. soluble carbohydrate and maybe free amino acids). There is, however, conflicting evidence concerning the fate of cell wall material in the stomach of the horse (Hintz *et al.*, 1971; Meyer *et al.*, 1983; Morris *et al.*, 2003). It is suggested that some ester linked cell wall components could be utilised in this region of the stomach. Furthermore, the conversion of soluble carbohydrate and some proteins by microbial communities to lactic acid, short chained fatty acids and amino acids can also occur yielding carbon dioxide (CO_2), hydrogen (H) and potentially methane (Meyer, 1995). Recent work by Varloud *et al.* (2003/4) has demonstrated that the apparent digestibility of OM, starch, NDF and ADF in the stomach is variable and dependent on the method used to estimate the digesta pool. The preferred method of estimation of digesta pool was acid insoluble ash (AIA) in the diet (Sutton et al., 1977; Cuddeford and Hughes, 1990; Miraglia et al., 1999; Table 2.8).

Table 2.8 Apparent digestibility of organic matter and dietary carbohydrate (g/g) in the stomach of horses offered high fibre or high starch diet using two methods of estimation of digesta pool size (Miraglia et al., 1999).

Feed fraction	Stomach			
	High fibre AIA	High starch AIA	High fibre ADL	High starch ADL
OM	-0.042	0.460	0.201	0.197
Starch	0.686	0.604	0.757	0.410
NDF	-0.142	0.321	0.120	-0.020
ADF	-0.103	0.319	0.151	-0.040

In the fundic region gastric juices are secreted in conjunction with hydrochloric (HCl) acid and pepsinogen. Fats and structural carbohydrates are probably not degraded in this region even though the microbial community is diverse and extensive (Table 2.9). The feed-soup (chyme) passes into the pyloric region towards the exit of the stomach where glandular secretion of mucus and gastric acid (gastrin) reduces the pH to as low as 1.8 (de Fombelle et al., 2003).

Table 2.9 Physio-chemical composition of the stomach contents of the horse (Morris et al., 2002).

	DM (g/kg)	NDF (g/kg DM)	pH	Fermentation acids (mM/g digesta)				
				Lactic	Acetic	Propionic	n-butyric	i-butyric
Saccus caecus	181	774	5.9	12.7	1.7	0.2	0.1	<0.1
Fundic	182	722	5.1	60.4	17.0	1.1	10.1	0.1
Pyloric	168	674	3.8	40.7	8.3	0.1	0.1	<0.1
s.e.d	8.6**	12.7***	0.49*	8.1**	2.2**	0.32*	1.2**	0.12

$P<0.05$; ** $P<0.01$; *** $P<0.001$

In contrast to the equine stomach, the only region in the ruminant fore-gut that has secretory tissue is the abomasum (Merchen, 1988). In the ruminant, the masticated food enters the reticulo-rumen where coordinated contractions of the musculature leads to a mixing of ingesta and development of a distinct stratification within the digesta (Forbes and France, 1993). This process allows the large population of microorganisms (anaerobic bacteria, protozoa and fungi) to commence the degradation of the feed yielding relatively high concentrations of volatile fatty acids. The inner surface of the rumen is lined with a high density of ruminal papillae, which absorb the VFA and ammonia rapidly thus maintaining the pH of the rumen fluid at approximately 6.4 to 6.8 (McDonald et al., 1995). The by-products of fermentation, methane (CH_4) and carbon dioxide (CO_2), are lost by eructation. The clearance of VFA from the stomach of the horse was examined in some detail by Argenzio et al. (1974). Isolated stratified squamous epithelia do not absorb or transport VFA whereas the mucosa of the fundic and pyloric regions can transport significant levels of VFA (up to 25 meq/litre/hour).

Recent work by de Fombelle et al. (2003) and Varloud et al. (2004) has investigated the effect of feeding high starch or fibre on microbial, chemical and digestive processes in different parts of the digestive tract of the horse. The impact of feeding high levels of starch on the production of D+ and L- lactate and various VFA in the stomach are in Table 2.10.

Table 2.10 VFA and lactate concentrations in mixed digesta from the stomach of horses (de Fombelle et al., 2003).

	High fibre diet	*High starch diet*
pH	4.5	5.1
D-lactate	1.5	0.5
L-lactate	3.0	0.7
Acetate	9.7	15.7
Propionate	0.1	1.5
Butyrate[1]	0.2	1.9
Valerate[1]	0.0	0.4
(C2+C4)/C3	85.1	14.4
D/L lactate ratio	4.2	2.2

[1] total of n and i-isomers of butyrate and valerate

Dietary fibre plays an important role in maintaining the physicochemical environment in the stomach of the horse. The ratio of soluble to insoluble fibre entering the stomach of any mammal alters the viscosity of digesta, the water holding capacity of the feeds and potentially the rate of emptying (Bach Knudsen, 2001). Therefore, the entry of feed to the stomach and the distribution of particles within the stomach are important criteria that control both voluntary intake of the horse and the flow and utilisation of feeds further down the gastrointestinal tract. Recent work on particle size indices for the three regions of the stomach has suggested that the ingesta may be depleted in long particles (greater than 2.0 mm) compared to faecal indices (Kailalathi and Hill, 2003 *unpublished data*). These data may reflect the dual motility theory of particles suggested by Meyer (1995).

The small intestine

The small intestine joins the stomach to the large intestine. The anterior small intestine begins at the pylorus and the proximal junction is the point of entry to the hindgut in the lesser curvature of the caecum. The small intestine is divided into the fixed part (duodenum) and the mesoenteric part (arbitrarily divided into the jejunum and ileum). The small intestine of the horse is about 21 to 25 m (in a horse of approximately 450 kg body weight; Frape, 1998). In comparison, the small intestine of the cow is about 40 m. The duodenum of the horses is only about 1 to 1.5 m in length whereas in the cow it is about 3 to 4 m. Bile and pancreatic secretions drain into the duodenum of the horse approximately 15 cm distal to the pylorus via a common duct (*diverticulum duodeni*). The mesoenteric section of the small intestine is conventionally subdivided into the jejunum and the ileum. However, no distinctive junction can be identified.

The pH of digesta entering the small intestine ranges from 2.5 to 3.5. The action of bile buffers the pH to approximately 7 to 7.5 (de Fombelle *et al.*, 2003). Duodenal glands (*glandulae duodenales* or Brunner's glands) secrete bicarbonate (HCO_3^-) to the lumen of the small intestine neutralising the digesta further (Argenzio, 1993). A further increase in pH is observed in the proximal jejunum and ileum as a result of bicarbonate secretion raising the pH to 7.8 to 8.2 (Merchen, 1988, Meyer *et al.*, 1993). The neutral or slightly alkaline conditions within the small intestine are essential for active transport of nutrient substrates across the intestinal mucosa and the optimal activity of many enzyme systems (e.g. amylases and lipases). The construction of the wall of the small intestine is similar in many ways to the oesophagus. However, to increase the surface area of the wall, the small intestine is lined with a high density of villi (0.5 to 1 mm long) and crypts covered by columnar epithelium

(Hofmann, 1988, and Meyer, 1977). Crypts of Lieberkühn lie at the bottom of the villi and secrete various enzymes and mucus to cover the intestinal surface. The absorption of nutrients in the small intestine is not uniform, with the greatest absorptive capacity in the proximal jejunum (Singer, 1998). This lack of uniformity in absorptive capacity is most apparent in mineral nutrition. The greatest variation in electrolyte balance was observed in the stomach, but no substantial differences between the glandular and non-glandular regions are generally reported (Argenzio et al., 1977). However, the concentrations of electrolytes such as sodium and potassium in the lumen of the small intestine are higher in the anterior duodenum and thereafter decline. Ileal outflow of electrolytes (sodium, potassium and chloride) to the large intestine is about 50% of that entering the small intestine four hours post prandial (Argenzio and Stevens, 1975).

The small intestine is an important site for the breakdown and absorption of sugar, starch, amino acids and lipids (Roberts, 1974 and Roberts et al., 1974). However, the rate of flow of dietary fibre has been suggested to alter the viscosity and water holding capacity of digesta, thus altering the dynamics of flow and therefore uptake of nutrients by the small intestine. Observations by Drogoul et al. (2000a) have also suggested that the rate of flow through the ante-caecal phase of the digestive tract were altered by the variation in particles size entering the small intestine. It is not clear from the studies of Drogoul et al. (2000b) if the digesta was depleted in soluble dietary fibre. Soluble dietary fibre affects the viscosity and flow of digesta in the small intestine in other mammals for instance pigs and humans (Bach Knudsen, 2001). Recent work by de Fombelle et al. (2003) has demonstrated the presence of cellulolytic bacteria (relative low numbers in the jejunum and ileum), lactobaccili, streptococci and lactate-utilising bacteria in lower numbers than was observed in the stomach. Varloud et al. (2003/4) suggested that the digestibility of starch in the jejunum and ileum was about 88% (a value higher than those reported by Hintz et al., 1971 or Potter et al., 1992).

The utilisation of starch is almost certainly the result of degradation by pancreatic amylase, brush border disaccharidases and limited microbial utilisation. However, horses are not well adapted to diets with high concentrations of starch (Richards et al., 2003; Kienzle, 1994; Table 2.11). Furthermore, substantial variation between animals is observed in the capacity to absorb glucose in the small intestine (Mair et al., 1991; Church and Middleton, 1997). This may reflect the low but variable concentration of α-amylase (Alexander and Choudray, 1958; Comline et al., 1969; Roberts, 1974 and Kienzle et al., 1998). Starch digested (reflecting amylolytic enzyme) in the small intestine is absorbed as glucose pre-caecally. Starch digestion is the result of a three-step process. Starches are degraded, initially by α-amylase releasing maltose, maltotriose and α-dextrin. Hydrolysis of maltose, maltotriose and α-dextrin is mediated by intestinal brush border glycanases (especially amylogluosidase) yielding glucose (Gray, 1992). The reported activities of these glycanases are comparable to those observed in other species e.g. pigs and dogs (Kienzle and Radicke, 1993). The glucose released is then transported across the small intestinal epithelium by Na^+-dependent and Na^+-independent transport mechanisms (active transport and facilitative diffusion respectively, Bird et al., 1996; Thorens, 1993).

Table 2.11 Activity of α–amylase derived from jejunal fluid (after Richards et al., 2003). In vitro starch digestion (% loss of starch in 15 minutes).

	Standard assay (B. lichenformes α-amylase)	Jejunal fluid assay (equine α-amylase)
Cracked barley	25.7	12.7
Expanded barley	39.5	19.2
Oats	40.6	27.2
Unprocessed corn	15.8	8.2
Extruded corn	73.9	40.4
Micronised corn	34.0	13.2

The ileum has been suggested as the major site of protein digestion and absorption of amino acids in the horse. A high proportion of the luminal microbial population in the jejunum and the ileum is proteolytic in activity (Kern et al., 1973; Mackie and Wilkins, 1988). However, these processes can be limited by rapid rates of passage of digesta (plug-flow) through the small intestine. Rapid digesta flow reduces the residence time in the small intestine which can lead to some of the more complex sugars and starch escaping to the large intestine. The importance of the physical and chemical composition of feedstuffs on passage rate has been recognised recently as a major factor in nutrient absorption in the small intestine of the horse (Amici, 1997, Cuddeford, 2002, Coenen, 1986). Further, the theory that large particles leave the stomach and small intestines at a faster rate, to be processed in the hindgut, while small particles (<1.6mm) are retained longer was suggested by Meyer (1986) from the data collected from boluses and faeces. However, there is still a lack of knowledge in this area, especially regarding the complex inter-relationships between rate of food intake, particle dynamics and digesta composition and flow.

The large intestine

The large intestine is divided into the caecum, the great colon, the small colon and the rectum. The average length of the caecum of the horse is about 1.25 m and its capacity about 25 to 30 litres. The caecum has four longitudinal bands (*taeniae caeci*), one on each side (dorsal, ventral, right and left). These bands form four rows of sacculations (*ilaustra*). In the cow there is no banding or sacculation of the caecum. Flow of digesta to (via the *ostium ileale*) and from (via the *ostium caecocolicum*) the caecum is regulated by *sphincter ilei* and the valvular fold of the caeco-colic orifice. The colon in the cow is approximately 3 to 3.7 m in length, whereas the length of the colon in the horse is about 10 m. The capacity of the colon in the horse is approximately 50 to 60 litres. The folding of the colon is important in determining digesta flow and functionality. The colon can be divided into four parts (de Fombelle *et al.*, 2003; Varloud *et al.*, 2003/2004). The first, the right ventral colon, begins at the base of the caecum and is directed upward and backward in the body cavity. The colon then passes downward and forward and along the floor of the abdomen. A sharp left and backward flexure of the colon then occurs; the sternal flexure. This flexure determines the start point of the second part of the colon, the left ventral colon. The pelvic flexure determines the terminus of the second part of the colon. The left dorsal colon passes forward in the body cavity from the pelvic flexure to the diaphragmatic flexure. The final section of the colon, the right dorsal colon passes backward from the diaphragmatic flexure to the small colon. Many bands (*taeniae coli*) are observed on the colon. These bands have a similar function to those of the caecum, that is, to develop sacculation along the organ.

The large intestine of the horse is the major site of microbial fermentation and absorption (Leek, 1993; Drougoul *et al.*, 1996; Meyer *et al.*, 1997). The delivery and composition of nutrients to the large intestine is an important factor in understanding the flow and utilisation of nutrients from the digesta. If soluble dietary fibre (or sugars) escapes absorption in the small intestine, rapid fermentation of these products occurs playing an important in the overall energy balance of the animal (Potter et al., 1992; Garner et al., 1978). Insoluble dietary fibre components also undergo extensive degradation and fermentation, dependent on microbial activity and the compartmentation of the large intestine (Juilland et al., 2001; Frape, 1998). A system of compartmentation can be identified in the large intestine of the horse. Within each "compartment", (defined by the position of the flexures and degree of sacculation), muscular contractions aid the mixing of digesta. This process is essential for the maintenance of microbial health within the large intestine (Argenzio and Stevens, 1975; Bailey et al., 2002). The caecal-ventral colonic valve prevents retrograde flow from the large right ventral colon to the caecum and therefore entry of digesta into the colon is regulated by flow from the small intestine and the caecum. The degree of restriction of the colon decreases from the anterior pelvic flexure (tight closure of the lumen of the colon) to the relatively wide diaphragmatic flexure.

The capacity of the caecum in the horse, as a percentage of total tract volume, is about 16%. A further 45% of digestive tract volume is accounted for by the colon and rectum (Pond et al., 1995). In comparison, the rumen accounts for approximately 70% of the tract volume and may contain microbial communities of a higher fermentative capacity than those observed in the equine hindgut (Pond et al., 1995). However, the lower capacity for fermentation does not mean the horse is not "competitively inferior" in digestion and metabolism of nutrients compared to the ruminant (Table 2.12).

Table 2.12 Fermentative capacity of segments of the total digestive tract of herbivore species (after Parra, 1978).

	Reticulorumen	Caecum	Colon and rectum	Total fermentative capacity (%)
Horse		15	54	69
Sheep	71	8	4	83
Cow	64	5	5 – 8	75
Rabbit		43	8	51
Pig		15	33	48
Dog		1	13	14

Digestive physiology of the horse

The large intestine of ruminants does not possess the marked external demarcation noted in the horse and is a much narrower s-shaped, spiral colon. The microbial populations in the large intestine ferment any fibrous material and starch that escapes fermentation or digestion in the upper tract. The process of fermentation produces VFA and methane (Yokoyama et al., 1988). The extent of fermentation can be quite great when ruminants are fed diet containing high levels of maize silage as starch escapes digestion in the upper tract and spills-over to the caecum and colon. This can lead to ulceration of the organ and blood in the faeces. The main function of the colon in the ruminant is the absorption of water to produce the faeces.

Hyslop (1998) demonstrated that the microbial communities in the large intestine of the horse have the ability to degrade fibre to a similar extent to those identified in ruminants, but the major limiting factor in degradation was the rapid rate of digesta flow through the large intestine. There is considerable variation in the apparent digestibility of NDF in different segments of the large intestine (de Fombelle et al., 2003; Varloud et al., 2003/2004). Using acid insoluble ash as an internal marker to determine digesta pool, the sites of the greatest extent of NDF degradation were in the dorsal colon. These observations are in contrast to those of Bertone et al. (1989) who suggested that the right ventral colon was critical to the fibre degradation in the horse. The digesta outflow from the caecum of horses is reported at around 0.20 of total content per hour (Hyslop, 1998), whereas comparable figures for outflow from the rumen range from 0.02 to 0.08 of total content per hour (Pond et al., 1995). Therefore, the rapid flow of digesta from the site of fermentation reduces the period of time the feed particles are available for microbial colonisation and degradation.

Retention times of digesta in the different fermentation compartments of horses and ruminants have been measured. Sheep retained fibrous feed particles for about 35 hours in the rumen and liquid for 19 hours, while horses retained fibrous particles for only 10 hours and liquid for 9 hours in the caecum (van Soest, 1994). Fibrous material with long particle length (size not defined) seems to leave the caecum and ventral colon of the horse at a faster rate than small particles (Meyer, 1984). This is maybe the result of the degree of flexure in the organ decreasing the resistance to flow towards the terminal end of the large intestine (Meyer et al., 1997, Frape, 1998). Meyer et al. (1997) also suggested the rapid flow of large indigestible (lignified) particles leads to a more efficient degradation of smaller particles. However, further research is necessary to verify this opinion. The need for a rapid rate of digesta flow in the colon can also be explained by the position of the 'fermentation centre' in the horse.

Gases (CH_4, CO_2 and H_2) produced in the rumen as results of microbial utilisation of feed nutrients are released by eructation. The horse does not have a similar mechanism to remove large quantities of gases from the caecum and large colon and either, a limited fermentation takes place or there are microbial communities possessing biochemical adaptations to produce low levels of methane and hydrosome metabolism (Russell and Gahr, 1999). The over-production of gases in the large intestine does occur in horses, especially when the animal is offered abrupt dietary changes or diets containing feeds that ferment rapidly (Drogoul et al., 2000b).

The concentration of starch reaching the large intestine is directly related to the extent of ante-caecal utilisation. It is the general opinion that total tract digestibility of starch is 100%. However, the level of feeding of starch and the degree of processing of the feed can alter the amount entering the large intestine. For instance, Varloud et al. (2003/4) reported 4.6 times (37 vs. 8 g/100 kg BW) more starch entering the large intestine when horses were offered high starch diets compared with high fibre diets. Inevitably, this influx of starch will depress the pH of the large intestine fluid matrix and can lead to significant biochemical and microbial dysfunction (Bailey et al., 2002; Dawson et al., 1999; Julliand et al., 2001) commonly leading to colic and eventually leading to intestinal damage. Furthermore, glucose yielded as a result of starch degradation will not be absorbed across the intestinal lining and will be utilised by gut microflora leading to the formation of VFA and lactate.

Small colon and rectum

The small colon (*colon tenue*) of horses begins at the termination of the colon and ends by the entry to the rectum at the pelvic inlet. The length of the small colon is approximately 3.5 m – about 30% longer than that observed in the cow. The small colon is spiral in nature and is one of the main sites of water and mineral absorption. The exact nature of the processes of water secretion and absorption within the entire colon is still not clear (Meyer, 1992). The rectum is the terminal part of the bowel from the pelvic inlet to the anus. It is approximately 30 cm in length and responsible for storage and expulsion of faeces. Faeces are expelled in large loosely joined 'pellets' with an average DM of 15-25%.

3

Feed chemistry and digestive processes

The chemical composition of feedingstuffs for horses and other herbivores has been reviewed extensively in many texts, for example, Bacon (1988), van Soest (1994) and McDonald *et al.* (1995). These excellent treatises cover many issues important to feed evaluation and feeding of herbivores. They do not, however, appraise critically the role of various evaluation methods used to determine the chemical composition of feeds and their relative merits or deficiencies when viewed in context to equine nutrition. This chapter on chemical composition of feed related to digestive processes will, together with the following chapters on feed analysis and nutrient requirements, lead into chapters on feed evaluation systems for horses. These chapters will present information essential to understand the processes involved in formulation of diets for energy and protein.

A key concept in feed biochemistry is the contribution of carbon, hydrogen, nitrogen, oxygen, phosphorus and sulphur to form nutrients (water, carbohydrates, protein and fatty acids) in feeds. These elements make up around 95 % of the horse's body. The major elements are required to form organic matter and other elements such as calcium, magnesium, potassium and sodium are also essential for biological processes in the animal. The trace elements (also known as micro-nutrients) are also important in animal nutrition. The functions of trace elements are diverse, for instance many are critical co-factors for certain enzymes (e.g. copper, molybdenum, zinc), play specialist roles in physiological systems and specialist roles at cellular, tissue and organ level. The role and function of minerals and vitamins will not be reviewed in this chapter, but are presented in Chapters 8 and 9.

Carbohydrate and dietary fibre

The current classification for carbohydrate is directly related to chemical structure, and loosely associated with feed evaluation methods. It is not the purpose of this book to describe in detail the different chemical classifications in relation to detailed methodology used to determine each but we will discuss carbohydrate substrates in terms of availability to the horse and the integration of certain fractions in feed evaluation systems.

The dry matter of plant material is composed of approximately 70 to 80% carbohydrate, whose structure and function varies considerably. It is, therefore, very difficult to provide an accurate definition of the different classes of carbohydrate in feeds. For instance, structural carbohydrate, insoluble carbohydrate, dietary fibre or structural fibre is frequently referred to as "fibre" depending on the context of the description. The use of the term "dietary fibre" or "structural polysaccharide" is also not clear in the literature related to herbivore nutrition (Bach-Knudsen, 2001). Jung and Allen (1995) noted that dietary fibre, roughage, and even lignin content were synonymous and interchangeable when discussing structural polysaccharides in plant cell walls.

The division of non-structural and structural carbohydrate is artificial as there is overlap in the role and function of each class. We have, therefore, chosen to distinguish between sources of carbohydrate that are available for processing by mammalian enzymes (digestible carbohydrate) and those carbohydrates which have to be fermented by microbial populations in the digestive tract of the horse. In the latter category we also include lignin (Figure 3.1).

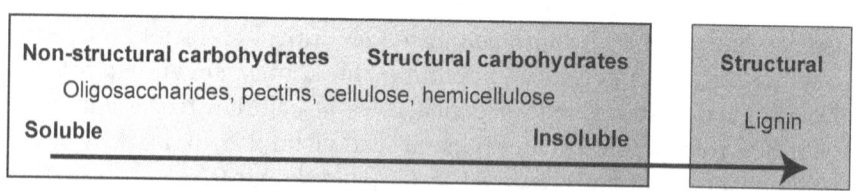

Figure 3.1 Characterisation and solubility of carbohydrate in animal feeds.

Feed chemistry and digestive processes

Non-structural carbohydrates

The characterisation of monosaccharides or simple oligosaccharides in feed evaluation systems is relatively simple. The preferred methods are either colorimetric or enzyme linked assays. However, the proximate analysis system incorporated the indirect measure of monosaccharide in the nitrogen free extractive (NFE). The assumption that the NFE was highly digestible carbohydrate is not true as it contains varying amounts of soluble carbohydrate, some hemicellulose, cellulose and lignin as a result of cumulative errors and incomplete characterisation of the fibre fraction (van Soest, 1994). For instance, the NFE of corn grain is over 80% simple carbohydrates but NFE of wheat straw contains about 60% hemicellulose and very little simple carbohydrate (Table 3.1).

Table 3.1 Monosaccharides and related compounds and their sources.

Type	Sugar	Source
Pentoses	Xylose	Hemicelluloses, pectic substances
	Arabinose	Plant gums (gum arabic), hemicelluloses
	Ribose	Nucleic acids (RNA), nucleotides
Hexoses	Glucose	Blood sugar in animals, storage in structural polysaccharides in plants
	Fructose	Semen / foetal fluids, storage polysaccharide in plants
		Lactose, glycoproteins, hemicelluloses
	Galactose	Glycoproteins, storage and structural
	Mannose	polysaccharides in plants
Deoxy-sugars	Deoxy-ribose	Nucleic acids (DNA)
	Rhamnose	Plant glycosides
Uronic acids	Galacturonic acid	Pectic substances
Amino-sugars	Glucosamine	Chitin fungi, mucopolysaccharides
Sugar alcohols	Sorbitol	Fruits
	Mannitol	Honeydew
	Glycerol	Fats

(Bacon, 1988)

The first products of photosynthesis are simple monosaccharides. The incorporation of simple monosaccharides into various non-structural and structural carbohydrate polymers is important for the characterisation of nutrients and formulation of diets. However, the total yield of glucose, xylose or any monomeric sugar from a feed after decomposition during analysis does not have a direct application to equine nutrition as the current methods of formulating rations do not consider the individual carbohydrate fractions. The non-structural carbohydrates form a large group of compounds based chemically on derivatives of pyranose or furanose. There are eight chemically distinguishable six-carbon sugars, of which one, glucose, has a central position in metabolism.

The polymers formed from monosaccharides are an integral component in the cell wall and storage compounds in plants. Easily digestible or fermentable storage polysaccharides in plants, such as amylose, are a readily available source of energy to the horse if they can be released from the cell. However, amylolytic activity in the digestive tract of the horse is relatively limited and the extent of digestion of starch in the small intestine is dependent on the botanical structure of the feed and the chemical structure of the starch (Kienzle et al., 1992).

Starch is the most important storage carbohydrate in plants. It can contribute up to 70% of the dry matter in cereal grains. Two types of polymer are observed; the linear α 1-4 linked glucopyranose chains and the branched chain α 1-4 linked amylopectin (Smith, 1981). The proportions of amylose and amylopectin vary in cereals used for animal feeds with potato and maize having higher concentrations of amylopectin than cereals (Fredrikksson et al., 2000; Frigård et al., 2002). The rate of enzymatic degradation of the two different types of starch differs and therefore the effect of feeding starch *per se* on the overall utilisation of the nutrient is variable (McAllan and Lewis, 1985). For example, in untreated maize there is a strong relationship between starch granule structure and the limitations of enzyme degradation of starch in the small intestine (Kienzle et al., 1998).

There is a further group of relatively simple oligosaccharides that have variable availability for digestion by mammalian enzymes, the ß glucans and fragments of amylopectin. Long-chained polysaccharides (eight or more monosaccharide units) provide the structural integrity to the cell walls of the plant. These are a rich source of energy that has to be fermented by microorganisms, as the animal does not possess cellulases, hemicellulases or pectinases. Pectic substances are often referred to as the 'intercellular cement' of plants (Fahey, 1988). They are mainly composed of galacturonic acid residues and are closely related to partially soluble hemicellulose. Pectin is also one of the major components of middle lamella of the cell wall conferring the ability of the cell wall to bind cations such as calcium and copper. Pectinases naturally occur in fungi, plants and bacteria. These enzymes catalyse the hydrolysis of pectin resulting in degradation of the middle lamella and separation of plant cell walls from each other. Pectin esterases convert pectins to pectic acid generally releasing Ca^{2+} ions (Fahey, 1988) and polygalacturonase degrades soluble pectin and pectic acid.

The processes of digestion and absorption of non-structural carbohydrate

Carbohydrate can only be absorbed across the intestinal mucosa if it is broken down to a simple monomeric compound, for instance glucose or fructose. Glucose is central to carbohydrate metabolism in horses; the regulation and routes of entry are essential to the understanding of diet formulation and the potential link to health problems (for example, acute laminitis). This is in contrast to the ruminant where the products of fermentation are the main energy source for metabolism. Three main routes of entry of glucose to intermediary metabolism occur: direct absorption of the monosaccharide, enzymatic digestion of di- and oligo-saccharides to yield glucose and the fermentation of dietary carbohydrate yielding volatile fatty acids that can be converted to glucose in the liver via gluconeogenesis (Table 3.2).

Table 3.2 Non-structural carbohydrate in feedstuffs and forages.

Carbohydrate	Solubility	Availability to mammalian enzymes	Fermentability
Sucrose	+++	+	+++
Galactans	++	0	++
Fructans	+	0	+++
ß glucans	++	0	++
Pectins	+	0	++
Starch	0	+	+
Soluble hemicellulose	+	0	+

(van Soest, 1994)

The lack of amylase activity in saliva means that only free water-soluble monosaccharides, or those which were released during the chewing process, can be absorbed immediately on entering the gastrointestinal tract. The viscosity of the ingesta can be affected by the chemical composition of the feed (especially the ratio of dietary fibre to starch) and secretions from the stomach wall. This will alter the dynamic of flow and the rate of acidification of the digesta in the pyloric region of the stomach. The impact of these dietary factors on the release of secretin in the duodenum of the horse still needs to be examined in detail but indirect evidence from de Fombelle et al. (2003) suggests that high starch diets lead to a higher pH in the duodenum compared to high fibre diets. The role of secretin in the duodenum is to stimulate the pancreas to release copious amounts of isotonic bicarbonate solution, thus neutralising the digesta.

The relatively mild, neutral pH conditions of the duodenum and the jejunum establishes ideal conditions for saccharidase activity attached to the brush border of the small intestine (Table 3.3). Monosaccharides are absorbed through the intestinal wall and the development of intestinal capacity and absorptive ability is essential for utilisation of carbohydrates. The secretion of fluids and enzymes into the intestinal lumen is also equally essential for optimal gut activity. In mammals, digestive enzymes have several sites of origin; the salivary glands, the stomach (especially the pyloric region), the pancreas and the small intestine *per se*. The mature horse possesses a full array of carbohydrase (amylase (from the pancreas), sucrase and maltase) with the exception of lactase (the enzyme system required to split lactose to glucose and galactose). Simple oligosaccharides are rapidly cleaved, by the action of enzymes secreted into the intestinal lumen, to their individual subunits and absorbed through the gut mucosa. The more complex oligosaccharides and starch also need to be broken down into monosaccharide units by enzymatic activity in the glandular region of the stomach or in the small intestine via the pancreatic juices. The released monosaccharides can then be absorbed as glucose and fructose. Fructose is further converted to glucose in the liver. A proportion of monosaccharides in the feed are utilised in the stomach as a result of microbial conversion to lactic acid or volatile fatty acids. This process is may be relatively important if the diet contains a relatively high level of sucrose or water-soluble carbohydrate.

Table 3.3 Carbohydrate digestion in the stomach and small intestine of the horse.

Amylose → α amylase (pancreas only) → maltose, iso maltose and → various enzymes → glucose

Amylopectin → α amylase (pancreas only) → maltose, iso maltose and → various enzymes → glucose

Sucrose → (sucrase) glucose
Lactose → (lactase) glucose
galactose

Feed chemistry and digestive processes

In cereal grains, starch is "protected" from digestion by the presence of the seed coat. Processing of cereal grain can effect the pre-caecal digestion and absorption of products of digestion in the horse (Kienzle *et al.*, 1998; Table 3.4). However, starch release is also affected by the granule structure, the endosperm cell wall and protein matrix as well as the biochemical structure of the starch *per se* (Rowe *et al.*, 1999; Kotarski *et al.*, 1992). The effects of disruption of the granule and chemical change as a result of feed processing of concentrate feeds containing cereal products have been evaluated extensively in horses (McLean *et al.*, 1999a and 1999b; Meyer *et al.*, 1993; Kienzle *et al.*, 1992).

Table 3.4 Proportion of pre-caecal starch digestibility of various feeds.

Author	Treatment	Oats	Maize	Barley	Sorghum
de Fombelle *et al.* (2001)	whole	0.993	0.662	0.814	
Meyer *et al.* (1995)	whole	0.835	0.288	0.215	
Meyer *et al.* (1993)	whole		0.290		
	crushed		0.470		
	heat processed		0.900		
Kienzle *et al.* (1992)	whole	0.800			
	crushed	0.850			
	ground	0.980			
Radicke *et al.* (1991)	ground	0.980	0.708		
Hinkle *et al.* (1983)	ground		0.607		
Arnold *et al.* (1981)	crushed	0.911	0.782		0.943
Householder *et al.* (1978)	rolled	0.480			0.360

The negative effects on digestibility of dry matter resulting from excessive levels of feeding of concentrate diets are exacerbated by the low intake of dietary fibre. This situation leads to the reduction in production of saliva (Meyer *et al.*, 1980), increasing numbers of colony forming units of lactobacilli (Garner *et al.*, 1978; Goodson *et al.*, 1988) and increased acidity in the stomach (de Fombelle *et al.*, 2003). The main physiological effect of the overload of starch in the digestive tract is an increased risk of ulceration of the gastric mucosa (Murray *et al.*, 1996; Nadeau *et al.*, 1998) and has been related to triggering the lamellar ischemia leading to acute laminitis (Bailey *et al.*, 2002 and 2003). Starch that is not digested in the small intestine will be readily degraded by bacteria in the hind-gut of the horse (a process of "spill-over"). Therefore, the total tract apparent digestibility of starch is approximately 100%

(Meyer *et al.*, 1993). However, the impact on the microflora in the hind-gut can be extensive. Starch entering the large intestine undergoes bacterial fermentation yielding volatile fatty acids and lactic acid (Garner *et al.*, 1978). This process is inefficient and it has been suggested that the yield of net energy to the animal from starch is reduced by between 35 and 40% compared to energy yielded from absorbed mono and disaccharides (Livingstone and Fowler, 1987).

An excess of soluble carbohydrate entering in the large intestine leads to a dominant community of microflora producing lactic acid (*Streptococcus bovis* and *Lactobacillus* sp.) developing a highly acidic environment (Garner *et al.*, 1978; Rowe *et al.*, 1995; Juilland *et al.*, 2001; Table 3.5). This situation can lead to lactate acidosis (Garner *et al.*, 1975), colic, laminitis (Pollitt, 2002; Pollitt and Davies, 1998; Rowe *et al.*, 1995) and diarrhoea in horses (Pickersgill and Marr, 1998). Furthermore, it can reduce cellulytic activity thus reducing the fermentation of dietary fibre (de Fombelle *et al.*, 1999). The by-products of microbial utilisation of starch may not be transported rapidly from the lumen of the intestine to intermediary metabolism increasing the acidity of the digesta. These conditions may lead to microbial death and release of endotoxins implicated with laminitis (Kruegar *et al.*, 1986; Meyer, 1995; Garner *et al.*, 1975; Valberg, 2000). Although microbial death has been indirectly implicated with the development of laminitis, intravenous injections of endotoxins produced by such processes have not led to the induction of laminitis. Furthermore, it has also been recently suggested that amine production in the caecum as a result of carbohydrate overload may lead to laminitis in the horse (Bailey *et al.*, 2002; Bailey *et al.*, 2003).

Table 3.5 Effect of diet on the pH and production of VFA (mmol/l) and lactate in the hindgut (A) or caecum (B).

Diet		Acetic	Proprionic	Butyrate	Lactate	Total	pH
A	Hay	43	10	3	1	57	6.9
	Concentrate	54	15	5	21	95	6.25
B	Hay	76.2	14.8	8			
	Hay: Concentrate 3:1	70.4	21.2	7.2			
	Hay: Concentrate 1:4	61.2	26	10.2			

(after Frape, 1998 (A); Meyer, 1995 (B))

Feed chemistry and digestive processes

The level of roughage in the ration of the horse will alter the digestibility of starch in the small intestine (Table 3.6). When green meal replaced hay in a diet containing ground maize, a significant increase in pre-ileal starch digestibility was noted (Meyer et al., 1993). The structural 'effect' of the fibre was lost in green meal due to the grinding process and thus pre-ileal retention time was likely to increase, leading to increased starch digestibility (Drogoul et al., 2000a; Kleffken, 1993). The results of Meyer et al. (1983) complement those of Hinkle et al. (1983) who changed the starch:roughage ratio of feed offered to ponies. At low levels of starch in the diet pre-ileal digestibility of starch was high but then reduced with increasing intake of starch despite a reduction in roughage intake. This response is likely to reflect the structural properties of alfalfa hay and a reduction in retention time of digesta.

Table 3.6 Effect of roughage on digestibility of starch (ground maize) in the small intestine.

Starch intake (g/kg BW/ meal)	Type of roughage	Roughage intake (g/kg BW/meal)	Starch/ Roughage ratio in feed	Starch digestibility (g/kg)	Reference
1.1	Alfalfa hay	12	11	650	Hinkle et al.
2.2	"	9	4	603	(1983)
3.2	"	6	1.9	547	
3.4	"	3	0.9	660	
2.2	Green meal	4.9	2.2	473	Meyer et al.
2.2	Grass hay	3.9	1.7	200	(1993)

Table 3.7 Effect of addition of α-amylase and amyloglucosidase (AMG) on mean and peak concentrations of glucose in blood plasma (mmol/l) of horses offered 670 g starch derived from steam treated triticale (Richards et al., 2003).

	Control	α-amylase	AMG	α-amylase +AMG
Peak glucose concentration	8.8^a	10.0^{ab}	8.8^a	10.8^b
Mean glucose concentration	6.9^a	7.9^b	7.0^a	8.4^b
Peak-basal glucose concentration	3.3^b	4.6^{ab}	3.6^{ab}	5.5^a
Time to peak concentration (hrs)	1.6	1.9	1.6	2.2
Slope to peak concentration (mmol/l/h)	2.2	2.5	2.4	2.8

[ab] values in same row with different superscripts are significantly different (p<0.01)

Recent studies by Richards *et al.* (2003) have examined the role of addition of α-amylase to concentrate diets offered to horses in an attempt to overcome the deficit in endogenous enzymes (Table 3.7). The addition of exogenous α-amylase elevated the peak concentration in blood and the average concentration of glucose 5 and 8 days after steam-rolled triticale was added to the diet of standard-bred and Thoroughbred geldings and mares. The study also confirmed that amyloglycanase activity did not lead to any improvement in the digestion of starch and peak concentration of glucose (similar glycaemic responses to the control diet)

Recently, fructans have been identified as important non-structural polysaccharides (up to 30 fructose molecules per fructan polysaccharide) in equine nutrition (Longland and Cairns, 1998; Longland *et al.*, 1999). There are two types of fructan, the ß 2-6 linked levans and the ß 2-1 inulins. The levans are relatively soluble in water, however the inulins have a much lower degree of solubility. Even though fructans are soluble in water, there is little evidence that the molecule is processed by mammalian enzyme systems (Bailey *et al.*, 2002; Garner *et al.*, 1975). Even though fructans are rapidly fermented by the gut microflora it is thought that low concentrations may be beneficial to balance the intestinal lumen matrix (Rao, 1999). However, in situations where excess fructan is available to the hind-gut microflora, there is evidence that the proliferation of gram positive microorganisms can lead to an environment where the epithelial mucosa is compromised (Weiss *et al.*, 1998). This situation may lead to carbohydrate-induced laminitis (Pollitt *et al.*, 1998; Pollitt and Davies, 1998; Mungall *et al.*, 2001; Pollitt, 2002). The chief function of fructans in grasses is to act as a storage polysaccharide with elevated concentration occurring in herbage grown under low environmental temperatures. High concentration of fructans in herbage has been associated with increased incidence of seasonal laminitis in horses and it is proposed not to turn susceptible animals out to pasture during the first few hours after dawn on winter mornings or while there is still frost on the land (Longland *et al.*, 1999).

Structural carbohydrate and lignin

Structural carbohydrates in nutritional terms are those polysaccharides which are not soluble in water and are associated with the plant cell wall. The term of "dietary fibre" or "structural polysaccharide" is not clear in the literature related to herbivore nutrition. Jung and Allen (1995) noted that dietary fibre, roughage, and even lignin content was synonymous and interchangeable when discussing structural polysaccharides in plant cell walls. The approach of van Soest (Goering and van Soest, 1970; van Soest and Wine, 1967) was to improve the definition of dietary fibre leading to the concept that structural polysaccharides associated with the cell wall could be divided into two classes based on their biological associations and availability of nutrients. Therefore, structural polysaccharides that lack covalent linkage to a lignin core are generally more soluble and will ferment in the rumen whereas those that are partially or fully linked to the lignin core are partially or incompletely digested (van Soest, 1994). However, the fundamental problem facing the equine nutritionist is to make a meaningful decision on the availability of information from chemical fractionation of the cell wall from ruminant data sets.

The majority of studies concerned with the utilisation of feeds by horses assume that crude fibre, neutral detergent fibre (NDF) or acid detergent fibre (ADF) are appropriate measures of the cell wall content of feeds. Studies that report the digestion of NDF and ADF by horses suffer from the problem that the measurement of NDF or ADF in feed or faeces may not be biologically relevant in equine nutrition (Andrieu and Martin-Rosset, 1995; Martin-Rosset *et al.*, 1990 and 1994; Miraglia *et al.*, 1999). The main reason for questioning the relevance of NDF and ADF as measures for feed composition in equine nutrition is that they were specifically designed for ruminant systems and thus may not reflect the chemical changes occurring during the passage of feed through the digestive tract. A further problem in the definition of dietary fibre is the underestimation of non-starch polysaccharide (NSP) by NDF. For instance, the underestimation of NSP by NDF in feeds containing high levels of legume can be as great as 15% (Chesson, 2000). This is important in the calculation of energy supplied by the feed to the animal as well as the efficiency of production of VFA by the gut flora. Lignin is not a carbohydrate but is generally listed as a component of fibre and therefore the description by van Soest (1994) of fibre as 'polymers that are unavailable to animal digestive enzymes' is applicable. Further information and details on the biochemical and physical nature of structural carbohydrates can be found in Bach-Knudsen (2001), van Soest (1994) or Aspinall (1980).

Cellulose is a ß1,4-linked polymer of glucose containing approximately 10000 glucose monomers per molecule. It is the most abundant carbohydrate polymer in biological systems amounting to between 20 and 40% of total dry matter and the principal component of dietary fibre. Holo-cellulose is deposited in primary cell wall of plants with pectins and xylans. This cellulose has a high digestibility *in vivo*. Cellulase enzyme complexes, produced by microorganisms in the large intestine of the horse or the rumen of the cow, are responsible for the cleaving of the ß 1-4 linkages. Cellulases are secreted by microorganisms once the microflora have attached to the cell wall and colonised. Very few cellulases are found in strained rumen liquor, however, substantial levels of hemicellulase activity can be observed (Dekker, 1976).

Hemicellulose is a heterogenous mixture of polysaccharides generally composed of ß 1-4 linked xylose chains with side-chains of arabinose, xylose or uronic acid with linkages of 1-2, 1-3 or 1-4. These ester linkages can be cleaved by hemicellulase but the degree of cross-linking to other sugar or polyphenol compounds modifies the availability of the molecule to fermentation. A high degree of cross-linkage to lignin or lignin like polymers in the cell wall confers hydrophobicity and can inhibit the action of xylanases, leading to an incomplete degradation of the cell wall (Jung and Allen, 1995). The digestion of hemicellulose and cellulose is not proportional in feeds. There are many instances in the literature on equine digestion where it is reported that the digestibility of cellulose is far lower than expected and the utilisation of hemicellulose is greater than expected (for example, Miraglia *et al.*, 1999, Dulphy *et al.*, 1997a). The reasons for this are not clear but may relate to the acidification and neutralisation of the cell wall in the fore-gut prior to entry into the large intestine and the processes of fermentation. Little or no hemicellulase activity has been recorded in the stomach of the horse (Hill *et al.*, 2002).

Lignin is probably the most important limiting factor in the availability of the cell wall to digestion. However, the characterisation of the compound is difficult and considerable variation in its composition has been observed between the major feed types and even during the growth of herbage (van Soest *et al.*, 1991; van Soest and Mason, 1991). The biosynthesis, occurrence and role of lignin in the degradation of cell walls has been reviewed by van Soest (1994). Lignin is a condensation product of various phenylpropanoid compounds for example, coumaric acid, ferulic acid and syringic acid and the various alcohol forms (Jung and Allen, 1995). During the biosynthesis and condensation of lignin, crosslinkages to hemi-celluloses can occur, reducing their degradability.

Degradation and fermentation of structural polysaccharides and lignin

The lack of an effective digestive enzyme in mammals that can cleave the β linkage in carbohydrate polymers (the exception is lactose) has led to the mutualistic arrangement between a wide range of microorganisms and the animal (van Soest, 1994). The arrangement allows the fermentation of plant cell walls and hence the utilisation of cellulose (or dietary fibre) by the horse.

Microbial fermentation of dietary fibre yields volatile fatty acids which are absorbed into intermediary metabolism across the wall of the large intestine and utilised as a major source of energy for the horse (Glinsky et al., 1976; Figure 3.2). Volatile fatty acids are waste products from fermentation and are removed from the large intestine through the epithelia. The pathway of absorption of VFA from the lumen of the caecum and colon has not been fully elucidated but may be dominated by the uptake of the anionic form of the individual VFA. It has been thought that uptake of the undissociated VFA was passive, however the rate of absorption is affected by lumen pH and type of VFA (chain length). The uptake of the anionic form would require active transport of bicarbonate across the epithelia of the caeco-colon complex and uptake of sodium (Argenzio and Stevens, 1975; Argenzio et al., 1977). The metabolism of absorbed volatile fatty acids produced during the fermentation is similar in horses and ruminants. Acetate and butyrate are generally incorporated into energy metabolism via pyruvate and acetyl Co A. Proprionic acid is the only VFA that can be converted directly into glucose (Mackie and Wilkins, 1988; Meyer, 1995).

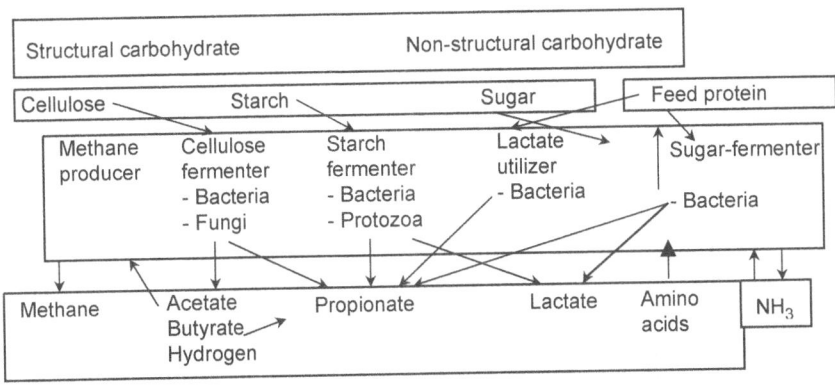

Figure 3.2 Microbial populations and their end products in the equine large intestine (adapted from Spring, 2000).

The structural carbohydrates (cellulose, hemi-cellulose, pectin) that enter the large intestine are largely intact, with little change in chemical composition. The number and range of microorganisms in the caeco-colon complex are comparable to those reported from ruminant species (Meyer, 1992; Michalet-Doreau et al., 2002).

The large intestine is generally populated by microflora associated with the digesta (lumenal based communities), as the rate of digesta flow in this compartment does not exceed the rate of turnover of microbial communities (Mackie and Wilkins, 1988). The community structure of the caeco-colon microflora varies considerably according to sources of carbohydrate entering the organ. Enumeration and characterisation of the microflora of the caecum and colon of the horse has received limited attention (for example, Kazunori et al., 1984; Moore and Dehority, 1993; Juilland et al., 1999, Drogoul et al., 2001; Michalet-Doreau et al., 2002; Medina et al., 2002). The microflora in the hind-gut is dominated by mixed communities of heterotrophs utilising structural carbohydrate (*Fibrobacter succinogene, Ruminococcus albus* and *R. flavefaciens*), lactic acid (e.g. *Veillonella*), undigested protein and non-structural carbohydrate (*Streptococcus* and *Lactobacillus*). The population of methane producing bacteria is much reduced in horses compared to ruminants presumably reflecting the process of acetogenesis (Spring, 2000).

Acetogenesis replaces methanogenesis in colonic fermenters (Yang et al., 1970; Prins and Lankhorst, 1977; Breznek and Kane, 1990). In the anoxic environment of the hind-gut microbial formation of acetic acid from H_2 and CO_2 is common. Large quantities of H_2 can be produced during fermentation and in ruminants the formation of methane results from the terminal electron sink reaction (Breznek and Kane, 1990). However, in equines there is considerable evidence that H_2 is consumed by bicarbonate to form acetic acid.

Ruminant: $\quad 4H_2 + HCO_3^- \rightarrow CH_4 + 3H_2O$

Equine: $\quad 4H_2 + 2HCO_3^- \rightarrow CH_3COO^- + 4H_2O$

Although this process yields a lower level of energy for the microbial community ($\Delta G^{0'} = -135.6$ kJ for ruminants compared to $\Delta G^{0'} = -104.6$ kJ for equine), the process will allow a greater retention of energy derived

Feed chemistry and digestive processes

from fermentation of carbohydrate than VFA (acetic acid) thus increasing the efficiency of carbohydrate utilisation by the animal (Russell and Gahr, 2000; Hill, 2002). Even though the apparent digestibility of feeds offered to horses is lower compared to ruminants, the ability of the horse to utilise non-structural carbohydrate before fermentation and the reduced loss of carbon as a result of acetogenesis is one of the reasons why the horse can compete with grazing ruminants. This scenario is also modified by rate of passage of digesta (Kern *et al.*, 1973; Koller *et al.*, 1978; Hyslop and Cuddeford, 1996; Hyslop, 1998). The outflow from the caecum of horses is reported at around 20% of digesta per hour, whereas rumen outflow to the abomasum ranges from 2 to 8% per hour (van Soest, 1994). This difference in rate would reduce the time structural carbohydrate resided in the site of fermentation. The microflora in the small intestine is likely to be composed of communities closely associated with the mucosa (e.g. *Lactobacillus mucosae*), adhering to epithelial surfaces and the mucus layer of the small intestine. Mackie and Wilkins (1988) also suggested that microbial processing of substrates in the duodenum, jejunum and ileum could occur. However, recent work by Morris *et al.* (2002) and de Fombelle *et al.* (2003) suggests little or no ante caecal utilisation of structural carbohydrate for hay-based diets. However, the situation may be different for haylage. Extremely high OM digestibility coefficients (greater than 0.74; Smolders *et al.*, 1990; Ellis *et al.*, 2003) and high quantities of fibre retained in the stomach after a period of 12 hours of fasting (Boswinkel *et al.*, 2004) may indicate some structural carbohydrate utilisation occurring pre-caecally.

Recent studies by Michalet-Doreau *et al.* (2002) demonstrated that the changes in cellulolytic bacterial community structure occurred in the caecum and the rumen of sheep after feeding hay:starch diets could be investigated by using molecular techniques (16S rRNA; Table 3.8).

Surprisingly, only 4.6% of rumen and caecal total bacterial communities were identified as the major cellulolytic species *Ruminococcus* and *Fibrobacter*. Michalet-Doreau and co-workers (2002) also reported the activity of polysaccharidases and glycosidases associated with solid-adhered microorganisms in rumen and caecal fluids (Table 3.9). Considerable differences in activities of fibrolytic enzymes in both organs were observed. It was suggested that the physico-chemical environment in the caecum was less favourable for enzyme production, and mean particle retention and concentration of potentially degradable substrates entering the caecum were lower than that of the rumen. These differences were measured in sheep, but comparable studies are essential in horses to improve our understanding of the microbial and enzymatic activities present in the hind-gut.

Table 3.8 Cellulolytic bacterial communities (μg/g DM) of the rumen and caecum of sheep) (after Michalet-Doreau et al., 2002)

Bacterial concentration	Location	Time after feeding (hr)				SE
		-1	3	6	9	
Total bacteria (μg/g DM)	Rumen	925.9	339.8	937.3	803.3	169.8
	Caecum	464.0	314.5	257.9	319.8	
Cellulolytic bacteria, rRNA % total bacterial rRNA						
Sum	Rumen	4.5	5.0	4.1	4.8	1.2
	Caecum	2.9	3.3	5.7	6.6	
Ruminococcus albus	Rumen	0.9	1.4	1.0	1.0	0.4
	Caecum	0.6	0.7	0.9	1.1	
Ruminococcus flavefaciens	Rumen	1.6	1.4	1.2	1.4	0.9
	Caecum	1.6	1.9	2.9	3.3	
Fibrobacter succinogenes	Rumen	2.0	2.3	1.9	2.3	1.1
	Caecum	0.8	0.7	1.9	2.2	

Table 3.9 Polysaccharidase (μmoles of reducing sugar.mg protein^{-1}.h^{-1}) and glycosidase (μmoles of p-nitrophenol.mg protein^{-1}.h^{-1}) specific activities in solid-adherent microorganisms in the rumen and caecum.

	Location	Time after feeding (hr)				SE
		-1	3	6	9	
Polysaccharidases						
Xylanases	Rumen	8.95	3.84	4.96	5.43	1.00
	Caecum	0.65	0.98	0.55	0.48	
Avicelase	Rumen	0.64	0.02	0.46	0.05	0.08
	Caecum	0.01	0.08	0.06	0	
Glycosidases						
ß-D-xylosidase	Rumen	2.26	1.19	1.80	1.82	0.60
	Caecum	0.45	0.45	0.24	0.22	
ß-D-glucosidase	Rumen	3.14	2.58	2.66	2.48	0.80
	Caecum	0.17	0.23	0.17	0.13	

The rate of flow of digesta, differential flow of feed particles and processes involved in the degradation of the structural carbohydrates in the horse have not been explored in detail. Chapter 4 examines the *in vivo* response of nutrient absorption to digesta flow. However, some aspects of the interactions between digesta flow and nutrient digestibility have to be examined. Drogoul *et al.* (1996) examined the impact of different methods of processing of hay on total tract digestibility of nutrients. Substantial differences in the rate of flow of particles from the mouth to the caecum were observed with long particles entering the caecum within an hour of feeding and residing for more than 8 hours. However, particles of ground, pelleted hay entered the caecum after approximately 2.5 hours after feeding and remained for less than 4 hours before passage to the colon. Interestingly, the total tract digestibility of dry matter was not affected by method of feed processing but there was a reduction in the cellulolytic microflora in diets containing ground, pelleted hay. It was suggested that a reduction in microbial attachment and colonisation occurred on the fine particles but the processes of fermentation were more efficient. An increase in the molar ratio of propionic acid to acetic acid occurred, highlighting important changes in the microbial ecosystem and it's processing of dietary fibre.

The physiological importance of dietary fibre to the horse has been highlighted in the past and more recently it has been suggested that variation in the fibre content of diets may alter behavioural processes of the animal. Wood chewing, coprophagy, restlessness, abdominal pain and development of stereotypical behaviour have been reported when horses are offered high levels of concentrate or have a high short-term intake rate (Willard *et al.*, 1977; Haenlein *et al.*, 1966b; Johnson *et al.*, 1988; Cuddeford, 1999). These behavioural changes are partly linked to the faster rate of ingestion of the concentrate diet and hence a greater period of time not feeding, a reduction in the production of saliva and higher production of volatile fatty acids and lactic acid in the stomach. Increased acidity of the digesta in the stomach may result in a greater risk of gastric ulceration (Pagan, 1997) and the increased production of VFA in the large intestine has been linked to restlessness (Cuddeford, 2000). The problems associated with high levels of starch in the concentrate can be managed by both the imposition of a maximum starch inclusion rate (generally suggested as 3.5 g/kg BW per meal; Potter *et al.*, 1992) and a recommended minimum fibre intake per day (5 g/kg BW - Meyer, 1987; or structural fibre intake of 1.5% of BW; Ellis, 2004). However, for starch levels there is considerable variation in the recommendations. The NRC (1989) recommends twice the amount at 10 g/kg BW, whereas Kienzle *et al.* (1992) suggested that small intestinal

Nutritional Physiology of the Horse

capacity for starch utilisation could be exceeded when 2 g/kg BW/meal was offered. Recent research confirms that 2 g/kg BW/ meal is the most realistic limit to prevent hindgut disturbances (Julliand *et al.*, 2003).

The recent trend towards increasing rates of inclusion of fibre in concentrate pellets/feed does reduce starch intake per meal but does not address aspects of behavioural problems. Ground and/or processed fibre is eaten at the similar short-term intake rates as concentrate feed (Ellis, 2003a), leading to reduced saliva production and possibly decreased rates of passage (Drogoul *et al.*, 2000a). Thus this processed form of fibre does not have the same 'protective' effect against acidification of the intestinal environment as large particulate structural fibre (Ellis, 2003a). It is therefore recommended that the concentrate to roughage (structural fibre) ratio of a diet is considered as well as the starch intake *per se*.

In conclusion, a model system can be presented that examines the fate of structural and non-structural carbohydrate in the digestive tract of the horse (figure 3.3). The model system is a modification of the model presented for pigs by Bach Knudsen (2001).

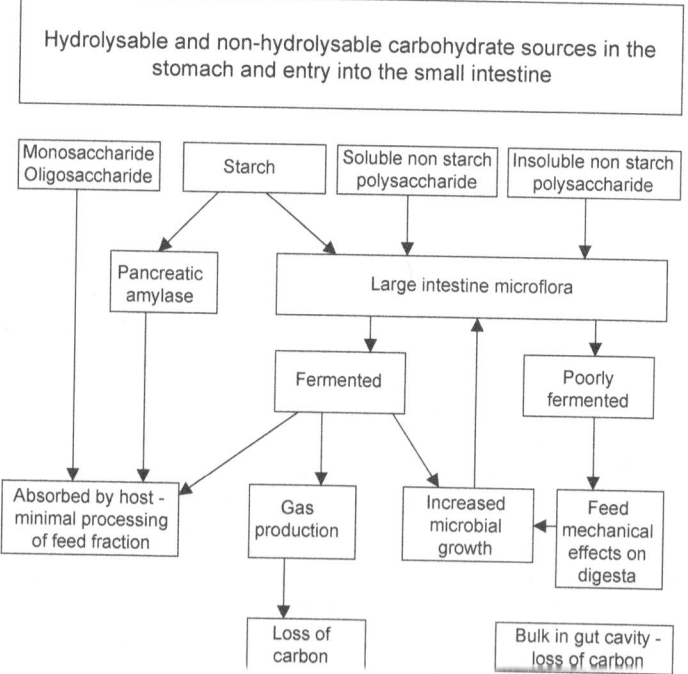

Figure 3.3 Proposed fate of structural and non-structural carbohydrate in digestive tract of the horse.

Feed chemistry and digestive processes

Protein and other nitrogen compounds in feed

Nitrogen occurring in feeds is broadly classified as true protein or non-protein nitrogen. The distinction is relatively simple and has an application in equine nutrition. The concentration of protein *per se* in total nitrogen ranges from 60 to 80% depending on source of feed. The residual nitrogen is either soluble non-protein nitrogen compounds (e.g. ureides, nitrate, low molecular weight peptides and amino acids), nitrogen in lignin or nucleic acids (4 or 5% of total N).

Proteins are constructed from the combination of amino acid monomer units (Metzler, 1977). Generally, protein is constructed from 20 to 21 individual major amino acid monomers, however, inclusion of minor amino acids into protein does occur. The processes involved in protein synthesis are not reviewed in this text (see any standard biochemistry textbook; e.g. Metzler, 1977). However, a brief discussion of the peptide linkage is essential in understanding of proteolytic enzymes and amino acid nutrition of the horse. Individual amino acids are linked together by the peptide bond (-CONH- linkage) to form peptides, polypeptides and functional proteins. The peptide linkage is susceptible to hydrolysis in acid and alkaline conditions as well as being the site of degradation mediated by proteases.

Many proteins are polymers of 100s to 1000s of amino acids. The architecture and structure of proteins is three-dimensional and is related to their role and function in mammalian systems. Mammals lack the ability to synthesise all amino acids required for protein synthesis and therefore they are dependent on intake of certain amino acids from dietary sources. In total, nine amino acids are believed to be essential for protein synthesis and metabolic function in the horse. These are lysine, threonine, leucine, isoleucine, valine, methionine, phenylalanine, tryptophan and histidine. Tyrosine and cysteine are thought to be "semi-essential" (Jarrige and Tisserand, 1984).

The processes of digestion of proteins and absorption of amino acids and non-protein nitrogen

Feed protein entering the digestive tract is denatured by acid (HCl) in the pyloric region of the stomach. The peptide linkages are cleaved by endopeptidases (proteolytic enzymes), for instance, pepsin in the stomach and trypsin in the anterior duodenum. Endopeptidases are secreted into the lumen of the digestive tract as inactive pro-enzymes (for instance pepsinogen) and are activated by the low pH, hydrochloric acid (HCl) and the presence of pepsin (autocatalysis) (Stevens, 1988). In the fundic region of the stomach of the horse, pepsinogen is released together with HCl, which facilitates proteolytic activity of pepsin (Argenzio, 1993). The digestion of protein here is limited by the passage rate. The main sites of protein digestion and absorption are the duodenum, jejunum and ileum. In these sections of the digestive tract pancreatic proteases (trypsinogen, chymo-trypsinogen, proelastases) are secreted and are converted to endopeptidases (trypsin, chymo-trypsin, elastase) and activated at the intestinal brush-border by trypsin (Argenzio, 1993).

A substantial proportion of microbial species residing in the lumen of the duodenum, jejunum and ileum of the horse are capable of proteolytic activity (Kern et al., 1973; Mackie and Wilkins, 1988). However, their activity is variable in relation to the quality of the protein entering the small intestine and the rate of passage of the digesta. The amino acids released after enzymatic digestion of protein and peptides in the stomach, duodenum and jejenum/ileum are absorbed across the intestinal wall. The transport of α amino acids to the blood across the intestinal wall is mediated by a number of amino acid transport proteins. These proteins allow the substrate (amino acid) to bind to a recognition site, assist the translocation of the amino acid through the membrane to the cell cytosol and release the amino acid to the cytosol during a process of re-orientation to allow further amino acids to bind (Matthews, 2000).

Three major pathways of amino acid metabolism can be identified in horses. Deamination is the main pathway used by animals to reduce amino acids to their carbon skeleton keto acid equivalent and glutamate. This pathway is important in the metabolism of all amino acids except lysine and threonine. Deamination is linked to a second pathway which then releases the nitrogen in glutamate in the form of ammonia via glutamate dehydrogenase. Deamination of amino acids can take place in the hindgut, where the exogenous (bacterial) D-amino acid oxidases convert amino acids to keto acids, hydrogen peroxide and ammonia (NH_3). Hydrogen peroxide is highly toxic and is immediately converted to water and oxygen by catalase. Bacterial action and excess supply of D-amino acids may affect the health of the horse, but there is little or no clear evidence. The only circumstantial evidence is that after microbial death D-amino acids can be released and are possibly connected to endotoxaemia causing laminitis (Bailey et al., 2002; Bailey et al., 2003).

Feed chemistry and digestive processes

All three pathways lead to the release of ammonia which must be cleared from metabolism rapidly. In horses ammonia is cleared from metabolism, as in the majority of mammals, via the formation of urea. The urea cycle occurs in the liver and consumes 3 mol of ATP for 1 mol of ammonia cleared. However, by-products of metabolism are recycled via the Krebs cycle thus making the clearance of ammonia energetically efficient.

Any protein passing the ileal-caecal junction will be exposed to the microbial community of the hind-gut. Feed protein and some microbial protein entering the hindgut will be degraded by exopeptidases released by the hind-gut microflora. The uptake of amino acids from the lumen of the caeco-colon complex to the blood is disputed. The opinion of the majority is that such absorption is unlikely (Meyer, 1995; Frape, 1998) and this is confirmed by recent research (see Chapter 7).

The concepts of biological value of protein and essentiality of amino acids to metabolism are important to note in equine nutrition. Biological value of protein attempts to link the quality of the protein in the feed to that of the animal product synthesised (muscle, milk, hide). In simplistic terms, the closer the match of feed protein amino acid composition to the product, the higher the biological value. This system is not appropriate for ruminants as the majority of feed protein is degraded in the rumen and incorporated into microbial protein. Therefore any measure of biological value in the ruminant is a measure of value of the feed protein to the rumen microflora and not the animal. However, the digestive tract of the horse has the main site of protein utilisation centred in the small intestine (Meyer, 1995). The process of denaturation and digestion of feed protein yields essential and non-essential amino acids as well as ammonia. Essential amino acids (EAA) are those that cannot be synthesised *de novo* by the horse but are essential for metabolic processes. The supply of EAA from the diet is especially important when physiological demand for EAA is high, for instance during heavy work, pregnancy and lactation. Any process of deamination of amino acids derived from feed protein reduces the supply of EAA but will provide precursors for non-essential amino acid (NEAA) synthesis. The supply of protein to the large intestine is also critical in equine nutrition. Rather than being a net supplier of amino acids to intermediary metabolism, nitrogen supplied will either be utilised by the microflora (thus providing an essential nutrient for microbial functionality) or be utilised via the synthesis of NEAA from ammonia (Potter, 2002).

Fats and oils (lipids)

Lipids are classified into compounds that are seed borne (triglycerides), leaf lipids (e.g. galactolipids and phospholipids) and waxes, pigments, essential oils and other ether soluble compounds (van Soest, 1994; Wiseman, 1984). Fatty acids are one of the most important energy reserves in animals. In general, the diet of the horse is relatively depleted in lipid, however supplementation of the diet with lipid from exotic sources (for example, animal by-products, seed extractives) has become common in equine nutrition (Lewis, 1995). Although fats and oils are generally more expensive than grain by weight, their energy content is generally twice or more than that of processed cereal grains. The other important function of lipid in the diet is the absorption of fat-soluble vitamins (e.g. vitamin A, D, E and K) as well as acting as a source of linoleic acid (an essential fatty acid).

Table 3.10 Energy density of fats and grain (after Lewis, 1995).

Source	Digestible energy (MJ/kg as fed)
Vegetable oil (source not cited)	37.5
Animal fat	33.1
Maize (cracked)	14.2
Oats (whole)	12.0

Lipids generally contain a glycerol molecule linked to one or more long chain alkanes terminating in a carboxylic acid functional group. The glycerol moiety can also be linked to a sugar for example galactose (galactolipids).

Table 3.11 Types of lipids and their composition.

Types of lipid	Composition
Fatty Acids	Long-chain carboxylic acids
Glycerides	Esters of fatty acids an glycerol
Waxes	Esters of fatty acids and long-chain alcohols
Cutin, suberin	Polymers of hyroxylated fatty acids
Steroids	Polycyclic hydrocarbons
Phospho, glycosyl-glycerolipids	Glycerides with phosphate or sugar constituents
Lipid amino-acids conjugates, peptide linked lipids	
Glycolipids	Substituted amide and other linkages

(Bacon, 1988)

The hydrocarbon chain can be composed of single bond carbon linkages (saturated) or single and double bond linkages (unsaturated) forms. Lipids are classified according to length of aliphatic chain, which may range from 1 to 30+ carbon atoms. Chain lengths of 1 to 6 carbon atoms are commonly referred to as volatile fatty acids (VFA) and are usually found in free undissociated form. Volatile fatty acids play an important role in the equine and ruminant nutrition, as they are by-products of microbial fermentation and major energy yielding substrates to intermediary metabolism.

Digestion and utilisation of fat

Fats are digested in the small intestine by lipases released into the lumen. The lipid is cleaved into its individual monoglycerides and these are absorbed efficiently (Meyer, 1995). The digestibility of fats and oils in the diet of horses ranges from 76 to 94% (Lewis, 1995). Fats and oils provide an important energy source for the horse under training and exercise, growth and lactation by increasing availability of energy without an increase in dietary energy intake (Geelen et al., 2001). The main reason for the increased availability of energy from fat (apart from its energy density) is the reduction in metabolic heat production and therefore, an increase in net energy available for maintenance and production (Scott et al., 1993). However, formulation of the diet must be optimal to prevent digestive disorders. High rates of inclusion of fat have been reported to reduce voluntary intake of the diet and reduce microbial efficiency ante-caecal and in the large intestine (Meyer, 1997; Jansen et al., 2000).

The reasons for the reduction in microbial efficiency are two-fold. Jansen et al. (2000) indicated that a high rate of inclusion of fat (381 g/day) led to an unfavourable environment for cellolulytic bacteria in the hind-gut rather than as a result of "coating" the feed with lipid. However, the alteration of the chemical composition of the fluid matrix in the gut and the toxic effects of high concentration of lipid on protozoa are the most possible effects to lead to negative associativity when the diet is supplemented with excess fat (Zinn and Ware, 2002). Meyer et al. (1997) also observed that high intake of dietary fat increased the rate of flow of jejuno-ileal chyme. Consequently, this increased rate of passage of digesta through the gastrointestinal tract could lead to a lower efficiency of fibre digestion as the residence time in the colon is reduced. When horses are supplemented with a range of inclusion of fat (corn oil: 0 to

15% of diet DM), digestibility of neutral detergent fibre, organic matter, crude protein and fat increases until 15% of the diet DM was lipid. Inclusion rates of 15% (750g/d) or greater lead to an increase in digestibility of oil but a decrease in NDF, OM and CP digestibility (Bush et al., 2001).

Physico-chemical properties of feeds

The physico-chemical composition of the feed is important in determining voluntary intake, nutrient release and the acceptability of a feed for ration formulation. The process of chewing of feeds to disrupt plant tissues has been examined in the previous chapter when we considered dentition. If the feedstuff is to pass from the fore gut to the large intestine in a form that allows microbial colonisation and utilisation, the process of chewing must disrupt the feed, thus altering the size, shape and specific gravity of particles (Faichney, 1986). Feeds utilised by horses contain plant material that is designed for specific roles and functions in the plant. Plant tissue can be divided into protective tissues (epidermis and periderm), the vascular tissues (phloem and xylem) and the basal tissues (parenchyma, collenchyma and sclerenchyma). The relative proportion of each tissue type within a feed depends on the date of harvest of the feed resource and the methods of processing applied during feed manufacture. Grazed grass is possibly the only form of feed that has not undergone processing and is harvested by the animal directly. Compound feeds, hays and silage have all undergone processing (physical or microbial) to some degree.

Basal tissues are the main sites of metabolic activity in the plant, providing a location for synthesis and storage of carbohydrate, lipid and protein. Basal tissues have a low resistance to chewing and therefore, the releases of nutrients are rapid and, generally complete (Jung and Allen, 1995). Cell wall material in plants is composed of primary and secondary tissues. The secondary cell wall contains a varying degree of sclerenchyma and hence a varying degree of lignin. The primary cell wall contains a considerable amount of pectin, xylan and cellulose. The availability of the cell wall to the animal is partly dependent on the chemical composition of the cell wall and partly on the physical disruption of cell wall during chewing or feed manufacture (including chemical and physical treatment of the cell wall; Harbers et al., 1981).

Chewing grinds and shears feed particles prior to entry to the stomach and intestinal tract. In ruminants, total chewing time has been related to concentration of fibre (NDF) in the diet (Welch and Smith, 1969; Sudweeks *et al.*, 1981; de Boever *et al.*, 1993). If the total chewing time is affected by the concentration of fibre in the diet, it will also potentially be altered by the physical structure of the fibre. It is therefore clear that a greater degree of lignification of the cell wall will alter the fracture properties during chewing. Various measures of physical structure have been developed for ruminants (for example, fibrousness index, Chenost, 1966); roughage value index (fibrosity index), Balch 1971, Sauvant *et al.*, 1996; physically effective NDF, Mertens, 1997; and structural value, de Brabander *et al.*, 1996). These methods have been useful in determining the voluntary intake of cattle and sheep when offered forage and concentrate diets. Little or no work has been performed to identify if the relationships developed for ruminants are appropriate for horses.

Apart from a negative effect on digestibility, the increasing maturity of forage leads to changes in chemical composition of the feed and the fracture properties of the tissues. Fracture properties of feeds and the methods to measure fracture properties of plant material have been reviewed by Vincent (1990), Lucas and Pereira (1990) and Wright and Illius (1995). Vincent distinguished three levels of fracture of feedingstuffs: organ, tissue and cell. The latter category is of particular concern to equine nutrition as the cell provides the majority of energy and protein supply to the animal. As mentioned, lignification of the cell wall tends to increases rigidity and therefore the cell wall is more likely to break or shatter than bend. The degree of shatter and bend of a feed during chewing will lead to considerable variation in the surface area to volume ratio of the digesta entering the gastrointestinal tract (Lowman *et al.*, 2002). Furthermore, the particle density and characteristics of flow within the lumen of the gut will be altered, thus leading to an alteration in the processes of digestion (Poppi *et al.*, 1981; Lowman *et al.*, 2002). For instance, legume particles tend to shatter into small, spherical or near-spherical particles whereas grass particles are needle shaped.

Processing of forages can adversely affect the voluntary intake of horses. Alteration of physical form will alter the rate of ingestion and potentially alter the response of the animal to certain feed factors (for example, NDF content). In Europe, the use of "chops" and "chaffs" as admixtures to concentrates are popular on the basis that "they slow" the rate of eating of concentrate diets. Undoubtedly physical form of forages alters the rate of eating (for example, wafering or pelleting of alfalfa hay elevated voluntary intake by 0.17 and 0.24 compared to "loose" hay; Haenlein *et al.*, 1966) but may not alter the digestibility of the feed (see for instance Gallagher *et al.*, 1984).

Wetting of particles during chewing is also affected by the degree of fracture. Two characteristics of the fractured feeds have to be assessed; the water-holding capacity of the cell wall and the bulk volume of the particle. Bulk volume is a measure of the space trapped within the particle and therefore the three-dimensional structure of the feed. Chewing and particle fracture generally reduces the bulk volume thus altering the hydration (wetting) capacity. Few studies examining the hydration capacity of particles entering the digestive tract of the horse have been performed. One such study (Hughes and Hill, 2004, *unpublished data*) showed differences in the rate of hydration of particles from different regions of the stomach of the horse. Particles collected from the pyloric region possessed a greater rate of hydration (0.078 ml/g/min) than those of the saccus caecus (0.037 ml/g/min). These differences may reflect one of two processes, the removal of soluble substances from the feed as a result of fermentation and the secretion of mucus in the pyloric region affecting the cation exchange capacity of the fibre. Little research investigating the fracture properties of forages offered to horses has been performed and should remain a priority for equine digestive physiologists. For instance, differences noted in eating behaviour, pattern of chewing and nutrient acquisition from grazed forages are not easily explained without an understanding of the physico-chemical interactions of feeds (Ellis, 2003a).

4

Feed and feed evaluation *in vivo*

Feed classification and the feed industry

The horse is, by nature, an animal adapted to the grazing environment. However, many horses are managed in the stabled environment and are offered conserved roughages and concentrate sources of feed for the majority of the year. The conserved roughage diets are low to medium energy density and contain varying levels of dietary fibre and protein. They are subdivided into field-dried (hays and straws), high temperature dried (ryegrass or lucerne products) or ensiled (haylage and silage) grassland products. In order to meet the additional demands for energy by work, reproduction, lactation and growth, additional energy is provided by offering concentrates containing a variety of energy (e.g. wheat, barley, oats, fat supplements etc.) and/or protein rich (e.g. soya, peas, beans etc.) feedingstuffs. During periods of grazing, feed allowances are based on pasture production with limited supplementation with high energy feed. The production of horse feeds in Europe is an important sector of agriculture (Figure 4.1).

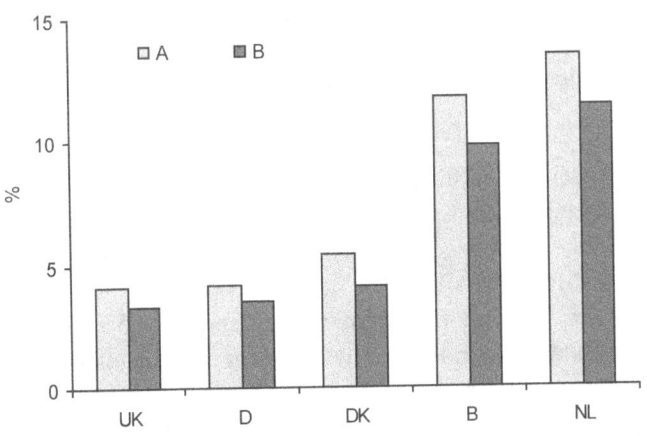

Figure 4.1 Proportion of agricultural land utilised for horse feed production, estimated according to horse numbers per European country and according to a high concentrate diet (A) or a high fibre diet (B) (Source: The Horse Industry in the European Union, Working Report, EU Equus 2001, Sweden).

Generally, horse feed can be divided into green and conserved plant material often referred to as roughages or forages and concentrate feeds (grains, seeds or by-products) fed either as straights or as part of processed mixed feed. Some feed processing by-products are also used as cheap raw fibre supplements (for example, coconut fibre, bran). There is also a range of pre mixes, containing minerals and vitamins, oils and further additives such as herbs (Figure 4.2).

Detailed descriptions of individual feed stuffs from this list have been published previously (see Frape, 1998). Some additional details of the major horse feed in relation to the feed industry in the UK are provided in this chapter.

Hay and silage

The production of hay and silage for livestock production has been reviewed recently by Wilkinson *et al.* (1996) and Wilkinson and Toivonen (2003). The area of grassland harvested for hay varies considerably from year to year depending on the weather conditions. The areas of grassland harvested in the UK for hay in 1984, 1989 and 1994 were 660,000, 768,000 and 641,000 hectares. The estimated total production of hay in these three years was below 3.5 million tonnes freshweight whereas silage production increased from 38 m tonnes fresh weight in 1989 to over 53 m tonnes fresh weight in 1994. The economic output from the UK hay industry is also difficult to determine. Prices for hay can vary between £30 per tonne to £80 per tonne (British Hay and Straw Merchants Association) however the cost to the individual owner of a horse can be considerably higher (up to £125 to £150 per tonne).

Silage production for horses has been limited in the UK, partly in response to a lack of knowledge of feeding the forage and partly reflecting the many and varied methods of production of silage. However, the production of high DM silage for horses is beginning to become popular. The production of high DM silage (greater than 45% dry matter) is a specialist grassland operation. High dry matter silages can be marketed in small bales, enough for feeding to less than 5 horses per day, or produced in large bales for yards with relatively high numbers of horses. The main problem with the production of high dry matter silage is the low stability on feed-out of the product during feeding.

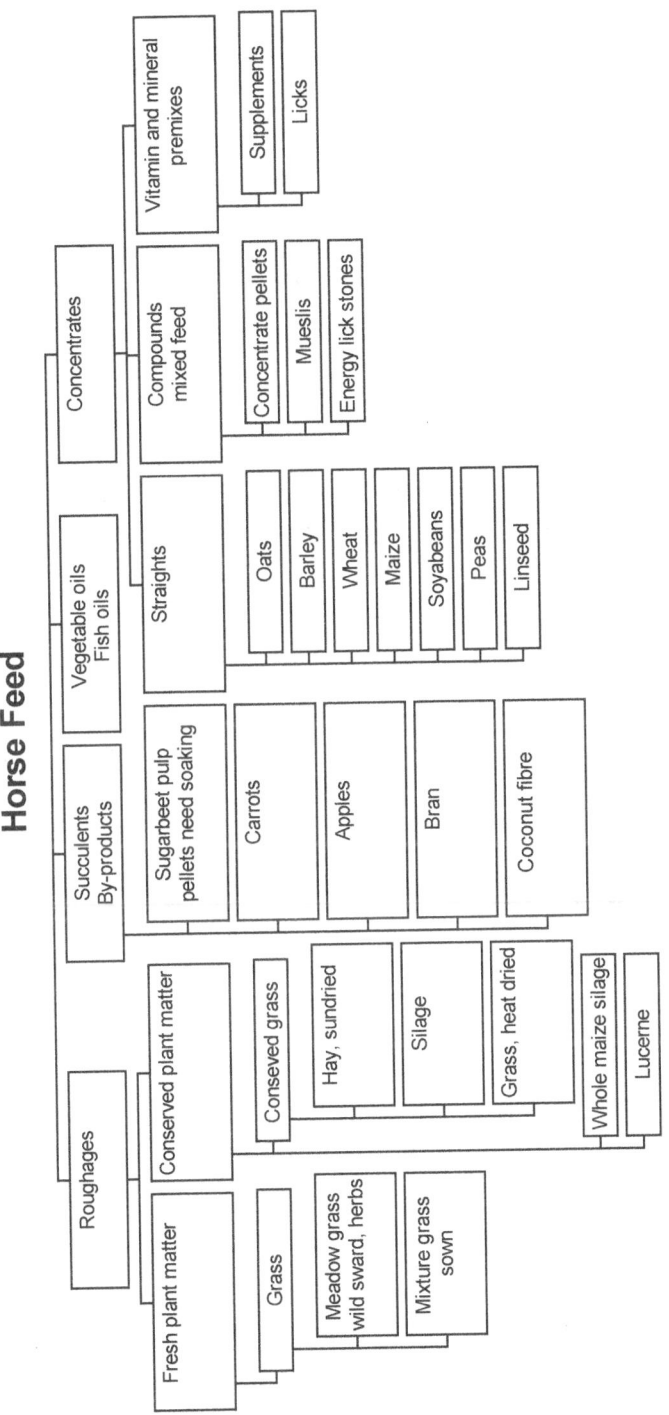

Figure 4.2 Range of equine feed.

Secondary fermentation following exposure to the air can lead to extensive mould development and hence a potential risk of mould and fungal contamination as well as mycotoxicosis (Smith et al., 2002). If the dry matter of the silage is too low, the development of potentially deleterious microbial populations is high (McDonald et al., 1991). There have been a number of cases of botulism and listeriosis in the horse industry ascribed to silage production (Ricketts et al., 1984). Recent studies on voluntary intake of silages have demonstrated differences between clamp and big-bale silage (Moore-Colyer and Longland, 2000; Hale and Moore-Colyer, 2001) and silages of different chop length (Morrow et al., 1999). In general, the voluntary dry matter intake of silages is lower than that observed for hay made from the same crop (McClean et al., 1995). Studies assessing the voluntary intake of maize silage are limited. Martin-Rosset and Dulphy (1987) noted very low voluntary intake of maize silage compared to hay (40.6 g/kg $BW^{0.75}$ for maize silage and 99.1 g/kg $BW^{0.75}$ for hay) even though the silage had good fermentation characteristics.

Table 4.1 Feed intake, nutrient consumption and *in vivo* apparent digestibilities of grass and oat silages offered to horses (after Särkijärvi and Saastamoinen, 2001).

	Grass silage	Oat silage	SEM[1]	Significance[2]
Intake				
DM intake (kg day^{-1})	7.95	6.63	0.457	*
DMI (g kg $LW^{0.75}$)	70.8	57.8	2.43	*
Crude protein intake (g day^{-1})[3]	1023	766		
Digestibility				
DM (g kg^{-1})	523	426	3.11	
Crude protein (g kg^{-1})	590	701	2.68	*
Neutral detergent fibre (g kg^{-1})	417	310	4.52	
Crude fat (g kg^{-1})	163	498	4.17	***
Crude fibre (g kg^{-1})	300	304	5.40	

[1] Experimental data based on 4 x 3 switch back design with four horses (Finnhorse mares). Grass silage (561 g kg^{-1} DM; 129 g CP kg DM^{-1}; pH 4.93) and oat silage (302 g kg^{-1} DM; 116 g CP kg DM^{-1}; pH 4.25).
[2] significance *p<0.05; ** p<0.01 and *** p<0.001 respectively
[3] calculated data

Feed and feed evaluation in vivo

The voluntary intake of hay, fresh herbage and silage has been reviewed recently by Cuddeford (2002) who outlined the various factors that could influence the process of voluntary intake (hay type, chemical composition and animal factors) and concluded that it is difficult to establish predictive equations. The poor relationship between voluntary intake of hay, and cell wall content and diet digestibility has been demonstrated by several authors (for example, Cymbaluk, 1990; Hyslop *et al.,* 1997 and 1998; Dulphy *et al.,* 1997a and 1997b). Recent studies by Lawrence *et al.* (2001) have generated relationships between NDF and voluntary intake of hays, however these relationships were derived from only a very limited range of forages (two orchard grass hays and two timothy hays in four horses). In studies that have offered legume hay, good relationships between dry matter digestibility and intake have been developed (Crozier *et al.,* 1997). This may reflect the reduced physical resistance to comminution and differences in cell wall composition in legumes with respect to grass hays (Minson, 1990).

There is little data concerning the voluntary intake of fresh herbage or grazed grass. Studies at INRA (Dulphy *et al.,* 1997b) examined zero-grazed fresh forages and observed estimates of voluntary intake similar to those obtained for hays containing similar concentrations of NDF (90 to 117 g/kg $BW^{0.75}$ with forages containing between 300 to 610 g NDF/ kg DM). Cuddeford (2002) suggested that the voluntary intake of fresh herbage ranged from 19 to 22 g DM/kg BW. Voluntary intake of straw is generally lower than that of hay. This may reflect the high mean retention time of digesta or a low intake as a result of poor oro-sensory quality of the feed (Pearson and Merrit, 1991; Pearson *et al.,* 2001; Hyslop and Calder, 2001 and Forbes, 1988) Voluntary intake at grass has been poorly researched. Grace *et al.* (2002) demonstrated that grazing of perennial ryegrass dominated pasture lead to a reduction in apparent dry matter digestibility compared to the grazing situation. This is not surprising as zero-grazed herbage rapidly deteriorates after cutting and, possibly of greater importance, the horse shows a strong degree of selection at pasture (Naujeck *et al.,* 2005). Intake at pasture has been examined by several authors, for instance Friend and Nash (2000), McMeniman (2000) and Grace *et al.* (2002). These studies have lead to highly variable voluntary intakes of horses at pasture reflecting unreliable estimates of faecal output resulting from absorption or poor recovery rates of inert (n-alkane) markers used.

Concentrate feeds

The equine feed industry produces feeds that can be classified as concentrate or compound feeds, chaffs, hay replacers, feed supplements and straights. The total production of horse feed in the UK in 2001 – 2002 was 160,600 tonnes. In comparison the ruminant feed industry produced 3,385,700 tonnes.

Feed manufacturers have to respond to global trends in raw material commodity supply and demand and market economics. The demand for raw materials by the equine feed compound industry in the UK is dictated by the ruminant and monogastric feed manufacturing sector. The use of raw materials in the production of compounds and blends for the UK livestock industry vary from year to year (Table 4.2), however the industry is still based on cereal production and soya (Table 4.3).

Table 4.2 Classification of compound feeds used in the UK equine industry.

Classification of feed	Examples
Concentrate or compound feed	Coarse mixes, cubes, balancers etc.
Chaffs	Alfalfa, molassed hay or straw based feeds
Hay replacers	Haylage, dehydrated alfalfa or grasses
Feed supplements	Vitamins and minerals, balancers, nuetraceuticals, herbal products.
Straights	Cereals, sugar beet pulp

Arguably the equine feed industry has a greater degree of diversity within its products than any other sector of the feed industry as a result of the segmentation and targeting of products to the customer. As a significant proportion of compounded feed is sold to the individual with less than five horses, product innovation is great leading to attractive packaging and branding of feeds. Furthermore, the composition of the feed also is important from a visual point of view to the horse owner. Feeds that look more attractive to the eye may have a competitive advantage to the average owner. This modifies the decisions on pricing and has led to "exotic" feeds being used in the equine industry, for instance dehydrated carrots added to the feed to improve the visual attributes of the product.

Feed and feed evaluation in vivo

Table 4.3 UK raw material usage in 1997 and 2001 – animal feed sectors.

Raw material	Usage ['000 tonnes in 1997] (%)	Usage ['000 tonnes in 2001] (%)
Wheat	3267.6 (30.8)	2631.0 (27.5)
Barley	720.2 (6.8)	827.6 (8.6)
Oats	44.8 (0.4)	26.5 (0.2)
Whole/flaked maize	79.8 (0.8)	74.3 (0.8)
Other grains	5.5 (0.1)	
Rice bran extractions	81.4 (0.8)	29.9 (0.2)
Maize gluten feed	443.1 (4.2)	480.8 (5.0)
Cereal by-products	1111.1 (10.5)	1142.3 (11.9)
Whole oilseeds	86.3 (0.8)	65.1 (0.7)
Rapeseed meal/cake	581.0 (5.5)	511.4 (5.3)
Soybean meal/cake	1170.2 (11.0)	1016.7 (10.6)
Sunflower meal/cake	538.2 (5.1)	319.0 (3.3)
Other seed meals	448.8 (4.2)	540.2 (5.6)
Field beans	34.3 (0.3)	83.0 (0.8)
Field peas	117.0 (1.1)	74.9 (0.7)
Sugar beet pulp	269.2 (2.5)	149.8 (1.6)
Molasses	344.4 (3.2)	316.4 (3.3)
Citrus and other fruit pulp	100.9 (0.9)	70.9 (0.7)
Animal products (poultry products)	19.2 (0.2)	12.0 (0.1)
Fish meal	218.7 (2.1)	152.7 (1.6)
Oils and fats	262.2 (2.5)	224.5 (2.3)
Protein concentrates	30.0 (0.3)	17.7 (0.2)
Other ingredients	639.6 (6.0)	798.2 (9.0)
Total	10613.5	9564.7

Feed characterisation

Provision of a balanced diet for the horse is based on current methods of feed characterisation and requirements of the horse. Feed evaluation provides the first step towards ration development for the nutritionist.

Rations are composed according to digestive processes of the animal (Chapters 1 and 2) and the demand for energy, protein and minerals. The main chemical components of feed have been described in Chapter 3. Feed characterisation is important to assess and predict the supply of nutrients to the animal thus ensuring the provision of a balanced diet for the horse. Proximate analysis of feeds is a series of arbitrary and, often,

Nutritional Physiology of the Horse

empirical tests that allow some prediction of nutrient supply from a particular feed and hence the performance of that feed offered to the animal. However before the characterisation of feeds can be linked to the process of feed formulation, the individual nutrients supplied and animal response to those nutrients must be examined.

The typical basis of analysis of feeds for herbivores has been an expression of moisture content, mineral matter, oil, protein and fibre (e.g. the Weende feed evaluation system). This analysis can be criticised. The analysis does not consider the whole range of non-structural polysaccharides that are important in herbivore nutrition. Originally the use of the nitrogen-free extractive (NFE) was important in the overall evaluation of non-structural polysaccharides but it suffers from a lack of repeatability and a lack of a consistent relationship with the various chemical characteristics of plant material (Chesson, 2000). The development of more refined methods of characterisation of structural polysaccharide occurred during the 1960s and 1970s with the methods of van Soest et al. (van Soest, 1967; van Soest et al., 1991). These methods refined our understanding of dietary fibre and non-structural polysaccharides in animal nutrition. Further advances during 1980s and 1990s led to the development of methods based on biological or physico-chemical approaches (e.g. enzymes and microbial incubation methods). These methods of characterisation were shown to mimic the processes of nutrient utilisation to a far greater extent than previous methods. The existing tables of feed composition for equine nutrition are based on proximate (Weende) analysis, fractionation of the cell wall (so-called van Soest approach) and occasionally data on vitamin, mineral and fatty acids (Figure 4.3). These data do not provide a complete basis for prediction of animal performance, however.

Feed evaluation aims to ensure efficient utilisation of biological resources by the animal and the feed industry. The whole evaluation process is based on specific chemical entities of feeds and the processes in which those entities are utilised or modified by the animal. The Achilles' heel of feed characterisation systems for the equine industry is that some data used in formulation have been collated for ruminant or mono-gastric species and little or no research into new characterisation methods for the horse have been developed. From a ruminant point of view, for example, feed characterisation has split feed components into categories according to their potential energy yield during fermentation. However, in the horse, feed first passes through the stomach and small intestine

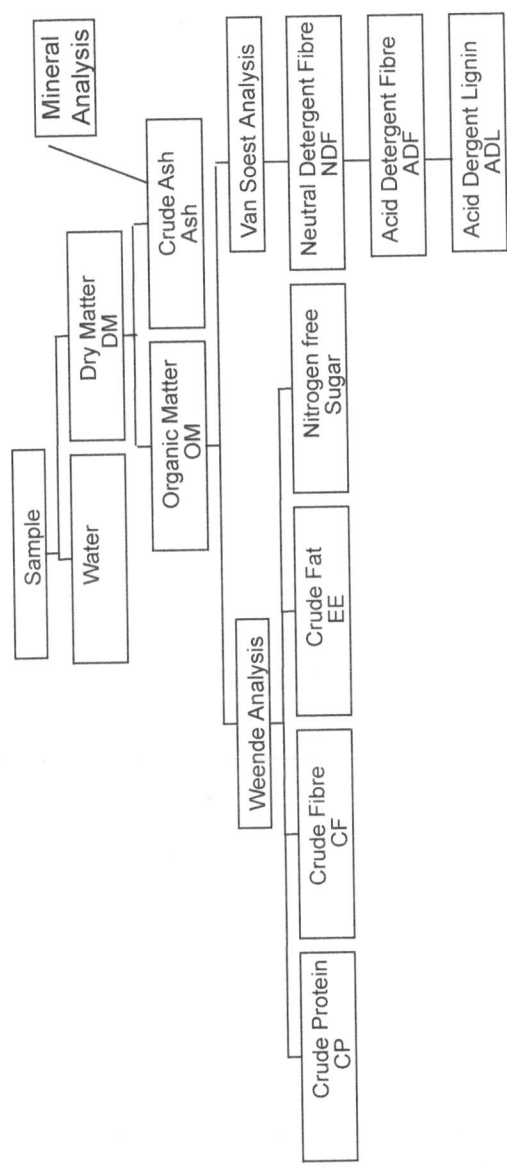

Figure 4.3 Chemical characterisation of animal feeds.

before it reaches the major 'fermentation' site and a distinction between pre-caecally and post-caecally digested feed components would be more logical.

Characterisation of structural and non-structural carbohydrate in feeds

The main problem facing feed evaluation is the accuracy of feed composition data. This is especially true for non-structural and structural carbohydrate where the quality of data is compromised by the lack of standard methods of analysis (NRC, 1987).

Non-structural carbohydrate can be characterised as total non-structural carbohydrate (NSC) or the individual components of NSC, such as starch, sugar and fructan. Total NSC is assessed by total decomposition of the extracted NSC fraction and measured using the ferricyanide colorimetric method (Smith, 1981). This method has been used in the prediction of DE to estimate "soluble carbohydrate" (see for instance Pagan, 1994). The individual chemical components of NSC are assessed using enzyme-linked methods. For instance, total starch in a feed can be measured using the methods of Salomonsson *et al.* (1984) or Herrera-Saldana *et al.* (1990). These methods do however suffer from a lack of specificity as the crude enzyme extracts used in the analytical procedure may have a greater range of activity than first supposed. Therefore, in the UK, there has recently been a shift back to the use of polarographic methods for evaluation of starch and soluble sugars.

The characterisation of cell content (sugars, starches, soluble carbohydrates, pectin, non protein nitrogen, proteins, lipids) and cell wall content (often referred to as 'fibre'; hemicellulose, cellulose, lignin; Zeyner, 1995) seems to be relatively clear. Proximate analysis of feeds leads to problems when integrating chemical methods and *in vivo* evaluation. Structural carbohydrate in feeds has been traditionally measured using the crude fibre method appropriate in the Weende analysis. This approach has been criticised by many authors as being unrepresentative of the fibre fraction present in the feed, not reflecting the cell wall fraction of the feed and being inappropriate as the method does not reflect the digestive processes in the animals' digestive tract (van Soest, 1994). Crude fibre is still a legal requirement for feed evaluation but interpretation of the feed component *in vivo* is inaccurate and does not reflect cell wall composition. Crude fibre, as a measure of cell wall content, has been replaced by neutral detergent fibre (NDF), acid detergent fibre (ADF) and acid detergent liginin (ADL; van Soest and Robertson, 1977).

The current methods used to evaluate the cell wall fraction and "structural carbohydrate" of animal feeds were developed by van Soest (1965 a and b), van Soest and Wine (1967) and Goering and van Soest (1970).

The measures include neutral detergent fibre (NDF), acid detergent fibre (ADF) and acid detergent lignin (ADL). There are two major modifications to the original method of van Soest (1965) to determine the plant cell wall content (neutral detergent fibre; NDF). The problem facing the nutritionist is that these methods generate different values depending on the type of feed assessed. The original method for NDF included the use of sodium sulphite to remove protein crosslinked to the cell wall faction. This method did not however remove all the starch from feeds such as maize silage or cereal grains. The use of heat-stable α-amylase and the removal of sodium sulphite was an important modification that prevented contamination of the cell wall with residual starch (Undersander *et al.*, 1993). This method is however not adequate for high-temperature dried feeds (such as dried grass and lucerne) as the lack of sodium sulphite leads to a contamination of the cell wall fraction with heat damaged proteins. It is therefore recommended that NDF analysis be conducted using both amylase and sulphite. Acid detergent fibre is the fraction of a feedingstuff that includes cellulose and lignin as primary constituents. However, the residue also contains variable concentrations of nitrogen associated with cell wall compounds. The modification of ADF (MADF) as developed by Clancy and Wilson (1966) refers to changes in the drying procedure for the feed from an "as received" feed to the dried sample required for analysis. Lignin is classified as a non-carbohydrate, high molecular weight compound that is a constituent of the cell wall. There are a variety of methods used to estimate lignin content of feeds of which, acid detergent lignin is probably the most applicable to feed evaluation systems (van Soest, 1965a). Klason lignin is probably more accurate to estimate total lignin in the cell wall (Hatfield *et al.*, 1994; Lowry *et al.*, 1994) but from a commercial laboratory point of view, more complex in its procedural analysis (Table 4.4).

Table 4.4 Methods for chemical evaluation of structural carbohydrates in feedstuffs.

	Crude Fibre	NDF	ADF	ADL	In vitro gas production
Cellulose	+	+	+	-	Digested +
Hemicellulose	+?	+	-	-	Digested +
Pectins	-	+?	-	-	+
Lignin	+?	+	+	+	+

Characterisation of the nitrogen content of feeds

The current procedures used to determine the concentration of protein in feedingstuffs for herbivores are inadequate and cannot be used to accurately predict the animals' response to feed protein. The nitrogen fraction in animal feeds has traditionally been assessed by digesting the feed and determining total nitrogen, the Kjeldahl method. The assessment of crude protein is not adequate, as it does not describe the total concentration of protein, the quality of the protein and its availability to digestion. The typical calculation from nitrogen content to crude protein (6.25 times total N) does not reflect the true concentration of nitrogen in protein. For instance the factors for conversion of nitrogen to CP in alfalfa and maize stover are 6.33 and 6.9 respectively (Table 4.5). The characterisation of non-protein nitrogen is also inadequate for accurate formulation of diets.

Table 4.5 Composition of soluble non-protein nitrogen in fresh forage

	Grass (% DM)	Alfalfa (% DM)
Total NPN	14-34	25-38
Non amino acid bases	1-25	-
Basic amino acids	1-15	3-4
Glutamic acid and derivatives (inc. aspartic acid)	16-49	30-63
Other amino acids	7-25	7-12
Nitrate	10-25	2-4

Non-protein nitrogen can be an important source of nitrogen to the animal and the gut microflora. In ruminant feed evaluation systems non-protein nitrogen is considered as non precipitable and therefore of high availability to the rumen microflora and also the animal.

The approach of using total nitrogen as a measure of crude protein does not consider the fractionation of protein or nitrogen in feeds (Table 4.6). The development of neutral detergent insoluble nitrogen (NDIN) and acid detergent insoluble nitrogen (ADIN) are important in feed evaluation as they consider nitrogen substrates associated with the cell wall (Fry, 1988; Krishnamoorthy et al., 1982) and heat damaged protein (van Soest and Mason, 1991). Both these fractions have been correlated with slowly solubilisable nitrogen (NDIN) and nitrogen indigestibility (ADIN).

Table 4.6 Distribution of protein and nitrogen in feeds (% of crude protein).

Feed	Crude protein %	NPN	True protein (soluble)	Slow degradable protein	ADIP
Maize gluten meal	66	3	1	94	2
Sugar beet pulp	8	4	0	85	11
Maize silage	9	48	6	38	8
Alfalfa	20	27	3	60	10
Soyabean meal	52	13	14	71	2

Characterisation of fats, oils and related compounds

The extraction of ether soluble compounds from feeds has been considered as a measure of fats and oil (Table 4.7).

Table 4.7 Fatty acid composition of selected feeds.

	Fatty acids (%)	Individual fatty acids (g/100g fatty acid)						
		14:0	16:0	16:1	18:0	18:1	18:2	18:3
Barley	1.6		27.6	0.9	1.5	20.5	43.3	4.3
Oats	3.2	Trace	22.1	1.0	1.3	38.1	24.9	2.1
Dehydrate alfalfa	1.4	0.7	28.5	2.4	3.8	6.5	18.4	39.0
Perennial rye grass		Trace	11.9	1.7	2.2	14.6	68.2	
Soya bean meal[a]	18.0	Trace	10.7	Trace	1.5	21.4	14.2	7.0
Maize gluten	1.3		17.2	0.9	0.8	26.7	53.0	1.4
Lard		0.9	24.4	6.5	10.6	38.4	19.3	
Palm oil		1.5	42.0		4.0	43.0	9.5	

[a] soyabean meal also contains substantial levels of 20:1 (12.3%) and 22:1 (38.9%)

However, ether extract also contains numerous non-lipid compounds, for instance plant pigments, cuticular waxes and some vitamin and pro-vitamin compounds. In general, two methods for extraction of ether soluble compounds have been applied to animal feeds, the extraction using ether as the sole solvent and extraction after treatment with weak acid (in an aim to solubilise lipids conjugated with protein and cell wall components). Further analysis of the ether extract can be conducted. This involves the characterisation of individual fatty acids (both saturated and unsaturated fatty acids) to produce a fatty acid profile to determine the occurrence and concentration of essential fatty acids (e.g. linoleic acid).

Feed evaluation *in vivo*

Feed evaluation *in vivo* has been based on a relatively limited number of studies with horses (in comparison with the extensive literature concerning ruminants and monogastrics). This approach has been enhanced by the use of ruminants in appraising animal responses to diets.

Measurement of digestibility in vivo

The measurement of digestibility of nutrients *in vivo* is the ideal situation in feed evaluation. However, the procedures used to measure digestibility *in vivo* are expensive, require large quantities of feed of uniform quality and a relatively large number of animals. The inherent variation of individual animals and their response to a feed can also lead to difficulties in the interpretation of results. Furthermore, the recent refinements in *in vitro* methods have lead to a further reduction in use of animals in digestion experiments on the basis of animal welfare.

A number of digestibility trials using horses were performed by Kellner and others during the late 1880s, yielding data on the apparent total tract digestibility of protein and the development of starch equivalent values for a number of feeds. These early data provided the basis of the relationship between nutrient supply and level of exercise (for instance, light, medium and heavy work for cavalry horses). More recently, the focus of digestibility trials performed with horses have been to develop relationships for feeding standards that can be measured using small ruminants (e.g. sheep; Martin-Rosset *et al.*, 1996) or to validate new *in vitro* methods (Macheboeuf and Jestin, 1997; Lowman *et al.*, 1999). The approach of using sheep and *in vitro* methods allows an accurate prediction of nutrient availability from feed that is cost and labour efficient.

The calculation of apparent digestibility is relatively simple. The proportion of a nutrient that "disappears" in the animal and is not excreted is assumed to be digestible and this defines its digestibility. This is a measure of the apparent digestibility of a feed and not the true digestibility of the nutrient. True digestibility of a nutrient has to consider the sources of "contamination" of the faecal output from the animal. The loss of gut mucosa and lining and the incorporation of microbial biomass in the faeces can account in ruminants from 0.098 to 0.129 g g^{-1} DM intake (van Soest, 1994). Gaseous losses of methane would also have to be considered if a measure of true digestibility were made for feed evaluation. However, no advantage in the precision of formulation has been shown for true digestibility compared to apparent digestibility and therefore, for technical reasons, apparent digestibility is used for purposes of evaluation (Minson, 1990). Direct measurement of apparent digestibility involves the complete collection of faeces excreted over a period of time and analysis of the faecal output for the nutrient of interest. The actual amount of dietary nutrient ingested by the animal is also required for calculation of apparent digestibility. Therefore:

$$\text{Apparent digestibility} = \frac{\text{intake} - \text{faecal output}}{\text{intake}}$$

The measurement of true digestibility of nutrients is relatively rare in horses. True digestibility takes into consideration the contribution of non-feed substances voided into the faeces (for example, gut mucosa, microbial biomass). For example, the true digestibility of N can be calculated as:

$$\text{True N digestibility} = \frac{\text{Intake of N} - [\text{Faecal N} - \text{non-feed N}]}{\text{Intake of N}}$$

Digestibility coefficient can also be calculated accurately using indigestible markers (e.g. Miraglia *et al.*, 1999) or by feeding a small amount of indigestible marker as a 'pulse dose' in daily feed (Cuddeford and Hughes, 1990). If the marker is totally indigestible then:

Apparent digestibility =

$$1 - \frac{1 \times \text{concentration of marker in feed}}{\text{concentration of marker in faeces}} \times \frac{\text{concentration of nutrient in faeces}}{\text{concentration of nutrient in feed}}$$

This method for apparent digestibility can eliminate lengthy periods of time for total collection of faeces, by estimation of total faecal excretion per day, from marker excreted in 'grab-samples' (Kotb and Luckey 1972).

The typical apparent digestibility coefficients reported for feeds offered to horses are dry matter (DMd), organic matter (OMd), cell wall (NDFd, ADFd or CFd), crude protein (CPd) and occasionally digestible organic matter (DOMd). Other methods (e.g. difference, regression and indirect) have been used in ruminants and horses to evaluate the digestibility of feeds (Rymer, 2000). A number of comparative studies have been performed between horses and ruminants. However, these are difficult to interpret. The formulation of identical diets for horses and ruminants is possible but differences in the feeding strategy and body size need to be considered. For instance in comparisons between sheep and horses, the apparent digestibility of a diet can be confounded by differences in metabolic losses and the varying ability of the microflora to digest fibre. Feeding strategy may also affect the comparison of digestibility studies. Rate of passage and retention of digesta can confound any comparison of digestibility coefficients.

The differences in digestibility coefficients between ruminants and horses could be interpreted as differences in anatomical and digestive efficiencies with horses having a lower digestive capacity than ruminants. Individual animal variation within and between trials can be considerable and can lead to further difficulties in comparison. Finally comparisons between species and especially groups (hind gut *vs.* ruminant) are also affected by the quantification of chemical composition (Table 4.8). For instance, is NDF the same feed entity in ruminants and equids? New feed evaluation techniques are being developed such as near infrared spectroscopy to evaluate if certain chemical entities are comparable between species (e.g. the application of detrended NIRs in horses and sheep; Hill and Ellis, 2001).

The use of species other than ruminants in digestion trials to predict nutrient values of feeds for horses has been considered. The rabbit is potentially a good candidate as the digestive system (by physiology alone) can be interpreted as similar to horses (Schurg, 1977; Cheeke, 1987).

Table 4.8 Digestibility coefficients* reported in equine and equine-ruminant *in vivo* experiments. Source: Ellis, 2003a.

Author	Animals	Feed and feeding level	DMd	OMd	CFd	NDFd	ADFd
Chenost and Martin-Rosset (1985)	5 horses, trotters	Fresh hybrid ryegrass				77.3	67.5
	6 sheep					80.4	69.4
Martin-Rosset and Dulphy (1987)	Heavy horses, 377kg (10 months old)	Hay low intake		53.4	55.1		
		medium intake		49.8	48.7		
		ad libitum		52.8	49.8		
	Sheep	low intake		63.6	72.7		
		ad libitum		64.3	71.8		
	Horses	Hay + maize/barley (2:1) low intake		61.7	52.7		
		medium intake		61.5	52.6		
		high intake		59.3	46.2		
	Sheep	low intake		69.6	69.7		
		ad libitum		64.8	61.3		
Cymbaluk (1990)	6 horses, 334kg	Altai wild rye hay	47.0			49.9	39.4
	6 steer, 221 kg		58.8			64.0	53.4
	6 horses	Bromegrass hay	47.7			44.4	29.1
	6 steer		59.7			61.5	42.7
Smolders *et al.* (1990)	4 saddle horses	Grass hay early cut		62.3			
		Grass hay medium cut		54.1			
		Grass hay late cut		45.7			
		Grass silage		64.6			
	Sheep	Grass hay medium cut		62.1			

Table 4.8 Contd.

Author	Animals	Feed and feeding level	DMd	OMd	CFd	NDFd	ADFd
Istasse et al. (1996)	4 sports-horses	Silage (43% DM)	63.7	64.5			66.5
		Silage (66 % DM)	67.5	67.1			57.7
		Silage (79 % DM)	58.8	59.7			48.4
Vermorel et al. (1997)	6 standardbreds	Hay late cut (high ADF)	43.8	45.0			
		Hay + barley (1.5:1)	58.6	61.6			
		Hay (medium NDF)	52.4	54.1		41.4	39.1
		Hay + maize pellets (2:1)	63.2	65.2		44.7	40.8
		Hay (high NDF) restricted	47.5	47.2		48.6	44.4
		Hay ad libitum	47.2	47.5		48.5	45.3
		Hay restr. + barley (1.5:1)	60.2	61.6		44.6	39.5
		Hay ad lib. + barley	59.9	61.5		45.1	40.9
Palmgren Karlsson et al. (2000)	4 standard bred	Hay	48	49	44	37	29
		Hay + oats (4:1)	55	56	46	39	32
		Hay + oats (1.5:1)	58	59	42	43	35
		Hay + oats (1:1.5)	58	60	51	36	26

*DMd = Dry matter digestibility, OMd = Organic matter digestibility, CFd = Crude Fibre digestibility, NDFd = Neutral detergent fibre digestibility, ADFd = Acid detergent fibre digestibility.

However, rabbits are not a suitable animal for equine feed evaluation for the following reasons. Studies by Uden and Van Soest (1982) comparing faecal and ruminal/caecal particle size suggested that equines and rabbits passed much larger faecal particles in relation to bodyweight than the ruminant animals. This observation was made despite the fact that the rabbits received a ground and pelleted hay while horses received the same hay untreated, thus suggesting that rabbits are less efficient at particle breakdown. Second, the rabbit's digestive mechanisms are quite different from those of horses. Rabbits are caecotrophs and produce two types of faeces (soft for re-ingestion and hard faeces). It is therefore difficult to ensure that total collection of faeces from rabbits is not compromising gut health and function. Removal of soft faeces may lead to protein malnutrition of the rabbit. Several studies comparing rabbits and horses have been performed. Rabbits derive less digestible energy (DE) from roughages than horses (digestibility coefficients for horses versus rabbits respectively: Schurg, 1977 (0.70 *vs.* 0.47); Slade and Hintz, 1969 (0.64 *vs.* 0.54); Wolter, 1980 (0.51 *vs.* 0.26).

An interesting "indirect measurement" of digestibility of starch was performed by Hoekstra *et al.* (1999). The effect of grain processing on the digestibility of starch in the small intestine of horses is difficult to measure. Hoekstra *et al.* (1999) used the glycaemic response as an "indirect measure" of small intestinal response to diets containing different maize products. Steam flaking of maize led to higher mean and peak concentrations of glucose in the plasma in horses compared to animals offered cracked or ground maize. These data reflect the observations by Meyer *et al.* (1993) for whole, crushed and steam treated maize.

Any discussion on digestibility must also consider voluntary intake. Normally digestibility trials are conducted with animals being offered forages and concentrates at maintenance level of feeding. As the level of feeding increases, the rate of passage or digesta through the gastrointestinal tract will increase, thus reducing the residence time of digesta in the small intestine and the hind-gut.

Diet presentation and composition

Diet presentation and composition are important considerations before feed evaluation and digestion studies are performed. Diet presentation (for example, pelleted feeds, chopped or long hay) has some effect on the fill of the gut as there will be differences in the mean particle size of ingesta entering the digestive tract (Lowman *et al.*, 2002). However in studies by Ellis (2003a) only small differences in mean faecal particle size and distribution were observed between horses offered identical late cut threshed ryegrass hay long (greater than 20 cm) and chopped short (less than 5 cm) (Figure 4.4). It is notable, in view of the previous discussion (Chapter 2) that over 60% of particles did not pass the 2 mm sieve layer.

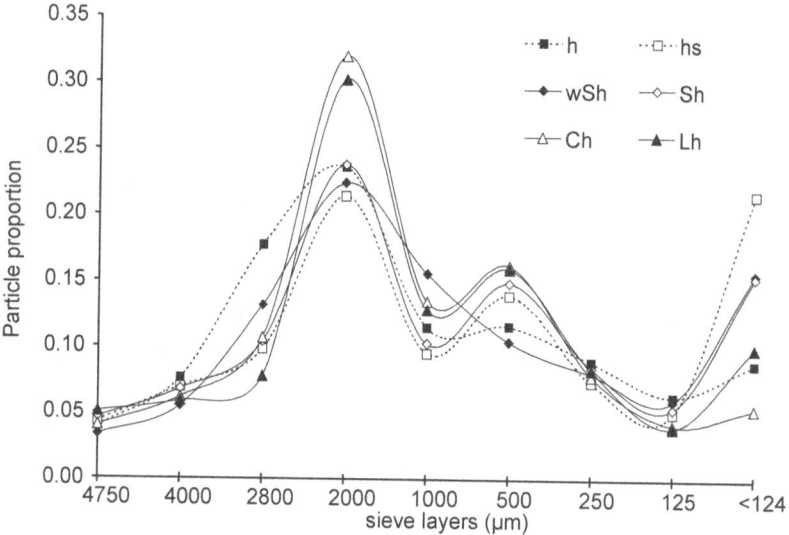

Figure 4.4 Mean particle distribution of faecal samples among sieve layers for English rye grass forages (medium cut: **h**-hay; hs = **hay**-silage and late cut, threshed: **Lh** = long hay; **Ch** = chaffed hay) and for mixture hay fed soaked (**wSh** = wet hay) and dry (**Sh** = dry hay) (Source: Ellis, 2003a).

Pelleting and wafering of feeds has however been shown by many authors to alter the apparent digestibility of diets. Hintz and Loy (1966) noted that pelleting of rations containing hay only or hay-concentrate mixtures led to inconsistent increases in the rate of passage of digesta, leading to a mean marker-recovery of 75% for the pelleted and only 50% for the non-pelleted rations 33 hours post feeding. The marker was not however attached to feed particles and the faecal dry matter of horses on pelleted feed was considerably lower, indicating a change in water metabolism presumably reflecting the altered physical structure of the feed. In contrast, the digestibility of diet and microbial activity of the caecum did not change if a hay diet was pelleted, extruded or semi-extruded (Wolter et al., 1978). The study by Wolter et al. is difficult to explain as surface area to volume ratio of feeds has been suggested as one of the most important limiting factors for digestion (Lopez et al., 1995; Poppi et al., 1981). However, this approach is too simplistic and van Soest (1994) provided six arguments why increases in surface area may not lead to an increase in digestibility. First, the process of grinding of feeds in the mouth may be selective with less lignified material being more easily disrupted. The very nature of the cell wall does not lead to an increase in surface area *per se* as the cell wall is porous and grinding only exposes internal space. Furthermore, the finely ground cell wall can lead to a reduction in digestibility as there is a "trade-off" between rate of flow of digesta and rate of fermentation of the feed by microflora. Chemical modification of the cell wall by the action of grinding, pelleting and extrusion can lead to unpredictable differences in apparent digestion and these differences in physical properties may not be uniform throughout the whole feed. Finally, there may also be substantial differences between particles of different size and shape and the aforementioned effects may not be uniform.

Digesta flow, particle dynamics and degradation

An important aspect that has to be considered when feed evaluation methods are developed is the movement of feed particles (particle kinetics) and their degradation in the digestive tract. Measurements of passage rates (PR) and mean retention times (pooling of ingesta in the digestive tract; MRT) of particles in the digestive tract have given an insight into the effect of the physical composition of feed on particle dynamics and degradation. The net capture of nutrients (digestibility) and the flow of undigested ingesta are important processes in understanding gut function of the horse. However, the majority of studies on digesta flow have been reported in ruminant species and the comparison and applicability of models developed have to be examined carefully. Some excellent reviews of the development and application of methods appropriate for ruminants and horses are available (Kotb and Luckey, 1972; Kennedy and Murphy, 1988; Dove and Mayes, 1991; Forbes and France, 1993; Aharoni et al., 1999).

The methods used to determine digesta flow involve the feeding of a measurable, totally indigestible/inabsorbable substance (called marker/ indicator/ tracer). The marker can be either not associated with feed particles (for example, titanium dioxide or chromic oxide) or chemically attached to feed particles (e.g. chromium mordanted fibre). The most common used markers include titanium dioxide (Ellis *et al.*, 2001), chromium mordanted fibre (Cuddeford and Hughes, 1990), chromium ethylenediamine tetraacetic acid (Cr-EDTA; Kobt and Luckey, 1972), cobalt ethylenediamine tetraacetic acid (Co-EDTA; Medina *et al.*, 2002), ytterbium mordanted fibre and alkanes (Uden *et al.*, 1982; Dove and Mayes, 1991; Pearson and Merrit, 1991; Afzalzadeh *et al.*, 1997). Other feed-based markers could be used, for instance indigestible acid detergent fibre (IADF), acid detergent lignin or acid insoluble ash (Miraglia *et al.*, 1999; de Fombelle *et al.*, 2003). Unfortunately, no marker fulfils the conditions of being totally indigestible and inabsorbable (especially in the pre-caecal compartment of the gastrointestinal tract of the horse; Hertel *et al.*, 1970). A problem with rare earth markers is the potential migration of the marker from the mordanted feed to the liquid phase. This leads to a substantial error in the estimation of the rate of passage for solid particles or estimates in total faecal output (Owens and Hanson, 1992).

Further errors associated with the timing of recovery of a marker (chromic oxide) for estimating total volume of chyme were presented by Kienzle (1994). If the concentration of marker was monitored after 3, 6 or 9 hours post feeding of oats or maize starch, pre-ileal digestibility coefficients of 70, 89 and 96% (oat starch) and 75, 58 and 18% (maize starch) were recorded. These data demonstrated that there can be considerable over or under prediction of digestibility of different starch sources depending on sampling time. The same problem was highlighted by Ellis (2003) who investigated the mean retention of a hay-based diet using two sampling regimes. When sampling faeces every 4 hours up to 120 hrs, in comparison with collecting 4-hourly at first and then 6 hourly and finally 12 hourly up to 80 hours, a considerable reduction in mean retention time was calculated for the reduced sampling method.

The recovery of markers in faeces or from canula in the digestive tract over a period of time allows the calculation of various flow parameters. These include rate of flow of digesta, transit time (point of time, first or last appearance of ingested marker) and mean retention time of digesta (Kotb and Luckey, 1972; Balch, 1956; Blaxter *et al.*, 1956). Turnover and flow of ingesta are important concepts in digestive physiology. Turnover is the mixing of digesta entering a section (pool) of the digestive tract that has one or more exits to balance the input of ingesta (van Soest, 1994). In ruminants, turnover, by definition, is applicable to

Feed and feed evaluation in vivo

sections of the digestive tract that may retain feed particles from previous meals. Turnover is an appropriate measure for processes involved in the caeco-colon complex but may not be useful for descriptions of particle movement in the stomach, small intestine or even the large intestine of the horse. Flow of digesta is biphasic. Digesta contains two main phases, the liquid and solid ingesta. In general, the liquid fraction flows faster than the solid ingesta and therefore rate of flow during one 24-hour period may alter diurnally in relation to the pattern of feeding. There is a lack of literature on the diurnal pattern of digesta flow in ruminants and horses as the majority of studies concerned with passage rate reported mean flow in relation to daily intake of dry matter. The various compartments within the digestive tract of the horse have been defined previously as the stomach, the small intestine (including the jejunum and ileum) and the caeco-colon complex.

Typically, the models used to determine MRT in the horse have been derived from Grovum and Williams (1973). This model seems to be relatively robust when considering the flow of digesta in the gastrointestinal tract of the horse. However, there have been no studies to date that have compared the robustness of Grovum and Williams' model with those of Ellis *et al.* (1979), Pond and Ellis (1988) or Dhanoa *et al.* (1985). The mathematical description of flow described by Grovum and Williams (1973) is:

$$Y = 0 \text{ when } t < TT$$

$$Y = Ae^{-k1(t-TT)} - Ae^{-k2(t-TT)} \text{ when } t > TT$$

where: Y and A are adjusted marker concentrations in the faecal DM

k1 and k2 are rate constants

TT is the calculated time for the first appearance of the marker in the faeces

T is the sampling time (h) after a single dose.

When the log concentration of marker is plotted against time after dosing, the intercept (A1) of the regression line of the descending slope is k1. Fitted values can be calculated from the regression analysis that correspond to the ascending phase and peak concentrations of marker. The anti-logarithm of the fitted values minus the actual concentrations of marker at those times gives a residual value. Regression through the residual values against time allows the calculation of k2, the rate of decline and the intercept A2. The transit time (TT) is therefore calculated as:

$$TT = (A2 - A1) / (k2 - k1)$$

The estimation of the mean retention time (MRT) is:

$$MRT = 1/k1 + 1/k2 + TT$$

This value has been used to compare results between experiments although, as showed earlier, sampling technique may affect results (Table 4.9).

If a liquid marker (for instance Co EDTA) is used the concentration in the faeces declines rapidly and therefore:

$$Y = Ae^{-kt}$$

This allows the calculation of rate of flow of liquid marker from the gastrointestinal tract.

Recent studies by Moore-Colyer et al. (2003) examined the fit of faecal excretion of ytterbium to the models of Pond et al. (1988). The best fit was achieved using the G3 model.

$$F = C_2 (\delta^3 e^{-k2TD} - e^{-\lambda1TD} (\delta^3 + \delta^2\lambda_1 TD + \delta^2\lambda_1 TD^2/2))$$

where F is the fractional concentration of marker,
C_2 is the initial concentration in the second compartment (V),
k_2 is an exponentially distributed rate parameter,
λ is the rate parameter for γ-distributed residence times,
$\delta = \lambda_1/(\lambda_1 - k_2)$ and
TD is the time delay (t – λ: time post – dose to first appearance of marker in faeces).

Even though the original models of Pond et al. (1988) were developed for ruminants, they allow accurate modelling of flow through a simple tubular digestive tract as the initial rate function increases from zero to a finite value within a known period of time. The most important issue to ensure accurate modelling of digesta flow in horses is adequate sampling of faeces during the period from dosing to 20 hours post dosing.

Feed and feed evaluation in vivo

Table 4.9 Mean retention times (MRT; h^{-1}) for different feedstuffs in horses (Ellis, 2003).

Feed	Marker	MRT	Author
Short oat-straw and concentrates	Cr-EDTA (fluid)	22	Orton et al., 1985
Lucerne chaff and barley			
unpelleted	Styrofoam	33	Hintz and Loy et al.,
pelleted	Coloured Beads	25	1966
Meadow hay	Coloured Beads	36	Wolter et al., 1974
Chopped meadow hay		25	
Pelleted meadow hay		31	
Timothy hay	Co-EDTA (fluid)	18	Uden et al., 1982
	Cr-mordanted	23	
Hay	Cr-mordantex	30	Pearson and Merritt,
	Co-EDTA	31	1991
Straw	Cr-mordanted	35	
	Co-EDTA	34	
Lucerne cubes			
at maintenance	Dysprosium (Dy)	25	Todd et al. 1995
1.4 x maintenance	Dy	16	
Lucerne : Straw	TB horse		Cuddeford et al. 1995
1 : 0	Cr-mordant	52	
0.67 : 0.33		44	
0 : 1		38	
1 : 0		64	
0.67 : 0.33	Pony Cr- mordant	50	
0 : 1		51	
1 : 0		51	
0.67 : 0.33	TB fluid marker	44	
0 : 1		43	
Ponies			Drogoul et al.
Chopped hay,	Yb – labelled solid	47	(2000a)
Ground pelleted hay		52	
Chopped hay,	Cr-EDTA fluid	28	
Ground pelleted hay		43	
Horses			Ellis (2003)
Chopped late cut hay	Cr-mordant solid	46	
Long late cut hay		45	
Medium cut hay: concentrate (3:1)		49	

Table 4.9 Contd.

Feed	Marker	MRT	Author
Chopped late cut hay	TiO_2 – fluid marker	39	Ellis (2003a)
Long late cut hay		37	
Medium cut hay: concentrate (3:1)		32	
Range for solid phase markers		25-64	Mean: 42.3
Range for fluid phase markers		16-43	Mean: 31.6

Failure to collect adequate numbers of samples leads to a poor fit of the multi-compartment models and leads to inaccuracies in estimation of the mean retention time. A multi-compartment model is an adequate description of the equine digestive tract (Moore-Colyer et al., 2003).

Drogoul et al. (1996) noted that, when using ytterbium as a marker of solid phase, the transit times through the small intestine and between the caecal and colonic compartments of the digestive tract were significantly different. The large particles of chopped hay arrived in the caecum within 1 hour of feeding and remained there for over 8 hours. In contrast when ground-pelleted hay was offered, the digesta arrived at the caecum 2 ½ hours after feeding but remained in that compartment for less than 4 hours before passing on into the colon. Total tract digestibility was not altered by grinding of the feed although cellulolytic activity was reduced as a result of grinding. Drogoul et al. (1996) suggested that this reflected the likelihood of microbial attachment to the feed and the higher concentrations and proportion of propionic acid resulting from the fermentation process occurring in response to grinding of the feed.

The data presented by Moore-Colyer et al. (2003) suggests that the size and position of the caecum would lead to a short retention time (that is a "fast compartment") in the caecum in comparison to the colon, however the sac like nature of the caecum would lead to mixing and possibly retained digesta. The colon however, is sacculated (four sections and three flexures) and this would predispose the organ to a "time-dependent" compartment (Argenzio et al., 1974). This may allow mixing of digesta within the distinct regions of the colon but the process of mixing is suggested as rapid.

Feed and feed evaluation in vivo

Previously it has been suggested that both physical and chemical compositional factors of a feed may affect the retention of the chyme along the different compartments of the digestive tract. Hyslop *et al.* (1999) examined the flow rate of digesta from the caecum by offering chromium mordanted feed as a pulse dose and calculating the kinetics of outflow by using a simple negative exponential model. Over a range of diets composed of hay cubes, oatfeed and molassed sugar beet feed the calculated outflow rate ranged from 0.240 to 0.387 h^{-1} with calculated MRT ranging from 2.61 to 4.76 h. Particle size of ingested feed has been demonstrated to affect the passage rate of hay diets offered to ponies (Wolter *et al.*, 1974). The mean retention time of long, unchopped hay was 37 hours, ground hay 26 hours and ground hay pellets 31 hours (Table 4.9). Furthermore, average total excretion time of marker offered with forage diets (various quality hay diets) has been reported to be approximately 96-98 hours in horses (Drogoul *et al.*, 1996; Wolter *et al.*, 1974; Vander Noot *et al.*, 1967).

The development of the *in situ* nylon bag method by Ørskov and McDonald (1979) for prediction of nutrient release in the rumen has led to the application of such techniques in equine nutrition (Noziere and Michalet-Doreau, 2000). The technique is based on the incubation of feeds in a nylon bag (generally 43 µm pore size) for varying periods of time in the rumen or caeco-colon complex. The pore size is a compromise between retention of feed particles and the complete penetration of gastric fluid, enzymes and microbial biomass. The ruminant technique does not involve a pre-incubation phase as the technique is applied in the rumen and pre-incubation with saliva and gastric fluids have been used successfully in pigs (Cherian *et al.*, 1989). Little or no research into pre-incubation with saliva or intestinal fluids has been performed with horses.

McClean *et al.* (1998) investigated the effect of physical processing on the *in situ* degradation of barley in the caecum of the horse. Micronisation of the barley increased the degradation rate of starch during the first 20 h of incubation compared with the unprocessed barley. However, by 40 h of incubation, no differences in extent of degradation of starch were observed between unprocessed, micronised or extruded barley. The application of mobile feed bags inserted orally, or through canulas, allows detailed knowledge of degradation rates of nutrients within specific compartments of the gastrointestinal tract. Mobile feed bags were used by Hyslop *et al.* (1998) to examine the degradation of various dehydrated grassland products. The mobile bag technique was successful in allowing the modelling of dynamics of fibre (NDF) degradation in the equine digestive tract however a great range in transit time (10 to 154 h) was observed.

Similar *in situ* techniques have been applied by Moore-Colyer *et al.* (1997); Hyslop *et al.* (1998); McLean *et al.* (1999b, c and g); Todd *et al.* (1995) and Palmgren-Karlson *et al.* (2001). However, the differences in digestive physiology of the horse compared with the ruminant may mean that new mathematical models for degradation and digesta flow need to be developed. It is also not known how much impact canulation of the caecum of the horse has on the particle kinetics and the particle flow within this 'compartment' of the gastrointestinal tract. The value of horses and the physical challenge to animal-health and welfare through this procedure further excludes extensive research to collect reliable data in horses (Varloud *et al.*, 2004; de Fombelle *et al.*, 2003).

Associative effects

The chemical and physical composition of feed and the digestion and absorption of nutrients have been discussed in some depth in Chapters 2 and 3. Also the effects of different physical treatments on digestibility of individual components have been described in light of rate of digesta flow, fluid metabolism and intestinal 'climate' (pH, substrates, bacterial composition; Drogoul *et al.*, 1996; Cuddeford, 2000; Meyer, 1997; Pagan, 1997). However, the effect of feed-to-feed interaction may influence the pattern of nutrient release derived from feedstuffs: the question of associativity.

The majority of rations offered to horses are composed of a mixture of different feeds. These can be divided into concentrate-type feeds (high in soluble carbohydrate, starch, fat) and roughages (high in hemi-celluloses, celluloses and possibly lignin). Current feeding systems are additive. Additive feeding systems simply summarise the contribution of nutrients of the various components of the ration to obtain total feeding values. In ruminants associative effects between feeds do occur and are relatively well understood (for example, Oldham *et al.*, 1977). The argument about associativity in the digestion of nutrients by the horse has not been resolved yet. Hintz *et al.* (1971) concluded that associative effects were unlikely to occur in horses as the animal possessed a 'split-level' digestive tract (i.e. a section which allowed the utilisation of simple carbohydrate, protein and lipid (fore-gut) and the site of fermentation). The proportion of concentrates in the diet and level of feeding was also shown to have no systematic effects on the organic matter digestibility in horses (Martin-Rosset and Dulphy, 1987). These observations were made at concentrate feeding levels of 0, 0.3 and 0.6 of total dietary intake (hay or maize silage diets offered at maintenance, 1.4 maintenance and *ad libitum*). However, the level of feeding (g/kg $BW^{0.75}$) was reduced as increasing level of concentrate was added to maintain iso-energetic intake. The reasons for the apparent lack of associativity may relate to the variability in rate of digesta flow through the small intestine, thus altering the residence time of the concentrate in the small intestine. In a further series of experiments with 12 forages and mixed diets, Vermorel *et al.* (1997a) concluded that there were no associative effects between concentrate and cereals on digestibility. Evidence of associative effects between various nutrients in hay and oat diets was reported by Thompson *et al.* (1984). Addition of oat grain to the diet resulted in increases in the apparent digestibility of crude protein, gross energy, acid detergent lignin and ether extract of the total diet and the fibre fraction. There was also a decrease in the apparent digestibility of holocellulase (acid detergent cellulose) and ADF. Observed and expected apparent digestibility coefficients are in Table 4.10. Substantial differences between observed and expected coefficients were observed for crude protein, holocellulose and ether extract. As the level of oats in the diet increased, crude protein digestibility increased but below expected levels, while digestibility of holocellulose and ether extract initially increased above expected levels.

Table 4.10 Associative effects in apparent digestibility of various nutrients (after Thompson *et al.*, 1984).

Diet inclusion of oats (%)	DM digestibility (g/kg)		CP digestibility (g/kg)[3]		Ether extract digestibility (g/kg)[4]		Holocellulose digestibility (g/kg)[3]	
	Obs.[1]	Exp.[2]	Obs.	Exp.	Obs.	Exp.	Obs.	Exp.
20	560	553	554	695	257	279	513	408
40	567	563	685	714	542	418	357	339
60	572	574	696	736	662	569	298	265
80	598	588	721	761	768	755	173	173

[1] Four geldings (492 to 549 kg BW) in a complete randomised design.
[2] Expected digestibility calculated according to Kromann (1967) and Schneider and Flatt (1975) *i.e.* on the presumption of unchanged digestibility of chemical components.
[3] $P<0.05$
[4] $P<0.10$

The large reduction in digestibility at 80% inclusion rate suggests a deterioration of the hindgut environment. Potter *et al.* (1992) indicated that starch digestibility declined as starch intake increased and the effect of high levels of concentrates on a reduction in fibre digestibility was observed. This reduction was suggested to reflect lower numbers of cellulolytic bacteria in the hindgut as a result of carbohydrate overload in the small intestine and "spill-over" of starch to the caecum and colon. Starch is rapidly fermented and the pH of the digesta declines to below 5.8 thus reducing cellulytic microbial populations (Julliand *et al.*, 1999). Similarly, the effect of increasing fat in the diet on microbial populations can reduce microbial activity in the hind-gut (Jansen *et al.*, 2000; Bush *et al.*, 2001).

The ratio of concentrate to roughage and its effect on carbohydrate and protein digestion has recently been investigated by Palmgren Karlsson *et al.* (2000). Diets containing meadow hay and oats were formulated to include 0, 0.2, 0.4 and 0.6 of the total diet as oats (Figure 4.5).

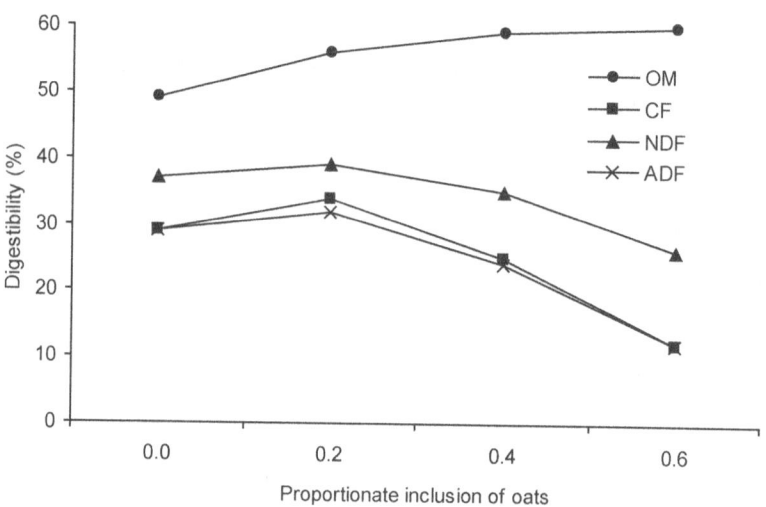

Figure 4.5 Effect of increasing level of feeding of oats on the digestibility of OM, CF, NDF and ADF in the horse. Source: Ellis, 2001. (adapted from Palmgren-Karlsson *et al.*, 2000).

Palmgren Karlsson *et al.* (2000) demonstrated that organic matter digestibility (OMd) was increased (but not linearly) as a result of the increased inclusion of oats in the diet. However, the increasing level of feeding of oats reduced the apparent digestibility of crude fibre, NDF and ADF similar to observations of Thompson *et al.* (1984). Furthermore, the negative associativity of oat starch on fibre utilisation was curvilinear and hence greater than would be expected in an additive model.

The sequence in which rations are offered and timing of feeding in relation to exercise, have also been discussed recently. Several theories are currently in favour but remain to be verified. Feeding fibre before or separate from concentrates was recommended by Tisserand (1992) and Cuddeford (2000). This may prevent starch from transiting through the small intestine at a rate which does not allow optimal utilisation. Palmgren Karlsson *et al.* (2000) however argued that offering a diet containing an inclusion rate of oats of 60% 15 minutes after the hay ration, may have reduced organic matter digestibility of the total diet. Furthermore, Meyer (1995) recommended that feeding concentrates about 15 minutes after offering roughage to increase saliva flow and therefore buffering of digesta ensured mixing of concentrates with the roughage component of the diet, thus 'diluting' the impact of the high concentrate intake.

An elevated rate of passage may also result from mixed feeding of concentrate and fibre, thus reducing the pre-caecal digestion of starch and leading to a reduction in the digestibility of fibre. This may also lead to a reduction in cellulytic microflora in the hindgut. This is an area of equine nutrition, which would benefit from further research to understand the synchronisation of nutrient flow in the digestive tract thus minimising negative effects of asynchronous diets on the process of digestion.

The arguments implicitly linked with associativity have not been fully resolved. It has been demonstrated that within the digestive tract of the horse, passage rates, buffering and water metabolism are adapted in response to chemical composition (e.g. starch, complex carbohydrates etc.) as well as physical characteristics (particle size and fracture properties) of feed. This minimises associative effects at a total tract digestibility level but does not preclude associativity within each compartment of the digestive tract (Figure 4.6).

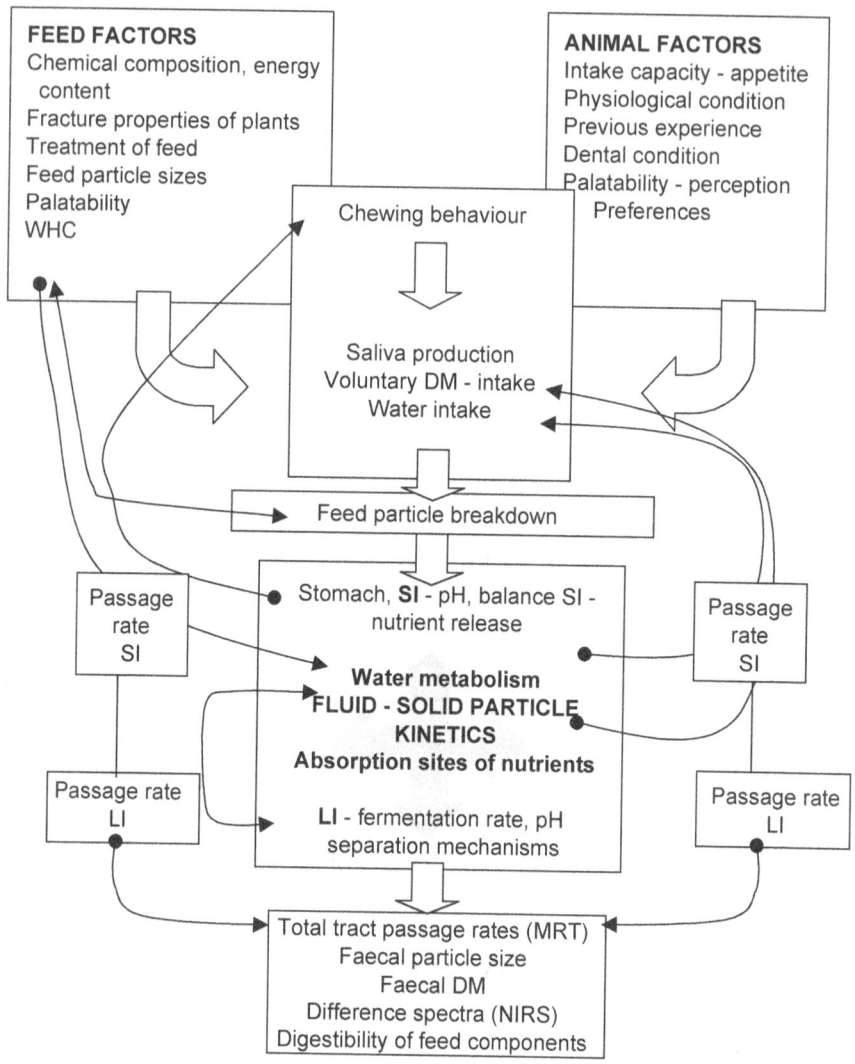

Figure 4.6 Factors involved in the ingestive and digestive processes of horses – a holistic approach (Ellis, 2003a).

5
Energy from feed

Introduction

The previous chapter on feed evaluation introduced the methods used to measure chemical composition of feedstuffs and concluded with the evaluation of feed *in vitro* and *in vivo*. In order to predict the energy derived from a feed in the practical situation, the conversion of chemical compositional characteristics into an energy value has been performed when developing the various feeding systems. An energy value of feeds is not particularly difficult to measure however, difficulties arise when expressing the quantity of the energy in the feed available for metabolism. This chapter will evaluate the methods available for prediction of energy value in feeds, the systems currently used and introduce the concepts of energy partition into maintenance and productive function (growth, exercise, pregnancy and lactation). This chapter will not give a detailed description of individual systems, as these can be found in great depth elsewhere (NRC, 1989; GEH 1995; INRA, 1990; ENESAD, 2002). It will, however, incorporate some comparisons, evaluations and discussion on the prediction of energy at various levels according to the published systems.

Predicting energy value of feed

The methods developed for predicting energy values of feeds offered to horses are based on chemical analyses or *in vivo* evaluation. The basis of all feed evaluation systems to predict energy content of feeds is gross energy (GE or heat of combustion of feed DM). Gross energy reflects the total heat yielded from combustion by burning the lipid, carbohydrate and protein fractions of the diet. The respective GE values are approximately 39.3, 17.5 and 23.6 MJ/kg DM. However, as not all feed components are digested equally, GE is not a satisfactory descriptor of energy value of a feed for horses or other species, as it does not consider the processes of digestion.

The integration of chemical methods and *in vivo* evaluation of energy utilisation has led to the development of the concepts of digestible energy (DE = GE minus faecal energy), metabolisable energy (ME = DE minus gaseous and urinary energy) and net energy (NE = ME minus heat increment reflecting energy losses due to the digestive and metabolic processes). In ruminants a further distinction is made for NEm (NE available for maintenance) and NEp (for production) by partitioning between requirements for maintenance and production. This is not attempted for feed prediction in any equine feeding system but accounted for under the animal's requirements. This is an important distinction which can lead to misunderstandings when discussing validity of systems.

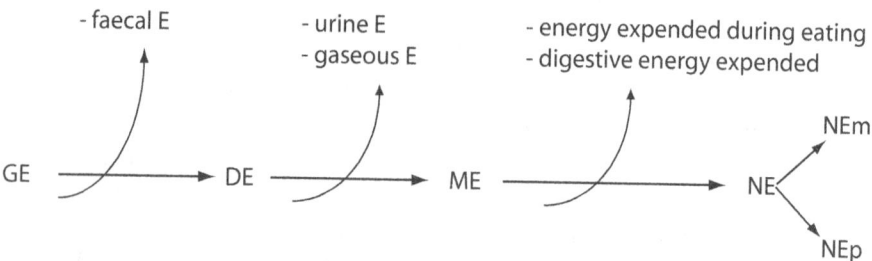

Several systems are currently available to predict energy availability of foodstuffs for horses as well as their requirements. Within the EU and the United States, systems based on DE, ME and NE evaluation exist. These can be grouped as:

1. The digestible energy systems (NRC, 1989; GEH 1995) used in the United States of America, Great Britain and Germany.

2. The metabolisable and net energy systems based on the French Net Energy System for horses (INRA, 1997) with adaptations used in France, Spain, Portugal, Scandinavian Countries and Italy (INRA, 1994), and the Dutch NE system developed in co-operation with INRA (1994) in the Netherlands (CVB, 1996).

In order to express a level of energy derived from a feed a measurement unit has to be applied. For GE and DE the calorific value of combustion

Energy from feed

measured in calories (Mcal) or megajoules (MJ; 1 Mcal = 4.184 MJ) is generally used. Although this would also be possible for further measurements or estimations of ME and NE, most countries using these energy values have converted the final NE MJ to feed units, by using a common denominator, in order to avoid comparisons between MJ DE or MJ ME or MJ NE values. It is also argued that units expressed as a ratio to a set feed give a better indication of a feed value in comparison to others for commercial evaluation and that previous research can be converted and compared more readily (Vermorel and Martin-Rosset, 1997). This approach is occasionally challenged especially if comparisons are attempted between systems. However, the argument that this conversion makes a system less valid is unfounded. In fact, as NE systems for horses express only 'relative' or 'potential' NE derived from a feed a 'unit' rather than an absolute energy value (MJ) may be more appropriate.

A short overview of the different systems or combination of systems used in various countries is presented in Table 5.1.

Table 5.1 Energy systems currently used in European Countries, their basis system and energy units.

System	Energy Unit	Country of use		
		DE	ME	NE
NRC (1989)	Mcal DE	USA; GB;		
GEH (1994)	MJ DE	DEU; AUT;		
INRA (1990)	UFC NE			FIN; ESP; POL; ITA;
CVB (1996)	VEP NE			NL; BEL;
CVB (1996) &	UFC NE;			DNK;
INRA (1990)	MJ ME;			NOR;
	FU ME;		SWE;	ISL;
			FIN;	

UFC = French horse Feed Unit
VEP = Dutch horse Feed Unit
FU = Feed Unit (Scandinavian)

The importance of chemical composition of feeds in the prediction of energy value is apparent when considering different components of feeds. For instance the ratio between cell content and cell wall content is not constant in plants and processed animal feeds. Therefore before prediction of energy value of a feed, characterisation of the feed using validated analytical methods must occur. The characterisation of cell content (sugars, starches, soluble carbohydrates, pectin, non protein nitrogen - NPN, proteins, lipids) and cell wall (often referred to as 'fibre'; hemicellulose, cellulose, lignin) seems to be relatively clear, but there are numerous analytical methods to quantify the concentration of each chemical fraction. In order to predict the energy value of complex, multi-component feeds, a factorial approach has to be taken to correlate the various combinations of feed components with *in vivo* data sets. This approach is exceptionally difficult to conduct in practice and is generally not used as a result of prohibitive cost.

Which predictors for energy?

For systems using digestible energy, feed energy values for horses from *in vivo* trials (GE – faecal energy) have been used. In Europe, organic matter digestibility (OMd) has become the common denominator to compare results of different *in vivo* experiments and develop the various prediction equations for digestible energy content of feeds in the absence of *in vivo* data. Organic matter (OM) can be divided into cell wall and cell content of feed *viz*

$$OM = \text{cell wall} + \text{cell content} = NDF + (\text{soluble carbohydrates} + CP + EE) \text{ (van Soest, 1967)}$$

Or more simply:

$$OM = DM \text{ (g/kg)} - Ash \text{ (g/kg DM)}$$

Crude fibre as an indicator of digestibility has proven to be variable and inaccurate (Zeyner, 1995). Crude fibre content can reflect the concentration of ADF in forages but gives little indication of hemicellulose content or total cell wall (NDF). Zeyner (1995) also noted that the estimation of energy content in feed from all components derived by the Weende analysis (ash, crude protein, crude fibre and ether extract) is not reliable, as the digestibility of crude fibre can range from 100 g/kg to 700 g/kg. The use of ADL and ADF in multivariate equations to predict energy content of feeds have led to most accurate predictions for fibrous feeds for horses (Smolders *et al.*, 1996; Zeyner, 1993; Zeyner, 1992; Zeyner *et al.*, 1995).

Proximate analysis of feeds can also face the problem that certain measurements of individual components of a feed are not relevant when considering the digestive processes of the horse. For instance, in digestion the availability of starch, sugar and the different fibre fractions is more important in relation to the energy derived by the animal from the feed but this is not addressed by proximate analysis. In net energy systems (INRA, 1990; CVB 1996) cytoplasmic content, nitrogen free extract, sugar and starch content have been incorporated.

Predicting GE and DE

The calculations derived from *in vivo* studies of energy balance at maintenance in ruminants have been modified for horses. From these studies, the digestible energy content of a feed is based on the apparent digestibility of gross energy:

DE (MJ) = GE (MJ) x Apparent digestibility of GE (as proportion)

where: Apparent digestibility (proportion of DM) = (GE $_{feed}$ − GE $_{faeces}$)/ GE $_{feed}$

Although GE can be measured accurately through actual combustion in a calorimeter, there is a paucity of such measurements of GE and initially estimates were used for different feedstuffs. Recent studies on grass silage have reported considerable variation in the concentration of GE (AFRC, 1993). Therefore a factorial approach using chemical composition has been used to calculate GE of feeds (for instance, the use of crude protein, crude fibre, nitrogen-free extract, ether extract or fat in the estimation of GE). This approach was used by Nehring *et al.* (1970).

GE (MJ/kg DM) = 0.0239 CP (g/kg) + 0.0398 CF (g/kg) + 0.0172 NFE (g/kg) + 0.0172 EE (g/kg)
(Nehring *et al.*, 1970 quoted in Zeyner, 1995)

where CP = crude protein, CF = crude fibre, NFE = nitrogen free extractive and EE = ether extract.

The French (INRA, 1990) and Dutch (CVB, 1996) systems use various modified equations to calculate the GE of a feed. The approach used in the French system uses crude protein and three different coefficients to calculate GE of forages depending on origin, for instance a separate equation is used for fresh lucerne, lowland permanent pasture, hays from lowland and upland permanent pastures compared with fresh red clover, sainfoin, upland permanent pasture, whole plant immature cereals and hays from leys. In addition, the French system uses multiple equations for concentrates and by-products with crude protein, ether extract, crude fibre and nitrogen free extractive as well as *in vivo* data (Vermorel *et al.*, 2000 pers.com). In contrast, the Dutch system (CVB, 1996) uses one equation for maize silage, based on ash content and one equation for all other feed based on crude protein, ether extract, crude fibre and nitrogen free extractives with additional adaptations for feed which contain more than 80 g sugar/kg DM.

Several energy evaluation systems used for ruminants have used a generalised value of 18.8MJ/kg DM as the basis of calculation of digestible, metabolisable and net energy (AFRC, 1993). The German (GEH, 1994) and American (NRC, 1989) systems have circumvented the difficulties of calculating GE by using an equation derived from *in vivo* studies evaluating the digestibility of dry matter.

In Germany the approach used to calculate DE for equine feeding systems was adapted from ruminant methods (DLG-Futterwerttabellen für Pferde, 1995; GEH 1994). Digestible energy values were calculated from *in vivo* estimates of digestibility of crude protein, crude fibre, ether extract and nitrogen free extractives in horses where possible. In the feed evaluation tables used to formulate rations, digestibility values for these chemical components and organic matter digestibility are presented:

DE (MJ/kg DM) = 0.0230 CPd +0.0381 EEd + 0.0172 (CFd + dNFE)

This calculation, although still based on the Weende analysis, was derived from *in vivo* studies. However, not all feedstuffs have been evaluated with horses and for those a conversion formula is applied (Meyer *et al.*, 1993). The calculation for digestible energy of diets containing less than 180 g crude protein/kg DM less than 50 g ether extract/kg DM and less than 120 g ash/kg DM):

DE (MJ) = 11.1 + 0.0034CP +0.0158CF-0.00016 CF^2

The German system is based on proximate analysis methods, which do not take structural components (cellulose, hemicellulose and lignin) of feeds into account. This has been criticised recently and work has begun to improve the system (Zeyner and Kienzle, 2002).

In the USA, Fonnesbeck (1981) developed the approach of using total digestible nutrients (TDN) to predict the digestible energy content of feeds based on 108 digestibility trials in horses. This method was originally developed for ruminant systems:

$$TDN\% = -64.2 + 2.61\, CP\% + 0.561\, CF\% - 3.03\, EE\% + 1.47\, NFE\%$$
$$(R^2 = 0.87,\ RSD = 0.04,\ n=108\ \text{experiments})$$
$$DE\ (Kcal/kg\ DM) = 255 + 3660 \times TDN$$

The feed composition tables published for equine formulation by the NRC (1989) base all estimates of digestible energy supplied by the listed feedstuffs on equations using the calculations of Fonnesbeck (1981) or modified equations:

Class 1-2 feeds: Forages, feeds high in fibre

$$DE\ (Mcal/kg\ DM) = 4.22 - 0.11\,(\%ADF) + 0.0332\,(\%CP) + 0.00112\,(\%ADF)$$

Class 4-5 feeds: Concentrates – seeds, grains, peas, feeds high in starches

$$DE\ (Mcal/kg\ DM) = 4.07 - 0.055\,(\%ADF)$$

The formula for feed classes 4 and 5 (concentrates) does not however incorporate starch, ether extract or crude protein content of feeds. The use of TDN has come under criticism, when Moore *et al.* (1953) estimated that 1 kg of TDN of corn (maize) had a greater net energy value than 1 kg of TDN of lucerne (van Soest, 1994). This observation not only highlighted the importance of the efficiency of energy utilisation, but also the effect of feed composition and the physiological state of the animal.

Recent advances in equine feed evaluation suggest the prediction equations will be updated in the near future. An example of a more recent equation to predict DE from components of feeds for horses used in the USA (Pagan, 1994) was devised after combining *in vivo* data from 30 experiments:

$$DE \text{ (kJ/kg DM)} = [2260 + 14.17 \text{ (CP \%)} - 11.48 \text{ (ADF \%)} - 4.88 \text{ (hemicellulose \%)} + 57.2 \text{ (fat\%)} + 24.38 \text{ (soluble carbohydrate \%)} - 31.77 \text{ (ash \%)}] \times 4.1855$$

$$(R^2 = 0.88)$$

This equation highlights the incorporation of predictors which may be more relevant to the digestive processes in the horse.

Having calculated an estimate of the GE of a feed, the French and Dutch systems measure or estimate OMd. From this energy digestibility (ED) is derived. The measure of energy digestibility has been validated using *in vivo* estimates of organic matter digestibility of 114 feedstuffs in joint experiments conducted in The Netherlands and France during the early 1990s (Smolders *et al.*, 1990; Vermorel *et al.*, 1997; Vermorel and Martin-Rosset, 1997). The French and Dutch system, however, take a slightly different approach than the German and American systems by using *in vivo* organic matter digestibility data for the majority of feed in their published tables:

$$ED \text{ (\%)} = 0.034 + \Delta + 0.9477 \text{ OMd (\%)} \quad RSD = 1.1 \quad R^2 = 0.95$$

$$GE * ED(\%) = DE \text{ (kg/DM)}$$

$\Delta = -1.1$ for forages
$\Delta = +1.1$ for concentrates

If *in vivo* data for organic matter digestibility are not available, equations relating OMd horses to OMd sheep are applied. Comparative studies were conducted with horses and sheep (Martin-Rosset *et al.*, 1984; Martin-Rosset and Dulphy, 1987; Smolders *et al.*, 1990). Based on experiments with 57 forages in France and The Netherlands an acceptable linear relationship was developed for forages:

Forages (INRA, 1990):

$$OMd_{Horses} = -14.91 + 1.1544 \text{ OMd}_{Sheep} \text{ (\%)} \quad RSD = 2.3 \quad R^2 = 0.96$$

Fresh grass and hays (CVB, 1996; n=27):

$$OMd_{Horses} = -16.71 + 1.1436 \text{ OMd}_{Sheep} \text{ (in \%)} \quad RSD = 1.8 \quad R^2 = 0.98$$

Energy from feed

The equation published by CVB (1996) is more reliable reflecting the larger number of forages evaluated. This system has taken the estimation of organic matter digestibility one-step further and when data for sheep is not available the estimate of organic matter digestibility in horses is calculated from *in vitro* methods (Tilley and Terry, 1963) for forages:

$$OMd_{Horses} = -8.66 + 0.9712\ OMd_t + 9.07*V\ (\text{in }\%)$$

V = 0 for fresh grasses, hay, artificially dried forages

Vermorel and Martin-Rosset (1997) suggested that with increasing concentration of crude fibre in the feed, the greater the difference between the estimates of organic matter digestibility between species (Table 5.2).

Table 5.2 Comparison of estimates of organic matter digestibility in vivo in horses (H) and sheep (S) and calculated data using published equations in CVB (1996) and INRA (1990) (Ellis, 2001).

Diet	Intake level	OMd in vivo		OMd_{Horses} from sheep	
		OMd sheep	OMd horses	Dutch equation	French equation
Martin-Rosset and Dulphy (1987)					
hay	low	63.6	53.4	56.0	58.5
	ad libitum	64.3	52.8	56.8	59.3
hay + maize/	medium	69.6	61.5	62.9	65.4
barley (2:1)	high	64.8	59.3	57.4	59.9
Smolders *et al.* (1990)					
grass hay medium	50 g/kg $BW^{0.75}$	62.1	54.1	54.3	56.8
fresh grass	50 g/kg $BW^{0.75}$	80.1	72.1	74.9	77.6
dried roughage	50 g/kg $BW^{0.75}$	59.4	55.1	51.2	53.7
compound feeds	50 g/kg $BW^{0.75}$	79.8	76.2	74.5	77.2
Ellis (2003a)					
hay and conc., 4:1	Medium	61.1	56.3	53.2	55.6
haylage - conc. 3.8:1	low$_S$/ medium$_H$	71.0	59.3	64.5	67.0

The French equation (INRA, 1990) seems to slightly overestimate the organic matter digestibility, while the Dutch equation underestimates slightly. Correlation is acceptable apart from the final trial by Ellis (2002) where a greater overestimation for the haylage (DM 56%) concentrate diet occurs. This may reflect the level of feeding and the use of very mature (late cut) ensiled rye grass haylage that was not readily eaten by sheep. The problem of using another species is that tight control of voluntary intake of feeds must be maintained. Smolders *et al.* (1990) also note that the sheep in the French experiments were fed *ad libitum* while in the Dutch experiments, a restricted level of feeding was used for both horses and sheep.

For the majority of feedstuffs used in the French and Dutch feeding systems, *in vivo* organic matter digestibility data are included which is a considerable improvement over other systems. However, much of the *in vivo* data was based on digestibility trials with as little as two horses offered an individual feedstuff.

The estimation of organic matter digestibility and digestible energy within all systems can, therefore, be greatly improved by including a range of chemical descriptors and a greater reliance on *in vivo* data. This should be available from recent extensive studies conducted in Europe and the USA, possibly leading to the setting up of an international feed database and an agreement on the method of calculating DE.

Predicting metabolisable energy

There are considerable problems associated with the measurement of urinary and gaseous outputs from animals. Continuous urinary collection and housing animals in calorimeters can compromise the welfare of the animal and considerable difficulties arise when trying to assess these measures in large species (for example cattle and horses). Therefore the majority of trials have been conducted with sheep and pigs.

In ruminants, the prediction of metabolisable energy (ME) is based on digestible organic matter digestibility (DOMD = $[OM_{in} - OM_{out}]/DM_{in}$. This approach has been shown to provide a more consistent estimate of metabolisable energy as the GE of DOMD is relatively constant and the proportions of energy lost via urine and methane are constant in relation to DOM, thus strongly correlated with ME. However, there are many different systems for ruminants throughout Europe. For instance in the UK, prediction systems are based on *in vivo* evaluation of digestible organic matter digestibility (DOMD) and vary according to feed type (AFRC, 1993).

$$\text{ME (MJ/kgDM} = 0.0157 \text{ DOMD (g/kg DM)} \quad r^2 = 0.83$$

In the Netherlands the system to predict ME of feeds for ruminants has been developed from *in vivo* data sets which were correlated with digestible crude protein (dCP), digestible ether extract (dEE), digestible crude fibre (dCF) and digestible nitrogen free extract (dNFE) based on equations by Van Es and Van der Honig (1977) and Benedictus (1977):

$$\text{ME (kJ/kg)} = 15.90 \text{ dCP} + 37.66 \text{ dEE} + 13.81 \text{ dCF} + 14.64 \text{ dNFE} - 0.63 \text{ sugar*}$$

[*if sugar higher than 80 g/kg DM]

This would be an ideal approach to formulate a direct relationship for ME for horses, but there is a lack of *in vivo* ME studies in horses to implement such a complex relationship reliably.

Estimates of ME *in vivo* with horses have been made (Fingerling, 1931 and 1939; Hoffmann *et al.*, 1967; Kane *et al.*, 1979). However, these studies used a limited number of horses (1 to 4 per feed). Nevertheless, the results highlighted that there were considerable differences in utilisation of energy at the ME level between forages and concentrates and justified the distinction made between feed values at this level. The Dutch system used these data sets to estimate ME based on crude fibre and crude protein content of the diet, but the limitations of a small number of replicates led to relatively inaccurate predictions (CVB, 1990).

$$\text{ME/DE} = (93.96 - 0.02356 \text{ CF} - 0.0217 \text{ CP}) / 100$$
$$R^2 = 0.5184 \quad RSD = 2.02$$

where values for chemical composition were reported as g/kg DM

In order to validate these data the estimates of urinary and gaseous losses in the French system were measured in digestibility trials using 6 to 8 horses per feed and 12 different diets were examined at one or two levels of feeding (Vermorel *et al.*, 1997). These studies confirmed the estimates derived for ME from different feeds.

$$\text{ME/DE (\%)} = 84.07 + 0.0165 \text{ CF} - 0.0276 \text{ CP} + 0.0184 \text{ CC}$$
$$R^2 = 0.45 \quad RSD = 1.37$$

where CC = cytoplasmic carbohydrates, i.e. cell contents (starch, water soluble carbohydrates) and all chemical compositional data were reported as g/kg DM.

for protein rich feed (greater than 300 g crude protein/kg DM)

$$ME/DE\ (\%) = 94.36 - 0.0110\ CF - 0.0275 CP$$
$$R^2=0.17 \quad RSD=1.75$$

Both systems then calculate ME as the product of DE and the ratio of ME/DE. The data sets were not sufficiently extant to predict methane and urinary loss associated with various feeds but a relationship between ME and DE was established, even though the correlation was relatively weak. The extremely weak correlation for the 'protein-rich' feed formula reflects the very low number of feeds evaluated. The estimates of ME/DE ranged from 78 to 80% for oilseed meals, 84 to 88% for forages, legume seeds and cereal by-products and 90 to 95% for cereals. This suggests that when using DE only, an 8% difference between the ME derived from cereals versus forages is not accounted for (Table 5.3). This is the major argument of those in support of a ME system, although they concede that further research is necessary for verification.

Table 5.3 ME as % of DE derived from various formulas used by CVB (1996) and INRA (1990) (Source: Ellis, 2002a).

	Barley	*Maize*	*High temp. dried lucerne*	*Soya beans*	*ESM[a]*	*Hay*	*Straw*	*Grass*
French								
normal	93.01	95.30	85.36	77.50		86.02	90.52	86.57
high CP				85.15	81.92			
Dutch	90.13	91.22	92.65	84.99	82.95	83.01	82.56	85.13

[a] (Fat) Extracted Soya Meal

The French system generally has a higher estimate of ME as a percentage of DE for feed with diets containing high levels of complex carbohydrate. This is a reasonable conclusion, as complex carbohydrate will produce lower volumes of gas as a result of inefficiencies in fermentation and contains lower concentrations of nitrogenous compounds which are excreted as urinary energy. In contrast the correction to the French equation necessary for feeds containing more than 30% crude protein, highlights that an overestimation of ME from DE may occur for concentrate feed. Neither equation applies a detailed analysis of cell wall component although this may be important in methane production and synthesis of microbial protein.

Both systems have yet to validate their estimates for ME and variation of each estimate is fairly high. There is a higher degree of variation in the Dutch system, and in light of recent research using respiration chambers in France, the methods used to estimate the ratio of ME to DE must be re-evaluated (Ellis, 2002a) (Table 5.4).

Table 5.4 Comparison of in vivo ME data and ME estimates using the French and Dutch Feed Evaluation Systems (data source: Vermorel et al., 1997). Adapted by Ellis, 2002a.

	in vivo					Equations for ME	
	CP	CF	CC	OMd	ME as % DE	French	Dutch
hay late cut (high ADF)	58	381	31	45	87.16	89.33	83.73
hay + barley (1.5:1)	91	247	246	61.6	90.10	90.16	86.17
hay (medium NDF)	86	312	50	54.1	89.05	87.76	84.74
hay + maize pellets (2:1)	98.3	227	254	65.2	90.23	89.78	86.48
hay (high NDF) restricted	116	336	50	47.2	87.21	87.33	83.53
hay *ad libitum*	116	336	50	47.5	88.16	87.33	83.53

The comparison demonstrates that the application of the French equations lead to fairly accurate estimates of ME. The Dutch equations seem to underestimate the proportion of ME in DE. However, the possibility of an overestimation by the French system is still likely with diets containing high levels of dietary fibre (see for instance the diet hay late cut: high in ADF).

The criticisms of an ME system for horses are based on the system being constructed on limited data sets. However it can be argued that such a system does provide the distinction for energy utilised at ME level between different feedstuffs (e.g. concentrates *versus* roughages). It is suggested that further studies are conducted to measure ME in horses and to develop studies leading to a greater understanding of the effect of protein digestion. This would be interesting both in view of improving predictability of ME, and in view of increasing knowledge of protein digestion and absorption (Figure 5.1). A direct relationship between crude protein content of feed and energy loss in urine could not be identified previously, as the relationship is partially dependent on ration composition. Future experimental studies should include analysis of non-protein N to quantify any relationship between crude protein content of feed and energy excretion via the urine. This was partially attempted by Macheboeuf *et al.* (1995) who made a distinction between N trapped in fibre (N in NDF), which will not be released until it reaches the hindgut.

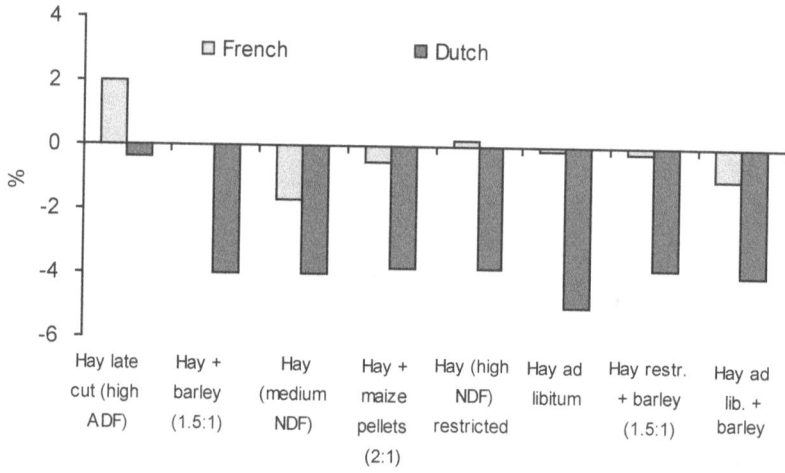

Figure 5.1 Difference of calculated ME as % DE from *in vivo* ME (= set at zero) (Ellis, 2002a).

Prediction of Net Energy

Any evaluation of a feed for net energy using *in vivo* methods is difficult to perform and expensive. Generally these studies require the use of calorimeters or serial slaughter techniques. Small ruminants are easier to manage for experimentation aiming to describe the energy requirements of the animal and the utilisation of energy from feeds by the animal. These experiments can also provide valuable information on the energetics of milk production. However, these trials rarely provide information on work output, milk production or medium and long-term tissue accumulation, which in ruminants has become an integral part of NE prediction (van Soest, 1994). The majority of experiments reporting ME or NE utilisation *in vivo* have been conducted with sheep at maintenance level and very few with horses, but these studies have been used to derive the basis for calculations of ME and NE requirements in many species including the horse (Reynolds, 2000; Zeyner, 1995). For horse NE systems the energy lost through heat combustion of feed (fermentation, enzymatic breakdown) at maintenance and the energy cost of eating (chewing) need to be estimated or measured. The latter has been measured successfully *in vivo* (Vermorel *et al.*, 1997).

The French and Dutch NE systems adjust energy expenditure data for ingestion and digestion by estimating the efficiency (k) of digestion of end-products (glucose, lactate, amino acids, long chain fatty acids and volatile fatty acids) absorbed and the ME available for maintenance (m). Therefore NE = ME x k_m. From the oxidation of these end-products of metabolism, ATP becomes available for maintenance and work. Vermorel and Martin-Rosset (1997) explained that they derived the estimated concentrations of glucose, long chain fatty acids, amino acids and volatile fatty acids from several *in vivo* data sets with fistulated or slaughter horses including data of Webster *et al.* (1975), Gibbs *et al.* (1981), Jarrige and Tisserand, (1984) and Potter *et al.* (1992). Vermorel and Martin-Rosset (1997) also used data generated from studies using ruminants and pigs to develop the relationships required to calculate heat lost as a result of fermentation and release of end products. Furthermore *in vivo* data on rate of passage of digesta, plasma long chain fatty acids and volatile fatty acids, and starch, sugar content and cell wall composition of feeds were used to estimate site of digestion and amount of absorption of end products (Roberts, 1975; Hintz *et al.*, 197; Wolter and Gouy, 1976; Potter *et al.*, 1992; Meyer *et al.*, 1993; Martin-Rosset *et al.*, 1996, Swinney *et al.*, 1995).

An important aspect affecting the net energy derived from feed is the quantity and composition of volatile fatty acids produced from digestible organic matter (DOM).

VFA produced (g/kg DM feed) = (DOM − OM digested in small intestine) x 0.92

Data for derived efficiency (k_m) of utilisation of ME was provided for a range of feeds for example, maize (whole grain), barley, oats, good and poor quality grass hay and lucerne hay (Vermorel and Martin-Rosset, 1997):

Concentrate feeds:

$$k_m = 0.85\ E_{Gl} + 0.80\ E_{LCFA} + 0.70\ E_{AA} + (0.63\ to\ 0.68)\ E_{VFA}$$

Forages:

Concentrate feed:
$k_m = 0.85\ E_{Gl} + 0.80\ E_{LCFA} + 0.70\ E_{AA} + (0.63\ \text{to}\ 0.68)\ E_{VFA}$

Forages:
$k_m = 0.85\ E_{Gl} + 0.80\ E_{LCFA} + 0.70\ E_{AA} + (0.63\ \text{to}\ 0.68)\ E_{VFA}\ \overbrace{-\ 0.14\ (76.4 - Ed)}^{\text{Energy cost of eating}}$
..........or $-\ 0.20\ CF + 2.50$

(where E_x equals percentage of absorbed ME supplied from 'x'; Ed and CF given in %; end products of fermentation (glucose long chain fatty acids, amino acids and volatile fatty acids) as per g/kg DM per feed).

From these equations the prediction of k_m from feed composition was performed for the French System:

	RSD	R^2
Forages		
$100k_m = 71.64 - 0.0289\ CF + 0.0148\ CP$	0.94	0.88
$100k_m = 65.21 - 0.01780\ CF + 0.0181\ CP + 0.0452\ CC$	0.53	0.96
$100k_m = 57.56 - 0.0110\ CF + 0.0105\ CP + 0.0270\ CC + 0.0150\ DOM$	0.40	0.98
Cereals – legume seeds		
$100k_m = 82.27 - 0.0248\ CF - 0.0160\ CP$	0.66	0.96
$100k_m = 72.34 + 0.0119\ CF - 0.0081\ CP + 0.0112\ CC$	0.35	0.99
$100k_m = 93.18 - 0.0490\ CF - 0.0101\ CP + 0.0127\ DOM$	0.59	0.97
$100k_m = 77.45 - 0.0060\ CP - 0.0106\ CC + 0.0054\ DOM$	0.32	0.99

A further refinement of the Dutch System was the development of a separate coefficient for fat in the feeds to compensate for the efficiency of utilisation of that substrate by horses.

In theory the measurement of NE for horses makes the distinction between feeds, which may at DE and ME level have similar values, but have very different responses when considering the composition and concentration of end-products of digestion. This approach is, in principle, a further step in estimating the actual supply of energy from a feed. The distinction at NE level takes into account the importance of technological treatment of feed as well as effects from changed rates of passage in the digestive tract. It was indicated in previous chapters that the release and absorption of glucose in the small intestine will yield a greater supply of energy to the animal than the released glucose or starch in the hindgut

Energy from feed

producing volatile fatty acids. However, validation of the system remains difficult. The conversion from ME to NE will always remain an educated estimate, unless extensive studies with horses in respiratory chambers are performed. One of the few studies at that level was conducted to adjust the equation for energy lost during chewing (Vernet et al., 1995). Vernet et al. (1995) analysed the energy expenditure of eating, showing a high increase in metabolic rate and energy expenditure during the chewing process.

Harris (1997) and Cuddeford (2002) noted that net energy systems assume the horse converted feed energy to work at the same efficiency (k) as for maintenance. This approach is however not correct but confusion can arise as there are difficulties in determining feed factors *per se* and metabolic processes *per se*. At the current theoretical definition of NE, based on previous ruminant systems of NE_m (and k_m) for maintenance, the metabolic factors are included (see following Chapter) (Brody, 1945). These theoretical considerations used in NE systems applied for ruminants are relevant to horses but as there are very limited data sets this further partitioning of energy at present is not feasible and is not attempted by current NE systems for horses. Thus, the terminology used (NE and $k_{maintenance}$) may be contributing to the confusion. Martin-Rosset and Vermorel (2002) recently pointed out that the potential generation of ATP from feed substrates is the same for maintenance and work but the actual utilisation will be at different efficiencies by different tissues under different circumstances. Only the potential energy available for ATP production from the raw substrate directly after absorption is estimated by k_m for horses. This explains why the NE system used for horses does not partition energy to the extent that equivalent ruminant systems do (Ellis, 2001). The metabolic increases in requirements for work are therefore accounted for in an increased maintenance requirement for the working animal. The diagram below illustrates the current level reached by NE systems for horses (Figure 5.2).

In this respect, it may be prudent to revise the terminology used in the system by calling the *efficiency* factor k_{feed} and changing the name of the NE system for horses to the pNE_{feed} (potentially absorbed Net Energy from feed) thus avoiding some unfounded criticism or confusion (Ellis, 2002). The use of DE, ME and NE systems to formulate for energy requirements remains controversial. However, the true test of a system is to ensure the health, condition and performance of the horses. In practice all current systems succeed in achieving these goals.

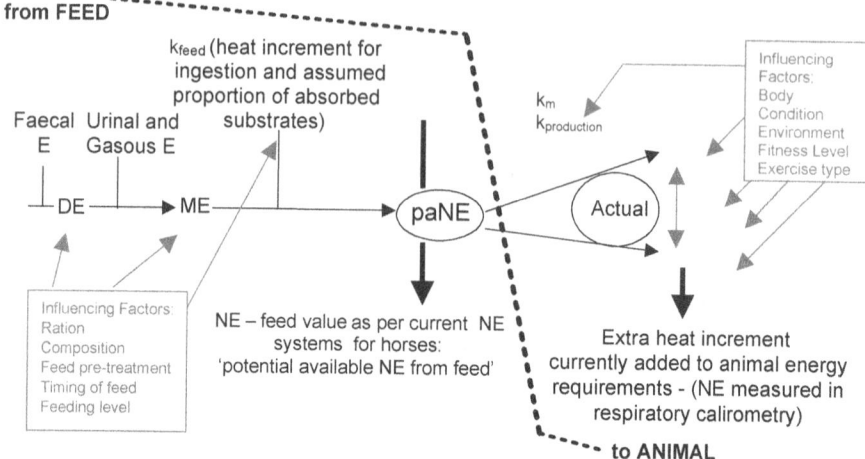

Figure 5.2 Distinction between feed and animal factors affecting digestibility at various levels with suggestion of new terminology to identify current net energy systems for horses (Ellis, 2002a) (where paNE = potentially absorbed net energy).

6
Energy metabolism

Maintenance requirements of the horse

The energy requirement of an animal at rest and in fasting post absorptive state maintained in a thermo-neutral environment is referred to as basal metabolism. Energy requirements for maintenance generally exclude the post absorptive condition and have been derived in thermo-neutral environments (where environmental conditions do not increase metabolism). It has also been assumed that the energy requirement for maintenance is approximately twice basal metabolism (Barth *et al.*, 1977). The energy needs can therefore be defined as the net energy required to maintain body tissues (weight and composition) at a state of rest (Armsby, 1903; Brody, 1945). Traditionally, systems devised for farm animals have considered the energy requirements for maintenance to include energy expenditure for:

- Ingestion, digestion and assimilation of food (including urine production and excretion)

- Temperature regulation

- Circulation and respiration

- Minor movements and 'incidental muscle work' (standing, lying)

- Glandular requirements

- Cellular requirements

The yield of energy from a feed is directly related to the oxidation of substrates with concurrent production of CO_2, H_2O and heat. Measurement of output of faeces, urine, methane and heat production forms the basis of net energy (NE), that is, the energy of a feed that is utilised by the animal for net bodily maintenance and production in a thermo-neutral environment. However the conversion of energy from diet sources and body reserves is inefficient with approximately 80% of the energy intake "wasted" as heat. Body composition, ambient temperature and level of feeding also affect the maintenance requirement of an animal. For instance, correction for level of feeding is important as the NE actually available to the animal is reduced at high levels of feeding due to the increased outflow rate from sites of digestion, and thus a reduced retention time. Various methods have been adopted to correct for this effect in ruminant systems, which attempt to partition between NE for maintenance and production, however the methods developed for ruminants are not relevant in current horse NE systems. If net energy is used as the basis for calculation of energy value of feed or requirement, the efficiency at which energy available from ME for net productive function may vary – *i.e.* the 'k' value may be different for a working horse (k_w) compared to a horse at rest (k_m) (Harris, 1997). However, as discussed before, the NE systems used for horses do not provide a distinction between k_m or k_w and simply define NE from feed for absorption. Even when assessing energy requirements at DE level the effect of feed should be taken into consideration. Potter *et al.* (1990) showed that horses fed on a fat-rich diet had a lower DE requirement for maintenance of constant bodyweight than horses fed on a control diet.

Correction for metabolic bodyweight

It has been demonstrated that the energy requirement for maintenance per unit body weight decreases as the weight increases and therefore a correction for "metabolic bodyweight" should be applied (AFRC, 1993). Heavy horses will therefore have a different relationship between maintenance requirements for energy and bodyweight compared to ponies. Most systems correct the energy requirements according to metabolic bodyweight as $BW^{0.75}$. Pagan and Hintz (1986) suggested that $BW^{0.87}$ improved the precision of the estimate for energy utilised under maintenance conditions in horses. However, their study used only four horses of different body size and conformation to evaluate maintenance requirements.

Requirements for maintenance estimated by the DE and NE systems

The maintenance energy requirements for horses according to the major evaluation systems are in Table 6.1. For ease of comparison the daily recommendations for a 500 kg gelding/mare are presented.

It is apparent that the systems based on net energy have different base requirements for maintenance according to sex and type of horse. All systems apart from the NRC (1989) give requirements according to metabolic bodyweight and the French system distinguishes most between breed of horses. Further, it is interesting to note that the German system (GEH, 1994) describes the requirements for maintenance of horses at rest as 0.65 MJ/kg $BW^{0.75}$, but uses 0.60 MJ/kg $BW^{0.75}$ in summary tables. If a comparison between the NRC and GEH systems (both based on DE) is made, horses are predicted to have a lower maintenance requirement using the GEH system compared to identical animal requirements calculated using the NRC approach (approximately 8% lower for a 500 kg horse and 11% less for a 600 kg horse; Figure 6.1).

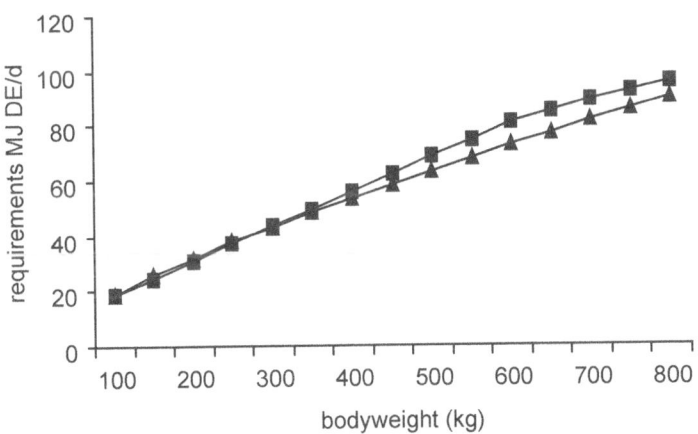

Figure 6.1 Comparison of maintenance requirements (DE/per day) calculated using the German (▲ GEH, 1994) and American (■ NRC, 1989) systems.

Comparisons between systems used to calculate requirements are always complex and difficult to perform. Ellis (2002) examined the current requirements for NE and DE of a 600 kg Warmblood mare offered a standard forage – concentrate diet based on medium quality hay (DM content 83%, ash 10%, sugar 5%, ether extract 1.5%, crude fibre 30%, nitrogen free extractive 76.5%, ADF 32% and crude protein 12%) and barley (Figure 6.2).

Table 6.1 Maintenance energy requirements for horses (all values are cited in MJ/kg BW or MJ/kg BW$^{0.75}$ depending on recommendation) (adapted from Ellis, 2002a).

	Requirement calculation as given per day		Unit per day	Daily requirements 500 kg Warmblood gelding	Experimental Basis
INRA 1984	NE in kJ/kg BW$^{0.75}$ Base 352		0.038 UFC	MJ NE/d	Taken from Vermorel et al. (1984): Voit (1901); Knox et al. (1970), Zuntz and Hagemann (1898), Benedict (1938), Wooden et al. (1970), Doreau et al. (1988), Martin-Rosset et al. (1990), Vermorel et al. (1997a,b), Martin-Rosset and Vermorel (1991)
	Mares/Gelding	Stallion			
Cold-blood	+0%	+10%			
Riding horse	+5%	+15%		37.18	
Thoroughbred	+10%	+20%		39.08	
				40.94	
CVB 1996	NE in kJ/kg BW$^{0.75}$		M/G St.		see Vermorel et al. (1984) as INRA (1990), but does not distinguish between riding horse and Thoroughbred
	Mare/Gelding	Stallion			
Cold-blood	351	386	37 41 VEP	37.11	
TB and X-breeds	367	404	39 43 VEP	38.80	
NRC 1989	DE in Mcal/kg BW		(500kg)	MJ DE/d	
Stalled	DE = 0.975 + 0.021 BW		11.5 Mcal/d	48.03	Pagan and Hintz (1986a)
Stable rest	DE = 1.4 + 0.03 BW		16.4 Mcal/d	68.64	
Above 700 kg	DE = 1.82 + 0.0383 BW - 0.000015 BW^2		21.3 Mcal/d		Potter et al. (1987)
Stallions	1.25*DE$_{maintenance}$				
GEH 1994	DE in MJ/kg BW$^{0.75}$				Hoffmann et al. (1967);Knox et al. (1970) Wooden et al. (1970); Argenzio and Hintz (1971); Barth et al. (1977)
General stalled	0.48–0.62				
Stabled	0.65			63.44	
(100-800kg)	0.60				

Nutritional Physiology of the Horse

Energy Metabolism

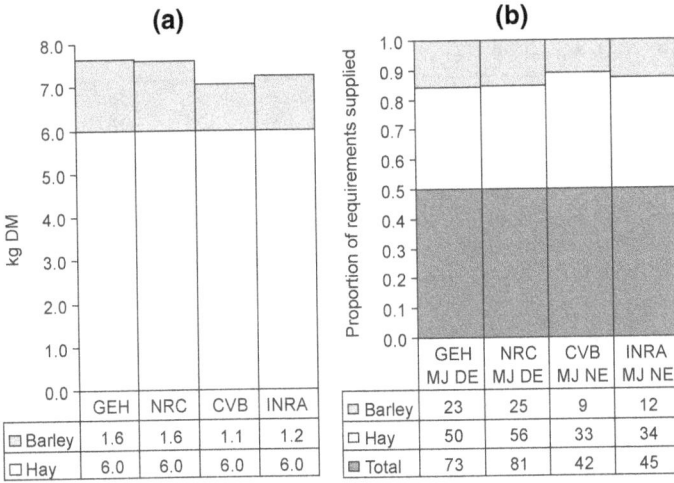

Figure 6.2 (a) Amount of barley necessary to reach maintenance requirements for a 600 kg Warmblood mare per day, when fed 6 kg DM hay and (b) energy supplied per feed (tabulated data) and proportion of energy supplied per feed (columns) of total requirement when feeding according to (a) (Ellis, 2002).

The analysis demonstrates that there is little difference within the two NE systems. However the total requirement for DE estimated by the NRC system is nearly 10% higher than the German system. In practice, at this level of feeding, both DE systems would require a higher level of supplementation with concentrate feed (approximately 0.5 kg in this case). It is difficult to discuss the requirements and feed values separately for two reasons. First in DE systems the hay component of the diet supplies less energy than in the NE systems compared to concentrates (under or overestimation depending on system) and secondly the estimations of energy requirements calculated by the DE system are higher than those estimated by the NE system. Theoretically the energy supplied by one kilo DM of feed as a percentage of total requirements per system would suggest that the supply from barley is around 2% higher in the NE system whereas the energy supplied by hay is only 1% higher in NE systems than in DE systems. These theoretical differences are low and suggest that in practice there is little difference between systems at maintenance.

Requirement for maintenance predicted *in vivo*

Assessing DE requirements for maintenance

A summary of studies using *in vivo* methods to measure the requirements for maintenance for horses is given in Table 6.2.

Nutritional Physiology of the Horse

Table 6.2 Summary of *in vivo* studies assessing DE requirements of horses for maintenance (Ellis, 2002).

Author	Animals	Diet	Daily kJ DE/kg $BW^{0.75}$	Daily kJ DE/kg BW
Barth *et al.* (1977)	3 Shetland Stallions (190kg) Tie stalls, faecal collection bags, no work	Lucerne, Orchard grass fed at estimated maintenance	612	165
Hoffman *et al.* (1967)	2 heavy Warmblood horses mean results	Hay 60%, Oats 20%, Wheat bran 10%, Linseed 10%	514	109
In Vermorel *et al.* (1984):	Draught horses (500kg)		627 - 702	132 – 148
Jesperson (1949)	Draught horses (700kg)		581 - 716	113 – 139
Morrison (1937)	Saddle horses (500 to 700kg)		619 - 816	130 – 158
In Hintz *et al.* (1971) Winchester (1943)	not known use calculation for 500kg BW	Maintenance	648	137
Pagan and Hintz (1986)	4 equines: 125, 206, 500, and 856 kg metabolism crates face-masks short term oxygen production of indirect calculation of heat production increase by 0.29 according to previous literature (NRC 1978)	3 levels of intake per horse 0.75 lucerne meal 0.25 oats basal - in stall: at 500kg activity in stable: (x1.29) at 500kg	DEkcal/d=975+21BW 460 DEkcal/d=1375+30BW 648	97 137

The wide variation in estimation of DE for maintenance is partially due to type of horses used in the experiments and effect of level of feeding. As mentioned previously type of feed and level of feeding will effect the estimation of maintenance energy requirement. In current equine feeding systems this is not addressed either at feed evaluation or at animal requirement level. Two approaches to the problem of increased rate of passage and reduced retention time at the higher levels of feeding have been applied for ruminants; the linear correction (-1.8% per unit increase in feeding level) for lactating animals or the exponential correction applied to growing and fattening animals. If the exponential correction is applied, the relationship between retention of energy and intake of ME is curvilinear for different values of q_m (AFRC, 1993).

The equation developed by Pagan and Hintz (1986) provides an identical estimate to that of Winchester (1943; quoted in Hintz *et al.*, 1971) for maintenance requirement in DE for a 500 kg horse, when the average increment of 1.29 from basal metabolism to maintenance is applied. It is also notable that the data from Hoffman *et al.* are similar to the stall-feeding trials by Pagan and Hintz (1986a) and are likely to represent an estimate close to basal metabolism. This is illustrated by the divergence in Figure 6.3 which occurs when trying to formulate a linear relationship from experiments limited to one type of horse only. It is apparent that results from a single trial using one type of horse cannot be used to extrapolate requirements for horses of a different body size accurately, even when using metabolic bodyweight.

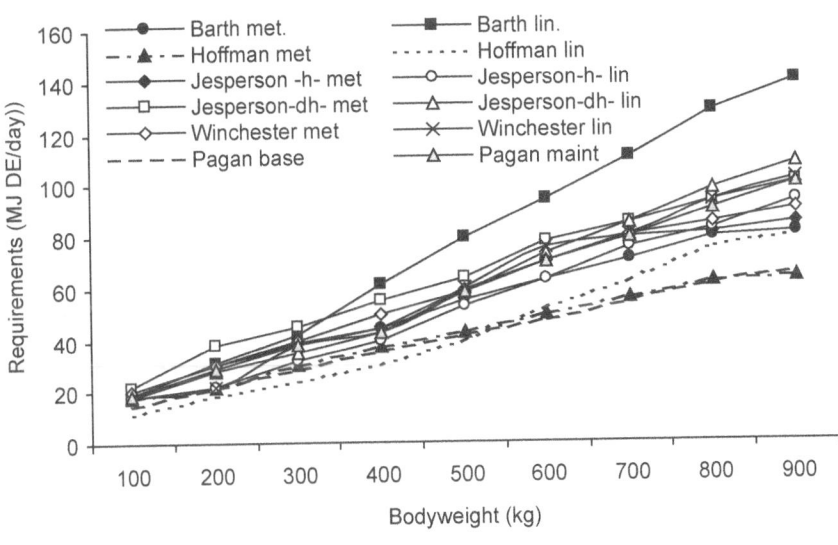

Figure 6.3 Comparison of maintenance DE requirements using results from various *in vivo* trials, giving requirements per kg metabolic bodyweight (met) and live bodyweight (lin) (values for Jesperson distinguish between horse results (h) and draught horse results (dh))
Source: Ellis, 2002.

When the same results are not extrapolated over a range of bodyweights but restricted to weights similar to those recorded in the *in vivo* experiments, it becomes clear that the maintenance equation by Pagan and Hintz (1986) unifies the data from all other trials (Figure 6.4).

Nutritional Physiology of the Horse

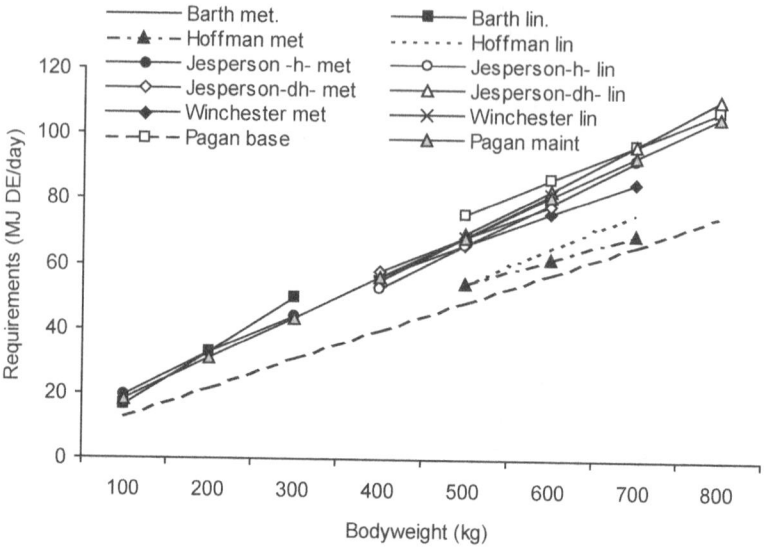

Figure 6.4 As Figure 6.3 but restricting each *in vivo* result to the range of bodyweights of horses used in trial, apart from equation line from Pagan and Hintz (1986) (Source: Ellis, 2002).

The calculation by Pagan and Hintz (1986) was derived from four types of horses and the intercept of the model was used to correct for the increasing body weight, thus allowing an improved estimate of energy requirement for a range of types of horse. This approach allows a unification of a series of equations published by INRA (1990) and other data sets produced to estimate the requirements for energy.

The NRC has adopted the equation from Pagan and Hintz (1986) for all horses up to 700 kg but above this BW a calculation based on a feeding trial for draught horses is used (Potter *et al.*, 1987).

Assessing ME requirements for maintenance

A number of studies have investigated the ME requirements of horses *in vivo* (Table 6.3).

The observations estimating the ME requirements for maintenance in horses demonstrate the effect of type of feed and level of feeding to a greater extent than that observed for similar studies concerned with the estimation of maintenance requirements based on DE.

Energy Metabolism

Table 6.3 Daily ME requirements of horses. Source: Ellis, 2002.

Author	Animals	Diet	Daily kJ DE/kg BW$^{0.75}$	Daily kJ DE/kg BW
Hoffmann et al. (1967)	2 horses, heavy Warmblood, Respiratory calorimeter Chambers	Hay 60%, Oats 20%, Wheat bran 10%, Linseed 10%	Exp.1: 435 Exp.2: 488	91.8 102.5
In Vermorel et al. (1984): Voit (1901)	Basal metabolism		209	43
Knox et al. (1970)	Draught basal metabolism		297	63
Zuntz and Hagemann (1898)	Draught		360	76
Benedict (1938)	Draught		364	77
Wooden et al. (1970)	2 geldings		435	92
Knox et al. (1970)	4 geldings		477	100
Vermorel et al. (1997a)	6-8 saddle horses/ diet (475kg) Open circuit respiration chambers, 7 days, no work throughout	hay late cut (high ADF)	632	135
		hay + barley (1.5:1)	542	116
		hay (high NDF) restricted	522	112
		hay restr. + barley (1.5:1)	461	98
		hay ad lib. + barley	461	98
Vermorel et al. (1997b)	6 pony geldings (208kg) Open-circuit respiration chambers, 7 days, no work 5 pony-geldings (remove nervous animal)	Feed level (m): Meadow hay 0.91M	428	112
		Meadow hay 0.98m	431	113
		0.7hay-0.3maize 1M	352	92
		0.7hay-0.3maize 1.15M	348	91
		Meadow hay 0.98M	414	109
		Hay-Maize 1M	340	90

M = maintenance

The studies of Vermorel and co-workers (1997a and 1997b) demonstrated this point most elegantly. If horses are offered hay with a high cell wall content those animals had an elevated ME requirement for maintenance reflecting the extra energy expenditure of mastication of the feed. In a similar fashion the studies by Vernet et al. (1995) estimated the energy cost for eating forages as ranging from 10% (high quality, low cell wall content hay) to 28% (straw; high cell wall content) of ME intake. This cost is, in the net energy systems, expressed as part of k_m (efficiency of utilisation of energy for maintenance), however in the DE-based systems it is not considered (Figure 6.5).

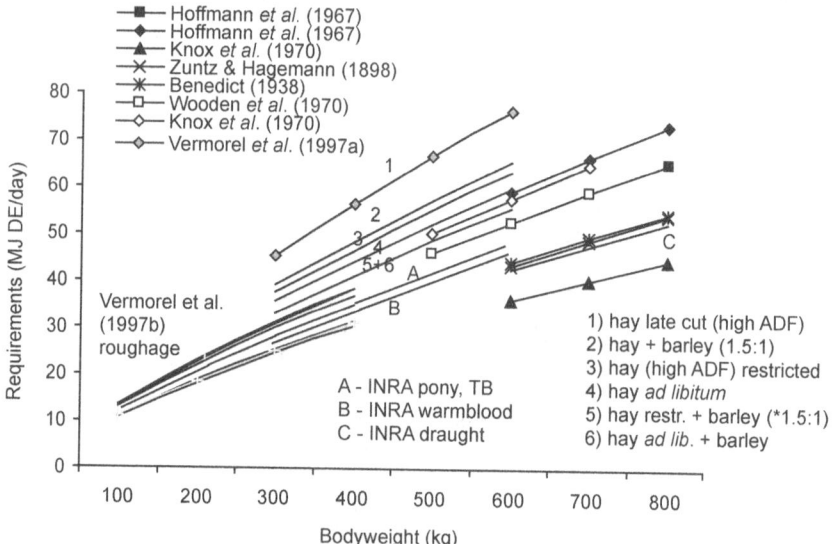

Figure 6.5 Daily ME requirements (MJ) using metabolic bodyweight resulting from in vivo research and NE requirements as recommended by INRA (1984) (Source: Ellis, 2002a)

Assessing NE requirements for maintenance

The net energy requirements for horses have been based on studies measuring DE and ME in vivo by digestibility trials and by calorimetry. In Figure 6.5 the recommended NE requirements by INRA (INRA, 1984), have been included for three types of horses (annotated as INRA A, B, and C). These requirements also form the basis for the Dutch system. These requirements are set considerably lower than the ME_m data reported by Vermorel *et al.* (1997a). This is to be expected at the NE level as the energy units of feed are adjusted for nutrient absorption and the energy cost of eating. In order to evaluate the NE requirements with *in vivo* ME data, the NE data need adjusting for nutrient absorption and cost of eating. For example, the NE of medium hay as percentage of ME is approximately 66% (see Chapter 5). By applying the ME to NE conversion to the ME values measured *in vivo* the resultant NE requirement is almost identical to those recommended by INRA (Figure 6.6).

Energy Metabolism

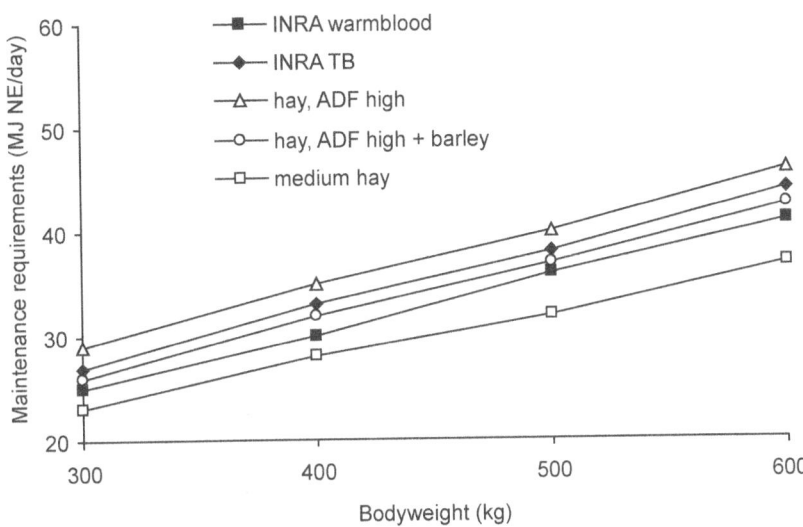

Figure 6.6 Energy requirements according to INRA (1984) and ME requirements derived from 3 *in vivo* feed trials after converting to NE requirements* using published conversion factors (Vermorel et al., 1997a) (*whereby: NE was calculated for: the high ADF hay at 63% ME; the 1.5:1 high ADF hay + barley at 69%, and the medium hay at 66%) (Ellis, 2002).

In conclusion, the estimates of energy requirements for maintenance in horses in the majority of systems currently used have been described by single or multiple linear regression equations based on average bodyweight (in some instances, metabolic body weight). The types of horse and sex have been incorporated into the methods used to estimate requirements for maintenance in the net energy systems used in France (INRA) and The Netherlands (CVB). The development of predictive equations from all systems has been based on several *in vivo* studies, however in all cases there have been a low number of horses used for the evaluation (Pagan and Hintz, 1986) leading to problems in the validation of each system. The most extensively validated system is the French system for ME prediction of feedstuffs in relation to NE requirements (Martin-Rosset and Vermorel, 1991; Vermorel *et al.*, 1997a, b). Recent research has highlighted changes in energy requirements reflecting post absorptive state, level of feeding, composition of ration and, potentially, timing of feeding (Ott, 1981; Thompson *et al.*, 1981; Palmgren-Karlson, 2000). The inclusion of these factors will influence the estimation of maintenance requirements and this emphasises that the assessment of the requirement must be conducted in conjunction with a systems' prediction of energy derived from a feed.

Energy requirements for work

The horse is one of two species of animal (the racing Greyhound being the other) that has had its requirements for energy adjusted for physical work (exercise) and production. Therefore, instead of converting nutrients into energy for maintenance and 'storing' excess supply in the form of body fat, it has been recognised that the horse also expends a considerable amount of energy in work (exercise).

Work is defined as the force required by the animal to move a certain distance in a discrete period of time. Originally, work was measured in Newton per metre (N/m) but it is relatively easy to convert these units to joules (1N/m = 1 joule). There are, however, a number of difficulties in quantifying work by horses, such as the definition of the period and intensity of exercise (e.g. a quiet hack to speed (sprinting, show jumping) or endurance work or a combination of both. Current knowledge of energy metabolism and nutrient requirements for performance by the horse is limited and focussed on Thoroughbred racehorses, trotters and occasionally event horses (Markus, 1998; Hiney and Potter, 1996). However, if these data are extrapolated to horses in less intensive levels of exercise, excess feeding and related problems can emerge as an important issue for the nutritional management of the horse.

In order to evaluate the current literature related to exercise, this chapter must review in some depth the energetics of muscular activity, the biochemical processes underlying the responses to exercise, dietary manipulation and the various studies that have attempted to measure the efficiency of utilisation of energy *in vivo*.

Energetics of muscular work

Muscular contraction is dependent on energy supply from feed and body tissue. The primary substrates for energy production in the horse under exercise are carbohydrates and fats. There is evidence that protein has a role to play in the overall energy budget, but the degree of importance of protein as a fuel is low (about 5 to 15% overall; Lawrence, 1994). At rest oxidation of lipids supplies the majority of energy required by the animal, however as exercise levels increase, glucose becomes the major substrate of energy metabolism (Hiney and Potter, 1996). The energy derived from the metabolism of food is converted into adenosine

Energy Metabolism

triphosphate (ATP) according to the cellular requirements of the muscle and any excess energy can be stored in muscle or liver as glycogen and as trigylcerides in adipose tissue. The catabolism of ATP releases energy (about 7-12 kcals per mol; Mathews and Fox, 1976). Several scenarios have been developed to examine the role of glucose and fat oxidation during exercise. Hiney and Potter (1996) suggest that at initiation of exercise, there is a mixture of fat and glucose oxidation supporting the generation of ATP for muscle utilisation. As the duration of sub-maximal exercise increases, the proportion of fatty acid oxidation increases as glucose oxidation decreases. This is reflected in a shift in the respiratory quotient (RQ) as exercise progresses.

Several metabolic pathways ensure the continuous replenishment of ATP during and immediately following exercise, for instance ATP-Creatine phosphate pathway (ATP-CP), the Krebs (or tricarboxylic acid [TCA]) cycle, the lactic acid pathway and ß-oxidation (oxidation of fatty acids) (Table 6.4). In very hard and fast exercise a further short-term pathway for re-synthesising ATP from ADP without oxygen in the muscle is also available; the myokinase pathway.

Glycolysis requires two ATP to activate and produces four ATP and two NADH. The conversion of one mole of glucose to two moles of pyruvate is accompanied by the net production of two moles of ATP and NADH.

$$\text{Glucose} + 2\ \text{ADP} + 2\ \text{NAD}^+ + 2\ P_i \longrightarrow 2\ \text{Pyruvate} + 2\ \text{ATP} + 2\ \text{NADH} + 2\ H^+$$

The NADH generated during glycolysis is used in mitochondrial ATP synthesis via oxidative phosphorylation leading to the generation of two or three ATP depending on the pathway i.e. if the glycerol phosphate shuttle or the malate-aspartate shuttle transports electrons from cytoplasmic NADH to the mitochondria. The net yield from the oxidation of 1 mole of glucose to 2 moles of pyruvate is therefore 6 or 8 moles of ATP. Complete oxidation of the 2 moles of pyruvate through the Krebs cycle yields a further 30 moles of ATP. The total yield of ATP is therefore 36 or 38 moles of ATP from the complete oxidation of 1 mole of glucose to CO_2 and H_2O.

Enzymes, co-enzymes, availability of nutrient substrates (glucose, oxygen, ADP, creatine phosphate) and accumulation or processing of intermediates and end products of metabolism (heat, lactic acid, CO_2,

Table 6.4 Overview of important metabolic pathways supplying energy for muscular activity. Source: Ellis, 2002b.

Pathways	Substrate (chemical fuel)	Energy – Capacity ATP	Time – moles ATP/min	Energy availability	End-product
ATP-CP anaerobic	Creatine phosphate Utilises ADP and creatine phosphate	Low (0.7 moles)	3.6	Rapidly available for seconds only – sprint	Creatine; Pi; ATP
Glycolysis anaerobic	Glucose	8 ATP		Breaks down glucose to be used in lactate or TCA cycle, rapid if glucose available – otherwise gluconeogenesis	Pyruvate
Gluconeogenisis aerobic	Glycerol, lactate, pyruvate, alanine			Slow, long endurance work	Glucose
Lactic acid –pathway anaerobic	Glycogen – glucose – (pyruvate)	1.2 moles	1.6	Rapidly available for minutes only – intermittent and sprint	Lactic Acid; ATP
TCA cycle aerobic	Glycogen-glucose Oxygen (pyruvate)	38 ATP per glucose molecule or 90 moles, liberates 674 kcal	1	Slow – takes approx 15 minutes to produce same amount as lactic acid-cycle Medium-long exercise	CO_2, H_2O, ATP
β-oxidation aerobic	Fatty acids, oxygen with glucose into TCA (pyruvate)	129 moles		Very slow, but used during slow long distance exercise	Acetyl-Co-A (needed in TCA cycle)

(adapted from: Mathews and Fox, 1976; Eaton, 1994; McMiken, 1983; Lawrence, 1990; Hiney and Potter, 1996)

Energy Metabolism

H$_2$O and pyruvate) are part of the complex regulatory system controlling the availability of energy for muscular work.

Environmental temperature is another important factor, especially when the requirements for exercise are calculated separately from the requirements for maintenance. Within the thermoneutral zone (TNZ), the horse can regulate its body temperature without altering its metabolic rate. However, below the TNZ (-5°C to 25°C, mean estimated at 18.2°C; Morgan, 1995; Meyer, 1996), extra feed is required to supply the increase in heat production to maintain the body temperature. The level of extra feed required has been estimated as 0.15 kg hay/1°C below the lower critical temperature (Hiney and Potter, 1996). Furthermore, if the animal is maintained above the upper critical temperature (about 30°C), extra energy is required to dissipate the heat.

At the outset of any exercise energy is provided by the ATP stores and the ATP-CP pathway, while concurrently glycolysis begins to produce glucose for all other pathways. As exercise intensity increases the lactic acid pathway takes over until the aerobic pathways match requirements for energy. As exercise continues at low to medium level the aerobic pathways will play the most important role and over time ß-oxidation takes place. This energy partitioning is described below in Figure 6.7.

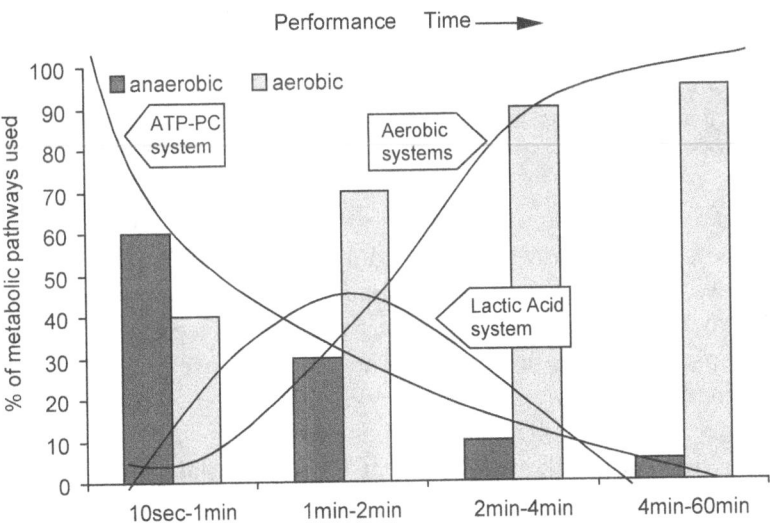

Figure 6.7 Estimated partitioning of energy into proportion of aerobic and anaerobic pathways used in performance horses (adapted by Ellis (2002) from Hodgson and Rose, 1994; Lindner, 1997; Fox, 1986).

Muscle biochemistry

The current understanding of muscle contraction is the sliding filament model of muscle contraction. The model is applicable to smooth, skeletal, cardiac and other contractile activity including mechanochemical events such as single cell locomotion and receptor endocytosis. Skeletal muscles comprise about 40 to 50 % of the mass of the average horse and are formed of long multinucleate, cylindrical cells or muscle fibres.

Each muscle is made up of bundles of fibres embedded in a matrix of connective tissue (endomysium). The bundle of fibres with its endomysium is surrounded by fibrous connective tissue (perimysium). The composite of the perimysium and its contents is the fasciculus. A complete muscle consists of numerous fasciculi surrounded by a thick outer layer of connective tissue or perimysial septa. Within the sarcolemma (the plasmamembrane of the muscle cell) is the sarcoplasm, containing long myofibrils.

Each myofibril is composed of bundles of filamentous contractile proteins. Myofibrils are the most conspicuous elements in skeletal myofibres comprising 60% of myofibre protein. A single myofibril is composed of many short structural units or sarcomeres arranged end to end. The proteins at the junctions between sarcomeres form the Z line, therefore the sarcomere extends along a myofibril from one Z line to the next. Sarcomeres are composed mainly of actin thin filaments and myosin thick filaments. Sarcomeres represent the minimal contractile unit of a muscle and it is the coordinated contraction and elongation of sarcomeres in a muscle that gives rise to mechanical skeletal activity.

The organisation of the sarcomere is a key feature of the sliding filament model with each sarcomere composed of hundreds of filamentous protein aggregates or myofilaments. Two kinds of myofilaments occur. Thick myofilaments are composed of several hundred molecules of the fibrous protein myosin and thin myofilaments are composed of two helically intertwined, linear polymers of the globular protein actin. Proteins of the Z line including α-actinin act as an embedding matrix or anchor for the thin filaments. The distal end of each thin filament is free in the sarcoplasm and is capped with the protein ß-actinin. The M line, a protein aggregate, is located in sarcomeres. Like Z line protein, the M line protein aggregate acts as an embedding matrix for myosin thick filaments. Thick filaments extend from their point of attachment on both sides of the M line toward the two Z lines that define a sarcomere.

Energy Metabolism

Within a sarcomere the thick and thin filaments interdigitate forming a hexagonal lattice so that 6 thin filaments are arrayed around each thick filament and the thick filaments are also arranged in groups of six. During contraction and relaxation the distance between the Z lines varies, decreasing with contraction and increasing with relaxation. The M line remains central to the sarcomere. The thin and thick filaments retain their extended linear structure except in extreme situations.

The biochemical basis of muscle activity is related to the enzymatic and physical properties of actin and myosin and the accessory proteins that constitute the thin and thick filaments. In a rested, non-contracting muscle myosin binding sites on actin are obscured and myosin exists in the high-energy conformational state (M*). ATP hydrolysis is used to drive myosin from the low energy conformational state (M) to the high-energy state.

$$(M\text{-}ATP) \longleftrightarrow (M^*\text{-}ADP\text{-}P_i)$$

When the concentration of calcium increases in the cytosol, myosin-binding sites on actin become available and an actomyosin complex is formed. Sequential dissociation of Pi and ADP with conversion of myosin to its low energy conformational state then occurs. These events are accompanied by simultaneous translocation of the attached thin filament toward the M line of the sarcomere.

$$(M^*\text{-}ADP\text{-}P_i) + A \longleftrightarrow (M^*\text{-}ADP\text{-}A) + P_i$$
$$(M^*\text{-}ADP\text{-}A) \longleftrightarrow (M\text{-}A) + ADP$$

At the end of the power stroke the actomyosin complex remains intact until ATP becomes available. ATP binding to myosin releases energy and ATP displaces from the actin. Energy in form of ATP is also required for muscle relaxation.

$$(MA) + ATP \longleftrightarrow (M\text{-}ATP) + A$$

Enzymes involved in glycolysis are located in the sarcoplasm and substrates such as glycogen and lipid are also present. The mitochondria in horse muscle are in close association with blood capillaries in the sarcolemma and their volume density varies in different muscles from 2 to 24 % (Hodgson and Rose, 1994).

Muscle tissues have two distinct types of fibres which, when working in unison, lead to optimum performance of the muscle while minimising energy use (McMiken, 1983). The two types of fibre are distinguished by their speed of contraction and relaxation and have generally been described as slow twitch (type I) or fast twitch muscles (type II). Slow twitch muscles have a high myosin-ATPase activity and are rich in mitochondria as well as oxidative enzymes. Fast twitch muscles are subdivided into high (IIa) and low oxidative muscles (IIb) (Snow and Valberg, 1994). Both have a high contraction speed and the low oxidative muscles are particularly designed for high-speed work.

It was always assumed that the composition of muscle fibre was predetermined genetically. Foals are born with more mature muscle tissue than most other species and differences in muscle fibre type are apparent at 158 days gestation (Lopez Rivero, 1997). However, some adaptation is possible between types of fast twitch muscle and training can result in an increase in high oxidative fibres leading to an increase in ratio of type IIa and IIb fibres (Lopez Rivero, 1997). Further adaptations of the muscle fibre during training can occur, such as in oxidative capacity (increase of oxidative enzymes), number of mitochondria and blood supply.

During maximal exercise glucose oxidation is responsible for over 90% of ATP synthesis with the other 10% contribution from free fatty acid oxidation (Snow and Valberg, 1994). However, during high-speed work (sprint racing) approximately 75% of the glycogen stores in the muscle are depleted (Lopez Rivero, 1997). If exercise is intense and of long duration type IIB low oxidative fibres may suffer 'complete' glycogen depletion. Depletion of glycogen may be one factor controlling the onset of fatigue or decreased performance, however the total glycogen reserves never deplete lower than 400 to 500 mmol glycogen/kg freeze dried muscle (Essén-Gustavsson et al., 1991). Under continuous endurance exercise, fatigue will set in before lipid supplies are depleted, as glycogen depletion in the liver and muscle reduces pyruvate production, necessary for free fatty acid utilisation in the TCA cycle. Therefore, feeding at racing checkpoints in endurance events is necessary to maintain reasonable concentrations of circulating free fatty acids and glucose.

Eaton (1994) suggested that oxygen supply is one of the most important regulation mechanisms for muscular activity. For a long time, it was assumed that as long as O_2 stores are replenished or sufficient, the aerobic metabolic pathways are utilised and as oxygen is depleted, the lactic

Energy Metabolism

acid pathway becomes the dominant energy production pathway. This theory is still propagated widely by many authors (Eaton, 1994; Hodgson and Rose, 1994; Frape, 1995). However, Lindner (1997) suggested that much evidence exists that there is always enough oxygen available for metabolism in healthy muscle cells, even during intensive work. The rise in lactate concentration and use of the lactic acid pathway is more likely to reflect a 'lack of time', i.e. the aerobic pathways are too 'slow' to supply the energy. However, another of the main limiting factors to aerobic metabolism in muscle tissue is the rapid turnover of enzymes and the surface area available on the mitochondrial membrane (Green et al., 1987; McMiken, 1998). Armstrong et al. (1992) demonstrated that VO_2max and O_2 transport to the muscles in horses remains sufficient throughout all types of exercises and therefore the oxygen capacity of the blood is unlikely to be a primary cause of muscle fatigue in a healthy horse. McMiken (1998) also suggested that the mitochondrial membrane surface may be a determining factor in maximum aerobic power depending on fitness of horses. This is supported by observations that increased training can improve the muscle storage capacity, by increasing mitochondrial volume density and oxidative enzyme activities (thus increasing the so called 'lactic acid threshold'). Therefore circulating lactic acid following strenuous exercise, and its speed of decline (from 8-15 minutes post exercise) is a good measure of body condition (Lindner, 1997).

The importance of lactic acid in limiting the performance of horses has not yet been fully defined. In general, short-term high velocity exercise in horses increases the production of lactic acid but to concentrations that do not seem to be detrimental to health or induce fatigue (Lindner, 1997; Ivers, 2002; Topliff et al., 1985). It is, however, likely that repeated intense bouts of exercise, or long-term medium intensity exercise may lead to increases in the concentration of lactic acid which may have an effect on muscle homeostasis (Walsh et al., 2002). Excess production of lactic acid through strenuous continued exercise leads to an acute H^+ overload. The muscle manages the high concentrations of H^+ by increased rate of respiration. Other buffering systems involve carnosine and bicarbonate. Carnosine may account for up to 50% of buffering in type IIb fibre muscles at a pH range of 7.1-6.5 (Sewell et al., 1992). The ingestion of sodium bicarbonate through nasogastric intubation pre exercise, has been shown to decrease adenosine 5-triphosphate loss and lead to a higher glycerol 3-phosphate formation in muscles, suggesting that a metabolic alkalosis may delay the onset of fatigue (Greenhaff et *al.*, 1991). There is however limited inter-species research available to confirm these observations, and not all species respond in the same way. In greyhounds, for example, the increase of lactic acid and acid-base disturbance is much greater in sprint racing than in horses (Snow and Harris, 1985). Finally, one has to take into account that lactic acid is not an "end-waste" product but can be used by other tissues (e.g. heart) as an energy substrate (Van der Vusse, 1992).

Substrates for muscular work

Manipulation of nutrient intake to affect the availability of energy for metabolism has been attempted to enhance the performance of many animals. This approach has been a successful way of increasing human performance, but there is limited data published for horses. In humans, depletion of muscle storage polysaccharide resulting from high intensity exercise, followed by two days of rest, and offering a high carbohydrate diet has been shown to improve anaerobic performance in subsequent exercise by around 37 % (McMiken, 1983).

McMiken (1983) estimated that ATP, glycogen, fat and creatine phosphate supply varying amounts of energy (kJ):

ATP	– 38	Glycogen	– 75 300
Creatine phosphate	– 188	Fat	– 640000

Energy utilisation is often measured by respiratory calorimetry, as the oxidation of substrates leads to exhalation of carbon dioxide. The proportion of CO_2 produced in relation to oxygen consumption is known as the respiratory quotient [RQ]. The oxidation of fats (RQ=0.71) produces less carbon dioxide than the oxidation of glucose (RQ=1.00; Eaton, 1994) and the production of lactic acid (as a result of anaerobic metabolism of pyruvate) has an RQ value of greater than 1.00. In general, a mixed composition diet has RQ values ranging from 0.72 to 0.99 (Eaton, 1994). Further insight into adaptations to diet and substrate can be assessed by measuring biochemical parameters (glucose, alanine, free fatty acids, lactate) and muscle biopsy (glycogen, glucose-6-phosphate, lactate, triglyceride) (Essén-Gustavsson *et al.*, 1991; Lawrence, 1994; Pagan *et al.*, 1987). These measures should not be relied on as independent parameters for estimating the impact of diet composition on performance but may be incorporated into a multivariate

Protein

Amino acid metabolism plays an important role in muscle physiology during exercise. Amino acids are both substrates for the *de novo* synthesis of enzymes and for ATP production. Exercise leads to a net increase in the free amino acid pool, thus allowing limited deamination of amino acids for TCA cycle intermediates (Jahn *et al.*, 1991; Poso *et al.*, 1991; Miller-Grabber *et al.*, 1990; Lawrence, 1990). Protein synthesis however declines during short and long term exercise bouts (Young, 1986; Lawrence, 1980; Schott *et al.*, 1995; Custalow, 1991). Many of the amino acids can be deaminated to intermediates used in the TCA cycle, thus sparing carbohydrate reserves (Lawrence, 1990; Miller-Grabber *et al.*, 1991a, 1991b and 1991c), but there is still a considerable lack of information concerning the use of protein as an energy source during exercise. Many authors report that contribution of protein to energy metabolism for horses under exercise is relatively minor, approximating to a maximum of 10% under long duration sub-maximal exercise regimes (Meyer, 1987; Patterson *et al.*, 1985; Glade, 1983, Lawrence, 1991).

Some metabolic evidence exists via the synthesis of alanine via transamination of pyruvate in the muscle (Lindner, 1997). Alanine is then transported to the liver where it is deaminated and the carbon residue (via α ketoglutarate) is used in gluconeogenesis, while the amino group is excreted via urea synthesis (Jahn *et al.*, 1991; Poso *et al.*, 1991; Miller-Grabber *et al.*, 1991b and c). This may play a role in providing further energy during moderate to long-term endurance exercise (mainly aerobic metabolism). In humans, endurance athletes show increased alanine formation (Graham *et al.*, 1997) but further research in horses is necessary as results are inconclusive (Lindner, 1997). During exercise the concentration of branch chained amino acids deaminated increases, providing a useful energy supply to the muscle. However, the fate of branch chain amino acids is not clear, for instance leucine is catabolised to a keto-acid, whereas valine yields glycogenic precursors (Murray *et al.*, 1993).

Lawrence (1994) points out several factors, which indicate that an increased protein need is necessary for working horses, such as N-loss in sweat, increased N-retention in horses during training and changes in concentrations of urea and alanine in plasma. Deamination of adenosine nucleotides to inosine phosphate occurs under sustained high intensity exercise, resulting in an increase in plasma ammonia concentration. Ammonia is known to inhibit isocitrate dehydrogense and pyruvate carboxylase leading to the accumulation of pyruvate. This situation could hasten the onset of fatigue by the formation of lactic acid from the surplus of pyruvate (Beaunoyer et al., 1991). However, evidence that these indicators are elevated in untrained horses compared to trained horses is limited and hence the basis of protein supplementation for energy reserves must be considered carefully (Jones, 1985). Several authors have demonstrated negative effects in performance as a result of feeding excess protein to performance horses, including increased sweating, heat production, hypocalcaemia, increased water requirement, cost of urea synthesis and ammonia metabolism (Meyer, 1987; Meyer and Pferdekamp, 1980; Glade et al., 1985; Lewis, 1995). In humans the effect of increasing protein density in diet has been established with linear increases in heat production resulting from 15, 30 and 45% of daily energy requirement provided as protein (Belko et al., 1986). Theoretically the energy cost of absorption, transportation and subsequent integration of amino acids into tissues (for storage, enzymes or energy) is higher for protein than for other feed substrates (Belko et al., 1986). Furthermore, the effect of protein quality (composition of amino acids in diet) on performance of humans has been researched extensively while very little research has been conducted with horses. This area of exercise physiology has to be addressed in detail if the feeding standards for protein and energy are to be improved for horses under varying exercise regimes.

Carbohydrates and fat

During intense exercise energy derived from carbohydrate (glucose) is the primary fuel source for the muscle, while at rest, metabolism is supplied by fat (Lawrence, 1990). This situation is known as the "sparing of glycogen". Glucose, not needed for immediate use by the muscle, is stored in the form of glycogen in the muscle and liver. It is nearly impossible to separate glucose and fat as substrates for aerobic energy supply to muscles as the utilisation of free fatty acids yields acetate that is used in the TCA-cycle. Further, the availability of one substrate affects utilisation of the other. For example, a high glucose intake before exercise, and consequently the increase in insulin release, leads to an increase in the uptake of glucose by the muscle at the start of exercise and a reduction in concentration of circulating glucose (Febbraio et al., 2000). Concurrent increases in plasma insulin concentration reduce lipolysis leading to utilisation of muscle glycogen and a reduction in performance if exercise intensity is sustained. Therefore, apart from type/composition of feed (addition of fat or replacement of carbohydrates with fat), the time of feeding before a specific exercise event is important for optimal substrate availability to the muscle. In addition periods of time used for warming up before short duration performance tests (sprint racing or show jumping for example) may affect substrate utilisation by the muscle. A low intensity warm up before a sprint exercise was associated with increased use of aerobic energy, decreased glycogen utilisation and a longer running time to fatigue (McCutcheon et al., 1999).

During exercise the plasma free fatty acids constitute the most important energy source derived from fats. Lipids stored as triglycerides in the muscle and adipose tissue, need to undergo hydrolysis into glycerol and free fatty acids. The process takes time and is, therefore important in medium-intensity long duration exercise. This has been confirmed by a reduction in respiratory quotients during such exercise, indicating a mobilisation of fat stores. However, Snow et al. (1991) did not observe a depletion of muscle fat during an 80 km endurance ride. Furthermore, an adaptation of muscle to fatty acid oxidation as a result of a modification in enzyme profile over a period of time on high fat diets has been reported (Lindner, 1996; Green et al., 1991 and Geelen et al., 2001). Ivers (2002) suggests that this training adaptation together with glucose loading just before and during endurance races will lead to optimum performance.

The actual mechanisms that lead to the beneficial effects of a high fat diet are complex. Some authors have provided evidence of glycogen sparing when high fat diets were offered while others did not (Topliff et al., 1985; Valberg, 1986; Orme et al., 1997; Harris and Harris, 1998; Geelen et al., 2001a). Beynen and Hallebeek (2002) note that glycogen sparing may occur in fit horses during high intensity exercise only, while horses on maintenance or long periods of low intensity exercise had reduced levels of muscle glycogen. Many authors however, suggest that it is likely that the high fat diet leads to an increased circulation of free fatty acids by increasing the mobilisation of adipose tissue reserves (Frape, 1998).

However, in the experiments by Pagan et al. (1987) and Orme et al. (1997) the concentrations of plasma free fatty acids did not increase during intensive exercise on either a high fat diet or a control diet. These observations were confirmed by Geelen et al. (2001b) who reported a reduction in fatty acid mobilisation from adipose tissue and increases in lipoprotein lipase in highly oxidative muscles. Pagan (1988) argued previously, that it is the absence of a high starch diet or excess glucose loading, which leads to the utilisation of the 'slower' (but more effective) aerobic pathways, through different muscle fibre recruitment.

The interaction between free fatty acids and glucose must also be considered. One benefit of feeding fat is the reduction of plasma insulin concentration. Normally the concentration of glucose in blood rises within two hours of feeding a concentrate feed (a change from 4 mmol/l to approximately 6 to 7.5 mmol/l). Crandall et al. (1998) reported that horses offered a diet rich in fat had lower concentrations of glucose in the blood for three hours post feeding, compared to horses on a beet pulp or starch diet, with concurrent reduction in insulin. During exercise, horses offered fat rich diets also had lower concentrations of glucose in plasma at the beginning of the exercise (presumably a diet effect) and higher concentrations of glucose towards the end of the set exercise test and during recovery, than the control diet. Therefore, the lower yield of glucose from the high fat diet suppressed insulin production as exercise continued, and led to higher concentrations of glucose in circulation. Pagan (1988 and 2000) also noted similar positive effects when feeding a high fibre diet for one day before performance exercises.

Low carbohydrate - high protein - high fat diets have been shown to have a negative effect on muscle glycogen metabolism during anaerobic work (Topliff et al., 1985). These authors highlighted the need for feeding high levels of available carbohydrate in conjunction with fat. During aerobic respiration no benefit from a carbohydrate rich diet was observed in horses under moderate intensity exercise, although the levels of glycogen in muscle increased (Valberg, 1986). In humans, nutritional manipulation can delay the onset of fatigue, for example carbohydrate supplementation during or at later stages of long-term exercise has delayed the fall of glucose concentration in blood by providing additional carbohydrates for oxidation (carbohydrate – loading; Lawrence, 1994). In similar studies with horses, glycogen stores in the muscle can be increased, after a two-day depletion period (low carbohydrate diet and exercise) followed by a very high soluble carbohydrate diet and rest (Jones, 1988). However, performance was either unchanged or declined in horses, confirming the results of Valberg (1986). As mentioned earlier, timing of feeding and subsequent control of glycaemic response may be responsible for these results. This latter practice is no longer employed in human sport, since exercising with low carbohydrate stores has been shown to be detrimental to long-term fatigue.

The reduced performance after glycogen loading observed in horses may also be due to the equine muscle having double the muscle glycogen storage capacity than humans (Pagan, 1988). The enzymes responsible for muscle glycogen utilisation are located in the myofibrils of the muscle ensuring immediate breakdown of glycogen during contraction. Furthermore an overload of the site of deposition of glycogen may during high intensity exercise lead to excess glycolysis with the end product of pyruvate being converted to lactic acid for fast release energy substrate (Pagan, 1988; Topliff et al., 1985). Therefore, direct loading of the muscle with glucose before intense short-term exercise may lead to positive effects if correct timing is applied, while systematic glycogen loading may not.

An excess of glycogen storage in the horse's muscle in conjunction with a reduced activity or insufficiency of enzymes which control glycogenolytic-glycolytic pathways may lead to reduced performance and can lead to one type of recurrent rhabdomyolysis syndrome (ERS) namely equine polysaccharide storage myopathy (EPSM) in horses. These conditions have been given various names in the past (azoturia, tying up, Monday morning disease; De La Carte et al., 1999). Recurrent rhabdomyolysis syndrome may occur following a high soluble carbohydrate meal if glycogen loading occurs rapidly in the muscle in response to glycogen depletion from extensive exercise. This, in conjunction with a sudden rest period, i.e. no further utilisation of glycogen in the muscle can lead to the condition. Some horses have a genetic pre-disposition towards abnormal accumulation of storage polysaccharide in the muscle (Valberg et al., 1999) and diets with low soluble carbohydrates (high fibre and fat) are recommended for the management of these animals.

The influence of a mixed, low protein – high starch diet (crude protein 15 %; fat 3 %; starch 40 %) on maintaining high reserves of muscle and liver glycogen at rest and immediately after long low intensity exercise were demonstrated by Pagan et al. (1987). Lower reserves of glycogen in muscle and liver were observed if the horses were offered either a high protein (crude protein 25%; fat 2%; starch 24%) or high fat (crude protein 13%; fat 18.2%; starch 31%) diet. These observations confirm those of Topliff *et al.* (1985) and Valberg *et al.* (1986). However, when exercising at high intensity short-duration (anaerobic), horses offered the low protein – high starch diet had higher concentrations of lactate in the blood than when on the high fat diet or the high protein diet (lowest concentration of lactate). In previous studies high concentrations of lactic acid have been interpreted as 'reduced performance', however, a greater use of the anaerobic pathway may indicate that energy was available at a faster rate leading to increased speed over a short distance. Furthermore, on the control diet (also high starch diet) horses had a higher heart rate than when on the high fat or high protein diets. These authors also report a greater excitability of horses on the high starch diets, which may be linked to high glucose absorption rates. This research suggests that short-intense work is better supported by high starch/glucose diets, while long-term medium exercise favours high fibre and fat diets. For the general leisure horse high starch diets may lead to unwanted behaviour.

The effects of diet composition and feeding schedule on glucose metabolism is one area which has received more attention recently (Lawrence, 1994; Stull *et al.*, 1988; Arana *et al.*, 1989; Pagan and Harris, 1999; Pagan, 2000). Pagan (2000) conducted a study to determine whether feeding grain with or without hay at different times prior to a treadmill set exercise test (SET; total 60 minutes) would affect performance. Feeding grain 3 hours prior to exercise led to a decreased availability of free fatty acids with an increased disappearance of blood glucose during exercise (Pagan, 2000). Therefore, time of feeding before work is another important aspect of energy supply from nutrition for the working horse. This is an area where further research may be useful, especially in relation to assessing the true benefit of circulating tryglyceride for production of FFA derived from dietary fat. Orme *et al.* (1994) showed a beneficial effect of increased concentrations of circulating FFA and tryglyceride at the beginning of low intensity exercise (15% of VO_2 max – 1 hour). The RER was considerably lower compared to a control group and plasma glucose was considerably higher in the test group, suggesting that an elevation in pre-exercise plasma FFA concentration leads to glucose sparing in low intensity exercise. Whether horses are in a fasted or fed state (glycogen availability), for example, may also influence the rate of triglyceride clearance from the blood as well as the site of uptake (Lawrence, 1990) an observation confirmed by the results of Geelen *et al.* (2001a and 2001b).

Energy Metabolism

Structural versus soluble carbohydrate for performance

Several authors recommend reducing the structural fibre component of diets offered for high intensity performance in horses, as high levels of structural fibre in digesta in the gut may lead to a reduction of performance. This has been suggested to occur particularly in racehorses, show jumpers and dressage horses. However, data provided from the limited number of studies in this area suggest a possible effect of timing of fibre intake and gut fill in horses exercised in maximum speed tests, but not in slow or long term work. In order to measure differences in performance related to nutritional manipulation, heart rate and blood parameters, as well as sweating and respiration rate, have been used to measure the response in repeatable exercise tests (set exercise test; SET; Marlin and Nankervis, 2002).

Rice *et al.* (2001) attempted to assess these effects by offering Thoroughbred horses hay *ad libitum* during an adaptation period and then reducing hay intake to 1% of bodyweight for three days before a set exercise test. The animals on the restricted hay intake lost about 13 kg of body weight during the experiment, while the horses offered *ad libitum* hay maintained a constant weight. Horses managed under the *ad libitum* regime had a higher oxygen deficit during exercise, higher peak concentration of lactate in plasma and higher VO_2 max during recovery from exercise compared to the restricted fed animals. It is likely that the animals offered restricted levels of hay were in negative energy balance and therefore started to conserve energy (presumably as a result of glucose sparing) This would have led to elevated levels of free fatty acids mobilisation which were thus available for use during exercise (leading to a reduced respiratory coefficient and reduced oxygen deficit). What effect this would have had on speed cannot be determined.

A study by Smolders (1990) examined the effect of offering a high concentrate diet (80 % concentrates) and a high fibre diet (80 % fibre) at isoenergetic levels on the performance of the horses. No differences in heart rates were observed between treatments, both during a sub maximal test and a high-speed performance test on the treadmill. These results were partially confirmed by Ellis, D.M. *et al.* (2003), who also examined the effect of forage intake on bodyweight and performance of horses by increasing the inclusion rate of hay in four steps from 50% hay to 100% hay. When horses were trained using a set exercise test on the treadmill, it was observed that maximum heart rate was only increased in animals offered 100% hay diets compared to the inclusion rate of 50% hay (186 beats/min versus 165 beats/min).

Similar observations were made by Ellis *et al.* (2003) who recorded behaviour, blood parameters, faecal pH, bodyweight and heart rates of Dutch Warmblood horses offered isoenergetic diets comprising either of high fibre (concentrate to haylage ratio of 1:4) or low fibre (concentrate to haylage ratio of 4:1). Data were collected during a 15-minute exercise test on the treadmill at 3 training levels and a 72-minute exercise test on a circular training-mill (40m diameter). No differences in heart rate between the two groups in all phases of exercise were observed and biochemical parameters suggested that horses offered high fibre diets could perform as well as horses offered low fibre diets up to medium intensity exercise regimes. However, reduced variability in heart rate in animals offered the low fibre diets was observed, as well as an increased 'difficulty of handling score' which may suggest an increased incidence of chronic stress in horses managed under the low fibre regime (Sgoifo *et al.*, 1997).

Pagan and Harris (1999) reported a series of experiments examining the performance of horses following high and low fibre intakes before training. These authors observed a higher heart rate during the gallop only phase of a performance test for horses offered grain and/or *ad libitum* hay the evening before exercise. They concluded that for training purposes high fibre diets do not have a detrimental effect on performance, whereas time and type of feeding before a performance was important in relation to substrate availability. Pre-exercise increases in concentration of lactate in plasma, packed cell volume (PCV) and glucose concentration are likely in horses offered *ad libitum* hay as a result of increased migration of water to lumen of the gastrointestinal tract. This effect was not observed in horses grazing all night prior to exercise. Ellis *et al.* (2003) when conducting a similar experiment noted no increase in concentration of lactate in the plasma pre-exercise in horses offered high fibre diets.

Measuring energy expenditure during work *in vivo*

Much of the *in vivo* research available has been performed under varying conditions, using horses at different pre-experiment fitness levels, with particular emphasis on the racing industry. The following experiments form the basis for all the energy requirement recommendations for working horses currently available.

Energy Metabolism

Table 6.5 Literature used for estimation of *in vivo* energy expenditure in different feed evaluation systems (Ellis, 2002b).

Dutch System (CVB)	French System (INRA) German System (GEH)	American System (NRC)
• Pagan and Hintz (1986)	• Brody (1945) • Karlsen and Nadal'Jak (1964)	• Barth, Williams and Brown (1977) • Anderson, Potter, Kreider and Courtney (1983)
• Martin-Rosset (1990, 1994) • Smolders (1990)	• Hornicke *et al.* (1974) • Meixner *et al.* (1981) • Persson (1983) • Hornicke *et al.* (1983) • Pagan and Hintz (1986) • Zuntz and Hagemann (1988) • Martin- Rosset (1990)	• Pagan and Hintz (1986) • Hintz, Roberts, Sabin and Schryver (1971) • Rose, Knight, Bryden Persson, Lindholm and Jeffcott (1991)

The results of some of these experiments are in Table 6.6. When converting the data in Table 6.6 to a standard feed unit, the energy requirements for horses under exercise are fairly similar (Rose (133 200 kJ/day), Pagan (130 270 kJ/day), Anderson (129 452 kJ/day) and Hintz (138 928 kJ/day)]. However, differences in partitioning between maintenance and energy requirements (as a result of method applied in each experiment - digestibility trials, calorimetry or calculation by body weight change) are apparent and are an important area of future research in energy metabolism of the horse (Figure 6.8).

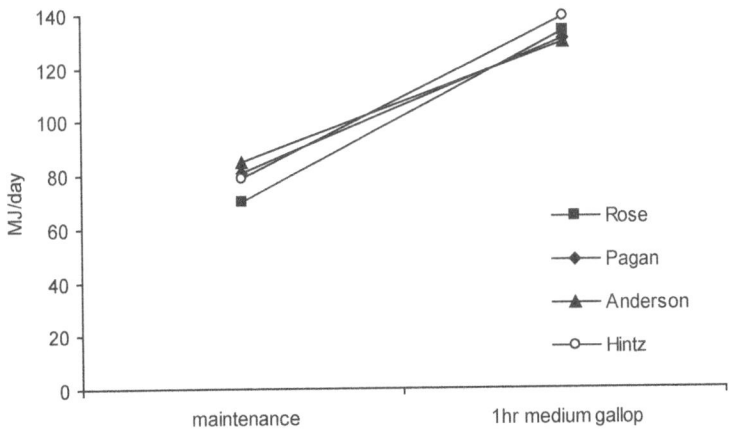

Figure 6.8 Total daily energy requirements for a 600 kg horse (kJ/day) kept at maintenance and or at heavy work (1 hour medium gallop) (Source: Ellis, 2002b).

Table 6.6 Summary of experiments measuring energy expenditure in horses. Source: Ellis (2002)

	Rose et al., 1991	Pagan and Hintz, 1986	Anderson et al., 1993	Hintz et al., 1971	Barth et al., 1971
Horses	4	4	4	16	5
Type	Thoroughbred (TB)	Quarterhorse, Appaloosa, TB and TBx	Quarterhorse	1/4 tot 5/8 Thoroughbred crosses	Shetlands
Weight	440–480 kg	433–520 kg	503 kg	Polo ponies: 475 kg; racing horses: 514 kg	190 kg
Work	Different speeds on treadmill: 3 minutes at 4 m/s 90 seconds at 6 m/s 60 seconds at 8 m/s 60 seconds at 10 m/s 60 seconds at 12 m/s	5 minutes running on an oval sand track 800 m at various speeds: from 40 m/min to 390 m/min	Treadmill with inclination of 9° at a constant speed of 155 m/min, with a medium heartbeat of 135 / minute for varying durations	Ridden in an indoor arena of 30 x 60 m for one hour Polo ponies: at the beginning of training, walk and then short gallop at the end, trotting for the rest of the training Later canter for around 15 to 20 minutes with sudden stops and starts up to 40 times per training; Horses are ridden by medium experienced riders	Pulling of weights up to 175 Kg meter per minute; 4 to 5 hours per day; 5 days per week
Results	**Maintenance:** 70 MJ DE/ day	**Maintenance:** 66.94 MJ DE /day	**Maintenance:** 70.92 MJ DE/day	**Maintenance:** 68.26 MJ DE/ day	**Maintenance:** 31.42 MJ/ day DE

Energy Metabolism

Table 6.6 Contd.

	Rose et al., 1991	Pagan and Hintz, 1986	Anderson et al., 1993	Hintz et al., 1971	Barth et al., 1971
	Work (AM) 75 min 79 MJ DE/day (112%)	**Work (AM):** slowwalk (59 m/min): 7.11 kJ DE/hour/kg BW fast walk (95 m/min): 10.46 kJ DE/hour/kg BW slow trot (200 m/min): 27.20 kJ DE/hour/kg BW medium trot (250 m/min): 39.75 kJ/hour/kg BW fast trot/ slow canter (300m/min): 57.32 kJ /hour/kg BW medium canter (350 m/min): 81.95 kJ/hour/kg BW	**Work (AM)** 0.89×10^3 kg.km: 82.76 MJ; 1.80×10^3 kg.km: 104.8 MJ; 3.56×10^3 kg.km: 118.1 MJ Very heavy: 163.2 kJ/ hour/kg BW	**Work (AM)** walk: 2.09 kJ/hour /kg BW light (trot slow canter) 21.34 kJ medium (fast trot, canter, jumping) 52.30 kJ/hour/kg BW heavy (stop start canter, gallop): 100.4 kJ/hour/kg BW	**Work:** 44.85 MJ/ day
Equations	Work (kJ) = 15.8 VO$_2$ + 4.86 VCO$_2$ VO$_2$ and VCO$_2$ in l/min	DE (kcal/kg BW/hour) = $\dfrac{e^{3.02 + 0.0065 X} - 13.92 \times 0.06}{0.57}$ X= speed (m/min)	DE (Mcal/day) = 5.97 + 0.021 (Wt$_{kg}$) + 5.036X − 0.48X^2 X= work in kg.km.10^3 Wt$_{kg}$= BW in kg	DE (Kcal) maintenance = 155 W$^{0.75}$kg	
Common Unit: 600 kg horse, medium canter, 1 hour	**Maintenance:** 70.000 kJ **Work:** 79.000 kJ **Total:** 70.000 + 79.000 = 149.000 kJ/day (75 min work) **60 min work:** 80% of 79.000 = 63.200 kJè 70.000 + 63.2000 = 133.200 kJ	**Maintenance:** **Work:** 81.95 * 600 = 49.710 kJ **Total:** 81.100+ 49.710 = 130.270 kJ/ day **Total:** 84.596 + 44.856 = 129.452 kJ DE(kcal/day) = 1.375 + 30.0W= 81.100 kJ	**Maintenance:** 600/503 =1.19; 70.920*1.19= 84.596 kJ **Work:** 3,56x 10^3 kg.km at speed 350m/min: 3.56 * 600 * (0,350*60) = 44.856 kJ **Total:** 129.452 kJ	**Maintenance:** 78.620 kJ **Work:** 100.4 kJ/ BW = 60.240 kJ **Total:** 138.860 kJ	n.v.t

149

Nutritional Physiology of the Horse

Energy systems for the working horse

The factors which affect energy requirements during work have been summarised by Martin Rosset (2000):

1) The duration of the work.

2) The intensity of the work (incline, pace, weight of rider and equipment).

3) The ancillary effects of work – extra energy expended for reverting to 'resting' state.

4) Extra energy expended from excitability/temperament.
5) General increase in metabolism during medium to hard level work (increased loss of energy from heat)

Additionally several authors suggest that body fat level (fat : muscle ratio) will affect the requirements for energy by horses (Webb *et al.*, 1991; Lawrence, 1990, Potter, 2002). Potter *et al.* (1990) demonstrated that horses in 'fleshy body condition' required 50% more than requirement of DE to maintain bodyweight under identical feeding and training conditions to horses that were deemed ideal condition. Such experiments are rare and further research in exercise physiology must also incorporate an estimate of fitness and body condition. As far as it can be understood from the study of Potter *et al.* (1990), the authors ensured that both normal and over-conditioned horses were at identical levels of fitness before 'fattening' of one group commenced.

Many current systems estimating energy requirement are based on research by Pagan and Hintz (1986). These workers determined the energy costs associated with exercise by measuring the amount of carbon dioxide produced during exercise. Energy expenditure was measured in four geldings (Quarter horse, Grade horse, Appaloosa, Thoroughbred; 433-520kg) using respiratory calorimetry with a total of 304 measurements taken. The data was used to derive a relationship between energy expended and activity:

$$X \text{ (net energy expended per hour per kg weight)} = e^{(3.02+0.0065 Y)}$$
$$\text{s.d.} = 0.105 \quad R^2 = 0.92$$
$$Y = \text{activity in meters per minute; } e = \text{exponential (2.7183)}$$

However, the intensity of the exercise (i.e. ground inclination and surface) was not incorporated into the model and the estimates are limited to short term exercise regimes as measurements were taken for 5 minutes at a time only. Although the respiratory quotient may be affected by substrate composition and supply, and only four horses, each of different body size were used, the equation developed by Pagan and Hintz (1986), is the most commonly applied method to estimate energy expenditure from work in current energy requirement systems for horses (NRC, 1989; CVB, 1994; GEH, 1994; INRA, 1990).

The NE equations were further converted to digestible energy (ratio of NE to 0.57DE) and corrected for basal maintenance and also considered rider weight and the speed in meters per minute (Y):

NE(kcal/kg (BW+rider+tack)/hour = $\{[e^{(3.02+0.0065\ Y)} - 13.92] \times 0.06\}$

DE(kcal/kg (BW+rider+tack)/hour = $\{[e^{(3.02+0.0065\ Y)} - 13.92] \times 0.06\}$ /0.57

OR

NE(kcal/kg (BW+rider+tack)/minute = $\{[e^{(3.02+0.0065\ Y)} - 13.92] \times \underline{0.001}\}$

DE(kcal/kg (BW+rider+tack)/minute = $\{[e^{(3.02+0.0065\ Y)} - 13.92] \times \underline{0.001}\}$ /0.57

The total energy requirements cited in NRC (1989) for work were calculated from these equations and those of Anderson *et al.* (1983) with the recommendation that an increase of 25, 50 and 100% above maintenance requirements are necessary for light (pleasure and equitation), medium (ranch work, barrel racing, jumping etc.) and intense work (race training, polo) respectively (Table 6.7).

Table 6.7 Total energy requirements (DE Mcal) for horses under exercise according to the NRC (1989).

Weight (kg)	Maintenance	Light work [a]	Medium work [b]	Intense work [c]
200	7.4	9.3	11.1	14.8
400	13.4	16.8	20.1	26.8
500	16.4	20.5	24.6	32.8
600	19.4	24.3	29.1	38.8
700	21.3	26.6	31.9	42.6
800	22.9	28.6	34.3	45.7
900	24.1	30.2	36.2	48.3

[a] Western – English pleasure riding, dressage, hacking, equitation.
[b] Ranchwork, roping, cutting, barrel racing, jumping, barrel racing.
[c] Race training, polo.

Although this approach seems to be user friendly for the general horse owner, the classifications are extremely limiting. It is recommended that data is also provided for an intermediate level of exercise between medium and intense work to reflect sports horse performance. Furthermore it is not known if, as bodyweight of horses increases, additional energy is required for work at similar increments (for instance will a 600 kg horse performing the same exercise as a 200 kg horse require the same increased increment of energy above maintenance). With the approach currently adopted in NRC (1989) feeding according to the 'eye' of the owner, is the only practical management option.

The German system (GEH, 1994) uses the equation from Pagan and Hintz (1986) as converted by the NRC (1989) to kJ/kg/ hour and thus rider and horse weight are taken into consideration:

$$DE(kJ/kg\ (BW+rider+tack)/hour = \{[e^{(3.02+0.0065\ Y)} - 13.92] \times 0.441$$

where Y = speed in m/minute

However, the summary table published by the German system (Table 6.8) reduces the classification of work to the three levels published in NRC (1989).

Table 6.8 Levels of work according to the German System (GEH, 1994).

Work		kJ Speed km/hour	DE/kg Weight/km*	kJ DE/kg Weight/hour
Walk	Slow	3.0-3.5	1.2-1.8	7
	Fast	5-6	1.8	10
Trot	Light	12	2.3	27
	Medium	15	2.7	40
	Fast (collected canter)	18	3.2	57
Gallop	Medium	21	3.9	81
	Fast	30	4-6	
	Racing	50-60	20-40	

* Weight = horse and rider combined

The French system for energy requirements in work is more refined and energy costs of locomotion per metre/minute have been calculated at standard velocities for different gaits. Furthermore, maintenance energy requirements are increased by 10% for standardbred horses in work. Data from early studies of horses exercised on treadmills in metabolism chambers or fitted with respiratory masks (Zuntz and Hagemann, 1898; Hornicke et al., 1974) and in later studies with riders and horses (Meixner et al., 1981; Pagan and Hintz, 1986) were incorporated into prediction equations. The French system based its energy requirements for work on energy expenditure measured during controlled exercise, with additional energy for ancillary effects of anticipation (Table 6.9).

The estimates for energy required for different intensities of exercise were validated in the field over six month periods using 104 horses at various levels of work (Vernet, 2002). The data also take into account that the efficiency of use of energy falls as velocity increases and that energy expenditure rises exponentially with increasing exercise (Martin-Rosset, 2000). Therefore, a precise description of work can be used, by subdividing exercise into duration (in minutes) of paces (walk, ordinary trot, ordinary canter, jumping) and into indoor or open-air work. For ease of application in the practical situation, intensity of exercise within hourly periods is determined according to paces used (very light, light, moderate, intensive) and assigned a cost of NE in UFC per hour.

Table 6.9 Energy expenditure at work and related proportionate increase of maintenance requirements as measured in a horse of 560 kg BW carrying a rider and tack of 100 kg.

Work level	Velocity m/min	Energy expenditure (kcal/ min/100kg BW)	Multiples of maintenance requirement
Maintenance	0	11.5	1.1
Waiting with rider	0	12	1.2
Walking	110	50	2.5
Trotting slowly	200	110	10
Trotting normally	300	160	15
Trotting fast	500	350	35
Cantering	350	210	20
Galloping	600	420	40
Maximum Speed		600	60

(Source: Martin-Rosset, 2000; Vermorel et al., 1994)

Duration:

Very light   horses assumed to work two hours per day manege, 1 hour outside hacking

Light   horses assumed to work two hours per day, 2 hours outside, 2- 4 h long slow hack

Moderate   horses assumed to work two hours per day, longer than 4 h long slow hacking

Intense   horses assumed to work 1 hour per day

Intensity (within work time– manege) approximately:

Very light: 45% trot; 55% walk

Light: 55% walk, 32% trot, 8% canter

Medium: 20 % walk, 60 % trot, 10% canter, 10% jumping

Intense: 12 % walk, 45 % trot, 18 % canter, 25 % jumping

Therefore, the precision calculations which can be applied by the professional owners have been simplified for the general horse owner. However, once again the description of light to intense work is ambiguous, but a greater precision can be achieved by using the French system than that published in NRC (1989) as duration of work is incorporated. This approach provides better guidelines for the general horse owner to predict energy requirements as the various intensities and durations of work both inside a manege and outdoors are described with a greater degree of detail.

The Dutch system for evaluating energy needs of horses at work is also based on Pagan and Hintz (1986). The efficiency of the energy metabolism for maintenance is adjusted by 5%, i.e. the horse will need 5% more net energy for maintenance if it is working (= 2 VEP/kg $BW^{0.75}$).

Work is then divided into very light, light, medium and heavy work and intensity is measured as velocity and duration of activity. Thus the French system has been combined with the NE calculations of Pagan and Hintz (1986). The NE (or ME) formula is adapted to Kcal/kg BW/min and then transformed to VEP.

Energy Metabolism

$$X = e^{(3.02 + 0.0065Y)} - 13.92 \quad \text{(in cal/ kg LG/ min)}$$

X^1 = net energy in Kcal per kg BW (rider, tack and horse) per minute

Y^2 = speed in m/min

$$VEP_{work} = ((e^{(3.02 + 0.0065Y)} - 13.92) \times 4.184 \times 10^{-3}) / 9.414$$

VEP_{work} = net energy in VEP / per kg weight (horse, tack and rider) / per minute

4.184 = factor for conversion from calories to joules

9.414 = net energy of 1 kg barley in MJ

However, the summary table published by the German system (Table 6.8) reduces the classification of work to three levels (light, medium and hard).

Initially this system seems to provide a precise definition but the level of work is calculated per hour. This may be misleading and horse owners might be inclined to arbitrarily increase the amount of feed offered if more than an hour is worked. In this context the recommendations provided by the French system are more user friendly (Table 6.10).

Table 6.10 Characterisation of work according to intensity and duration (CVB, 1996).

	Walk	Trot	Canter	Gallop		Jumping	Total
Km/hour	7	14	32	22		43	24
m/min	120	240	540	360		720	400

→ minutes

	Walk	Trot	Canter	Gallop		Jumping	Total
Walk	57	3	-	-	-	-	60
Light	29	29	-	2	-	-	60
Medium	14	34	-	7	-	5	60
Heavy	14	23	-	10	-	13	60
Very heavy	12	15	12	9	2	10	60

Comparing recommendations

A comparison of systems described is difficult as there are differences in the definitions of speed and work levels between the American, French, German and Dutch system (Figure 6.9).

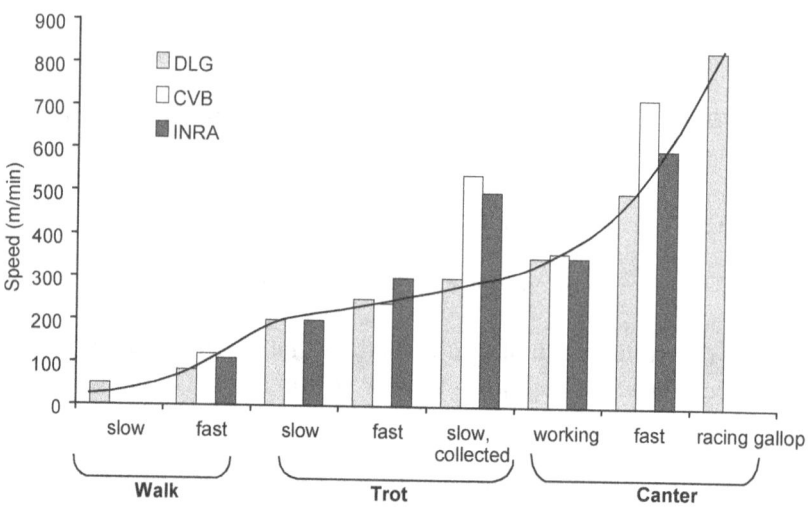

Figure 6.9 Comparison between velocities (m/min) given per work characterisation for different systems (Ellis, 2002b).

One approach to compare systems is to measure the increases of energy expenditure for various levels of work above maintenance requirement. However, once again the definition of work causes some differences and we incorporated the 100% increment described in NRC (1989) as 'very heavy' work. All other 'definitions' remain the same as per system.

The distinction between medium work (medium work – long term) and heavy work (intense – short term) described by the French system leads to a greater expenditure of energy for medium work – long duration (e.g. eventing, long distance work) than for heavy work – short duration (e.g. flat racing). This point seems to be omitted by other systems. Furthermore levels of work in relation to maintenance are set at different stages, i.e. expenditure of walk (INRA, 1990) is similar to light work for CVB (1996) and NRC (1989), and the same difference seems to occur for the next level of exercise described in the French system. This highlights the differences between the definitions of 'light' 'medium'

Energy Metabolism

and 'heavy' exercise between the systems, and such an ambiguity as this makes energy requirement systems for work nearly impossible to apply in practice when purely based on these three levels (Table 6.11) (Ellis, 2002b).

Table 6.11 Increments of maintenance requirements for the Dutch, French, American and German Energy Systems for horses (Ellis, 2002b).

	CVB	INRA	NRC	GEH
Maintenance	1	1	1	1
Walk	1.2	1.3		
Light	1.3	1.6	1.3	1.1
Medium	1.4	1.9	1.5	1.4
Heavy	1.5	1.7		1.8
Very heavy	2.2		2	

It has also been argued (Cuddeford, 2002) that with racehorses, the energy requirements additional to maintenance will be under-estimated when applying the approach of Pagan and Hintz (1986). However, this does not occur in the Dutch system, which uses these equations as 2.2 × maintenance is applied for horses working under racing sprint situations. One of the interesting issues that need further debate is whether the French system's approach towards short-term intensive exercise is more realistic, as it provides estimates which suggest a greater energy expenditure for horses working long term at medium level of exercise. The difference in estimates between medium and heavy work do seem too low in the Dutch system unless the system is applied exactly as described (within 1hr exercise). In general and for the practical application in rationing individual horses, a 'sliding' scale from 1.2 to 2.2 × maintenance is appropriate depending on both duration and intensity of work.

Another approach to compare systems is to examine the net energy requirements for working horses between the systems using work as defined in each system. The NE requirements for a 600 kg horse were derived by applying the 0.57 conversion factor (Pagan and Hintz, 1986) to calculate NE requirements from DE for the American and German systems. This method demonstrates a similar discrepancy in results, again mainly reflecting the definition of work (Table 6.12).

Nutritional Physiology of the Horse

Table 6.12 Energy requirements (MJ NE) according to NRC, INRA, CVB for various activities of a 600 kg horse (Ellis, 2002).

	CVB, 1996	INRA, 1990	NRC, 1989	GEH, 1994
Very light work	51.55	56.48		
Light work	57.81	70.61	57.85	51.82
Medium work	64.51	80.09	69.42	62.13
Hard work	97.88	73.43	92.56	82.65

The final comparison at a practical level can only take place by using the energy units given within each system (both for requirements and feedstuffs) and devising a diet comprising of hay and barley for a 600 kg horse at medium working level. This is demonstrated by using a forage intake of 7 kg of good quality hay (Figure 6.10). In this appraisal the lower recommendations estimated by the French system have been used and the calculations show that the estimates produced by the French, Dutch and German system are similar but the NRC system leads to a higher intake of feed.

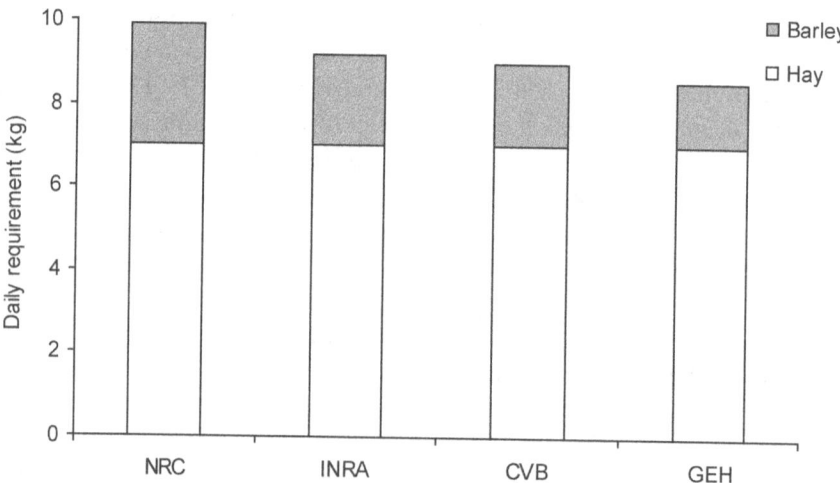

Figure 6.10 Daily additional requirements of barley for a 600kg horse at medium work, fed 7 kg hay.

Although energy recommendations are based on the same experiments and one equation, the main problem when comparing the systems and in practical rationing arises from the individual definitions of work. The Dutch and French systems have a clearer definition of exercise but neither system incorporate duration, repetition, and intensity of exercise accurately in order to define energy requirements for working horses in practice.

7
Protein metabolism

Mammals do not have a requirement for protein *per se* but they do have a requirement for amino acids which are either derived from feed protein or synthesised from nitrogenous compounds and intermediary substrates produced during carbohydrate and lipid catabolism. Protein is one of the most important components of the diet of any animal and receives the most attention from horse owners. Hiney and Potter (1996) also noted that frequently owners of horses will select a feed on the basis of its protein content rather than the energy value of that product, seemingly regardless of the performance of the animal.

Nitrogen metabolism

Mammals are dependent on other organisms for conversion of atmospheric nitrogen to nitrogen compounds available for mammalian metabolism. Nitrogen fixation is performed by microbial nitrogenase leading to the production of a reduced form of nitrogen (ammonium NH_4^+) that is then used to synthesise amino acids. Reduced nitrogen sources generally enter metabolism as dietary free amino acids, protein and the ammonia produced by gastrointestinal microflora. Glutamate dehydrogenase and glutamine synthatase are the two principal enzymes, found in all organisms that convert ammonia to amino acids (glutamate and glutamine respectively). Amino and amide groups from these molecules are transferred to other carbon skeletons by transamination and transamidation reactions thus forming other amino acids.

Aminotransferases exist for all amino acids (with the exception of threonine and lysine). However, the most common compounds involved in transamination are glutamate and α-ketoglutarate. Serum aminotransferases (e.g. serum glutamate-oxaloacetate-aminotransferase

(SGOT) also known as aspartate aminotransferase (AST) and serum glutamate-pyruvate aminotransferase (SGPT) also known as alanine transaminase (ALT)) have clinical implications as markers of tissue damage with increasing concentration in the serum indicating increased damage.

Glutamate dehydrogenase utilises nicotinamide (NAD^+ and $NADP^+$) for nitrogen release or incorporation. In the forward reaction free ammonia and α-ketoglutarate are converted to glutamate. However, the reverse reaction is an important anapleurotic process linking amino acid metabolism with energy metabolism (Krebs cycle). In the reverse reaction, glutamate dehydrogenase provides carbon for the production of energy as well as the reduced electron carrier NADH. The enzyme is regulated by the change in energy status of the cell where ATP and GTP are positive allosteric effectors in glutamate synthesis. ADP and GDP, the by-products of the utilisation of ATP and GTP respectively are positive allosteric effectors of catabolism of glutamate. In mammals glutamine is important as it conveys ammonia to and from tissues (especially muscle). The principal function is the detoxification of ammonia derived in peripheral tissues and transported to the kidney. When glutamine enters renal metabolism, glutaminase regenerates glutamate and releases the ammonium ion, which is then excreted in the urine. The liver also contains glutamine synthetase and glutaminase. However, these enzymes are in different compartments and therefore the liver is neither a net producer nor consumer of glutamine. The compartmentation of the enzymes allows the liver to scavenge ammonia not previously incorporated into urea. The enzymes controlling the urea cycle are located in the same compartment as those containing glutaminase. The differential distribution of the two hepatic enzymes makes it possible to control ammonia incorporation to urea or glutamine and the latter can lead to excretion of ammonia after renal metabolism. Acidosis leads to the diversion of glutamine from the liver to the kidney. This conserves bicarbonate. Glutamine entry to renal metabolism releases one mole of ammonia after conversion with glutaminase and generates glutamate. Glutamate dehydrogenase releases further mole of ammonia by generating α-ketoglutarate.

Dietary protein

Glutamine, glutamate and non-essential amino acids can be synthesised by mammals. However, the majority of the amino acids required for

Protein Metabolism

normal function are derived from dietary sources. The process of digestion of dietary protein starts in the stomach. Pro-enzyme pepsinogen is secreted and converted to pepsin A by autocatalysis. Pepsin A is used in the first stage of protein digestion or proteolysis.

In horses the majority of proteolysis takes place in the duodenum as a consequence of pancreatic enzyme secretion. All serine proteases and zinc peptidases are of pancreatic origin and are released in the form of their respective pro-enzymes. These proteases are endopeptidase and exopeptidase and their combined activity in the intestine leads to the release of amino acids, di-peptides and tri-peptides. The released protein degradation products are taken up by enterocytes located in the intestinal mucosal wall. The regulation of secretion of pro-enzymes into the intestine is controlled by digesta in the intestinal lumen in mammals. Mucosal endocrine cells secrete cholecystokinin (CCK; a peptide hormone) and secretin into the circulatory system. CCK and secretin release lead to the exocrine secretion of a bicarbonate-rich, alkaline fluid containing protease pro-enzymes from the pancreas to the intestine. CCK also stimulates adjacent intestinal cells to secrete enteropeptidase, a protease that cleaves trypsinogen to produce trypsin (a paracrine function of CCK). Trypsin activates trypsinogen as well as other proenzymes in pancreatic secretions leading to activation of proteases and peptidases. Furthermore, about half of the lumenal microbial population in the jejunum and ileum is proteolytic (exopeptidases, capable of protein degradation; carboxypeptidases A and B) (Kern *et al.*, 1973; Mackie and Wilkins, 1988). In the large intestine, the fermentation process further degrades proteins to ammonia.

Small peptides and amino acids are transferred via enterocytes to portal circulation by three processes; diffusion, facilitated diffusion and active transport. A number of Na^+-dependent amino acid transport systems with varying degrees of specificity have been isolated from duodenum mucosa. These transport systems allow Na^+ and amino acids (from high luminal concentrations) to be co-transported down a concentration gradient across the plasmamembrane. ATP-dependent Na^+/K^+ proteins exchange accumulated Na^+ for extracellular K^+ thus reducing intracellular concentrations of Na^+ levels and maintaining the high extracellular concentrations of Na^+ hence ideal conditions to control the transport process. Small peptides are accumulated by proton (H^+) driven transport processes and hydrolysed by intracellular peptidases. Amino acids in the circulatory system and in the extracellular fluid are transported to cells of the body by ATP-requiring specific active transport systems.

Nutritional Physiology of the Horse

Prokaryotes can synthesise the carbon skeletons of all 20 amino acids and transaminate with nitrogen from glutamine or glutamate to produce all essential and non-essential amino acids. Mammals cannot synthesise branched chain amino acids, the ring structures of aromatic amino acids or incorporate sulphur. Therefore, the 10 essential amino acids must be supplied from the diet. However, the diet does not always contain an optimal balance of essential and non-essential amino acids (Table 7.1). Furthermore, different physiological states of the organism modify its requirements for essential and non-essential amino acids e.g. arginine is considered essential in neonate development as mature mammals can synthesise enough via the urea cycle.

Table 7.1 Essential and non-essential amino acids in equine metabolism

Non-essential	Essential
Alanine	Arginine*
Asparagine	Histidine
Aspartate	Isoleucine
Cysteine**	Leucine
Glutamate	Lysine
Glutamine	Methionine*
Glycine	Phenylalanine*
Proline	Threonine
Serine	Tyrptophan
Tyrosine*	Valine

*The amino acids arginine, methionine and phenylalanine are considered essential for reasons not directly related to synthesis. Arginine can be synthesised in mammalian cells but the rate of production is insufficient to meet the requirements of growth and the majority of the arginine synthesised is degraded to urea. Methionine is required in high concentrations to produce cysteine if cysteine is not supplied by the diet to adequate concentrations. In a similar fashion, phenylalanine is required in high concentrations to form tyrosine if the latter is not adequately supplied by the diet.

** Occasionally considered as essential by certain authors (Graham *et al.*, 1993; Jarrige and Tisserand, 1984).

Nitrogen has no designated storage depots in the body. Furthermore, the turnover of many proteins in metabolism is rapid and insufficient dietary supply of amino acids to form such proteins may occur. If one amino acid is limiting, protein synthesis can be restricted and alterations in the nitrogen balance can occur. Normally, nitrogen balance is maintained as zero (intake and excretion are in balance). However, positive nitrogen balance occurs in growing and pregnant animals. Negative nitrogen balance can occur as a result of insufficient nitrogen in the diet or if the level of nitrogen excreted is greater than intake in response to a failure of protein synthesis. The biological value of dietary proteins is therefore important. Biological value relates the quality of ingested protein to that deposited in the animal. Therefore, unsurprisingly proteins of animal origin have a high biological value and plant proteins have a range of biological values. In general, plant proteins are deficient in lysine, methionine and tryptophan.

All peptides, polypeptides and protein are polymers of α-amino acids. There are 20 α-amino acids that form mammalian proteins. Several other different amino acids are found in the body in free or in combined states not associated with peptides or proteins. These non-protein amino acids perform specialised functions; for instance, taurine is an amino acid with specialist function in cats. Several amino acids in proteins serve distinct functions, for example tyrosine in the formation of thyroid hormones or glutamate acting as a neurotransmitter. The α-amino acids (excluding proline) in all peptides and proteins consist of a carboxylic acid (COOH) and an amino (NH_2) functional group attached to the same α carbon atom. R groups (including H in the case of glycine) that distinguish the individual amino acids are also attached to the α-carbon. The fourth substitution on the α-carbon is H. All amino acids except glycine are chiral (L-shaped). The L- form occurs naturally in nature and in proteins. D- forms can occur as free amino acids but are not conferred to protein. Each of the 20 α-amino acids found in proteins can be distinguished by the R-group substitution. There are two broad classes of amino acids - hydrophobic or hydrophilic. The hydrophobic amino acids tend to reside in the interior of proteins and this class of amino acids does not dissociate to form H-bonds. The hydrophilic amino acids tend to form H-bonds and are generally located on the exterior surfaced proteins or in the active site of enzymes.

The structure of proteins

The formation of the peptide bond is a condensation reaction resulting in the polymerisation of amino acids into peptides and proteins. Peptides are small molecules consisting of few amino acids. Proteins are polypeptides of varying size. The simplest peptide, the di-peptide, contains a single peptide bond formed by the condensation of the carboxyl group of one amino acid with the amino group of the second and the elimination of water.

The primary structure of peptides and proteins refers to the linear number and order of the amino acids. The convention for the order of amino acids in a protein or peptide is the N-terminal end (i.e. the residue with the free α–amino group) is to the left and therefore number 1. The secondary structure of a protein is the ordered array of amino acids conferring a regular conformational form. Proteins fold into two general classes - globular proteins or fibrous proteins. Globular proteins fold and coiled into compact structures and fibrous proteins tend to be more filamentous or elongated. The α–helix is a common secondary structure encountered in globular proteins. The formation of the α–helix is spontaneous and stabilised by H-bonding between amide N and carbonyl groups of peptide bonds four residues apart. The orientation of H-bonding produces a helical coiling of the peptide backbone such that the R-groups lie on the exterior of the helix and perpendicular to its axis. Not all amino acids favour the formation of the α–helix. The constraints of stereochemistry of the R-groups prevent certain amino acid sequences from forming helices. Amino acids such as alanine, aspartic acid, glutamic acid, isoleucine, leucine and methionine favour the formation of α–helices, whereas glycine and proline tend to disrupt the formation of helices. Proline is a pyrrolidine based amino acid whose R group restricts rotation about the peptide bond and therefore disrupts the extension of the helix. This is important as it is necessary for the formation certain globular proteins.

ß-sheets are composed of 2 or more sequences of 5 to 10 amino acids. The alignment and folding of these sequences allow the formation of a sheet-like structure, stabilised by H bonding between amide N and carbonyl groups. ß-sheets are pleated as a result of the positions of a carbon in the peptide bond (above and below the plane of the sheet). Furthermore, the sheet can be parallel and antiparallel i.e. the direction of N-terminal and C-terminal either end at the same or opposite end. Some proteins contain an ordered organization of secondary structures that form distinct functional domains or structural motifs. These super secondary structures are important in regulation of transcription of certain proteins, for example, the helix-turn-helix domain of bacterial proteins that regulate transcription.

Protein Metabolism

Tertiary structure refers to the complete three-dimensional structure of the polypeptide units of a given protein. Secondary structures of proteins often constitute distinct domains which are governed by several interactions including H bonding, hydrophobic interactions, electrostatic interactions and van der Waals forces. Polypeptides contain numerous proton donors and acceptors. Furthermore, the cytosol also contains the ample H-bond donors and acceptors. Therefore, H bonding occurs not only within and between polypeptide chains but with the surrounding aqueous medium. The spontaneous folded state of globular proteins reflects the balance between hydrophilic R-groups and the aqueous environment and the repulsion of the aqueous environment by the hydrophobic R-groups. Therefore the majority of the amino acids found on the exterior surfaces of globular proteins contain charged or polar R-groups.

Many proteins contain 2 or more different polypeptide chains that are held in association by the same non-covalent forces that stabilise the tertiary structure. Proteins with multiple polypetide chains are termed oligomeric proteins and the structure formed by monomer-monomer interactions is known as the quaternary structure. Oligomeric proteins can be composed of multiple identical polypeptide chains or multiple distinct polypeptide chains. Proteins with identical subunits are termed homooligomers, whereas those containing different chains are heterooligomers. For example, haemoglobin contains two sub units (a and b) arranged to form a_2b_2 haemoglobin – a heterooligomer protein.

Proteins are also conjugated with carbohydrates and lipids to form glycoproteins and lipoprotein respectively. These modifications to the protein occur after translation and the modifications impart specialised functions upon the resultant proteins. For instance, glycoproteins are of two classes, N-linked and O-linked, referring to the site of attachment of the sugar moieties. N-linked sugars are attached to the amide N of the R-group of asparagines whereas O-linked sugars are attached to the hydroxyl groups of either serine or threonine.

In summary, the role of proteins in equine metabolism and physiology is extensive and essential for optimal performance of the animal.

Nutritional Physiology of the Horse

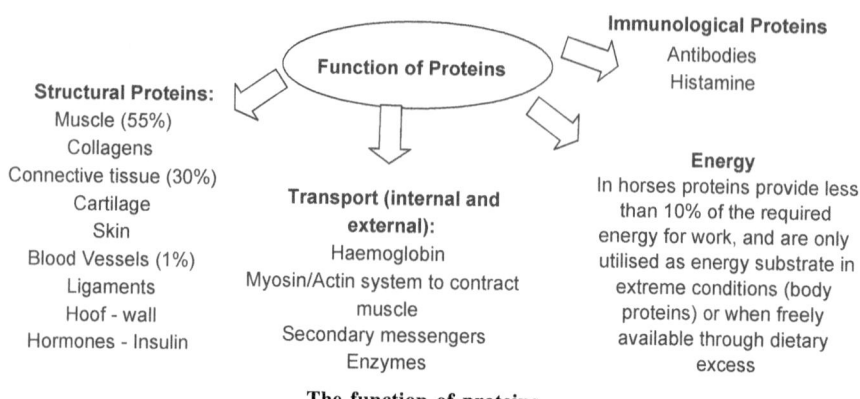

The function of proteins

Protein digestion

Proteins are in a dynamic state of degradation and synthesis in the animals' body and need to be replenished continuously. However, storage *per se* of protein is limited. Total dissection data suggests that approximately 17-19% of the horses' body comprises protein of which, about 55% is muscle and 30% in connective tissue (Martin-Rosset and Tisserand, 2000).

As described earlier the main site of digestion of proteins in the horse is the small intestine. The jejunum and ileum are, however, the most important sites of absorption of amino acids (Frank *et al.*, 1983). The total tract digestibility of crude protein can vary between 12-90% depending on feedstuff (Meyer, 1993). However, total tract digestibility data for crude protein is not particularly useful for diet formulation or rationing the horse. Digestibility of crude protein has therefore been reported as either pre-caecal digestibility or total tract digestibility. A number of invasive techniques have been used to measure the pattern and compartmentation of protein utilisation by the horse. Cannulation of the ileum and the caecum have been applied over the last 25 years to measure nitrogen uptake and utilisation in the horse. More recently, mobile bag techniques have been used in conjunction with canulas to measure compartmentation of digestion (Farley *et al.*, 1995; Gibbs *et al.*, 1996; Hyslop and Cuddeford, 1996; Hyslop *et al.*, 1997; Hyslop, 1998).

The digestibility in the hindgut of crude protein derived from dried grass or lucerne ranges from 60 to 79% whereas the pre caecal digestibility ranges between 2 and 40% (Gibbs, *et al.*, 1988; Frape, 1981; Glade *et al.*, 1984; Meyer 1983; Potter *et al.*, 1992). An overview of recent research findings on digestibility of crude protein is in Table 7.2.

Protein Metabolism

Table 7.2 Summary of apparent digestibility of DM, OM, CP, NDF and ADF of various diets offered to horses in studies examining protein metabolism (Ellis, 2002c).

Author	Animals	Feed / feeding level	DMd	OMd	CPd	NDFd	ADFd
Smolders et al. (1990)	4 saddle Horses	grass hay early cut		62.3	60.3		
		grass hay medium cut		54.1	73.4		
		grass hay late cut		45.7	59.3		
		grass silage		64.6	70.0		
Vermorel et al. (1997)	6 standard-Breds	hay late cut (high ADF)	3.8	45.0	48.3		
		hay + barley (1.5:1)	58.6	61.6	61.4		
		hay (medium NDF)	52.4	54.1	54.6	41.4	39.1
		hay + maize pellets (2:1)	63.2	65.2	64.8	44.7	40.8
		hay (high NDF) restricted	47.5	47.2	55.0	48.6	44.4
		hay ad libitum	47.2	47.5	54.3	48.5	45.3
		hay ad libitum + barley	59.9	61.5	63.8	45.1	40.9
		hay restricted + barley (1.5:1)	60.2	61.6	65.1	44.6	39.5
La Casha et al. (1999)	18 Quarter horse yearlings	Matua brome grass	51	64	74		
		Coastal bermuda grass	46	60	64		
		Lucerne hay	63	74	83		
Palmgren Karlsson et al. (2000)	4 standard bred	Hay	48	49	54	37	29
		hay + oats (4:1)	55	56	65	39	32
		hay + oats (1.5:1)	58	59	72	43	35
		hay + oats (1: 1.5)	58	60	76	36	26
Drogoul et al. (2000a)	10 ponies 4 with caec+ colocanulas	Lucerne + Cocksfoot Hay chopped	51.4	52.1	72.6	44.2	39.6
		ground and pelleted	53.8	55.2	71.5	47.0	39.6
Rey et al. (2001)	4 Shetland	Diets:		CF<u>d</u>			
		hay + conc. (low CP)	42.9	57			
		+ potato prot.(high CP)	38.1	71			
Farley et al. (1995)	3 ponies ileal fistulas diets – pelleted	soya+cotton seed hull	DMd	Total N-dig.		Pre-caecal*	Post ileal*
		+ soybean meal 0%	82.1	62.9		57.3	42.7
		+ soybean meal 11%	79.3	78.8		67.7	32.4
		+ soybean meal 23%	73.7	85.8		69.3	30.7
		+ soybean meal 35%	77.3	87.4		55.3	44.8
Gibbs et al. (1988)		Bermuda grass		56.5	17.2		83
		Luzerne low intake		66.0	2.1		97.9
		Luzerne high intake		74.2	28.6		71.4
Gibbs et al. (1996)	3 ponies 127 kg ileal fistulas	Bermuda grass hay (0.75) + 0.25 Corn (CP 9.8; NDF 38.4)	Total 88.5	Conc 98.1	Total 43.8	Conc 94.4	Total 56.2	Conc 51.6
		+ 0.25 Oats (CP 14.2; NDF 42.7)	84.6	88.5	55.3	60.9	44.7	39.1
		+0.25 Sorghum(CP 10.2; NDF 37.3)	84.6	93.1	66.3	75.9	33.7	24.1
		s.e.m	1.4	1.3	4.9	5.9	4.9	5.9

Table 7.2 Contd.

		Total	Conc	Total	Conc	Total	Conc
Corn and Bermuda grass hay		84.0		36.6		63.4	
+ Soyabean meal		88.4	92.2	48.0	57.0	52.0	43.0
+ Solv. Extr. Cotton Seed Meal		84.4	85.0	66.5	95.6	33.5	4.4
s.e.m		0.4	1.0	3.2	2.9	3.2	2.9
		Mean		Range			
Total tract mean	(n = 24)	65		48-83			
Pre-caecal mean Whole diet	(n = 10)	57		44-69			
Pre-caecal Forages only	(n = 5)	28		2.1-57			
Pre-caecal Concentrates only	(n = 5)	69		50-96			

* percentage of total N-dig.

Digestion of protein and subsequent absorption in the small intestine of amino acids is directly related to chemical composition of protein and the period of time the digesta is retained in one compartment in the digestive tract. There is an upper limit to the quantity of protein digested in the stomach and anterior small intestine as a result of the rapid flow of digesta through the small intestine of the horse. Differences in passage rates through the small intestine are therefore more important in relation to the absorption of amino acids than the process of protein digestion. Furthermore, the effect of the physico-chemical composition of feedstuffs on digesta passage rate has been recognised recently as a major factor in determining digestibility of crude protein in horses (Amici, 1997, Cuddeford, 1995, Coenen, 1986; Drogoul, 1996; McLean et al., 1999; Drogoul et al., 2000a and b).

The effect of passage rate on uptake of nitrogen from feeds has been demonstrated by Farley et al. (1995) and Gibbs et al. (1996) using ileal-cannulated Shetland ponies. When offering hay-concentrate diets 44 to 69% of total N disappeared across the small intestine. However, the calculated disappearance of nitrogen from the forage component and concentrate component only were 36.6% and between 48 to 67%. Therefore the higher estimates of disappearance of total N from concentrates and hays assumed by INRA (1984) (Table 7.3) may overestimate the supply of amino acids from the diet, available for uptake and use in intermediary metabolism.

Protein Metabolism

Table 7.3 Estimated N-digestibility in the small intestine as used in the French Protein Evaluation systems INRA (1984)

Hays	30-45
Dehydrated Lucerne	60
Grass	60-70
Concentrates	70-80

Data recorded by Gibbs *et al.* (1988 and 1996) clearly demonstrates the associative effect of concentrate and roughage components of the diet and probably reflects the variation in passage rate according to diet composition and volume.

The estimation of the impact of associative effects on amino acid supply for metabolism is an important issue for equine nutritionists.

The interaction between dietary fibre and protein is an important issue for equine nutritionists but, as with energy yielding substrates, there are limited data available to determine the effect of diet formulation. Cell wall bound proteins or those closely associated with indigestible cell wall components (for example, tannins) could enter the hindgut unprocessed by proteolytic enzymes in the small intestine. These proteins are degraded extensively by microflora with proteolytic activity (for example, protozoa and some *Enterobacteria*; Meyer, 1995). Amino acids are utilised by the microflora in the hindgut to synthesise microbial protein. The exact requirements for nitrogen for bacteria in the hindgut of the horse have not been determined but would be similar to those occurring in the rumen. However, energy supply would be the first limiting factor for microbial protein synthesis (AFRC, 1993). In equine nutrition there are no equivalent measures to "rumen fermentable organic matter" and the supply of energy substrates entering the hind gut will be depleted of readily fermentable carbohydrate. Therefore, any concept of microbially-available carbon has to be considered in light of substrate flow, composition of digesta post ileum and any "spill-over" of nutrients not utilised in the ante caecal section of the gastrointestinal tract. A further complexity is that nitrogen sources entering the hindgut are not well characterised. They will be comprised of partially digested protein that may be unavailable for microbial degradation (i.e. not digestible), products of metabolism from microbial populations that are endemic to the small intestine, urea, amino acids and intestinal protein (endogenic) in the form of mucins. Meyer (1993) attempted to estimate the ileo-caecal flow of nitrogen (in urea equivalents) and relate such a flow to daily dry matter intake (DMI), crude fibre and crude protein content of feed:

$$\text{Urea-N flow} = (6DMI + 1.02CF).(3+11.2CP)$$

The ability of the horse to absorb free amino acids through the wall of the hind gut resulting from exopeptidase action is still disputed. It has been suggested that the utilisation of microbial protein, free amino acids and non-protein nitrogen in the lower digestive tract (post caecal) may be important in horses with low intakes of dietary protein (van Soest, 1994). Free–ranging horses (feral or wild) often have to survive on very low-quality forages containing very low concentrations of crude protein (often less than 6% in the dry matter). Those forages also have a high level of crude protein associated with the cell wall thus reducing the digestibility of the protein available for digestion (van Soest, 1994). Disruption of the cell wall as a result of chewing is therefore essential for protein availability in such feeds and it is suggested that there may be more studies required to understand the interactions between protein and physico-chemical nature of feeds. Coprophagy may also play a role in the protein nutrition of wild and feral horses foraging on low protein rangeland. Coprophagy offers an additional means to ingest high quality microbial protein.

Active absorption of amino acids through the mucosa of the hindgut of sheep, dogs and pigs has been demonstrated, with limited or no further absorption into the bloodstream (from the mucosal lumen into serosal side), indicating that the amino acids were utilised in the mucosa only (Bochroder *et al.*, 1994). These observations may have lead to some of the contradictions noted in the literature concerned with the absorption of amino acids in the hindgut of the horse. Passive diffusion of some amino acids into the blood from the hindgut has been reported in rats (Binder, 1970), but no evidence of absorption of amino acids to circulation has been observed in pigs (Kravielitzki *et al.*, 1983; Schmitz *et al.*, 1991). Little evidence *in vivo* is available for transportation of amino acids via the hind gut mucosa by either passive or active mechanisms in horses. Slade *et al.* (1971) introduced ^{15}N labelled essential amino-acids (lysine) into the caecum of horses and observed transport of the label to circulation. It was concluded that the ^{15}N lysine was absorbed and transported across the caecal wall to circulation, but Bochroder *et al.* (1994) when reviewing the data suggested that it was likely that the ^{15}N ammonium was absorbed from the caecum and colon and this led to

^{15}N labelled lysine in the venous blood in caecal circulation. The experiment by Slade et al. (1971) has never been repeated successfully.

Absorption across the hindgut lining to circulation is unlikely due to the nature of the lining of the caecum and colon (Meyer, 1995; Frape, 1998). Schmitz et al. (1991) using homoarginine as an analogue assessed the absorption of amino acids from the caecum and colon to circulation. Negligible concentration (less than 10%) of homoarginine resulted in circulation suggesting that the level of amino acid absorption in the hindgut of the horse was insignificant. Further evidence for a lack of transport was provided by Bochröder et al. (1994). When using discs of stripped equine colon mucosa to study the possible transport of essential amino acids (lysine, histidine, arginine) and ammonia, it was demonstrated that the equine colon was not permeable to luminal free amino acids, but ammonia was transported across the mucosa at a rate comparable to similar studies with small ruminants. More recently Martin-Rosset and Tisserand (2002) reported preliminary results from studies examining the uptake of five different amino acids (threonine, valine, methionine, pheylalanine and lysine) via the colon wall. Again, as with the studies of Schmitz et al. (1991) and Bochröder et al. (1994) no increase in concentration of these amino acids were observed in the plasma sampled via the colonic vein.

Requirements for amino acids

In order to assess the dietary requirement of the horse for amino acid supply, the 'nitrogen balance' has been the traditional approach (the balance between N ingested in the feed and that excreted in the faeces and urine). If the supply of amino acids derived from dietary protein is deficient, the animal will commence breakdown of existing, mainly structural, protein to gain the necessary amino acids required to fulfil productive function. This results in a negative nitrogen balance where excretion of nitrogen exceeds intake. A positive nitrogen balance is common during growth of foals, youngstock, during fittening, heavy work and lactation. Intake of dietary nitrogen will exceed excretion as amino acids are utilised during growth for the laying down of new structural tissues. Positive nitrogen balances may also occur during recovery after illness or injury and following extreme exertion (replenishment of resources).

Many studies concerning nitrogen balance are confounded by the secretion of endogenous nitrogen into the digestive tract via saliva, gastric and pancreatic secretions, bile and exogenous nitrogen from microbial shedding. Thus, nitrogen balances do not indicate, in practice, whether the animal is receiving too much or too little protein from dietary sources. Excessive intakes of protein lead to greater urine volume associated with increased excretion of ammonia. Daily basal endogenous losses of nitrogen are, therefore, very difficult to measure as nitrogen output when feeding very low concentrations of dietary protein will not give true reflection of endogenous loss. Linear modelling has been applied to such data and estimates have been applied to the various feeding systems. The problems associated with measurement of endogenous nitrogen loss are highlighted by Reitnour and Salisbury (1976), who demonstrated that with increasing levels of protein offered in the feed, the apparent digestibility of crude protein increased (reduced excretion of nitrogen). These authors argued that the increase probably reflected a reduction in the endogenous nitrogen fraction in the faeces.

Requirements for maintenance

Traditionally, experiments examining the apparent digestibility of crude protein have been used to estimate the requirements for maintenance, work and lactation. However, these studies may not provide an accurate reflection of the protein "household" of the horse. Endogenous nitrogen losses and shedding of microbial protein distort the data from apparent digestibility studies and a variety of approaches have been used to ensure a realistic estimate of the requirement of protein for the horse (Hintz and Schryver, 1969; Slade *et al.*, 1970; Frape, 1981; Prior *et al.*, 1974; Jarrige and Tisserand, 1984; Meyer, 1983).

Meyer (1984) calculated the daily endogenous faecal nitrogen losses and urine nitrogen excretion as 180 mg N/kg $BW^{0.75}$ and 140 mg N/kg $BW^{0.75}$ respectively. A further 35 mg N/kg $BW^{0.75}$ was estimated to be lost as dermal losses as scurf (shedding of skin and hair). Meyer (1984) however, estimated that 40% of faecal N was derived from feed, reducing faecal endogenous nitrogen losses to 72 mg N/kg $BW^{0.75}$. It is unclear why the initial '180 mg' are included in so called '*endogenous*' faecal nitrogen loss by some authors, and not simply stated as total faecal nitrogen.

At maintenance, the daily requirement of nitrogen to replace endogenous nitrogen is 255 mg N/kg $BW^{0.75}$. From this the following calculation is published (Coenen, 2002; Table 7.4):

Protein Metabolism

Table 7.4 Calculation of nitrogen and digestible crude protein requirements using estimated endogenous nitrogen losses (Meyer, 1984) (table expanded from Coenen, 2002).

	Endogenous loss kg $BW^{0.75}$/day loss	Calculated endogenous (subtracting 60% as feed N) kg $BW^{0.75}$/day	Basal nitrogen requirements per kg $BW^{0.75}$/day
Faeces	180 mg	108 mg	72 mg
Urine	140 mg		140 mg
Dermal	35 mg		35 mg
Basal nitrogen requirements			250 mg/kg $BW^{0.75}$/day
In CP Intake (x 6.25)			1.6 g CP/kg $BW^{0.75}$/day
In DCP Intake (assuming digestibility of CP of 66% = 1.6/0.66)			2.4 g DCP/kg $BW^{0.75}$/day
Final recommendation to account for lower absorption rates (estimate)			3 g DCP/kg $BW^{0.75}$/day

This calculation is applied in practice by the German and Dutch (DCP = VREp) feed evaluation systems for requirements for maintenance. Digestible crude protein (DCP) data in the German and Dutch feeding tables are based on *in vivo* digestibility results where possible, thus the feed values are already corrected for digestibility leading to a 'double correction'. To allow for 66% crude protein digestibility we need to increase the intake of crude protein but this increase should then not be defined as DCP but as crude protein requirements of horses. However, these two systems present the increases in DCP and additionally convert crude protein concentration of feed to digestible crude protein, thus leading to a 'double digestibility effect' akin to assuming an actual digestibility of protein is 0.43 (0.66 x 0.66). As the apparent efficiency of absorption of nitrogen compounds yielded from dietary protein may be only 30% for roughage, the feed requirements calculated with this system may be fairly accurate, due to the 'double correction', while for concentrates with a digestibility coefficient of up to 90% an underestimation in supply will be observed.

In the USA and UK the NRC (1989) system is used for prediction of protein requirements. This approach includes a calculation to take into consideration endogenous losses by correcting for daily basal endogenous loss (leading to 0.6 g DCP/kg BW requirement). Further,

Nutritional Physiology of the Horse

the data for digestible crude protein is then converted back to CP, by assuming an average absorption efficiency of 46% for nitrogen derived from crude protein leading to maintenance recommendations of 1.3 g CP/kg BW. By applying the NRC recommendations to a 200 kg horse, the calculated requirement of 260 g CP/day would equate to 2.3 g DCP/kg $BW^{0.75}$. The same calculation for a 600 kg horse would lead to a recommendation of 2.9 g DCP/kg $BW^{0.75}$. Thus, despite the different approach, the requirement recommendations of the NRC (1989) and the GEH (1994) are similar when taken in isolation from feed evaluation.

The French protein system is based on digestible crude protein, but adjusts for the proportion of dietary crude protein that does not supply amino acids available for absorption in the small intestine (non-absorbable DCP). This is a modification of the approach taken by INRA for dairy cattle (Jarrige and Tisserand, 1984) and is known in the French protein system for horses as corrected digestible crude protein (MADC). As with the other prediction systems, protein requirements are calculated by considering endogenous loss in faeces and urine, exogenous loss as a result of shedding of micro-organisms and "integumental" endogenous N (dermal losses as scurf: hair and losses not associated with faeces and urine) (Slade *et al.*, 1970; Prior *et al.*, 1974 and Martin-Rosset *et al.*, 1994). As with the German and Dutch systems, the MADC requirements are increased slightly to build in a 'safety' margin to 2.8 g MADC/kg $BW^{0.75}$.

GEH (1994) and CVB (1996) requirements
in DCP (CP adjusted for DCP)   3 g DCP/kg $BW^{0.75}$/day

In DCP Requirements according to Slade
et al. 1970; Prior *et al.* 1974   2.7 g DCP/kg $BW^{0.75}$/day

INRA (1990) final requirements in MADC
(DCP adjusted for MADC)   2.8 g MADC/kg $BW^{0.75}$

In this case, the 'double' correction from crude protein to DCP or MADC is not made and the MADC correction factor (k) for absorbability of amino acids is only applied to feedstuff evaluation (MADC of feed = CP x dCP% x Correction factor [k]). At the same time the correction for digestibility (from CP to DCP) is only applied to the calculations for requirements. Table 7.5 provides examples of how the k-values for MADC have been derived.

Table 7.5 Amino acid absorption in the small and large intestines and total tract digestion values (INRA, 1990).

	Intake (g)		Small Intestine entry AA-absorbed	Large Intestine (g) entry	digested	AA Total tract digestion DCP	MADC
	CP	AA					
Concentrates	180	171	0.85	26	0.90	148	147
Spring grass	180	162	0.70	49	0.80	128	117
Barley/maize	110	105	0.85	16	0.90	90	90
Grass hay	110	99	0.50	49	0.75	65	54
Grass silage	110	82	0.50	41	0.75	65	44

Source (Jarrige and Tisserand, 1984; Frape, 1998)

The k- factor used for concentrate feeds is 1.0, 0.90 for green forages, 0.85 for hays and dehydrated forages, and 0.70 for good quality grass silages. The k-factor for amino acids utilised from hays initially seems a little high, but this is not so if we consider that the reduced digestibility factor is already included within the requirement recommendation. For instance, only 60% of protein is digested in the whole tract (according to the calculation for requirement) of which 70% of amino acids are absorbed in the small intestine (according to the feed), suggesting 42% of amino acids are available for uptake from forages. Equally, the coefficient of 100% availability of amino acids from concentrates is reduced by increasing requirements to DCP values, compensating for actual availability from concentrates. In view of the very low pre-caecal digestibility of some forages, the estimates for amino acid availability may still be too high. Finally, Martin-Rosset and Tisserand (2002) noted that the k-factors will need improving as greater knowledge on sites of absorption of amino acids becomes available.

Requirements for work

Work increases the requirement of the animal for dietary protein through increases in metabolism, losses of amino acids in sweat and muscle accumulation and repair. It is common to estimate and add to the requirements additional losses of nitrogen in sweat when calculating the requirements for work (Coenen, 2002). During intensive long-term exercise in humid conditions, a horse may lose up to 15 l sweat per hour: however, very low concentrations of nitrogenous products are found in the sweat of fit horses (Carlson, 1996). The contribution of protein to energy supply for working horses is minor, estimated at a maximum of 10% at long-term medium exercise (Meyer, 1987; Patterson *et al.*, 1985; Glade, 1983, Lawrence, 1991). Amino acids play an important role in the muscle under exercise as primary substrates for enzyme synthesis, as a substrate for ATP generation (limited) and as a building block for muscle tissue during training. This has been demonstrated by a net increase in free amino acid pool following exercise (Lawrence, 1990). The evidence reflecting the use of protein as an energy substrate is implied from studies of the glucose-alanine cycle. In humans, increases in synthesis of alanine is observed in muscles of endurance athletes but current data for horses are still inconclusive (Graham *et al.*, 1997, Lindner, 1997). The negative effects from feeding excess protein to performance horses have been reported as an elevated thermogenic effect, possible hypocalcaemia and an increased acidogenic effect (Meyer, 1987; Meyer and Pferdekamp, 1980; Glade *et al.*, 1985; Lewis, 1995; Graham-Thiers *et al.*, 2001). Very little *in vivo* research is available to confirm these observations concerning protein metabolism in working horses.

Protein metabolism has been demonstrated to decline during bouts of exercise (Young, 1986; Lawrence, 1980) and therefore protein 'requirements' are likely to be increased in untrained horses in response to increases in muscle mass rather than for utilisation as an energy substrate (Jones, 1985). It has therefore been concluded that horses at work do not require a higher concentration of protein in the ration compared to horses managed at maintenance (Frank *et al.*, 1987; Pagan, 1996; Hintz, 1996; Meyer, 1994). Little is currently known about real changes in protein requirements or the actual needs of essential amino acids for working horses. Therefore, protein requirements for work have been linked to energy requirements using linear relationships in all the published systems but this approach is likely to be an oversimplification as it is unlikely that the relationship would progress at the same rate at differing levels of exercise (NRC, 1989; INRA, 1984; GEH, 1994; CVB, 1996):

Total Protein Requirements for working horses per day per system

NRC (1989)   CP = 40 x Mcal DE
GEH (1994)   DCP = 5 x MJ DE

INRA (1990)   MADC = 60-70 x UFC or MADC = 24 x Mcal DE
CVB (1996)   VREp = 13 x VEP

This approach can lead to an overestimation of protein requirement with increasing work as the energy requirements increase to a greater extent than protein requirements. Furthermore, if elevated levels of concentrate are included in the diet, increased DCP absorption in the small intestine may further reduce the real requirements of crude protein.

Protein requirements for growth

The requirements for growth in young horses are higher than that for adult horses at the same bodyweight (DLG, 1982). Martin-Rosset et al. (1994) assumed that requirements for maintenance for young horses were the same for adult horses, apart from foals under 1 year old (a 25% increase in maintenance protein requirement). In the prediction systems used in The Netherlands, the maintenance requirement for stabled foals up to 6 months of 3.5 g /kg BW $^{0.75}$ VREp is used (that is approximately 15% above maintenance). However, for foals turned out to pasture, the requirement was increased by 20% above maintenance to compensate for greater contribution for exercise. For young horses from 7 months of age the same requirements (3 g /BW$^{0.75}$ VREp) for apparent digestible protein are used as for adult animals. The VREp requirements for growth are calculated from estimated protein gain of approximately 200 g per day from birth to 36 months and thereafter a reduction to 160 g per day. This approach is similar to the requirements used in the French feeding system described by Martin-Rosset et al. (1994). However the estimates for protein gain used in the French system are 202 g per day in the first year and 122 g per day in the second and third year. The systems used in the USA and the UK (NRC, 1989) do not change their requirements for maintenance for young horses. NRC (1989) recommends 12 g CP per MJ digestible energy per day for foals up to 1 year and 10.8 g for yearlings. These recommendations include maintenance. Both GEH (German) and INRA (French) calculate the efficiency of conversion of crude protein into body protein as 45% for foals. This may be considered as a low value. Similar estimates for calves range from about 75% immediately after birth to approximately 40% at an age of 1 to 1.5 years. AFRC (1993) has adopted 59% as an estimate for the utilisation of metabolisable protein by growing cattle.

Nutritional Physiology of the Horse

Lysine is an important essential amino acid, especially during growth of animals. The protein and lysine requirements recommended by various systems are in Table 7.6.

Table 7.6. Daily protein and lysine requirements for growing horses as predicted by the various feed evaluation systems (Ellis, 2002c).

	GEH (1994)	NRC (1989)	CVB(1996)	INRA (1994)
Protein			adult weight 600kg	
Up to 6 months			$3.5g/BW^{0.75}$	
4-6 months	680g DCP/day	160 g CP/kg DM	597 g/day	530 MADC
6-12 months	610g DCP/day	135 g CP/kg DM	317 g/day	MADC = $3.5BW^{0.75}$ +
				450.daily gain (kg)
Lysine				
4-6 months	0.6 g/MJ DE	2.1g/Mcal DE	5.8g/100g VREp	7 g/kg DM
6 - months	0.4 g/MJ DE	1.9g/Mcal DE	5.1g/100g VREp	4.5 g/kg DM
4-6 months	43.8 g/day	30 g/day	31.5 g/day	35 g/kg

The main problem with the estimates from the four systems examined is that protein needs before the age of four months are seldom specified. The Dutch VREp system does provide some data for this period by using daily additional protein retention during growth divided by a coefficient of 0.45 and incorporating % of final weight and adding this to the basic maintenance formula of 3.5 g/$BW^{0.75}$ for foals under 6 months of age (Figure 7.2).

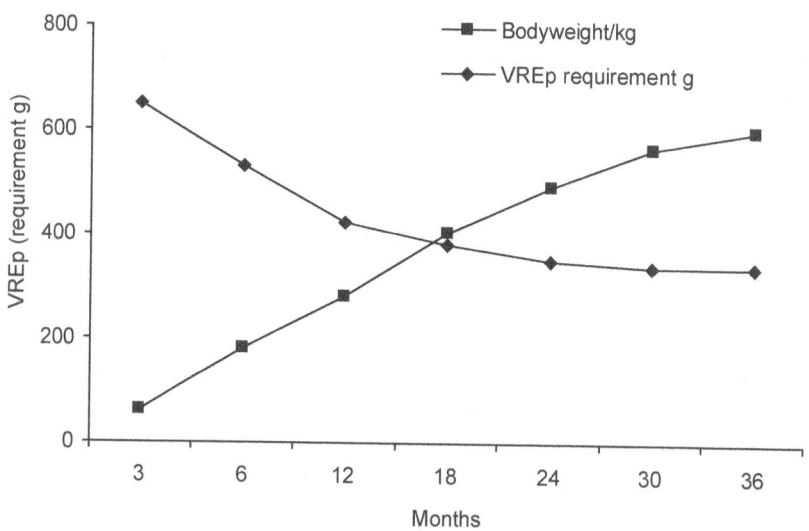

Figure 7.2 VREp Requirements in relation to bodyweight during growth of a foal (Ellis, 2002).

8
Mineral nutrition

Supply and utilisation of minerals are important aspects of the nutrition of the horse. The supply of minerals to the horse is derived from feeds offered (from pasture, conserved forage and concentrate feed sources), from anthropogenic sources (e.g. soil ingested) and, to a limited extent, water drunk. Minerals play an important role in the metabolism of the horse, for instance, during the development of bone, in growth and modelling of structural tissues, as co-factors to enzymes (e.g. iron, copper, magnesium), as regulatory roles in transport of energy in cellular systems (sodium and potassium in transport of ATP), as regulators (e.g. selenium) and for acid-base balance. Mineral supply to the animal is dependent upon interactions between various elements in the digestive tract. These interactions can be synergistic or antagonistic by nature and have a direct effect on the mineral balance of an animal (ARC, 1980; Bremner and Mills, 1979). Even though interactions between minerals are recognised, the majority of experiments studying the effects of different levels of minerals in a ration are generally based on single elements. The exception has traditionally been copper, molybdenum and sulphur.

There have been many in-depth reviews on the nature and functions of minerals in the nutrition of horses (Lewis, 1995; Meyer, 1995; Frape, 1998). This chapter aims to provide an overview of the important macro-minerals and trace elements, their function and role in the animal and to develop a short discussion of more recent research into mineral metabolism of the horse in relation to the current recommendations for feed formulation and requirements of the horse.

The concentration of minerals accumulated in the horse is estimated as approximately 4% of body weight (wet weight). Seven major minerals are essential for mammals; calcium (Ca), phosphorus (P), sodium (Na), potassium (K), magnesium (Mg), sulphur (S) and chlorine (Cl as chloride,

Cl⁻). A number of trace elements also play a key role in maintaining metabolic functions: cobalt (Co), copper (Cu), molybdenum (Mo), zinc (Zn), manganese (Mn), iron (Fe), fluorine (F as fluoride, F⁻), iodine (I), selenium (Se) and chromium (Cr).

Many feed manufacturers have started to adapt the national systems used to predict the mineral requirements of the horse and this text will not discuss to any great depth these modifications. There are three "official" systems; the American system (NRC, 1989), the French system (INRA, 1990) and the German system (GEH, 1994). The systems are not directly comparable as all use different units to express requirements, with some using requirements per kg DM intake per day (of which the estimates differ between systems), some using a direct relationship to DE-requirements and others using requirements per kg bodyweight or metabolic bodyweight per day. Even within a system different versions are used for different minerals. In order to compare current systems, the recommendations were converted into recommendations per kg BW/ day for small and large horses, by using the recommended daily DM intake as per system (Ellis and Boekhoff, 2003). The distinction between small and large horses did not always fall at the same point, due to limited data or information given within the respective systems. For the American system (NRC, 1989), and the German system (GEH, 1994) horses up to 400 kg were assumed as small, whereas in the French system horses up to 550 kg still constitute the 'small' animal (INRA, 1990). Quantities given after maintenance are incremental (i.e. include maintenance).

Calcium and phosphorus

The requirements and metabolism of calcium and phosphorus are closely related and therefore considered together in this chapter. The main functions of calcium in mammalian physiology are in Table 8.1.

Calcium has many roles in metabolism. One of the most important functions is the regulation of phosphorylase kinase activity and hence the regulation of glycogenolysis in muscle cells. Regulation of phosphorylase kinase activity is effected by two distinct mechanisms involving calcium ions. The regulation is mediated by calmodulin; a calcium binding protein. Binding induces a conformational change in calmodulin which in turn enhances the catalytic activity of the phosphorylase kinase towards its substrate, phosphorylase-ß.

Mineral Nutrition

Table 8.1 Role and function of calcium in mammalian physiology with special reference to the horse.

Metabolic / physiological function	Interactions with other minerals	Effects of shortages	Effects of excesses
• Main element of crystal apatite in bone matrix, skeletal integrity • Support of neural and muscular functions • Main element in matrix of teeth • Enzyme activity • Conduction of nerve impulses • Coagulation of blood and muscle contraction (mitochondrial and neuromuscular function) • Cell membrane function • Glandular secretion	Excess phosphorus has a negative influence on calcium metabolism	• Lameness, skeletal deformations (especially in long bones) • Malfunction of muscles and nervous system • Development of rickets in young horses • Decalcification of bones in mature horses, developmental orthopaedic disease (osteoporosis), fractures, lameness, stiffness • Big head syndrome Loss of weight • Long bone syndrome	• Not many effects known • Brittle bones through abnormal storage of calcium (if P concentration in diet is low) • Hypocalcaemic tetany skeletal diseases • Rickets in growing animals • Osteomalacia in adults

This activity enhances glycogenolysis in muscle cells when muscle contraction is stimulated by acetylcholine release in the neuromuscular junction. The effect of acetylcholine release from nerve terminals at a neuromuscular junction is to depolarize the muscle cell leading to increased release of sarcoplasmic calcium, thereby activating phosphorylase kinase. Therefore increased concentration of calcium in the muscle cell increases the rate of muscle contraction and increases glycogenolysis providing the cell with increased supply of precursors for ATP generation. The second calcium ion-mediated pathway to phosphorylase kinase activation is through activation of α-adrenergic receptors by epinephrine. Unlike ß-adrenergic receptors (coupled to adenylate cyclase), α-adrenergic receptors are coupled through G-proteins that activate phospholipase-C-γ (PLC-γ). The activation of PLC-γ increases the hydrolysis of phosphatidylinositol-4,5-bisphosphate (PIP_2) in the membrane, inositol triphosphate (IP_3) and diacylglycerol (DAG). Diacylglycerol binds to and activates protein kinase C (PKC). Inositol triphosphate binds to receptors on the surface of the endoplasmic reticulum leading to release of calcium ions. The calcium ions interact with calmodulin subunits of phosphoryase kinase resulting in activation.

In order to terminate the activity of glycogen phosphorylase, the enzymes need to be converted to their original (non activated) state. In the case of calcium-induced activation, the level of calcium ions released from muscle stores will terminate when the incoming nerve impulses for contraction cease. The removal of phosphate from phosphorylase kinase and phosphorylase-α is performed by phosphoprotein phosphatase-1 (PP-1). Calcitriol regulates calcium and phosphorus homeostasis in mammalian systems. Active calcitriol is derived from ergosterol (produced in plants) and from 7-dehydrocholesterol (produced in the skin). In the skin 7-dehydrocholesterol is converted to cholecalciferol (vitamin D_3) following UV irradiation. Cholecalciferol (or egrocalciferol) is absorbed in the intestine and transported to the liver bound to a specific vitamin D-binding protein. In the liver cholecalciferol is hydroxylated at the 25 position by a specific D_3-25-hydroxylase, generating 25-hydroxy-D_3 [25-(OH)D_3]. Conversion of 25-(OH) D_3 to its biologically active form calcitriol occurs through the activity of a specific D_3-1-hydroxylase present in the proximal convoluted tubules of the kidneys, the bone and the placenta. 25-(OH) D_3 can be hydroxylated at the 24 position by a specific D_3-24-hydroxylase in the kidneys, intestine, placenta and cartilage. Calcitriol functions with parathyroid hormone (PTH) and calcitonin to regulate serum calcium and phosphorus levels. PTH is released in response to low serum calcium and induces the production of calcitriol. In contrast, reduced levels of PTH stimulate synthesis of the inactive 24,25-(OH)$_2D_3$. In the intestinal epithelium, calcitriol functions as a steroid hormone in inducing the expression of calbindinD$_{28K}$, a protein involved in intestinal calcium absorption. The increased absorption of calcium ions requires absorption of a negatively charged counter ion to maintain electrical neutrality. That ion is generally phosphorus. When plasma calcium levels fall the major sites of action of calcitriol and PTH are bone where they stimulate bone resorption and the kidneys where they inhibit calcium excretion by stimulating reabsorption by the distal tubules. The role of calcitonin in calcium homeostasis is to decrease elevated serum calcium levels by inhibiting bone resorption. The main symptom of vitamin D deficiency is rickets and osteomalacia. Rickets is characterised by improper mineralisation during the development of the bones resulting in soft bones. Osteomalacia is characterised by demineralisation of previously formed bone leading to increased softness and susceptibility to fracture.

Mineral Nutrition

Acetylcholine is synthesised from choline and acetyl-CoA through the action of choline acetyltransferase in cholinergic neurons. When an action potential of the nerve reaches the terminal button of a presynaptic neuron, a voltage-gated calcium channel is opened. The influx of calcium ions stimulates exocytosis of the presynaptic vesicles and acetyl choline is released. Once released, acetyl choline must be removed rapidly in order to allow repolarisation to take place; this is performed by acetylcholinesterase thus preventing further non stimulatory signalling.

Calcium is carefully regulated and the concentrations in sera are maintained within a narrow range. Therefore serum calcium concentrations are not adequate to diagnose deficiency or excess (NRC, 1989). However, the concentration of calcium in urine may be an important indicator of deficiency (less than 15 µmol calcium/mOsm of urine solute), especially when urinary calcium to creatinine clearance ratios are greater than 2.5:1 (Caple *et al.*, 1982). Creatinine is formed in muscle from creatine phosphate by the non-enzymatic dehydration of the molecule and the loss of phosphate. The amount of creatinine produced is related to muscle mass and remains constant from day to day and the creatinine is excreted by the urinary pathway thus leading to the use of the creatinine clearance rate as an accurate measure of renal function.

The main site for absorption of calcium is the small intestine by passive or facilitated diffusion. A limited concentration of calcium is absorbed via the hind gut mucosa, however calcium is excreted actively via that mucosa into digesta and eliminated in faeces (Schryver *et al.*, 1970). The efficiency of absorption of calcium from the diet depends on type of calcium supplement, the effect of compounds that impair the uptake or release of calcium in the digesta (e.g. oxalate and phytate), the concentration of phosphorus and the age of the horse. Calcium absorption is also affected by zinc, manganese, copper, iodine, iron and cadmium. There is evidence from many species that the rate of absorption of calcium declines with age (McDonald *et al.*, 1995). The efficiency of absorption of calcium by the horse is estimated as 50% by NRC (1989), however it is acknowledged that in young horses the efficiency may be as high as 70%. The efficiency of absorption noted by the GEH, (1994) is 60%, although the German system suggests that the rate of absorption is reduced in diets containing high concentrations of phosphorus. The presence of oxalate in feeds affects the absorption of calcium. For instance a reduction of 66% in rate of absorption of calcium was observed by Swartzmann *et al.* (1978) when the diet contained 1% oxalic acid. Negative calcium balances were observed in horses offered diets containing between 2.6 and 4.3% oxalic acid, with faecal excretion doubling and clearance via the urine decreasing by about 30% (McKenzie *et al.*, 1981). These observations could reflect nutritionally-induced secondary hyperparathyroidism. However, if the concentration of calcium is adequate when elevated concentrations of oxalate are observed, the impact on calcium absorption is reduced. In general if the ratio of calcium to oxalate exceeds 1.5:1, negative calcium balances are rarely observed (Hintz *et al.*, 1984).

Phosphorus in feeds can be classified in two broad categories; inositol phosphate (phytate) or inorganic compounds (phosphate). Phosphate is important in several roles in the animal, for instance, acid-base metabolism of an animal, essential for energy transduction and utilisation in cells and integral to many biochemical compounds. Phosphorus is absorbed in the small intestine and the colon of the horse (Schryver *et al.*, 1971). However, phosphate is also recycled via the salivary pathway and via secretions of the intestinal mucosa. There are many elements that interact with phosphorus and alter the apparent absorption of the element, for instance copper, cobalt, calcium, iodine, zinc, manganese, molybdenum, iron and aluminium. Phytate has a relatively low digestibility compared with inorganic phosphate (Schryver *et al.*, 1972; Hill and Gutsell, 1998). The lower digestibility of phytate-linked phosphate reflects the formation of insoluble phytate-mineral complexes. However, phytase produced by the microorganisms endemic to the digestive tract of ruminants and pigs will degrade phytate-phosphate complexes, releasing phosphate leading to increased absorption of phosphate from the diet (Kemme, 1998). The main functions of phosphorus in mammalian physiology are in the Table 8.2.

Table 8.2 Role and function of phosphorus in mammalian physiology with special reference to the horse.

Metabolic/physio-logical function	Interactions with other minerals	Effects of shortages	Effects of excesses
• Stability of skeletal integrity • Component of nucleic acids and cell membranes • Supporting energy metabolism and buffering cellular systems.	Calcium, Magnesium	• Similar to effects of calcium deficiency	• Negative effect on calcium uptake (nutritional hyper-parathyroidism • Miller's disease, big head • Calcium deficiency

Mineral Nutrition

Requirements for calcium and phosphorus

There have been numerous studies concerning the calcium and phosphorus homeostasis of horses (for instance, Schryver *et al.*, 1971; Meyer and Ahlswende, 1976; Schryver *et al.*, 1986; Jarrige and Martin-Rosset, 1981). Many of these studies have reported apparent absorption coefficients (equivalent to digestibility coefficients for dietary constituents) and these data have been used to develop estimates of requirements for maintenance, growth, pregnancy and lactation. Recently, Van Doorn (2003) examined a range of feeds and demonstrated that the apparent absorption of calcium ranged from 26 to 48 %. The coefficients were affected by level of phosphorus intake, quality of phosphorus offered (i.e. the balance between phosphate and phytate-phosphate) by calcium intake and phytase activity. There was considerable variation between animals on the same dietary treatments and during the different phases of the experiments. In a similar fashion to Hintz *et al.* (1984), Van Doorn concluded that high concentrations of calcium (>2.5 calcium: 1 phosphorus) could lead to a negative phosphorus balance, as the absorption of dietary phosphorus was depressed. Thus diets which contain calcium to phosphorus ratios of 6:1 which previously were suggested acceptable as long as recommended phosphorus levels are reached, (Lewis, 1995; Jordan *et al.*, 1975) may be considered inadequate (Van Doorn, 2003).

The evidence on apparent absorption of calcium provided by Van Doorn (2003) also resulted in apparent absorption coefficients for phosphorus from 2.4 to 29 %. Crozier *et al.* (1997) also reported very low apparent absorption coefficients of phosphorus from forages ranging between 9% and 8%. These data were substantially lower than comparable findings reported in GEH (1994; estimated apparent absorption of 40%) and NRC (1989; estimated apparent absorption of 35 to 45% depending on type of feed and physiological state of the horse). Data provided by INRA (1990) suggests apparent absorption coefficients for phosphorus of 30%. The current estimates of requirements for horses (converted to mg/kg body weight as reported by INRA (1990), GEH (1994) and NRC (1989) are presented in Table 8.3.

There is little variation between estimated requirements for calcium between systems. If the horse is managed at maintenance levels, the predicted requirements for calcium are lower using the NRC method than those reported by the other published systems (GEH and INRA).

Nutritional Physiology of the Horse

Table 8.3 Estimates for calcium and phosphorus requirements for horses (data converted by Ellis and Boekhoff, 2003).

	Bodyweight	Calcium (mg/kg BW/day)			Phosphorus (mg/kg BW/day)		
		INRA	GEH	NRC	INRA	GEH	NRC
Maintenance	Small	49	50	40	29	30	28
	Large	50	50	40	30	30	28
Work							
Low	Small	58	51	55	34	30	40
	Large	59	51	49	34	30	35
Medium	Small	67	54	67	40	30	47
	Large	70	53	59	43	30	42
Heavy	Small	61	56	89	36	30	63
	Large	66	57	78	40	30	56
Pregnancy							
7-8 months	Small	75	0	0	49		
	Large	71	0	0	47		
9 months	Small	93	81	77	62	54	58
	Large	89	74	68	65	49	51
10 months	Small			78			59
	Large			69			52
11 months	Small	92		83	55		63
	Large	89		73	65		55
Lactation							
Month 1		140			90		
Month 2		125			75		
Month 3		113			68		
0-3 month	Small	127	116	136	78	86	89
	Large	126	100	112	78	75	72
3-weaning	Small		0	88			56
	Large		0	67			44

This reflects that the estimates for requirement do not consider urinary losses. In terms of extra requirements for work and reproduction the German (GEH) system provides lower estimates for the increases in requirement than both the other systems. Interestingly the estimated requirement for phosphorus for working horses is substantially higher, if calculated using the method published by the NRC (1989), than those estimated using the GEH or INRA systems. There are no reasons provided for the higher estimate, however as the recommendations for intake of phosphorus are linked to digestible energy intake, an elevated requirement would result compared to other prediction systems. This slightly contradicts the explanation given for pregnant mares, where a higher absorption rate for phosphorus is assumed (45% instead of 35%) reflecting the supplementation of inorganic phosphorus in high-energy diets offered to broodmares. The same argument should be applied to working horses, especially at heavy work level, as these animals also receive greater amounts of concentrate feed.

Requirements for growth

Recently considerable effort has been made to research the impact of nutrient supply in relation to the process of bone formation in foals (see for instance the 2nd European Workshop on Equine Nutrition at Dijon 2004: Harris *et al.*, 2004; Van Weeren, 2004; Jeffcott, 2004; Ellis, 2001; Coenen and Vervuert, 2004, Kienzle, 2004).

The importance of calcium and phosphorus in skeletal development is apparent. Bone is a metabolically active tissue that is constructed of many different cell types. They require a supply of calcium and phosphorus as well as other minerals such as fluoride, magnesium, manganese and zinc. The process of bone formation is initiated by chondrocytes from cartilaginous growth plates. Chondrocytes 'develop' in zones, starting at the chondrocyte resting zone, where the growth plate begins, followed by the zone of chondrocyte proliferation, leading into the maturation zone and followed by migration into the hypertrophic zone which develops into subchondral bone. The exact mechanism which triggers chondrocyte differentiation has not yet been fully defined but it is known that growth factors and hormones stimulate proliferation. Nutrition (as well as genetic pre-disposition) has also been directly linked to growth hormone secretory capacity in humans, horses, dogs and pigs (Wolter, 1996). Vitamin A has been identified as one cofactor stimulating chondrocyte differentiation (Orth, 1999). Deficiency of this vitamin leads to a poorly differentiated growth plate whereas toxicity related to massive ingestion of vitamin A has lead to a prematurely closed growth plate (Orth, 1999). New capillary sprouts/buds invade the subchondral area from below supplying further necessary nutrients to complete the formation of subchondral bone. In horses, type VI collagen has an interesting role, being concentrated along regions of hypertrophic chondrocytes, where capillary buds are invading, possibly acting as a strengthening matrix in the developing bone (Henson *et al.*, 1996). These cartilage canal vessels have been shown to disappear both in horses and other mammals after a certain age, partially explaining the 'window of opportunity' in which malnutrition or improvements in nutrient supply for the young foal can occur. In pigs, defects in cartilage canal blood supply have been repeatedly reported as a cause of osteochondrosis lesions (Kincaid *et al.*, 1985; Carlson *et al.*, 1989).

Equine cartilage canal vessels become necrotic from 4.5 months of age, depending on site, and disappear from all sites by the age of 7 months (Carlson *et al.*, 1995). Mineralisation in chondrocytes reflects the accumulation of inorganic calcium ions linked to inorganic phosphate and phosphatidylserine. These complexes are present in an amorphous calcium phosphate form which is stabilised by the presence of ATP and Mg^{2+}, preventing the formation of apatite (the crystallised form of calcium phosphate in bone). At this stage, the matrix must be pliable and soft and proteoglycans are implicated in the prevention of early mineralisation. A reduction in proteoglycan metabolism in osteochondrotic articular cartilage of foals has recently been reported (Van den Hoogen *et al.*, 1999). One of the key components of the bone matrix is apatite. Apatite is a calcium phosphate complex ($Ca_5(PO_4)_3 OH$) and is the primary component of the matrix. Calcium carbonate is also a substantial component of the bone matrix. Dietary lipid also has an important role in bone physiology. Lipid composition is important for the accumulation of calcium ions into matrix vesicles mediated by annexin V formed from phosphatidylserine. Annexins have a zinc binding site and an inhibition of the annexin-calcium uptake resulting from excess supply of zinc in the diet has been reported. Acidic phospholipid is also an integral part of the tissue matrix in epiphyseal cartilage and omega-3 polyunsaturated fatty acids are taken up by chondrocytes readily but omega-6 fatty acids are not concentrated in developing chondrocytes.

Concurrent with the development of the blood supply in the developing bone, osteoblasts and osteoclasts are deposited along the calcified septae. The osteoclasts secrete cathpepsin B and L which resorb bone and soft cartilage, completing the type II and VI degradation, while osteoblasts support the forming of type I collagen ossified bone (Lee *et al.*, 1995a). Lysyl oxidase plays a major role in cross-linking the lysyl residues of collagen and elastin into covalent structures. This enzyme is known to be copper dependent and zinc can attach to the copper binding site and inhibit its function.

Mineral Nutrition

Nutrition and endocrine regulation of growth

For adequate incorporation of calcium and phosphorus into skeletal tissue, hormonal control via parathyroid hormone (PTH), oestrogens and vitamin D must occur. Paracrine control of deposition is mediated by prostaglandins, cytokines and IGF-I and IGF-II. Mineralisation of new bone matrix and resorption of bone matrix during periods of physiological demand (e.g. lactation) are important regulatory mechanisms to ensure periods of negative calcium or phosphorus balance are minimised.

Rapid growth rates have been identified as one causative factor in the increased incidence of osteochondral lesions in fast growing breeds of pigs, dogs and sheep (Ellis, 2001). However, genetic predisposition, supply of nutrients and hormonal status of the animal have to be considered. A study by Savage et al. (1993) implicated a high-energy diet (129% of digestible energy requirement) in the higher incidence of osteochondrosis (all foals in the experiment; n=12) compared to a control group offered the recommended intake of DE (two animals developed osteochondrosis; n=12). Bruin and Creemers (1994) also observed that feeding excessive energy with restricted exercise under controlled experimental conditions led to an incidence of osteochondrosis similar to that reported in practice (about 20 %) and therefore, level of carbohydrate offered as well as intensity and duration of exercise are important factors in bone development. Growth hormone regulation is mediated by insulin-like growth factors (IGF) and receptors of IGF's are present in the majority of cells. Recently the genetic regulation of the IGF system has been investigated by Rhoads et al. (2000) by examining the 'acid labile sub-unit (ALS) gene' expressed in the liver. A delay in maturation of ALS, which together with growth hormone determines the maturation of the IGF system, can result from undernutrition during late foetal and early post-natal periods (Rhoads et al., 2000). Furthermore, over supply of nutrients during late pregnancy may lead to a faster maturation of the IGF system in the developing foetus (Bosclair, 2000). In studies examining the effects of undernutrition during the conception period (4 days) of rats, reduced embryonic and foetal hormone production was observed, leading to slower growth and development of the new-born (Kwong et al., 2000). This may reflect the effect of low concentration of insulin in maternal circulation leading to reduced sensitivity of foetal insulin receptors and impaired IGF-2 production. These mechanisms are likely to exist in horses, as ossification starts in the 9-week-old foetus, the patella cartilage is fully defined in the embryo before 2 months, and from as early as 10 days after ovulation, the equine conceptus secretes IGF-binding protein 3 (Ellis, 2001).

Bone resorption and remodelling

During periods of physiological stress the skeleton has two roles to play, that of structural integrity of the horse to support locomotion, and that of regulation of calcium and acid-base homeostasis. These roles are fulfilled through the processes of resorption and remodelling of bone and they may occur if dietary calcium and phosphorus intake do not meet requirements (for instance during gestation or lactation) or following increase in mechanical skeletal stress (for instance through training or through a traumatic injury to the bone). Potentially the hydroxyapatite crystals in bone represent a large reservoir of buffer from which carbonate and hydroxyl ions could be manipulated. It has been suggested that short-term acidosis or alkalosis could be a trigger for subchondral bone pathology. Petito *et al.* (1984) demonstrated a decline in bone weight in rats resulting from offering a negative dietary cation-anion balance (DCAB) diet after feeding ammonium chloride. Similar findings were observed in dogs when Kealy *et al.* (1993) reported a reduction in dyschondroplasia following a change of DCAB from +410 mEq/kg DM to +80 mEq/kg DM.

Dietary protein intake, especially of proteins rich in lysine, arginine, histidine, methionine and cysteine, leads to an increase in the production of protons (H^+) in circulation, which can be subsequently eliminated via the urinary pathway as a result of increased excretion of ammonia. Renal excretion of calcium and phosphorus has been demonstrated to increase in mature horses following a decline in blood pH resulting from diets containing imbalances in dietary cation-anion balance (Baker *et al.*, 1992; Ralston *et al.*, 1993).

The regulation of bone resorption and remodelling is critical if maintenance of bone mass and architecture is to be achieved. Parfitt (1990) described the resorption and remodelling process as four main events (Table 8.4) although initiation (Phase 1) of the process is not well understood. The concentration of calcium in serum initiates calcitriol, parathyroid hormone and calcitonin release (Klein and Coburn, 1991). Low concentrations of calcium in sera stimulate parathyroid hormone (PTH) secretion, leading to resorption of calcium and phosphorus from

Mineral Nutrition

the bone. PTH also stimulates the production of calcitriol in the kidney, which decreases calcium and phosphorus excretion via the urinary pathway.

Table 8.4 Processes of bone modelling and remodelling (adapted from Parfitt, 1990)

Activity	Bone remodelling	Bone modelling
Local coupling	Formulation and resorption are coupled	Formation and resorption are <u>not</u> coupled
Timing and sequence of activity	Cyclical: A1-RS2-RV3-F4; formation always follows resorption	F and RS are continuous and occur in separate Surfaces
Extent of surface activity	20% of surfaces are active	100% of surfaces are active
Anatomical objectives	Skeletal maintenance	Gain in skeletal mass and changes in skeletal Form

A1=Activation, RS2=resorption, RV3=reversal, F4=formulation

During phase 2, osteoclasts attach to the surface of the bone and resorption of bone occurs in discrete deposits of mineral.

This allows the release of calcium from the mineralised matrix. During phase 3, bone resorption is greatly reduced and osteoblastic recruitment occurs in preparation for deposition of new bone matrix. An excess of calcium stimulates the secretion of calcitonin, which decreases osteoclastic processes and also increases osteoblast activity (McGilvery and Goldstein, 1983). This reduces the losses of calcium and phosphate in the urine (Schoenmakers *et al.*, 2000). Excess phosphorus intake stimulates PTH to reduce phosphorus absorption, which in turn increases calcium absorption and, in conjunction with calcitriol, accelerates bone absorption. Phase 4 can be described as the final crystallisation process of the new matrix laid down by the osteoblasts within the affected areas and is identical to the process described as bone formation. A lack of vitamin D and/or calcium reduces renal absorption of phosphate and can cause a delay in growth and closure of epiphyseal plates (Westen, 1995).

Thus the resorption and formation of bone occurs in separate areas. The formation of bone during growth is initiated from the epiphyseal growth plates on the outer surface ends of the bone and through osteoblasts arriving through blood vessels which (up to a certain age only) reach into the inner surface of the bone. During re-modelling in adult horses, osteoclasts resorb bone on the endosteal (inner) surface (marrow cavity) and osteoblasts add mineralised matrix on the periosteal (outer) surface. As the bone grows osteoblastic and osteoclastic activities lead to the increase in bone size and changes in longitudinal and cross-sectional geometry.

Requirements for growth

The importance of calcium and phosphorus in skeletal development is apparent. Studies examining the role of calcium and phosphorus nutrition during growth of horses document the occurrence of mineral related metabolic bone diseases. For instance in a survey of 384 yearlings, highest incidence of mineral related metabolic bone diseases were associated with low levels or deficiency of calcium or phosphorus *per se* or extreme ratios of calcium and phosphorus (Knight *et al.* 1985). Studies conducted with Shetland ponies (a breed that is not likely to develop osteochondrosis) offered a diet comprised of calcium to phosphorus ratio of 6:1 for four years demonstrated a significant reduction in bone-mineral content over the duration of the study (Jordan *et al.*, 1975). Jeffcott summarised in 1993 that there was not yet any clear evidence of a link between excess calcium and osteochondrosis in horses and research by Savage *et al.* (1993) confirmed this opinion, when horses fed 345% of recommended NRC levels (NRC, 1989) for calcium showed no increase in osteochondrotic lesions. However, the group of foals fed elevated levels of phosphorus in the diet (388% of NRC recommendations; NRC, 1989) without increasing calcium supplementation accordingly showed increased incidence of osteochondrotic lesions and cortical bone porosity. Increased cortical metacarpal bone area and growth rate in calcium deficient Thoroughbred (TB) foals was observed after two months of feeding a low calcium diet (Thompson *et al.*, 1988b). However after a further period of offering a low calcium diet for two months (at 8 months of age) the processes controlling cortical metacarpal bone accretion were reversed and the rate of skeletal growth was retarded compared with foals offered diets containing sufficient calcium. This suggests a possible adaptation or switch in control mechanism and or absorption pathways; a similar process to that observed in dogs managed under similar dietary treatments (Hazewinkel *et al.*, 1991).

Mineral Nutrition

The effect of level of protein in the diet has been suggested as an important factor in calcium uptake and metabolism. Schryver *et al.* (1987) assessed the effect of varying levels of protein and calcium intake on calcium metabolism in foals from the age of four months. The group offered low protein (9%) diets had a reduced voluntary intake and therefore low intake of calcium and phosphorus. Foals achieving intakes of calcium of 125mg/kg body weight with low protein diets had higher rates of apparent absorption of calcium (77%) compared to foals offered medium or high levels of protein (14% and 20%) with intakes of calcium of 154 and 157 mg/kg body weight respectively (apparent absorption of calcium of 62 and 56% respectively). The differences between the medium and high protein diets were not statistically significant but a reduction in apparent absorption of 6% between the two diets could suggest an effect at the intestinal mucosa level or on the retention of calcium. In humans excessive intakes of protein have been linked to increased losses of calcium from metabolism but this theory has been disputed (Spencer *et al.*, 1988).

Practical implications

The whole body ratio for calcium to phosphorus is approximately 1.7:1 and therefore dietary inclusion rates of calcium and phosphorus have been recommended to be at least this for adult horses and 2:1 for growing horses. This approach seems to be redundant on two grounds, firstly, that apparent absorption will vary according to the diet offered and secondly there is a lack of information on the impact of the interactions between calcium, phosphorus and other major and trace elements. Therefore, in practice, the horse owner and feed manufacturer should first pay attention to the minimum requirements for individual elements. Formulation using the NRC approach (1989) never allows intakes of phosphorus to be greater than calcium, that is to avoid ratios less than 1:1 and with ratios greater than 2:1, adequate phosphate must be provided. In youngstock, adequate supply of vitamin D and access to exercise in sunlight (UV radiation) is also an important management procedure to ensure optimal bone development and growth.

In neonates the calcium and phosphorus levels are 18.2 and 9.7 g/kg body weight respectively (Meyer and Ahlswede, 1976) and therefore adequate supply of these two minerals is important throughout pregnancy.

During the tenth month of pregnancy the calcium and phosphorus content of the foetus increases by 38 and 34% respectively and is greater than those observed in neonates as the bone to muscle ratio is greater in the foetus than the neonate. Meyer and Ahlswede (1976) concluded that the intake of calcium and phosphorus by the pregnant mare should increase respectively from 36 g calcium/day to 45 g/day and from 25 g phosphorus/day to 30 g/day in the last two months of gestation. As most mares will be managed indoors during this period and voluntary intake of the mare decreases in late pregnancy, the calcium and phosphorus levels supplemented will have to be provided via a well formulated concentrate mix. Grazing will provide approximately 5 to 6 g calcium and 4 g phosphorus per kg DM herbage ingested (Smolders, 1990) and mares may be able to ingest up to 12 kg DM grass per day thus providing adequate concentrations of calcium and phosphorus for lactation (Houbiers and Smolders, 1990). However, supplements which supply a 2:1 ratio of calcium to phosphorus will be of little use in management of imbalanced diets.

Mare's milk contains approximately 1.2 g calcium/l fluid milk and 0.5 to 0.75 g phosphorus/l fluid milk (Baucus *et al.*, 1987; NRC, 1989). During the first four weeks of lactation a foal, with the potential to achieve a mature body weight of 580 kg, may achieve an average intake of 21.6 g calcium/day and 13.0 g phosphorus/day (equal to a 1.7 ratio). The NRC system recommends a minimum intake for a 4-month foal (to achieve a mature body weight of 600 kg) of 40 g calcium/day and 22 g phosphorus/day whereas the GEH (1995) recommends identical intake of calcium per day and 28 g phosphorus/day. It is therefore likely that limited supplementation of calcium and phosphorus via creep feeding may be necessary in order to achieve such levels of intake.

Magnesium

Magnesium is an essential mineral in cell metabolism. In mammals magnesium is essential for the function of the nervous system, cell signalling, the energy utilisation in muscles (for example in activation and formation of magnesium complexes of ATP), the activation of more than 300 enzymes (for instance, hexakinase in glycolysis and pyruvate dehydrogenase complex that serves to interconnect glycolysis, glucogenesis and fatty acid synthesis to the Krebs cycle) and stabilisation of macromolecules such as DNA and protein (Table 8.5). The magnesium content of the body is approximately 0.05 % of the body

Mineral Nutrition

mass, of which 60% is found in the skeleton. About 35 % of the magnesium is found in the heart, skeletal muscles and the liver, and 1to 5% in body fluids, such as blood, gastric juice, bile, lymph and urine.

Table 8.5 Metabolic and physiological role of magnesium in the horse.

Metabolic / physiological function	Interactions with other minerals	Effects of shortages	Effects of excesses
• Inter and intracellular processes • Muscular contraction • Functioning of enzyme systems • Skeletal integrity – closely related to calcium and phosphorus metabolism • Stabilisation of DNA and protein	Excess phosphorus depresses magnesium intake Magnesium competes for same binding sites as calcium: excess calcium can impair magnesium uptake	• Loss of appetite, nervousness, sweating, muscular tremors, ataxia, rapid breathing, convulsions, heart and skeletal degeneration, in chronic cases mineralisation of the pulmonary artery by deposition of phosphate and calcium salts	• Not known

Magnesium in plasma represents less than 1% of the total body load. However as plasma is easily sampled, the concentration of magnesium in samples is used to determine magnesium status of the whole animal. The concentration of magnesium in plasma only indicates short-term sufficiency and as approximately one third of magnesium in plasma is bound to protein, free ionisable magnesium status can be difficult to determine.

Furthermore, the concentration of magnesium in plasma provides little information on the level of intracellular magnesium concentration (Hinds et al., 1994). There are strategies to overcome this problem, for instance by the determination of magnesium in leucocytes, which are representative of cellular magnesium concentration (Ryan, 1991). It has been established that hypomagnesaemia can occur in tissue even though circulatory concentrations of magnesium seem to be normal. Muscle tissue contains a high proportion of intracellular magnesium and in particular, magnesium is essential for cardiac muscle function (Matthei, 1996). The number of studies investigating the requirements of the horse for magnesium is very limited.

Uptake of magnesium in monogastric animals occurs in the duodenum and anterior jejunum, however the process is not fully understood (Meyer, 1996).

Nutritional Physiology of the Horse

The apparent absorption of magnesium is affected markedly by the sources of supplementation of magnesium in the diet with ranges reported from 35 to 70% (NRC, 1989; GEH, 1994; Van Doom, 2003) and the endogenous excretion is estimated as 6 mg/kg body weight in mature horses. However, there is little data on the impact of other dietary elements on the apparent absorption (for instance uptake of magnesium is affected by manganese and fluorine). In contrast to calcium, magnesium uptake is not altered by the presence of oxalate. In a recent study in The Netherlands diets containing high concentrations of phosphorus led to a reduction in the apparent absorption of magnesium, however the mechanism for this is not understood (Van Doorn, 2003).

Table 8.6 Requirements for magnesium by horses under different physiological regimes (data converted by Ellis and Boekhoff, 2003).

	Body weight	INRA	GEH	NRC
			mg/kg BW/day	
Maintenance	Small	14	20	15
	Large	13	20	15
Work				
Low	Small	16	20	21
	Large	15	21	18
Medium	Small	19	21	25
	Large	17	22	22
Heavy	Small	27	26	33
	Large	24	25	29
Pregnancy				
7-8 months	Small	23		
	Large	24		
9 months	Small	23	20	19
	Large	24	21	17
10 months	Small			20
	Large			17
11 months	Small	23		21
	Large	23		18
Lactation				
Month 1	Large	35		
Month 2	Large	38		
Month 3	Large	38		
0-3 month	Small	38	24	24
	Large	36	25	22
3-weaning	Small			18
	Large			17

Mineral Nutrition

Although serum magnesium status does not accurately reflect the overall magnesium balance of the animal, symptoms of deficiency correlate well with serum concentrations of less than 2.0 mg/dl or 1.5 mEq/l (Worth, 2002). The normal status for magnesium ranges between 2.2 to 2.7 mg/dl however heavy exercise can decrease the concentration to less than 2.0 mg/dl (Riond, 2002). In cattle, serum concentrations of less than 2.0 mg/dl are associated with the onset of grass tetany, however horses appear to be more resilient to low concentrations of magnesium in circulation and very rarely develop the symptoms of grass tetany. Low magnesium status in horses is however associated with symptoms of impaired muscle or nerve function (Meyer, 1995; Harrington, 1974; Harrington and Walsh, 1980). Excessive intakes of calcium can also lead to temporary muscle tetany in horses.

The recommendations for requirements for magnesium by INRA (1990) assume that the apparent absorption of magnesium from the diet is approximately 40% and that milk contains 90 mg/l fluid milk during early lactation and approximately 45 to 60 mg/l in mid and late lactation (Barlet, 1990).

Magnesium requirements for growth and development

In bone formation, magnesium plays an important role in the regulation of the calcium binding protein Annexin V and hence regulation of calcium uptake into matrix vesicles. Magnesium also is important in maintaining copper attachment sites in the developing bone and excessive supply can lead to a reduction of copper binding (Chvapil and Misiorowski, 1980; Kirsch *et al.*, 1997). Furthermore, in the hypertrophic chondrocyte and later in the matrix vesicles magnesium prevents the premature crystallisation of apatite and therefore calcium, magnesium and phosphorus metabolism are closely interlinked in bone development.

Harrington (1974) assessed the indicators of magnesium deficiency in various tissues of foals from three weeks of age. There were no substantial changes in the concentrations of calcium and phosphorus in bone and no osteochondrotic lesions were reported, although growth rates of foals were reduced. As with other species (dogs and ruminants) mineralisation (focal calcium and phosphorus deposits) in the aorta was observed. The adverse effects of offering diets containing excessive concentrations of magnesium have not been reported in relation to bone development but elevated concentrations of magnesium inhibit parathyroid hormone secretion thus mimicking the action of calcium

(Habener and Potts, 1976, Brown, 2000). This may be important in the development of osteochondrosis in horses, although currently there is little evidence of a causal link.

The foetus deposits 120, 140, 160, and 180 mg magnesium/day in the 7, 8, 9, 10 and 11th month of gestation respectively (Meyer and Ahlswende, 1976). The requirements of pregnant mares for magnesium therefore increase by only 1 to 2g magnesium per day during late pregnancy (Meyer and Ahlswende, 1976). The current daily recommendations for a 600 kg pregnant mare in late pregnancy and during lactation are 13 g and 15 g magnesium respectively and for her foal 4 to 7g magnesium/day in the first year of life (Meyer and Tiegs, 1995; GEH 1994; NRC 1989). The requirements of the foal (as currently recommended by NRC and GEH) are not fully met by the intake of mare's milk (Csapo-Kiss et al., 1995) and therefore supplementation of the diet is necessary. Legumes (lucerne or clover) will supply high levels of magnesium, and medium quality hay or grass will also provide adequate levels of magnesium if the voluntary intake is greater than 4 kg DM/day. This is likely in foals of 5 months of age or greater. At that age, a creep pellet feed will supplement the animal adequately but if the foal is growing rapidly it is advised to use a mineral supplement rather than a creep feed as the latter will also provide energy that may not be necessary at that stage of growth.

Sodium, potassium and chloride

Sodium, potassium and chloride are important ions involved in maintenance of the acid-base balances of inter and intra-cellular fluids, osmotic regulation, as co-factors for enzyme reactions and affect the uptake of neutral amino acids and glucose by cells (Table 8.7). Sodium has a further important role in the processes controlling nerve impulse transmission. Additionally chloride is an important component of bile and HCl released into the gastric lumen. All these ions are also important in the process of influx and efflux of ions from cells via ATP-linked pump systems. The distribution of sodium, potassium and chloride differ from each other, thus maintaining the processes controlling fluid transport between the intercellular and extracellular fluid pools. It is estimated that 98% of potassium exists within the cell systems and approximately 90% of sodium is present in extracellular fluid. Chloride is almost exclusive to the extracellular fluid pool. The largest pool of potassium (ca 75%) is located in skeletal muscles. The myocardium accounts for

Mineral Nutrition

about 1% of the total body potassium, erythrocytes carry about 7% of total pool and 8% is located in bone (Sejersted and Sjogaard, 2000).

Table 8.7 Roles and function of potassium, sodium and chloride in mammals.

Metabolic/physiological function	Interactions with other minerals	Effects of shortages	Effects of excesses
Potassium			
• Regulation of osmotic pressure and water uptake by organs • Skeletal integrity, functioning of muscles	Excess sodium restricts potassium uptake	• Reduced appetite, depressed growth rates in young horses, muscular dystrophy, stiffness of the joints • Fatigue, weakness, lethargy, reduced feed and water intake, weight loss	• Potassium induced periodic paralysis – not reported clinically in horses
Sodium			
• Electrolyte (determines osmolarity of extracellular fluid) • Osmotic regulation • Conduction of nerve and muscle impulses	Potassium	• Decreased sweating and performance • Excess licking behaviour and constipation • Increased aldosterone activity • Reduced feed intake, ultimate cessation of eating • Muscular and nervous dysfunction (muscular tremor, gait and chewing co-ordination)	• Colic, diarrhoea, polyuria, weakness, staggering, posterior paralysis, recumbency
Chloride			
• Electrolyte • Osmotic regulation • Extracellular fluid – acid balance • Hydrochloric acid (digestion)	Sodium	• Possible blood alkaliosis	• Possible damage to central nervous system

As skeletal muscle is the largest pool of potassium in the body, changes or abnormalities in the functionality of muscle can lead to large and rapid changes in the distribution of potassium in body tissues. Tight regulation of potassium in skeletal muscle is therefore central to potassium homeostasis (Suwannchot, 2001; Hinchcliff, 1998).

Sodium, potassium and chloride are important in the calculation of the dietary cation-anion balance of diets and rations (Wall *et al.*, 1992; Baker *et al.*, 1992; Frape, 1998). Although there are several different equations currently available, the dietary cation-anion balance (DCAB) is most commonly defined as (Na + K + Ca + Mg) – (Cl + P + S) reported as milliequivalents per kg dry matter.

Dietary cation-anion balance is implicated in the regulation of blood pH and therefore the transportation of carbon dioxide and oxygen to tissues. Changes in blood pH as a result of changes in the loading of various cations and anions can have profound implications during periods of exercise. In mammalian systems the pH of blood is maintained in a narrow range from pH 7.2 to 7.5. Small changes in blood pH can lead to severe metabolic problems and therefore the buffering of the blood is extremely important in order to maintain homeostasis. Blood contains numerous cations (e.g., sodium, potassium, calcium and magnesium) and anions (e.g., chloride, phosphate and sulphate) but their contribution to the overall buffering capacity of blood is relatively low. The primary buffers in blood are haemoglobin (located in the erythrocytes) and bicarbonate in plasma. The dissociation of the imidazole ring of histidine in the haem protein acts as the buffer and the reaction above is the basis of the buffering of the plasma with bicarbonate.

The formation of bicarbonate ion in blood from carbon dioxide and water facilitates the transfer of relatively insoluble carbon dioxide from the tissues (as a result of the oxidation of carbon sources) to the lungs. Carbonic acid is formed when dissolved carbon dioxide reacts with water.

$$CO_2 + H_2O \longleftrightarrow H_2CO_3$$
$$H_2CO_3 \longleftrightarrow H^+ + HCO_3^-$$

These reactions occur predominately in erythrocytes as virtually all carbon dioxide leaving tissues via the capillary endothelium pathway is processed by the erythrocytes. The reaction is catalysed by carbonic anhydrase and the dissociation of carbonic acid occurs spontaneously yielding bicarbonate ion. Carbonic acid is a relatively strong acid (pK_a 3.8) but is in equilibrium with dissolved carbon dioxide gas. The release of a proton (free acidity) as a result of the formation of bicarbonate is buffered by haemoglobin which leads to a reduced affinity of haemoglobin for oxygen and the subsequent release of oxygen to the peripheral tissue is known as the Bohr effect. The equilibrium equation for the reaction is:

Mineral Nutrition

$$pH = 6.1 + \log [HCO_3^-/(0.03)(pCO_2)]$$

where the apparent pK_a for bicarbonate formation is 6.1 and 0.03 is a conversion factor accounting for the gaseous nature of carbon dioxide.

The difference in the partial pressure of carbon dioxide in peripheral tissue and blood favours the diffusion of carbon dioxide from the tissues into the blood. The opposite process occurs when oxygen is taken up from the alveoli of the lungs and carbon dioxide is expelled. Any free acidity (protons) produced in the plasma as a result of ionisation of carbonic acid can also be buffered by phosphate and by proteins, especially albumin. Furthermore about 15% of carbon dioxide is transported from peripheral tissues to the lung as haemoglobin carbamate. The transfer of carbon dioxide from peripheral tissue to plasma can lead to relatively low levels of dissociation of carbonic acid takes place. The resultant free acidity are buffered by proteins and phosphate ions in the plasma. The increased concentration of bicarbonate in the erythrocytes leads to imbalance in osmotic potential. This imbalance is removed as bicarbonate ion exchanges (when released from the erythrocyte) with chloride derived from the plasma (the so-called chloride shift; Coenen, 1992). Additionally, decreases in blood pH can trigger the processes to mobilise calcium from bone. Currently there have been no comparable studies in horses but research into the impact of alteration of DCAB has focussed on the demands on performance horses, particularly in the field of endurance and eventing. The recommended requirements of these minerals are given in Table 8.8. The German (GEH) system is the only one to provide recommendations for requirements for chloride.

The estimate for apparent absorption of potassium from dietary sources is approximately 100% but the true retention rate for the element is estimated as 50% (NRC, 1989). The German system (GEH, 1994) however estimates the true retention of potassium as about 80 %. Crozier *et al.* (1997) estimated an average apparent absorption of potassium ranging between 74 and 78% for forages fed *ad libitum*, supporting the observations made in the German system. No differences in maintenance requirements are made between these two systems, but the system published by INRA (1990) predicts a slightly higher requirement, possibly reflecting the higher predictions for voluntary intake of feeds.

Electrolyte (sodium, potassium, chloride, calcium and magnesium) losses through heavy sweating during intense exercise can contribute to the onset of fatigue and weakness (Rose *et al.*, 1980; Bergero, 2004).

Nutritional Physiology of the Horse

Table 8.8 Current recommendations for requirements of potassium, sodium and chloride by horses (data converted by Ellis and Boekhoff, 2003).

	Body weight	INRA	GEH	NRC	INRA	GEH	NRC	GEH
		mg/kg BW/day			mg/kg BW/day			
		Sodium			Potassium			Chloride
Maintenance	Small	24	20	16	60	50	50	80
	Large	25	20	16	57	50	50	80
Work								
Low	Small	54	45	54	72	66	69	120
	Large	48	46	54	65	65	61	121
Medium	Small	88	71	58	105	80	83	164
	Large	67	71	58	94	80	73	163
Heavy	Small	66	140	68	118	120	111	274
	Large	69	141	68	105	120	97	273
Pregnancy								
7-8 months	Small	26			61			
	Large	26			64			
9 months	Small	26	24	16	61	55	65	81
	Large	28	23	16	64	53	57	75
10 months	Small			16			66	
	Large			16			58	
11 months	Small	26		16	61		70	
	Large	28		16	62		61	
Lactation								
Month 1		31			94			
Month 2		29			101			
Month 3		28			101			
0-3 month	Small	29	26	23	101	75	106	94
	Large	30	26	20	97	69	92	90
3-weaning	Small			23			74	
	Large			20			66	

Coenen and Vervuert (2003) provided an excellent review on the current knowledge of electrolyte metabolism and water balance in working horses and confirmed the importance of an increased intake of chloride, potassium and sodium immediately after the period of exercise to replenish depleted reserves of these minerals. Therefore the evidence provided by Coenen and Vervuert (2003) explained the greater than expected recommendations for these electrolytes predicted by the German (GEH) system for working horses and the additional supplementation for very heavy long-term work such as eventing and long distance riding (Table 8.9).

Mineral Nutrition

Table 8.9 Electrolyte requirements for a 600 kg horse following intensive (very heavy) work load.

	Sodium (g/day)	Potassium (g/day)	Chloride (g/day)
Estimated requirements	115	90	213

These estimates are based on losses of sweat of 30 to 40 ml per kg body weight per exercise bout; a loss that could occur during intense long-term exercise (peak performance). However, the majority of horses eventing or performing endurance disciplines will only reach peak performance exercise around once a month. Coenen and Vervuert (2003) also highlighted the importance of electrolyte replenishment directly after exercise in heavily working horses. At the lower levels of work, the question arises whether these horses need such a high daily increase of electrolyte intake, or whether they require these increases in electrolytes only during the latter part of intensive training, or even only directly before and after a competition. For the supplementation to be adequate, correct estimation of workload has to be made and this is where there are considerable differences between the NRC, GEH and INRA systems. Currently, recommendations are given per day according to working level, but they are applied according to general work over a period of time and it is unlikely that horse owners will adjust mineral intake on a daily basis, depending on exercise performed.

Meyer (1995) suggests that horses will self regulate their intake of sodium in relation to their requirements. Therefore supplementation can be provided by using a salt-lick for horses. However, Jansson and Dahlborn (1999) reported that intakes of sodium from salt licks can vary considerably (0 to 62 mg/kg body weight per day) and a high proportion of horses would not ingest levels adequate to cover the requirements of medium to heavy work. It was also suggested that consuming concentrated salt solutions could lead to taste aversion and temporary inhibition of appetite in some horses (Jansson and Dahlborn, 1999). However, this may be affected greatly by previous experience of horses and the individual preferences (Ellis, 2003). A salt or mineral lick is therefore an uncertain method of supplementing horses under moderate to heavy exercise and supplementation via water and feed is essential.

Requirements for growth and lactation

There is little or no evidence that deficiencies in sodium, potassium or chloride are implicated in developmental orthopaedic disease in foals even though about 50% of the total body pool of sodium is located in the bone (Meyer and Ahlswende, 1976). There are also increased requirements for sodium, potassium and chloride during pregnancy and lactation (Table 8.10). These increases reflect the extra requirements of the developing foal for each mineral and the losses associated with secretion of milk (Lewis, 1995).

When comparing level of supply of sodium, potassium and chloride from milk and the recommendations for young foals, it becomes apparent that very little is known about the actual requirements for each mineral during the first few weeks of the foal's life. The recommendations for each mineral are based on apparent absorption coefficients based on adult horses but there is a lack of research conducted using foals under the age of three months to justify the use of the apparent absorption coefficients of adult horses. Milk composition during early lactation has a ratio of sodium: potassium: chloride of 1:4:1.6 and a low positive dietary cation-anion balance of 6.95 mEq/l. However the recommendations from GEH and elsewhere would suggest diets should be offered with a ratio of 1:2:3 for sodium, potassium and chloride respectively which leads to a negative dietary cation-anion balance of -91.3 mEq/kg DM. Further studies have to be conducted to provide accurate estimates for the various requirements for the three minerals and also ensure that the impact of grassland management regimes and mineral supplementation are not detrimental to the development of the foal (Table 8.10).

Table 8.10 Requirements and supply of sodium, potassium and chloride for growth and lactation (Source: Ellis, 2001).

	Na (g/day)			K (g/day)			Cl (g/day)
	GEH	INRA	NRC	GEH	INRA	NRC	GEH
Foals up to 12 months of age	6	11	6	12	-	13	18
Milk Composition Colostrum and fluid milk (after Csapo-Kiss, 1995 and Meyer, 1995)	0.32 g/l colostrum 0.18 g/l milk			0.93 g/l colostrum 0.71 g/l milk			1.00 g/l colostrum. 0.3 g/l milk
Feed (g/kg DM) *							
Mixed Grassland	2.4			36			
Hay	2.4			25			
Grass silage	2.4			33			
Barley**	1.2			5.4			1.2
Lucerne hay	1.2			27			

* CVB (1996); ** (CVB, 2000)

Sulphur

Sulphur is essential for metabolism in animals. It plays an important role in many biochemical compounds, for instance amino acids, vitamins (biotin and thiamine), haemoglobin, heparin, insulin, bile salts and heteropolysaccharides such as chondroitin sulphate. It is necessary for keratin formation and it may impair the uptake of various trace elements, such as copper, cobalt, selenium and molybdenum.

Sulphur metabolism

Sulphur occurs in the diet in the form of inorganic sulphur, sulphate and related chemicals and sulphur containing amino acids and other organic compounds. Mammals cannot synthesise branched chain amino acids, the ring structures of aromatic amino acids or incorporate sulphur into amino acids. This means that methionine (a sulphur containing amino acid) cannot be synthesised directly and has to be supplied via the diet as one of the ten essential amino acids. Methionine is essential for protein synthesis in mammalian species. Cysteine is another acid that is noted for its oxidation to form the "double-headed" amino acid cystine. Both of these amino acids contain sulphur and can be synthesised if sufficient methionine is present otherwise they become essential amino acids. The process of oxidation leads to a disulphide linkage between peptide chains and therefore is important in the tertiary and quarternary structures of proteins and enzymes.

The sulphur required for cysteine biosynthesis is derived from methionine. A condensation reaction between ATP and methionine is catalysed by methionine adenosyltransferase yielding S-adenosylmethionine. S-adenosylmethionine acts as a precursor for numerous methyl transfer reactions (e.g. the conversion of norepinephrine to epinenephrine) and methyl transfer of S-adenosylmethionine forms S-adenosylhomocysteine. S-adenosylhomocysteine is then converted by adenosylhomocyteinase to homocysteine and adenosine. Homocysteine can be converted either to methionine via methionine synthase (a methionine-sparing reaction) and requires N^5-methyl-tetrahydrofolate to methylate the compound, or cysteine via a condensation reaction with serine. The transsulphration reaction produces cystathionine which is converted by cystathionase to cysteine and α-ketobutyrate. α-ketobutyrate is decarboxylated and converted to propionyl-CoA. Cystathionine synthase and cystathionase (cystathionine

Nutritional Physiology of the Horse

lyase) both use pyridoxal phosphate as a cofactor and are under strict regulatory control. Cystathionase is controlled by negative allostery resulting from the production of cysteine. Furthermore, cystathionine synthase gene is regulated by cysteine concentration.

There are several pathways for cysteine catabolism. The simplest and least important is catalysed by desulfurase activity in the liver leading to the production of hydrogen sulphide, (H_2S) and pyruvate. However, of greater importance is the catabolism of cysteine via cytochrome-P_{450}-coupled enzyme cysteine dioxygenase. This reaction oxidises the cysteine sulphydryl group to a sulphinate leading to the intermediate cysteinesulphinate. Cysteinesulphinate serves as a biosynthetic intermediate undergoing decarboxylation and oxidation to produce taurine. As the catabolism of cysteinesulphinate proceeds through transamination to ß-sulphinylpyruvate, bisulphite and pyruvate are yielded (Metzler, 1985). The enzyme sulphite oxidase converts bisulphite to sulphate and hydrogen peroxide. The resultant sulphate is used as a precursor for the formation of 3'-phosphoadenosine-5'-phosphosulfate and is utilised in metabolism as a mechanism to transfer sulphate to other biological molecules, for example, sugars of the glycosphingolipids. The most important product of cysteine metabolism is the bile salt precursor taurine. This is used to form the bile acid conjugates taurocholate and taurochenodeoxycholate. The enzyme cystathionase can transfer sulphur from one cysteine molecule to another generating thiocysteine and pyruvate. Transamination of cysteine yields ß-mercaptopyruvate which reacts with sulphite to produce thiosulphate and pyruvate. Both thiocysteine and thiosulphate are utilised by rhodanase to incorporate sulphur into cyanide, thereby detoxifying the cyanide to thiocyanate.

The most abundant heteropolysaccharides in the body are the glycosaminoglycans. These molecules are long unbranched polysaccharides containing a repeating disaccharide unit. The disaccharide units contain either of two modified sugars; N-acetylgalactosamine or N-acetylglucosamine and a uronic acid such as glucuronate or iduronate. Glycosaminoglycans are located on the surface of cells or in the extracellular matrix and are highly viscous making them ideal for lubricating fluid in the joints. The rigidity of the molecule also provides structural integrity to cells and provides passageways between cells allowing for cell migration. The glycosaminoglycans of physiological significance are hyaluronic acid, dermatan sulphate, chondroitin sulphate, heparin, heparan sulphate and keratan sulphate. Hyaluronic acid contains no sulphur and is not covalently linked to proteins as a proteoglycan. It is, however, a component of non-covalently formed complexes with proteoglycans. Hyaluronic acid polymers are very large and can displace a large volume of water. This property makes them excellent lubricators of joints. This is of considerable interest to the equine nutrition industry as supplementation using compounds such as chondroitin sulphate for joint problems has become relatively common recently (Table 8.11).

Table 8.11 Incidence of glycosaminoglycans in the body of the horse.

Glycosaminoglycan	Location in body
Hyaluronate	Synovial fluid, vitreous humor, loose connective tissue.
Chondroitin sulphate	Cartilage, bone, heart valves.
Heparan sulphate	Basement membranes, components of cell surfaces.
Heparin	Component of intracellular granules of mast cells lining the arteries of the lungs, liver and skin.
Dermatan sulphate	skin, blood vessels, heart valves.

Proteoglycans

One of the recent developments in supplementation of diets is the use of proteoglycans or mucopolysaccharides. The glycosaminoglycans (GAG) are the basis of many supplements as they have an important role in cartilage development and integrity. Various supplements are now available for horses and dogs based on these substances, most of which are recommended for 'joint and connective tissue problems' and in particular as anti-arthritic compounds. Chondroitin sulphate has been examined extensively for its anti-inflammatory properties as a therapy for osteoarthritis in humans (Ronca *et al.*, 1998).

There are however many questions about the efficacy of these products. The first question, which needs to be assessed, is whether these substances, if taken orally, are absorbed without modification and if they are transported to sites of damage or repair. Ronca *et al.* (1998) reported the bioavailability of chondroitin taken orally as 12 and 15% for humans and rats respectively, resulting in strong anti-inflammatory effects and no side effects. These observations were similar to those of

Deal and Moskowitz (1999). In contrast the smaller sub-unit of glucosamine has a relatively low molecular weight and as glucosamine sulphate it can be absorbed rapidly in the small intestine with (90% uptake and subsequent excretion of 20% in urine and as much as 70% exhaled as CO_2). Incorporation of glucosamine into cartilage can occur as little as four hours after ingestion and approximately 8-12% is retained in the tissues to be incorporated by chondrocytes into proteoglycans (Deal and Moskowitz, 1999). Therefore, if developing lesions become osteochondrotic as a result of a depletion in inorganic sulphate it can be speculated that these substances will counteract these effects and support repair. Furthermore strong anti-inflammatory action and a protective action against cartilage degradation has been observed repeatedly *in vitro* and *in vivo* in humans but as yet there is no evidence of a curative effect (Deal and Moskowitz, 1999).

In horses limited research has been conducted examining the use of GAG supplements. One experiment examining the role of commercially available supplements based on chondroitin sulphate demonstrated no increases in serum GAG concentration after oral administration of the supplement (Bathe *et al.* 2000). It was concluded that there seems to be little justification for oral administration of chondroitin sulphate as an integral part of therapy or for prevention of osteochondrosis. Fenton (1999) examined the effects of glucosamine sulphate and N-acetyl-glucosamines on degradation of explant cultures of articular cartilage after various periods of induction. Glucosamine sulphate consistently inhibited cartilage degradation *in vitro* and may have chondroprotective properties, however little *in vivo* data is available to support these observations.

Hanson *et al.* (1997) did however examine the effects of administration of a mixed proteoglycan (9 g (twice daily) of a compound containing glucosamine hydrochloride (60%), purified chondroitin sulphate (20%), manganese (0.5%) and ascorbate (3.4%) to horses suffering from degenerative joint disease. Substantial improvements in lameness grade, stride length and flexion test were observed after two weeks of therapy which may reflect the anti-inflammatory properties of the substances. Whether a reparative effect of the supplements can be ascribed is still unclear.

Sulphur requirements

Although the requirements of the horse for sulphur have not been established, INRA (1990) and NRC (1989) provide recommendations based on other non-ruminants species (Table 8.12). The apparent absorption of sulphur from forage based diets show considerable variation from 28% in diets composed of Caucasian bluestem to 66% in lucerne based diets (Crozier *et al.*, 1997). It was noted however, that there was a close link between the apparent absorption of sulphur and the digestibility of crude protein from the diets. Finally sulphur is an important element in the diet of horses as it may well impair the uptake of various trace elements, such as copper, cobalt, selenium and molybdenum.

Table 8.12 Estimate sulphur requirements for horses (data converted by Ellis and Boekhoff, 2003).

	Body weight	INRA	GEH	NRC
		mg/kg BW/day		
Maintenance	Small	23		24
	Large	22		24
Work				
Low	Small	27		27
	Large	25		27
Medium	Small	32		29
	Large	28		29
Heavy	Small	32		34
	Large	28		34
Pregnancy				
7-8 months	Small	23		
	Large	24		
9 months	Small	23		24
	Large	24		24
10 months	Small			24
	Large			24
11 months	Small	23		24
	Large	23		24
Lactation				
Month 1	Large	35		
Month 2	Large	38		
Month 3	Large	38		
0-3 month	Small	38		23
	Large	36		20
3-weaning	Small			23
	Large			20

Trace elements

The trace elements or micro nutrients are, as with the major minerals, essential for life. It is generally accepted that 15 trace elements are essential for the biochemical and physiological processes in mammals (Underwood, 1981). Trace element disorders are widespread in livestock, ranging from sub-clinical conditions to severe deficiencies or acute toxicity. Rarely do deficiencies or excesses result from single trace elements but they reflect the complex biological interactions between the various major and trace minerals. Furthermore, trace element disorders are difficult to identify as deficiencies and toxicities can produce similar symptoms. In this section we will consider 10 of the trace elements for which there are published requirements. We do not consider tin, vanadium, silicon, nickel or arsenic. For the trace elements, INRA (1990) have adopted the recommendations of Meyer (1981) which are similar to those used in GEH (1994).

The only differences between the three systems are that the estimated requirements for iron, cobalt, selenium and iodine are slightly higher in the INRA (1990) system and the estimated requirements for copper for young horses have been increased in the GEH system (1994). The higher recommendations estimated by INRA (1990) are a result of adopting recommendations based on voluntary intake rather than body weight.

Copper

The literature concerning copper and its interactions with sulphur and molybdenum is extensive in farm livestock. It is not the aim of this section to review that literature but to provide an overview on the role and function of copper in equine metabolism (Table 8.13). Copper is involved in a number of enzyme systems, for instance urate oxidase (in nitrogen excretory pathway), metalloenzymes (important in iron and catecholamine metabolism), haemoglobin, complex IV of electron transport system used in oxidative phosphorylation, involved in the function of proteoglycans and phospholipids, lysyl oxidase (elastin and collagen synthesis) and superoxide dismutases. Cytosolic superoxide dismutase protects the lipid cell membrane from oxidation (Uauy *et al.*, 1985) and all superoxide dismutases (SODs) in animals contain zinc, copper or manganese. A further role of superoxide dismutase is the conversion of superoxide to peroxide and minimisation of the production of the hydroxy radical. Peroxides produced by superoxide dismutase are also toxic but they are detoxified by conversion to water via peroxidases such as glutathione peroxidase. The role of superoxide dismutase at the subchondral level of bone metabolism has not yet been investigated, but Van de Lest *et al*. (1999b) reported changes in lipid composition of equine osteochondrotic subchondral bone that were associated with free radical damage. The absorption of copper from dietary sources in the small intestine is relatively low, even in the absence of interference from molybdenum and sulphur. Excess copper is excreted in the bile with only small amounts being found in urine, unless renal damage is present.

Table 8.13 Role and function of copper in metabolism

Metabolic / physiological function	Interactions with other minerals	Effects of shortages	Effects of excesses (>800mg/kg DM in diet)
• Bone collagen stabilization, mobilization of body iron stores • Part of enzymes involved in iron metabolism • Synthesis of connective tissue proteins, melanin synthesis, mitochondrial integrity • Central nervous system function	• Molybdenum • Sulphur • Zinc	• In foals malfunctioning of osteoblasts, increased fragility of bones (erosion of articular cartilage of joints) • Anaemia and haemorrhage in parturient mares. Uterine artery rupture in aged, parturient mares	• Inhibition of collagen synthesis and loss of bone density in ruminants (not demonstrated in horses) • Acute haemolytic anaemia and icterus, lethargy and death. Hepatic and renal damage • Gastro-intestinal disturbances, hypercupremia, hemolytic crises, gastroenteritis, hemolysis, jaundice, hemoglobinuria, death

Molybdenum and sulphur interactions with copper occur at the digestive tract level by the formation of insoluble thiomolybdate, however there are numerous compounds and minerals that can affect the uptake of copper at tissue level (Woodbury *et al.*, 1999; Suttle *et al.*, 1974 a and 1974 b; Simpson *et al.*, 1982). Horses will tolerate higher concentrations of molybdenum than ruminants and therefore it is possible that interference in copper absorption does not occur until diets contain molybdenum greater than 3 mg/kg DM (Underwood, 1977; Cymbaluk *et al.*, 1981). The process of absorption is also reduced or inhibited by antagonists (zinc, calcium and iron) which compete for metalloprotein binding sites (present in albumin, amino acids or transcuprin) during transport across the gut mucosa (Cymbaluk, 1993). These antagonists are important factors in the development of secondary copper deficiency. About 50% of copper in the body of mammals is in red blood cells and most of the remainder is in plasma closely associated with caeruloplasmin. The concentration of copper in blood remains relatively stable as there is a dynamic equilibrium between the concentration of copper in liver, kidney and bone, and the blood. However the concentrations of copper in skeletal muscle and milk are independent of circulatory concentration and dietary supply (Georgievskii, 1982). Blood is therefore not useful to assess the copper status of the horse (Pearce *et al.*, 1997, Hurtig *et al.*, 1993). Furthermore Pearce *et al.* (1998a) demonstrated no differences in the concentration of copper in plasma, bone or soft tissue in supplemented and non-supplemented mares and foals.

The apparent absorption of copper in ruminants ranges from 4 to 6% (ARC, 1980). However, the apparent absorption of copper in horses is estimated as ranging between 14 to 50% (on average 28%), depending on the composition of the ration and the presence of any antagonistic minerals (Cymbaluk and Smart, 1993). Crozier *et al.* (1997) reported very low apparent absorption coefficients (ranging between 3 and 8%) for copper when horses were offered lucerne hay, tall fescue or Caucasian blue stem grass hay. Furthermore, there is evidence that the absorption of copper declines with age (Cymbaluk and Smart, 1993). As with other trace elements, there is lack of data concerned with copper absorption *per se* but a number of studies that consider the interactions of copper and other minerals in horses exists (Ralston, 1991).

Requirements for growth and development

Ellis (2001) and Harris *et al.* (2004) conducted in depth literature analyses of the function of copper in the metabolism in the growing horse. During the neonate stage supply and balance of nutrients to the foal may have an important impact on the risk of the development of osteochondrosis. During this stage of growth, the foal depends primarily on copper stored in body tissues (especially the liver). The supply of copper from mares' milk is relatively low and does not fulfil the requirements of foals. Pearce *et al.* (1998b) reported concentrations of 0.32 to 1.7 mg Cu/l at birth, decreasing to a mean of 0.2 mg/l after 14 days and remaining constant thereafter (a similar observation to Anderson, 1992). Manipulation of copper or zinc concentrations in milk is difficult to achieve via dietary supplementation and additional copper in the diet does not alter the concentration secreted in milk (Baucus *et al.*, 1987; Pearce *et al.*, 1998 b).

Table 8.14 Current estimated requirements for copper (Source: Ellis and Boekhoff, 2003).

	Body weight	INRA	GEH	NRC
			mg/kg BW/day	
Maintenance	Small	0.15	0.12	0.16
	Large	0.14	0.10	0.16
Work				
Low	Small	0.18	0.14	0.18
	Large	0.16	0.11	0.18
Medium	Small	0.21	0.20	0.19
	Large	0.19	0.16	0.19
Heavy	Small	0.21	0.27	0.23
	Large	0.19	0.21	0.23
Pregnancy				
7-8 months	Small	0.15		
	Large	0.16		
9 months	Small	0.15	0.17	0.16
	Large	0.16	0.13	0.16
10 months	Small			0.16
	Large			0.16
11 months	Small	0.15		0.16
	Large	0.15		0.16
Lactation				
Month 1	Large	0.23		
Month 2	Large	0.25		
Month 3	Large	0.25		
0-3 month	Small	0.25	0.22	0.23
	Large	0.24	0.18	0.20
3-weaning	Small			0.23
	Large			0.20

At birth, foals have relatively high concentrations of copper stored in the liver (ranging from 250 to 500 mg/kg DM). The concentration declines with age to 'adult' levels of approximately 16 to 30 mg/kg DM (Cupps and Howell, 1949; Egan and Murrin, 1973, Pearce *et al.*, 1998c; Meyer and Tiegs, 1995; Knaap *et al.*, 2000). Although the concentration of copper in the liver can be influenced by Cu intake by the mare during pregnancy, there is very high variation between individuals' independent of dietary status of animals or feeding levels between animals (Bridges and Harris, 1984; Pearce *et al.*, 1997; Pearce *et al.*, 1998 b and c).

Copper and osteochondrosis

As copper is the most researched mineral in equine nutrition in relation to the development of osteochondrosis, a short summary of this disease will be given here (Ellis, 2001). Osteochondrosis is a condition, which can only develop during growth when chondrocytes are active. It is described as the failure of the chondrocytes to ossify leading to soft, cartilaginous areas or 'islands' within bone. These symptoms may be visible as small lesions (islands) within the articular surface or as whole areas of thickened retained cartilage in x-ray or post mortem investigations. Dyschondroplasia is another term used in studies concerned with osteochondrosis and often refers to the early signs of localised abnormal bone formation, before proper lesions develop. Clinical signs in the foal may be swollen joints and lameness. Although clinical signs may not occur during growth, the areas of abnormal bone formation are likely to inhibit the weight bearing function of the bone and smooth operation of the joint during exercise of the mature horse. Detachment of the abnormal bone matter also may occur, exposing the underlying bone and leading to pain and excess fluid accumulation in the joint. This condition is called osteochondrosis dissecans.

Among the main causative factors, which have thus far been identified, are genetic predisposition as well as both external and environmental factors, which can be influenced during gestation and after birth (Ellis, 2001):

- Exercise
- Nutrition
- Nutrition + growth rate
- Nutrition + hormones
- Genetics: final height/growth rate
- Hormones (genetics/nutrition)
- Accidental trauma/injury

For instance in one study, foals examined at 90 days of age showed over twice as many osteochondrotic lesions than foals investigated at 150 days, suggesting that lesions are a naturally occurring process, which may recede over a period of time (Knight *et al.*, 1990). These observations were confirmed by Van Weeren and Barneveld (1999) who examined the development and pathology of the condition and the effect of exercise on the development of osteochondrosis in foals. Biochemical analyses of effected tissues have provided new insights into the development of osteochondrotic lesions (Supplement 32 of Equine Veterinary Journal, 1999). Osteochondrosis is very much a 'dynamic' condition, which may resolve in a large percentage of foals by around 8 months of age but with little chance of resolving after 11 months (Dik *et al.*, 1999).

Copper deficiency has been reported as a causative factor for skeletal diseases in humans and ruminants, but only limited case studies and little experimental data are available (Danks, 1980; Stark, 1988). In dogs, copper deficiency is unlikely as commercial diets are carefully formulated. However, Richardson and Zentek (1998) noted that if deficiency does occur, osteochondrotic lesions can be induced, particularly in the presence of high concentrations of zinc or calcium. This is supported by Wolter (1996) who emphasises that excess calcium in the diet leads to secondary copper deficiency as a result of reducing apparent absorption of copper, zinc and iodine in the small intestine. Evidence from many authors has also implicated molybdenum as an interacting element resulting in reduced absorption of copper (Cymbaluk *et al.*, 1981; Hintz, 1987; Strickland *et al.*, 1987; Ladefoged and Sturup, 1995; Soodan *et al.*, 2000).

Copper has been implicated in osteochondrosis through failure of subchondral bone formation in horses (Bridges and Harris, 1984; Hintz, 1987; Knight *et al.*, 1990; Cymbaluk and Smart, 1993; Hurtig *et al.*, 1993; Jeffcott and Savage, 1996; Pearce, 1998 a to c; Caure *et al.*, 1998; Woodbury *et al.*, 1999). The early work by Crupps and Howell (1949) concluded that 8 mg copper/kg DM was adequate supplementation for growing foals. These studies were based on weight gain, blood and serum parameters but did not link the occurrence of joint lesions (also noted by Hurtig *et al.*, 1993) and erosions to the low intake of copper (Cymbaluk and Smart, 1993). After re-appraisal of the data, the recommendations for copper supplementation were increased to 10 mg/kg DM for adult horses (NRC 1978).

Nutritional Physiology of the Horse

However, adequate supplementation of copper does not lead to prevention of the joint lesions. This would suggest that induced copper deficiency is unlikely to have a direct causative effect on osteochondrosis and mean intake of copper in feeding systems must be assessed. Furthermore Hurtig and Pool (1996) noted that lesions resulting from copper deficiency were "wholly unlike naturally occurring" lesions on closer examination. Closer examination, however, means euthanasia and dissection of the animal, as radiographic classification of lesions does not suffice and therefore, in many cases, distinction between lesions cannot be made *in vivo* (Ellis, 2001). This may also only be true for lesions resulting primarily from copper deficiency and not for inherent lesions which are probably less likely to recede due to copper unavailability (Table 8.14) (Ellis, 2001).

Copper supplementation

Knight *et al.* (1990) examined the effects of copper supplementation on the occurrence of post mortem cartilage defects in foals at 90 and 180 days of age. The concentrations of copper offered to pregnant (last trimester) mares were 13 mg/kg DM or 32 mg/kg DM and foals received creep feed containing 15 mg/kg DM or 55 mg/kg DM. After 180 days of growth, foals receiving the lowest level of supplementation had more articular and physeal cartilage lesions than other foals supplemented with higher concentrations of copper. The authors attribute the reduction and "near prevention" of lesions in the supplemented group of foals to elevated supplementation of the mare rather than the creep feed as creep feed intake before 60 days post partum was negligible. However, it was not possible to distinguish between the relative influences (Harris *et al.*, 2004).

The supplementation of mares with copper pre-partum led to an increased liver copper status of foals at birth compared to foals from an unsupplemented group (Pearce *et al.*, 1998a, b and c). A lower incidence of articular cartilage lesions in foals born from supplemented mares was observed at the age of 150 days in a post mortem examination and a significant reduction in radiographic physitis scores from supplemented mares' foals was also recorded compared to examination results at 21 days of age. Nevertheless, no relationship between radiographic physitis scores and accumulated concentration of copper in the liver could be established, probably reflecting a 'dilution' of sampling groups to insufficient numbers by further subdivision of treatment groups after birth (Pearce *et al.*, 1998c)

Mineral Nutrition

How effective the reserves of copper in the liver are in preventing osteochondrosis is still unclear. Furthermore the horses in the study by Pearce *et al.* (1998c) had relatively low calcium to phosphorus ratio in the diet (2.5 to 3.8 g calcium/kg DM and 2.3 to 4.3 g phosphorus/kg DM) which may have increased predisposition to bone metabolic dysfunction. Therefore, the copper mobilised from liver stores and/or supplementation may have had a beneficial effect in reducing osteochondrosis. This theory is supported by results of Knaap *et al.* (2000) and Van Weeren *et al.* (2001) who observed that foals with higher concentrations of copper in the liver at birth had increased recession of lesions before reaching the age of eight months. This may indicate that copper supply to the mare during pregnancy increases placental transport of copper and storage in the liver of the foetus and thus may increase the chances for repair of 'naturally occurring' lesions after birth.

Practical implications affecting supplementation of diets

If the voluntary intake of grass is estimated as 10 kg DM (Smolders, 1990) for Warmblood mares, the intake of copper (if herbage contained 10 mg/kg DM) would be about 50% of the recommended requirement. Grazed herbage, however, often contains concentrations of copper lower than 10 mg/kg DM (ranging between 2 and 15 mg/kg DM; Stark, 1988). Foals would also consume considerably less than the recommended levels of copper, although the concentration of copper in the liver may compensate for low dietary intakes. Milk intake ranges from 16 to 20l per day (Frape, 1998, GEH, 1994). However if the average concentration of copper in milk is 0.2mg copper/l from 14 days post partum, a total intake of copper of only 8 to 10 mg/day would be achieved. Adequate liver stores and supplementation via dietary means are therefore essential to maintain intakes of copper adequate for requirement.

There are several reports which recommend higher requirements for pregnant mares and foals than the currently published recommendations of NRC, INRA and GEH. The most recent recommendations from Cymbaluk and Smart (1993) and Suttle *et al.* (1996) suggest that a minimum inclusion rate of 20 mg copper/kg DM for broodmares and youngstock is necessary. Ellis (2001) also made recommendations following an in depth study on current literature (Table 8.15).

In practice many feed manufacturers already produce foal supplements and creep feed which fulfil the higher levels of supplementation.

Nutritional Physiology of the Horse

Table 8.15 Summary of recommended daily copper intake in feed for breedingstock (Ellis, 2001).

Author	Animal	Recommended levels (per kg DM fed) mg/kg DM	500 kg horse 1.6% BW (as DM intake) mg	in mg/kg BW
Cupps and Howell (1949)	Foals	8	64	0.13
NRC (1989)	Pregnant mare + youngstock	10	80	0.16
GEH (1994)	All	10	80	0.16
INRA (1990)	All	10	80	0.16
Gabel et al., (1987)	Foals	20	160	0.32
Cymbaluk and Smart (1993)	Susceptible ponies, draft	20-25 / 10-15	160-200 / 80-120	0.32-0.40 / 0.16-0.24
Suttle et al., (1996)	Mares, foals	20	160	0.32
Pagan et al., (2001)	Mares, 9 months + foals, up to 8 months			0.30 / 0.75-0.40
Ellis (2001)	Mares, pregnant 8 months + foals, up to 8 months			0.40 / 0.32

When considering these supplements, the risk of toxicity need to be taken into account.

Schryver (1990) demonstrated that horses had a much higher tolerance to copper than ruminants as absorption of copper declines rapidly if excess is supplied by feed. Oral supplementation offering 800 mg/kg (about 2 g per day or 0.8 mg/kg BW) for periods of 6 months had no adverse effect in pony yearlings. However an intake of 50 mg/kg BW led to toxicity in adult horses. Parenteral (for instance subcutaneous injections) administration of copper compounds can be very toxic and at supplementation of 4 mg/kg bodyweight can be fatal.

Zinc

Zinc (Zn) is an important trace mineral in mammals and is stored mainly in muscle but is also present in high concentrations in the brain, choroid and iris of the eye, pancreas, and adrenal and prostrate glands. Most of the zinc in circulation (about 80%) is present in erythrocytes. The rest is

Mineral Nutrition

albumin bound, bound to α-2 macroglobin and some to amino acids. Zinc is a component of many enzyme systems (for example carbonic anhydrase, alkaline phosphatases and carboxypeptidases) and other protein structures (for example in transcription activation factors) and therefore zinc is crucial for normal growth and maturation. Zinc also plays an important role in neural activity, especially the metabolic processes associated with synaptic vesicles (Table 8.16). The uptake of zinc is regulated through the intestinal mucosa by processes dependent on intracellular zinc binding proteins. However, these mechanisms are not fully understood. Zinc will interact with many other trace elements, for instance iron and copper (Stark, 1988; Georgievskii, 1982).

Table 8.16 Zinc metabolism in horses.

Metabolic/physiological function	Interactions with other minerals	Effects of shortages (<15ppm)	Effects of excesses (>70ppm)
• Enzyme activity; bone formation • Component of many metalloenzymes involved in protein and carbohydrate metabolism.	• Calcium, copper, molybdenum, sodium, phosphorus, potassium, iron, cobalt, chromium, selenium and tin	• Developmental orthopaedic disease • Reduced feed intake • Reduced growth (weanling <40ppm) • Parakeratosis, hair loss • Impaired reproduction	• Reduced uptake of calcium, anaemia, stiffness and lameness, breaks in the skin around the hooves • Weight loss, enlargement of the epiphysal ends of the long bones, stiffness, lameness, reluctance to bend spine laterally, "hopping" gait, increased amounts of joint fluid • Osteochondrosis

The current recommendations for zinc are in Table 8.17. As with the other trace elements the French system (INRA, 1994) has a higher recommendation than those estimated by the other two systems – both for maintenance and for pregnant mares.

Nutritional Physiology of the Horse

Table 8.17 Estimated requirements for zinc for various classifications of horses (Ellis and Boekhoff, 2003).

	Bodyweight	INRA	GEH	NRC
			mg/kg BW/day	
Maintenance	Small	0.76	0.70	0.63
	Large	0.72	0.58	0.63
Work				
Low	Small	0.89	0.83	0.72
	Large	0.82	0.68	0.72
Medium	Small	1.05	1.13	0.77
	Large	0.94	0.88	0.77
Heavy	Small	1.05	1.33	0.90
	Large	0.94	1.05	0.90
Pregnancy				
7-8 months	Small	0.76		
	Large	0.80		
9 months	Small	0.76	0.93	0.63
	Large	0.80	0.73	0.63
10 months	Small			0.63
	Large			0.63
11 months	Small	0.76		0.63
	Large	0.77		0.63
Lactation				
Month 1	Large	1.17		
Month 2	Large	1.26		
Month 3	Large	1.26		
0-3 month	Small	1.26	1.24	0.90
	Large	1.22	0.99	0.81
3-weaning	Small			0.90
	Large			0.82

Zinc metabolism

Zinc plays an essential role as a co-factor to many enzyme systems during growth and development (Brandao-Neto *et al.*, 1998). Little storage of the mineral occurs in tissue and therefore a reasonably constant supply of zinc is required to maintain sufficiency. Only approximately 8% of total body zinc is stored in the liver (Meyer and Ahlswede, 1976). Deficiencies related to reduced intake of zinc have been linked to inappetence, anorexia, parakeratosis of the lower limbs, alopecia and weight loss (Harrington *et al.*, 1973). In bone development, zinc is essential in calcium uptake by matrix vesicles and is up to 30 to 40% more prevalent than copper at sites of uptake (Sauer *et al.*, 1989) and therefore deficiency can lead to changes in chondrocyte, osteoblast and fibroblast activity and differentiation (Yamaguchi and Takahashi, 1984). In other species zinc deficiency has also been shown to reduce sulphate incorporation into the cartilaginous matrix at the epiphyseal plates leading to inadequate bone calcification (Lema and Sandstead, 1970).

At present there is no reliable indicator of zinc status in horses or other farm animals. In dogs however, low activity of serum alkaline phosphatase has been used as a good indicator of zinc deficiency (Richardson and Zentek, 1998). In general the symptoms of zinc deficiency *per se* in practical management systems differ from those induced under experimental conditions. In many instances zinc deficiency is noted by a reduced rate of growth and primary zinc deficiency is rare in horses offered high forage diets. However, much of the research on zinc has been focussed on its interaction with copper and its attachment to the binding sites on cell membranes leading to secondary copper deficiency (for example Baucus *et al.*, 1987; Spias *et al.*, 1977; Fisher *et al.*, 1983; Pearce *et al.*, 1998b; Knight *et al.*, 1990; Table 8.18).

Table 8.18 Concentration of zinc and copper in various studies examining incidence of zinc deficiency (Ellis, 2001).

Author		Concentration of zinc in diet	Copper retention	Zn:Cu	Daily intake as per experiment or estimated*
Spais *et al.* (1977)	Yearlings, ponies	26 mg/kg DM vs. 126 mg/kg DM	33% 20%	3.25:1 15.75:1	128 mg 604 mg
Graham (1940)	Mares				54 g/day 540 g/day
Pearce *et al.* (1998 c)	Mares, foals to 5 months	Pasture for all: 22 mg/kg DM Pregnant mares + 0.5mg/kg BW/day Control: Treatment:		5-2.5:1 1.5-1.3:1	176 mg* 250 mg* 176 mg 426 mg
Knight *et al.* (1985)	Mares and foals farm survey	40 mg to 140 mg		unknown	320 to 1120 mg
Caure *et al.* (1998)	survey/ experiment			unknown	584 and 632 mg

This was demonstrated in ponies by Spais *et al.* (1977) by showing increased zinc retention through dietary supplementation leading to a decrease in the retention of copper (from 33% to 20%). The interaction between copper and zinc has been studied in mare's milk (Baucus *et al.*, 1987) resulting in data demonstrating no effect of supplemental copper or zinc on the concentrations of either element in serum samples taken from foals or in mares' milk.

Requirements for growth

Several authors report that foals and youngstock managed on grassland contaminated with industrial pollutants (e.g. zinc or cadmium) had an increased prevalence of osteochondrosis as a result of either secondary copper deficiency or by interactions of excess levels of zinc with calcium and other mineral nutrients (Graham *et al.*, 1940; Gunson *et al.*, 1982; Eamens *et al.*, 1984). Kroneman and Goedegebuure (1980) also report one case of osteochondrosis in a foal resulting from the ingestion of grass contaminated with high concentrations of zinc, copper and lead.

Mares' milk contains about 3 mg zinc/l immediately post partum and the concentration slowly declines to about 2 mg/l after 8 to 10 days days (Csapo-Kiss *et al.*, 1995). There are very few reports of zinc deficiency in foals, although in sheep the deficiency has led to abortion and skeletal underdevelopment (Meyer *et al.*, 1997). The concentrations of zinc in the liver remain relatively constant after birth, however considerable variation between foals has been observed (Meyer *et al.*, 1997).

The optimum supplementation of zinc in the diet of horses is not readily determined from the literature and it is essential that the requirements for zinc are reviewed in the near future, especially in light of recent studies examining its role in bone growth and, if excessive, its adverse effect on bone growth (potential inhibition of copper metabolism). A farm survey conducted in the USA on 19 breeding farms (384 yearling foals) suggested that both deficiency and excess can be linked to higher osteochondrosis scores. (Knight *et al.*, 1985). However, the key question that needs to be addressed is whether, if supplementation of copper is increased, it necessary to increase zinc supplementation (Table 8.18).

An experiment in France attempted to balance these ratios, by changing

Mineral Nutrition

the diet of horses managed at two breeding studs (Caure et al., 1998). The ratios of the elements were changed from Zn : Cu of 6.28 to Zn : Cu of 2.99 by increasing daily intake of copper from 93 to 211 mg. A substantial reduction in osteochondrosis scores for horses managed at one of the breeding studs was observed but the general design of the experiment did not allow for firm conclusions to be drawn as there was a lack of controlled conditions at both sites. Nevertheless, it seems that increasing the concentration of zinc in the ration simultaneously with copper is not necessary as long as adequate supplementation of zinc is provided by the diet.

The current recommendations for the ratio of zinc to copper is 5:1 (NRC, 1989; GEH, 1994). When copper intake is increased to latest recommendations (see previous Cu requirements) the ratio would be reduced to 2.5:1. Whether this is adequate and how much zinc is ingested in the practical situation must be assessed (Table 8.19).

Table 8.19 Summary of recommendations for intake of zinc and Zn:Cu ratios in feedstuffs (Ellis, 2001).

Author		Recommended concentration of zinc in feed mg/kg DMI	Zn:Cu	Intake of zinc based on 8 kg DM intake/day mg
NRC (1989)	mare, foal	40	4:1	320
GEH (1994)	adult	50	5:1	400
INRA (1990)	adult	50	5:1	400
Feed Composition		mg/kgDM or l/WM	Zn:Cu	
Milk (Csapo-Kiss et al., 1995)	0-2 days	2.95/l	14.75-1.7	47.2
Milk	3-8 days	2.08/l	10.04	41.6
	8-45 days	1.95/l	6.1	
Pasture – fescue (Pearce et al., 1998)		19-25	2 - 5	200
Italian Ryegrass (INRA, 1990)		32.7	5.7	262
Hay (Pearce et al., 1998)		33	4.2	264
Grass hay – Italian ryegrass (INRA, 1990)		26	5.3	208
Lucerne hay (CVB, 2002)		17	1.7	136
Barley		20	6.6	160
Maize (CVB, 2002)		22		176
Grass (CVB, 2002)		80		

*Dry matter intake

The possibility of deficiency is unlikely on high forage diets or diets including grass. If however the diet contains high levels (greater than 60%) of cereal grains (oats, barley etc.), supplementation is required with a mineral premix. However, analysis of feeds should be conducted before feeding additional zinc as there is considerable variation in the concentration of zinc between forages (24 to 48 mg/kg DM in grass hay) (INRA, 1990).

Manganese

Manganese deficiency has been demonstrated using synthetic diets with laboratory species (for example rats and mice). It is an essential trace mineral that is concentrated primarily in the bone, liver, pancreas, and brain. This mineral is a component of several enzymes, for instance superoxide dismutase (prevention of tissue damage resulting from free radical damage to lipids), pyruvate carboxylase (important in catabolism of carbohydrate) and arginase (important for nitric oxide synthesis and the formation of urea).

Manganese also activates numerous enzymes, particularly glycosyltransferases which are involved in the formation of cartilage in bone and skin (Table 8.20).

Table 8.20 Role and function of manganese in mammalian physiology.

Metabolic/physiological function	Interactions with other minerals	Effects of shortages (<200ppm)	Effects of excesses
• Enzyme activity • Epiphysal cartilage and bone matrix formation • Essential for carbohydrate and protein metabolism, synthesis of chondroitin sulphate (necessary for cartilage formation)	• Calcium • Copper • Phosphorus • Iron • Cobalt • Molybdenum • Sodium • Magnesium	• Enlarged hocks, deformation of legs, lameness and incoordination in young horses, "tiptoeing" of suckling foals • Increased risk of resorption *in utero* or death at birth, irregularity of oestrus cycle in the mare • Brain function > • Glucose intolerance	• No known manganese intoxications in horses • At very high concentrations interference with phosphorus uptake • Rachitic changes reported in rats when low levels of manganese are offered in combination with low levels of phosphorus

In animals, manganese deficiencies produce abnormalities in brain function, impaired glucose tolerance, impaired reproduction (possible evidence of intrauterine malformation), and skeletal and cartilage formation. Concentrations in body tissues are extremely low and only a small amount

Mineral Nutrition

is absorbed through the intestine. Excess manganese is eliminated through the bile and there appears to be an efficient blood/brain barrier to the passage of this element.

Manganese can interact with iron in the digestive tract, preventing the absorption of iron, leading to anaemia (GEH, 1994). There is no recent research concerned with the supplementation of horses with manganese. Current recommendations are based on experimental data from other mammals (Schwarz and Kirchgessner, 1979) and therefore very little variation between systems is noted (Table 8.21).

Table 8.21 Manganese requirements for horses (data converted by Ellis and Boekhoff, 2003).

	Body weight	INRA	GEH	NRC	INRA	GEH	NRC
		mg/kg BW/day			for small: 300kg horse for large: 600kg horse in g/day		
Maintenance	Small	0.61	0.56	0.63	0.18	0.17	0.19
	Large	0.57	0.46	0.63	0.34	0.28	0.38
Work							
Low	Small	0.72	0.66	0.72	0.21	0.20	0.22
	Large	0.65	0.54	0.72	0.39	0.32	0.43
Medium	Small	0.84	0.90	0.77	0.25	0.27	0.23
	Large	0.75	0.70	0.77	0.45	0.42	0.46
Heavy	Small	0.84	1.06	0.90	0.25	0.32	0.27
	Large	0.75	0.84	0.90	0.45	0.50	0.54
Pregnancy							
7-8 months	Small	0.61			0.18		
	Large	0.64			0.38		
9 months	Small	0.61	0.74	0.63	0.18	0.22	0.19
	Large	0.64	0.58	0.63	0.38	0.35	0.38
10 months	Small			0.63			0.19
	Large			0.63			0.38
11 months	Small	0.61		0.63	0.18		0.19
	Large	0.62		0.63	0.37		0.38
Lactation							
Month 1	Large	0.94			0.56		
Month 2	Large	1.01			0.61		
Month 3	Large	1.01			0.61		
0-3 month	Small	1.01	0.99	0.90	0.30	0.30	0.27
	Large	0.97	0.79	0.81	0.58	0.47	0.49
3-weaning	Small			0.90			0.27
	Large			0.81			0.49

Manganese is required as a cofactor for enzymes essential for energy metabolism of chondrocytes, within the epiphyseal plate. It also is required for proteoglycan synthesis, such as glycosaminoglycan, chondroitin sulphate (Yang and Klimis-Tavantzis, 1998). Enlarged hocks caused by physitis, some lameness and imbalance in gait have been reported as symptoms of deficiency (Cowgill *et al.*, 1980; Frape, 1998).

In calves, manganese deficiency can result in similar disorders as well as musculo-skeletal problems (Hidiroglou *et al.*, 1990). Little storage of manganese occurs in body tissues. Spias *et al.* (1977) demonstrated that supplementation of the diet with manganese could increase the mean retention of manganese from 11 % to 21%. If however diets are offered that contain excessive concentrations of manganese, excretion of absorbed manganese can occur back across the intestinal mucosa (Grace, 1983). Further iron uptake will be inhibited.

The current recommendations for daily intake of manganese are 40 mg/kg DM for adult horses and 50 mg/kg DM for breedingstock (NRC, 1989; GEH, 1994). In general the concentrations of manganese in forage are adequate to fulfil the daily requirements.

Molybdenum

Molybdenum is an essential trace element required in the formation of molybdopterin, a cofactor essential to the function of the xanthine oxidase, sulphite oxidase and aldehyde oxidase. Primary molybdenum deficiency has been demonstrated in laboratory animals, but not in commercial livestock. The majority of studies considering the role of molybdenum have been focussed on its role in copper metabolism. The concentration of molybdenum in tissue is very low, but the highest concentrations are in the liver, kidney, adrenal gland and bone. In general molybdenum occurs in dietary sources as either the soluble hexavalent form (readily absorbed) or the insoluble form associated with calcium and magnesium (Table 8.22).

There are no requirements currently published for horses and little research has been conducted to rectify the situation. The only reports on molybdenum reflect its role in copper metabolism and its possible competition with copper (at the lysyl oxidase copper binding site) in bone metabolism increasing risk of developmental orthopaedic disease in foals (Osman and Sykes, 1990).

Mineral Nutrition

Table 8.22 Role of molybdenum in horse nutrition.

Metabolic/physio-logical function	Interactions with other minerals	Effects of shortages	Effects of excesses (if Cu:Mo=1:8)
• Co-factor in several oxidase enzymes, involved in purine metabolism	• Copper, zinc, manganese, phosphorus, iodine, sulphur	• Not reported	• Excess may cause secondary copper deficiency

Iron

Almost all the iron in the body of the horse is associated with proteins. The distribution of iron in the body is approximately 60% in haemoglobin, 20% in myoglobin, 20% in transport and storage proteins and about 0.2% in cytochrome and other iron requiring enzymes.

Iron metabolism

The key function of iron is its role in oxygen transport and cellular respiration through the protein haemoglobin. Haem biosynthesis is essential for the synthesis of haemoglobin. The first reaction in haem biosynthesis takes place in the mitochondria and involves the condensation of glycine and succinyl CoA by the pyridoxal phosphate-containing enzyme δ-aminolaevulinic acid synthase (ALA synthase). This reaction is the rate-limiting and the regulatory reaction of haem biosynthesis. Mitochondrial δ-aminolaevulinic acid (ALA) is transported to the cytosol where ALA dehydratase (porphobilinogen synthase or hydroxymethylbilane synthase) forms a dimer of ALA to produce the pyrrole ring compound porphobilinogen. Four molecules of porphobilinogen are joined using a head-tail condensation reaction (activated by porphobilinogen deaminase (PBG deaminase or uroporphyrinogen I synthase)) to produce the linear tetrapyrrole intermediate hydroxymethylbilane. Hydroxymethylbilane is converted to uroporphyrinogen III by the holoenzyme uroporphyrinogen synthase and the protein uroporphyrinogen III cosynthase. In the cytosol, acetate substitution of uroporphyrinogen III are decarboxylated (uroporphyrinogen decarboxylase) and the products are methylated to form coproporphyrinogens (of which coproporphyrinogen III is the important intermediate in haem synthesis). Coproporphyrinogen III is transported to the interior of mitochondria where two propionate residues are decarboxylated yielding the vinyl substitution groups on the two pyrrole rings. This colourless product (protoporphyrinogen IX) is converted to protoporphyrin IX by protoporphyrinogen IX oxidase. The oxidase reaction requires molecular oxygen and results in the loss of 6 protons and 6 electrons but yields the complete conjugated ring system characteristic to haem. The final reaction in haem synthesis takes place in the mitochondria and involves the insertion of the iron atom (by ferrochelatase) into the ring system generating haem ß.

Myoglobin and haemoglobin are haemproteins whose principal role is to bind molecular oxygen. Myoglobin is the monomeric haem protein in muscle tissue where it acts as an intracellular storage site for oxygen. During periods of oxygen deprivation oxymyoglobin releases its bound oxygen.

The oxygen is bound directly to the ferrous iron atom of the haem prosthetic group. Oxidation of the iron II to iron III renders the molecule incapable of oxygen binding. Further, a nitrogen atom (derived from histidine) is located above the plane of the haem ring, stabilising the interaction between the haem and the protein. In oxymyoglobin the remaining site on the iron atom is occupied by oxygen, and stabilised by histidine.

Haemoglobin is an [α(2):ß(2)] tetrameric haemprotein. It is found in erythrocytes where it is responsible for binding and transporting oxygen. Each subunit of a haemoglobin tetramer has a haem prosthetic group identical to myoglobin. Four peptide subunits (designated α, ß, γ and δ) are arranged in the functional haemoglobins in a unique fashion. The properties of haemoglobin resulting from the quaternary structure differentiate the oxygen binding properties of haemoglobin from myoglobin.

The curve of oxygen binding to haemoglobin is sigmoidal (typical of allosteric proteins). When oxygen binds to the first subunit of deoxyhaemoglobin the binding increases the affinity of the remaining subunits for oxygen. As additional oxygen is bound to the second and third subunits oxygen binding is strengthened, fully saturating haemoglobin with oxygen. As oxyhaemoglobin circulates to deoxygenated tissue, oxygen is unloaded and the affinity of haemoglobin for oxygen is reduced. Therefore at low oxygen tensions the binding affinity of haemoglobin for oxygen is very low allowing maximum delivery of oxygen to the tissue. In contrast the oxygen binding curve for myoglobin is hyperbolic indicating the absence of allosteric interactions. In addition to transporting oxygen from lungs to peripheral tissues, haemoglobin molecules transport carbon dioxide in the opposite direction. N-terminal amino groups of haemoglobin are available to react with carbon dioxide and about 15% of the carbon dioxide formed in tissues is carried to the lung covalently bound to the N-terminal nitrogens as the carbamate:

$$CO_2 + Hb\text{-}NH_2 \longleftrightarrow H^+ + Hb\text{-}NH\text{-}COO^-$$

In conditions of high oxygen partial pressure the reverse reaction occurs and carbon dioxide is released and exhaled.

The main transport protein of iron is transferrin, synthesised in the liver at a rate inversely proportional to body stores. Transferrin can bind two molecules of iron and is normally about one third saturated. Ferritin is an iron-storage protein found in most cells of the body, particularly the liver, and which provides a readily available reserve. Haemosiderin is an insoluble aggregate of ferritin deposited in many tissues from which iron is less readily available. Iron loss via the usual excretory routes is minute and apart from loss of blood, desquamation of intestinal and other cells is the only means of depletion. Serum ferritin concentration of supplemented horses ranges from 70 to 250 ng/ml (mean of 152 ng/ml) under normal dietary conditions (Smith et al., 1984).

The recommended daily intake of iron for horses is not based on studies with exercising horses, and extrapolation of studies from human athletes have been used to ensure adequate iron supply for equines (Tables 8.23 and 8.24). In humans during prolonged intense training iron losses may increase to 2 mg/day, which translated to the body weight of the horse would be equivalent to 15 mg/day for a 500 kg horse (or 0.03 mg/kg BW). Current increments of iron recommended for light work are more than adequate for the calculated depletion (Table 8.24). However, iron losses during training have never been measured in horses (Lawrence, 1994). The concentration of iron in mare's milk varies from early lactation (1.3 mg/l) to mid and late lactation (approximately 0.5 mg/l; Ullrey et al., 1974).

There are some slight differences in the recommendations for iron. The French system (INRA, 1990) suggests 80-100 mg/kg DM intake is sufficient, while the German system recommends only 60-80 mg/kg DM intake. The lowest recommendations are provided by NRC (1989) system at 40-50 mg/kg DM intake. These differences remain when converting to mg/kg BW. In general the requirement for iron is exceeded by the concentration in the diet. However, the apparent absorption will vary depending on the bioavailability of iron in the feed. High supplementation (500 to 1000

Nutritional Physiology of the Horse

Table 8.23. Role of iron in horse nutrition.

Metabolic/physio-logical function	Interactions with other minerals	Effects of shortages	Effects of excesses (rarely dietary)
• Haemoglobin formation, (support of oxygen carrying capacity of blood) essential constitute of molecules • Oxygen transport and use (part of blood haemoglobin and muscle myo-globin and cellular respiration)	• Copper, manganese, zinc, cadmium, cobalt, sulphur	• Anaemia, Iron deficiencies seldom occur, possibly in high performance horses leading to reduced performance	• Ingestion of a single large dose of ferrous fumarate causes death in newborn foals • Iron in excess depresses serum and liver zinc; reduced bacterial resistance • Chronic excess of iron results in reduced growth, impaired trace mineral metabolism, hepatic failure, liver necrosis • (ferrous iron relative less toxic than ferric iron)

Table 8.24 Recommendations for requirements of iron for horses (data converted by Ellis and Boekhoff, 2003).

	Body weight	INRA	GEH mg/kg BW/day	NRC
Maintenance	Small	1.37	0.98	0.63
	Large	1.29	0.81	0.63
Work				
Low	Small	1.61	1.16	0.72
	Large	1.47	0.95	0.72
Medium	Small	1.90	1.69	0.77
	Large	1.69	1.31	0.77
Heavy	Small	1.90	2.12	0.90
	Large	1.69	1.68	0.90
Pregnancy				
7-8 months	Small	1.37		
	Large	1.43		
9 months	Small	1.37	1.48	0.79
	Large	1.43	1.16	0.79
10 months	Small			0.79
	Large			0.79
11 months	Small	1.37		0.79
	Large	1.39		0.79
Lactation				
Month 1	Large	2.11		
Month 2	Large	2.27		
Month 3	Large	2.27		
0-3 month	Small	2.28	1.98	1.13
	Large	2.19	1.58	1.01
3-weaning	Small			1.13
	Large			1.01

mg/kg DM or up to 8 times the requirement) has been demonstrated to have no adverse effect on feed intake, daily gain, red blood cell count, concentration of haemoglobin and concentrations of calcium, iron, copper and manganese in the serum (Lawrence, 1986; Lawrence et al., 1987). However, excess iron supplementation can lead to death among foals and mature horses (Mullaney and Brown, 1988; Arnbjerg, 1981).

Iodine

Iodine is an important component of hormones secreted by the thyroid gland. Iodine conjugates with thyronine to form monoiodothyronine and diiodithyronine and is therefore part of triiodothyronine (T3), thyroxine (T4), and thyroglobulin (the storage form of thyroid hormones). The hormones T3 and T4 are controlled by the thyroid, pituitary, brain and various feedback signals from peripheral tissues (for example the extent of low density lipoprotein). The role of T3 and T4 are to influence the rates of oxidation of energy substrates in cells (Hetzel and Maberly, 1986).

Secretion of thyroid stimulating hormone (TSH) is stimulated by thyroid releasing hormone. Cyclic AMP increases the secretion of TSH by thyrotropes but it is not clear if cAMP is the signal that regulates TSH production. However circulating TSH binds to receptors on the basal membrane of thyroid follicles. The receptors are coupled through a G-protein to adenylate cyclase. The result of binding increases the secretion of thyroxin (T4) and triiodothyronine (T3) and chronic stimulation of the receptor leads to an increase in the synthesis of thyroglobulin. Thyroglobulin produced on rough endoplasmic reticulum contains more than 100 tyrosine residues which become iodinated and are used in the synthesis of T3 and T4. A Na^+/K^+-ATPase-driven pump concentrates iodide in thyroid cells and the iodide is transported to the follicle lumen where it is oxidised by thyroperoxidase. The addition of iodine to tyrosine residues of thyroglobulin is catalysed by the same enzyme producing monoiodotyrosyl and diiodotyrosyl residues. The main role of thyroid hormones is similar to steroid hormones, by binding to hormone response elements in nuclear DNA and up-regulating protein synthesis inducing a positive nitrogen balance (Tables 8.25 and 8.26).

Dietary iodine is absorbed in the small intestine with about 30% of absorbed iodine taken up by the thyroid gland. The remaining iodine is excreted in urine, faeces and sweat. Deficiency of iodine causes

Table 8.25 Role and function of iodine in metabolism.

Metabolic/physiological function	Interactions with other minerals	Effects of shortages (<0.01 mg/kg DM)	Effects of excesses (>5 mg/kg DM or 0.08 mg/kg BW)
• Synthesis of thyroid hormones: thyroxin, function of thyroid gland	• Copper, phosphorus, cobalt, chloride, molybdenum, calcium, fluorine	• Different pathological symptoms: • Foals of iodine deficient mares show enlargement and malfunctioning of thyroid gland (goitre) and other pathological signs, most often in new born • Stillborn or weak foals, DOD • Hyperthyroidism, goitre, rough hair, hair loss	• Iodine in excess is toxic, results in similar symptoms as deficiencies • Goitre in newborn foals

Table 8.26 Iodine requirements for horses (Ellis and Boekhoff, 2003).

	Bodyweight	INRA	GEH $\mu g/kg\ BW/day$	NRC
Maintenance	Small	3.04	2.10	1.58
	Large	2.87	1.73	1.58
Work				
Low	Small	3.58	2.48	1.80
	Large	3.27	2.03	1.80
Medium	Small	4.21	4.50	1.94
	Large	3.75	3.50	1.94
Heavy	Small	4.21	5.30	2.25
	Large	3.75	4.20	2.25
Pregnancy				
7-8 months	Small	3.04		
	Large	3.19		
9 months	Small	3.04	3.70	1.58
	Large	3.19	2.90	1.58
10 months	Small			1.58
	Large			1.58
11 months	Small	3.04		1.58
	Large	3.09		1.58
Lactation				
Month 1	Large	4.69		
Month 2	Large	5.05		
Month 3	Large	5.05		
0-3 month	Small	5.06	4.95	2.25
	Large	4.86	3.95	2.03
3-weaning	Small			2.25
	Large			2.03

hypothyroidism or goitre in mammals. The deficiency is characterised by an enlarged thyroid gland, stillbirths and abortions, prolonged gestation, abnormal oestrus, congenital malformations, stunted growth, skin problems, reduced metabolic rate and increased mortality (Driscoll et al., 1978; Kruzhova, 1968). Foals born from iodine deficient mares generally have a prominent enlargement over the anterior segment of the trachea. Effective therapy for this condition is difficult to achieve. Supplementation of mares during the last trimester of pregnancy is successful in prevention of hyperplasia of the thyroid (Rodenwald and Simms, 1935).

A form of hypothyroidism has been associated with selenium deficiency. Deiodinase (the enzyme that converts T4 to T3) contains selenium and induced hypothyroidism is observed by increased concentrations of T4 and decreased concentrations of T3 in the plasma. Iodine toxicity was characterised in horses by Drew et al. (1975) who observed that when pregnant mares received approximately 40 mg iodine per day, foals were born with enlarged thyroid glands and goitre. If this occurs, an alternative supply of milk is required to reduce the intake of iodine by the foal (Brown-Grant, 1957). Other symptoms of toxicity have been noted as iatrogenic iodinism and associated alopecis (Fadok and Wild, 1983).

Fluorine

The amount of fluoride in the body does not appear to be regulated and therefore concentrations in plasma reflect dietary intake, rate of excretion and turnover of bone. Fluorine is often included in formulation as an essential trace element, but there is little or no evidence for fluorine deficiency in horses or other animals. However, fluorine toxicity can be a considerable problem in animal management and horses tend to be more tolerant to excess fluorine in the diet than ruminants. The physiological properties of fluoride depend on it being present as an anion in circulation and therefore its tendency to form insoluble calcium fluoride can lead to a dramatic reduction in concentration of both calcium and magnesium in circulation. Excessive intakes of fluorine can lead to discolouration of teeth (fluorosis), lesions and sclerosis of bones (dysfunction in osteoblast metabolism) and ligament damage. There are no current recommendations for dietary supplementation for fluoride (Table 8.27). Fluorine plays a role in the formation of hydroxyapatite crystals in bone matrix and is reported to alter metabolism in the osteoblast (Frape, 1998). 'Splayed leg syndrome' and osteochondrosis have been reported in rabbits and dogs with excessive dietary intakes of fluorine (Santos *et al.*, 1994; Hedhammer *et al.*, 1974) and there may be limited evidence that fluorosis could occur in horses grazing contaminated pastures (Shupe and Olson, 1971).

Table 8.27 Role and function of fluorine in metabolism

Metabolic/physiological function	Interactions with other minerals	Effects of shortages	Effects of excesses (>50ppm or in water >8ppm)
• Incorporated in teeth and bone as fluorapatite, increases crystalinity and hardness • Formation of hydroxyapatite crystals decreases solubility	• Often comes as 'by-product' of P-supplements from rock phosphate • Magnesium, iodine and calcium	• Never reported, no evidence for benefit of fluorine for horses	• Teeth grow too slowly, mottled and pitted teeth, reduced feed and water intake • Chronic debilitation, stiffness, lameness • Abnormally increased bone density • rough, dry hair coat, failure to fully shed winter coat in spring; thickened, taut, less pliable skin; dental lesions during dental growth • Periosteal hyperostosis at tendon and ligament insertions of limb bones, skull, ribs

Selenium

Selenium is recognised as an essential trace element in animal nutrition. Selenium is present at the active site of two enzymes; glutathione peroxidase and phospholipid-hydroperoxide glutathione peroxidase which are found as distinct compartments intracellular and extracellular. The enzymes catalyse the destruction of hydrogen peroxide and organic hydroperoxides.

Mineral Nutrition

Selenium plays an important role with vitamin E and superoxide dismutase as part of the array of defence mechanism to prevent oxidative stress in the cell. Type 1 iodothyronine 5'-deiodinase, present mainly in liver and kidney, mediates conversion of thyroxine (T4) to 3,3" triiodothyronine (T3) and is effected by the supply of selenium to the cellular system. Selenium is generally bound in an amino acid form in circulation either as selenomethionine or selenocysteine. These selenoamino acids are analogues of the sulphur rich amino acids methionine and cysteine respectively and therefore can compete in protein synthesis. An additional extracellular Se-containing protein, selenoprotein-P, accounts for approximately 50% of human plasma selenium; its function is unknown (Table 8.28).

Table 8.28 Role of selenium in animal nutrition.

Metabolic/physio-logical function	Interactions with other minerals	Effects of shortages (<0.05ppm; if vitamin E deficient)	Effects of excesses (>52-5 ppm)
• Protecting body tissue (cell membranes, enzymes, other intracellular substances) against oxidation induced damage by detoxification of peroxides in extra cellular fluid, enzyme systems (glutathione peroxidase) • Support of muscle function and function of vitamin E	• Vitamin E and selenium jointly function in protection of body tissue • Sulphur, copper, zinc	• Reduced immunity, reduced growth, stiffness of limbs, listlessness, difficult nursing in foals, dyspnoea, lung oedema, increased salivation, white muscle disease • Combined selenium and vitamin E deficiency: progressive emaciation, painful subcutaneous swelling (steatitis), rough hair coat, ventral subcutaneous oedema, yellow, gritty fat, "wobbler syndrome" (equine degenerative myeloencephalopathy, degeneration of brain stem and spinal cord), stiff gait • Deficiencies seldom occur	• Selenium in excess has toxic effects • "Blind Stagger" syndrome, weight loss, listlessness, anaemia, hair of mane or tail rough and loose, fluid faeces, stiffness, painful feet, abnormal hoof growth and rings; respiratory distress, diarrhoea, prostration, death (3.3 g selenium per kg BW is lethal) • Sub acute poisoning results in alkali disease (emaciated, swollen, tender coronary band of the hoof, separation of integument from coronary band, loss of mane and tail hair

Selenium deprivation normally reduces the activity of the selenium-dependent enzymes for instance a reduction in glutathione peroxidase activity to lower than 25 enzyme units (EU)/dl and serum selenium concentrations of less than 60 ng/ml (Caple *et al.*, 1978; Gallagher and Stowe, 1980; Maylin *et al.*, 1980; Roneus and Lindholm, 1983). The clinical and morphological signs of selenium deficiency in animals depend on the vitamin E status of the animal and normally appear only when both nutrients are limiting. The symptoms vary according to species; for example, selenium and vitamin E deficient animals have symptoms of myopathy affecting the skeleton (sheep, cow and horse), cardiac muscle (pig) or smooth muscle (dog and cow) (Meyer *et al.*, 1995). The myopathies will affect locomotion, lead to respiratory distress and impaired cardiac function and therefore selenium has been highlighted as an important potential supplement for performance horses.

In each country areas of 'lower than normal' and 'higher than normal' concentrations of selenium have been identified and related to soil chemical characteristics. Sandy, peaty areas generally have low concentrations of selenium, while areas of marine and river silt (clay) provide adequate to high levels of selenium to grassland.

Horses grazing grassland and forage in Northern Germany (particularly on moorland and sandy soils) are likely to suffer from selenium deficiency and supplements are added to commercial feeds on a regular basis (Meyer *et al.*, 1995). However this practice has also led to some reported cases of toxicity due to errors in feeding and formulation of feeds (Coenen *et al.*, 1998).

The recommendations by the NRC (1989) are 0.1mg/kg DM for all horses while INRA (1990) recommend 0.1 to 0.2 mg/kg DM. The GEH (1994) recommends 0.15 to 0.2 mg/kg DM and a maximum concentration of 2 mg/kg DM should not be exceeded (Schryver 1990). There is still some controversy over the level of selenium that should be offered in the diets of horses. For instance there is concern that the apparent absorption of 77% suggested by NRC (1989) is an overestimate and may not reflect the processes in the horse (Ullrey, 1992; Hintz, 1999). For comparison, the apparent absorption of selenium by ruminants is about 30% (Stark, 1988). In contrast to these opinions, Wichert *et al.* (2002) reported that in practice many horses may have very low intakes of zinc and selenium, but few show clinical signs of deficiency. These authors suggest that as long as there is adequate vitamin E supplementation, the non pregnant adult horse managed at light working levels is unlikely to suffer from selenium deficiency (Table 8.29).

Table 8.29 Selenium requirements for horses

	Body weight	INRA	GEH	NRC
			µg/kg BW/day	
Maintenance	Small	2.28	2.45	1.58
	Large	2.15	2.01	1.58
Work				
Low	Small	2.68	2.89	1.80
	Large	2.46	2.36	1.80
Medium	Small	3.16	4.50	1.94
	Large	2.81	3.50	1.94
Heavy	Small	3.16	5.30	2.25
	Large	2.81	4.20	2.25
Pregnancy				
7-8 months	Small	2.28		
	Large	2.39		
9 months	Small	2.28	3.70	1.58
	Large	2.39	2.90	1.58
10 months	Small			1.58
	Large			1.58
11 months	Small	2.28		1.58
	Large	2.32		1.58
Lactation				
Month 1	Large	3.52		
Month 2	Large	3.79		
Month 3	Large	3.79		
0-3 month	Small	3.79	4.95	2.25
	Large	3.65	3.95	2.03
3-weaning	Small			2.25
	Large			2.03

Cobalt

The only role of cobalt in animal nutrition is as a cofactor to vitamin B_{12} and it is therefore an essential compound for energy and nitrogen metabolism. The cobalt requirements for the horse have not been studied but cobalt is required by the microflora in the hindgut in the synthesis of vitamin B_{12} (Saliminen, 1975; Clark and Miller, 1983). The GEH (1994) system suggests that the requirements for cobalt will always be fulfilled under feed or grazing management systems and that no reports of effects of over or undersupply symptoms exist in horses. Furthermore horses will maintain good health when grazing pastures that provide an inadequate supply of cobalt for sheep (Filmer, 1933). Diagnosis of potential cobalt deficiency is difficult in all animals as it manifests itself as a loss of appetite (Table 8.30).

Table 8.30 Recommended requirements for cobalt (Ellis and Boekhoff, 2003).

	Body weight	INRA	GEH µg/kg BW/day	NRC
Maintenance	Small	3.04	1.12	1.58
	Large	2.87	0.92	1.58
Work				
Low	Small	3.58	1.32	1.80
	Large	3.27	1.08	1.80
Medium	Small	4.21	1.80	1.94
	Large	3.75	1.40	1.94
Heavy	Small	4.21	2.65	2.25
	Large	3.75	2.10	2.25
Pregnancy				
7-8 months	Small	3.04		
	Large	3.19		
9 months	Small	3.04	1.85	1.58
	Large	3.19	1.45	1.58
10 months	Small			1.58
	Large			1.58
11 months	Small	3.04		1.58
	Large	3.09		1.58
Lactation				
Month 1	Large	4.69		
Month 2	Large	5.05		
Month 3	Large	5.05		
0-3 month	Small	5.06	2.48	2.25
	Large	4.86	1.98	2.03
3-weaning	Small			2.25
	Large			2.03

Chromium

Chromium is recognised as an essential nutrient involved in glucose metabolism (NRC, 1997). Chromium functions primarily by potentiating the action of insulin via glucose tolerance factor. There is considerable evidence that supplementation of chromium can influence carbohydrate metabolism in growing pigs by affecting glucose, insulin and lipid metabolism (Anderson *et al.*, 1997, Kornegay *et al.*, 1997). Insulin seems to become 'more effective' and therefore less is needed, avoiding

Mineral Nutrition

a reduction in thyroxine. Anderson *et al.* (1997) also report of an influence of chromium picolinate on nitrogen absorption leading to increases in protein metabolism (Lukaski, 1999). Among the many symptoms of chromium deficiency in mammals are impaired glucose tolerance, elevated concentrations of insulin in circulation and impaired growth.

Currently no daily requirements are published for horses. Ott and Kivipelto (1999) assessed the effect of chromium tripicolinate on growth and glucose metabolism in yearling horses. As with other mammals, they found that in supplemented yearlings, the concentration of glucose in plasma decreased more rapidly following a glucose challenge than in non-supplemented animals. This may mean that chromium supplementation is useful in rapidly growing foals ingesting excessive levels of carbohydrate in their diets. Pagan *et al.* (1995) also report that in working thoroughbreds, supplementation with yeast cultures containing high concentrations of chromium reduced the response to insulin and reduced lactic acid accumulation during a set exercise test.

9
Vitamins

Research concerning the role and function of vitamins in horses is relatively limited as experiments are difficult to conduct and do not always provide definitive results on sufficiency, deficiency and toxicity. Vitamins are organic compounds that are required in very low concentrations to promote and regulate many biological processes in the animal (Lewis, 1995). The requirements for vitamins are affected by age of animal, physiological state, exercise regime and health status. They are classified into two broad classes; the fat-soluble vitamins and the water-soluble vitamins. This classification reflects the properties of the vitamins, in the way they are absorbed, stored and excreted. The fat-soluble vitamins include vitamin A (and associated carotene compounds), vitamin D, E and K. The water-soluble vitamins are the B complex, pantothenic acid, biotin, folacin (or folic acid), vitamin C and choline. Formulation of diets for vitamins is complex and has its own nomenclature. For instance the use of international units (IU, also known as USP) can lead to interpretational errors when examining feed tables and requirements.

Fat-soluble vitamins

Vitamin A

There are over 600 different carotenoid type compounds in nature. Carotenoids are characterised by being a conjugated polyene structure which is efficient at absorbing light. The main colours of carotenoid compounds are yellow or red pigments and are responsible for the colour in fruits and vegetables (Ross, 1999). The term "carotene" refers to carotenoids which contain only carbon and hydrogen (*e.g.* ß-carotene), however "xanthophylls" are related compounds that contain hydroxyl groups (*e.g.* lutein and zeaxanthin) or keto groups (canthaxanthin) or both (astaxanthin; the colour in lobsters). As vitamin A is fat soluble, it is accreted in fatty tissues and the concentration is directly related to dietary intake.

Vitamin A complex consists of three biologically active molecules retinol, retinal (retinaldehyde) and retinoic acid. The horse is not able to synthesise vitamin A and therefore they have to be supplied entirely from dietary sources. Each of the three biologically active molecules is derived from the plant precursor ß-carotene. ß-carotene from the diet is converted in the small intestine by ß-carotene 15, 15' dioxygenase to yield retinal and the retinal is subsequently reduced to retinol by retinaldehyde reductase (an NADPH requiring reductase). This process is variable in mammals, with some species having a very efficient conversion (for instance chicks and rats) whereas the horse is relatively inefficient and cats do not possess any ability to convert ß-carotene to vitamin A (Ross, 1999; Lewis, 1995; Fonnesbeck and Symons, 1967). Furthermore, the uptake of vitamin A is affected by the fat content of the diet. Diets with very low concentrations of fat have a lower concentration of vitamin A and a lower efficiency of uptake by the horse (Lewis, 1995). The retinol produced is esterified to palmitic acid and delivered to the blood via chylomicrons (Britton, 1995). Transport of retinol from the liver to extrahepatic tissues occurs by binding of hydrolysed retinol to apo-retinol binding protein and the retinol protein complex is then transported to the cell surface, packaged and secreted. Plasma transport of retinoic acid is accomplished by binding to albumin. The process of cleaving of ß-carotene is not 100% efficient and some is bound to high-density lipoproteins and transported to various tissues (e.g. ovary, sub-cutaneous fat in the skin) where it plays a role as an antioxidant (Krinsky, 1993). The major storage site of vitamin A in the body is in the liver, primarily in the form of retinyl esters.

One of the major roles of vitamin A in animal nutrition is the utilisation of vitamin A metabolites in the retina. Photoreception in the eye is the response to light by rod and cone cells. Both rod and cone cells contain photoreceptor compounds; a protein opsin in cone cells and scotopsin in rod cells and a metabolite of vitamin A. The photoreceptor of rod cells is known as rhodopsin or "visual purple". Rhodopsin is a complex between scotopsin and 11-cis-retinal and is coupled to the G-protein complex transducin. When the rhodopsin is exposed to light it releases of 11-cis-retinal from the protein moiety opsin. The release of opsin results in a conformational change in the photoreceptor and activation of the transducin thus increasing GTP-binding by the α-subunit of transducin. This activation is required to maintain open conformation of sodium channels in the rod cells. Closure of the channels leads to hyperpolarisation of the rod cell and the propagation of nerve impulses to the brain and the basis of sight (Sporn, 1994).

The characteristic symptoms of deficiency of vitamin A in the horse are anorexia, sublingual salivary gland abscesses, a higher incidence of respiratory and intestinal disease or dysfunction, low rate of growth, weight loss, sub fertility (loss of libido and reduced semen production in stallions; Ralston et al., 1985, and reduced ovarian activity; Ahlswede and Konermann, 1980), dull hair, anaemia, tearing and night blindness (Stowe, 1968; Donoghue et al., 1981). Night blindness is one of the early signs of vitamin A deficiency. The classical symptom of vitamin A deficiency in horses is hyperkeratinisation of the cornea leading to clouding. Furthermore, bacterial infections and permanent scarring of the cornea can occur (xerophthalmia) as a result of a lack of vitamin A required for control of gene expression. Vitamin A deficiency of horses has not been implicated with skeletal problems (Hintz, 1986). Toxicity caused by excessive intakes of vitamin A is relatively rare in horses (Jarrett et al., 1987). Prolonged feeding (40, 000 IU/kg BW/day or 12 mg/kg BW) has been potentially linked to bone fragility, hyperostosis, exfoliation of the epidermis, teratogenesis and increased blood clotting time (Donoghue et al., 1981). The recommended daily requirement for vitamin A according to NRC (1989) ranged from 30 to 60 IU/kg BW (9 to 18 µg/kg BW) as retinol. If however the calculations are made on the basis of dietary ß-carotene, 120 to 240 IU/kg BW (72 to 144 µg/kg BW) of provitamin A is required.

Vitamin D

Vitamin D is a steroid hormone that regulates specific gene expression following interaction with its intracellular receptor. The biologically active form of the hormone is 1,25-dihydroxy vitamin D_3 (calcitriol). Calcitriol regulates calcium and phosphorus homeostasis (see Chapter 8). Active calcitriol is derived from ergosterol (produced in plants) and from 7-dehydrocholesterol (produced in the skin). Ergocalciferol (vitamin D_2) is formed by UV irradiation of ergosterol and in the skin 7-dehydrocholesterol is converted to cholecalciferol (vitamin D_3) following

UV irradiation (NRC, 1989). Vitamin D_2 and D_3 are processed to D_2-calcitriol and D_3-calcitriol by the same enzymatic pathways in mammals. Cholecalciferol (or egrocalciferol) are absorbed from the small intestine and transported to the liver bound to a specific vitamin D-binding protein. In the liver cholecalciferol is hydroxylated at the 25 position by a specific D_3-25-hydroxylase generating 25-hydroxy-D_3 [25-(OH)D_3]. Conversion of 25-(OH) D_3 to its biologically active form calcitriol occurs through the activity of a specific D_3-1-hydroxylase present in the proximal convoluted tubules of the kidneys, the bone and the placenta. Furthermore 25-(OH) D_3 can be hydroxylated at the 24 position by a specific D_3-24-hydroxylase in the kidneys, intestine, placenta and cartilage (Holick, 1994).

The major symptoms of vitamin D deficiency are decreased feed intake, reduced rate of growth, enlarged physis, bone demineralisation and very rarely rickets and osteomalacia (NRC, 1989). The level of supplementation for horses has however not been calculated (NRC, 1989). The deficiencies in vitamin D, if they are likely to occur, result from a lack of UV radiation and animals housed outside for any period or on a standard diet are unlikely to suffer deficiency (El Shorafa et al., 1979; Nieberle and Chors, 1954). Rickets is characterised by a dysfunction in the mineralisation of the bone during the development resulting in "soft" bones. Osteomalacia is characterised by demineralisation of previously formed bone leading to increased softness and susceptibility to fracture. Vitamin D_3 (cholecalciferol) and vitamin D_2 (ergocalciferol) are stored in body fat and it is estimated that the horse when supplemented adequately has between 3 and 6 months supply. Excessive supply of vitamin D can lead to similar symptoms to vitamin A toxicity with decreased feed intake and growth, dull hair anaemia and hyperostosis (Bille, 1970; Harrington, 1982; Lewis, 1995). The proposed maximum safe limit for vitamin D is 2200 IU/kg DM (NRC, 1987).

Vitamin E

Vitamin E is a mixture of several related compounds known as tocopherols. The most biologically active tocopherol is α-tocopherol, but there are eight different isomeric forms of the base molecule. Vitamin E is absorbed in the small intestine and packaged in chylomicrons; a similar system to that involved with the uptake of vitamin A. Vitamin E is delivered to target tissues via chylomicron transport and to the liver through chylomicron remnant uptake where the liver can export vitamin E in very low density lipoproteins (Miller and Hayes, 1982). Vitamin E is lipophilic and it therefore accumulates in cell membranes (where it can confer antioxidant activity), fat deposits (adipose tissue is the major site of storage) and circulating lipoproteins. The major function of vitamin E in metabolism is as an antioxidant scavenging free radicals and molecular oxygen. Vitamin E is important for preventing peroxidation of polyunsaturated membrane fatty acids. The roles of vitamins E and C are interrelated in their antioxidant capabilities and α-tocopherol can be regenerated by oxidation by vitamin C reduction, scavenging of the peroxy radical and conjugation to glucuronate with excretion in the bile.

The main symptoms of severe deficiency in animals are reproductive failure, nutritional "muscular dystrophy," reduced performance under exercise, steatites, haemolytic anaemia, and neurological and immunological abnormalities (Stowe, 1968; Jackson et al., 1983). It is however difficult to distinguish between selenium deficiency and vitamin E deficiency per se (Schougaard et al., 1972; Liu et al., 1983). Vitamin E is relatively safe (i.e. a relatively low toxicity) compared to the other fat-soluble vitamins, however toxicity has manifested itself as reduced performance and growth, hyperphosphotaemia, weight loss, anorexia, recumbency and debilitation. These symptoms do not however occur clinically (Roneus et al., 1986; Lewis, 1995) and diets containing 1000 IU/kg can be offered without apparent harm to rats and chicks (NRC, 1987; Corrigan, 1979).

Vitamin K

The K vitamins exist naturally as K_1 (phylloquinone) in green vegetables, K_2 (menaquinone) produced by intestinal bacteria and K_3 is synthetic menadione. When administered, vitamin K_3 is alkylated to one of the vitamin K_2 forms of menaquinone. The major function of the K vitamins is in the maintenance of normal levels of the blood clotting factors, protein C and protein S in the liver. Conversion from inactive to active clotting factor requires a posttranslational modification (carboxylation) and the enzyme responsible requires vitamin K as a cofactor.

Vitamin K is absorbed from the intestine in the presence of bile salts and other lipids through interaction with chylomicrons (Shearer et al., 1974). Synthetic vitamin K_3 is water-soluble and can be absorbed irrespective of the presence of intestinal lipids and bile. There are several reports linking reduced vitamin K uptake and coumarin based compounds (for instance dicoumarol) but these problems rarely manifest themselves during grazing (Blakley, 1985; Lewis, 1995). Vitamin K is a cofactor in the carboxylation of glutamine residues to γ-carboxyglutamate (the "gla" residue; Vermeer and Ulrich, 1982). Several of the gla proteins are essential for blood clotting and its regulation whereas others have a role in the regulation of tissue mineralization (osteocalcin, matrix gla protein; Kohlmeier et al., 1996) and cell proliferation (glas6; Suttie, 1992). Vitamin K deficiency has been defined as a disruption of blood clotting due to diminished gla content of the vitamin K-dependent coagulation factors. There is however little evidence of deficiency in horses. Toxicity is also rare, if not unknown, in natural diets (Lewis, 1995). Excessive intake of the synthetic K_3 form can however lead to toxicity in the form of acute renal failure, colic and haematuria (Green and Green, 1986; Rebhun et al., 1984).

Water-soluble vitamins

Thiamine

Thiamine is also known as vitamin B_1. Thiamine is derived from a substituted pyrimidine and a thiazole which are coupled by a methylene bridge. Thiamine is rapidly converted to its active form thiamine pyrophosphate (TPP) in the brain and liver by specific enzymes thiamine diphosphotransferases. Thiamine pyrophosphate is necessary as a cofactor for the pyruvate and α-ketoglutarate dehydrogenase catalysed reactions as well as the transketolase catalysed reactions of the pentose phosphate pathway. Deficiency in thiamine leads to a severe reduction in the capacity of cells to generate energy. Abundant synthesis of B vitamins can occur as a result of intestinal microbial synthesis (Carroll et al., 1949; Lindrode, 1967), however gastrointestinal motility is an important factor in the synthesis of thiamine with microbial synthesis being potentially reduced by high transit times. For deficiency to occur in horses, very low voluntary intakes of thiamine have to be observed, for instance 3μg/kg body weight was not adequate to prevent loss of weight, normal appetite, high performance exercise and optimal concentrations of thiamine in skeletal muscle (Carlstrom and Hjarre, 1939; Carroll, 1950; Topliff et al., 1981).

The dietary requirement for thiamine is proportional to the energy intake of the diet and if the carbohydrate content of the diet is excessive then

Vitamins

an increased thiamine intake will be required. The earliest symptoms of thiamine deficiency include constipation, appetite suppression and nausea as well as mental depression, peripheral neuropathy and fatigue. Chronic thiamine deficiency leads to more severe neurological symptoms including ataxia, mental confusion and loss of eye coordination. Other clinical symptoms of prolonged thiamine deficiency are related to cardiovascular and musculature defects (Diniz *et al.*, 1984). However, these symptoms are generally related to thiaminases and antithiamine compounds in poisonous plants ingested or as a result of amprolium (coccidostat) use in animals (Cymbaluk *et al.*, 1978). Toxicity is rare and is unlikely to result in conventional diets. The NRC (1987) notes that ingestion of greater than 1000 fold of requirement seemed to result in no adverse symptoms (MacKay, 1961; Stewart, 1972).

Riboflavin

Riboflavin is also known as vitamin B_2. Riboflavin has a broad distribution of flavin but little is present as free riboflavin. Riboflavin is the precursor for coenzymes flavin mononucleotide (FMN) and flavin adenine dinucleotide (FAD). Both classes of enzymes are involved in a wide range of reduction-oxidation reactions, e.g. succinate dehydrogenase and xanthine oxidase. As the catalysis site in flavocoenzymes, riboflavin participates in oxidation-reduction reactions in numerous metabolic pathways and in energy production via the respiratory chain. Flavoproteins participate in both one and two electron transfers as they operate in pyridine nucleotide-dependent and independent dehydrogenation reactions with sulphur containing compounds, hydroxylation, oxidative decarboxylations, deoxygenations, and reduction of oxygen to hydrogen peroxide following abstraction of hydrogen from substrates (Yagi, 1994). The normal daily requirement for riboflavin is probably less than 2 mg/kg DM ingested (NRC, 1989) for normal adult horses. Riboflavin deficiencies are rare in animals and have never been documented in the horse. However, unsupplemented soya-based milk replacers may be deficient in riboflavin. Furthermore, toxicity has not been observed in horses.

Niacin

Niacin (nicotinic acid and nicotinamide) is also known as Vitamin B_3. Both nicotinic acid and nicotinamide can serve as the dietary source of vitamin B_3. Niacin is required for the synthesis of the active forms of vitamin B_3, nicotinamide adenine dinucleotide (NAD^+) and nicotinamide adenine dinucleotide phosphate ($NADP^+$). Both NAD^+ and $NADP^+$ function as cofactors for numerous dehydrogenase, e.g., lactate and malate dehydrogenases (Jacob and Swendseid, 1996). Niacin is not a true vitamin in the strictest definition since it can be derived from the amino acid tryptophan (NRC, 1989; Carroll et al., 1949). However, the ability to utilize tryptophan for niacin synthesis is inefficient (approximately 60 mg of tryptophan is required to synthesize 1 mg of niacin). Also, synthesis of niacin from tryptophan requires vitamins B_1, B_2 and B_6 which under the conditions for synthesis would be limiting. No dietary requirement for niacin has been established for the horse and niacin deficiency has not been described. In other species diets deficient in niacin (as well as tryptophan) led to glossitis of the tongue, dermatitis, weight loss, diarrhoea, depression and dementia. Excessive niacin intake has also not been identified in horses (NRC, 1989). Nicotinic acid (but not nicotinamide) when administered can reduce plasma cholesterol concentrations as the major action of nicotinic acid in lipid metabolism has been demonstrated to reduce fatty acid mobilisation from adipose tissue. However, high levels of nicotinic acid would also lead to a depletion of glycogen stores and fat reserves in skeletal and cardiac muscle.

Pantothenic acid

Pantothenic acid is also known as Vitamin B_5. Pantothenic acid is formed from ß-alanine and pantoic acid and can be synthesised by the microflora in the gastrointestinal tract of the horse (Carroll et al., 1949; Linerode, 1966). Pantothenate is required for synthesis of coenzyme A and is a component of the acyl carrier protein (ACP) domain of fatty acid synthase (Annous and Song, 1995). Pantothenate is required for the metabolism of carbohydrate (via the Krebs cycle), fats and proteins. At least 70 enzymes have been identified as requiring coenzyme A or ACP derivatives (Song, 1990). Deficiency of pantothenic acid is extremely rare in horses if it occurs at all (Pearson and Schmidt, 1948). Symptoms of pantothenate deficiency are difficult to assess since they resemble other B vitamin deficiencies but have been reported as dermatitis, achromotrichia, enteritis and neuritis (NRC, 1989). Toxicity is also unlikely as the acute LD_{50} for calcium pantothenate administered parenterally is approximately 1 g/kg body weight (Cunha, 1991; Unna and Greslin, 1941).

Vitamins

Vitamin B_6

Pyridoxal, pyridoxamine and pyridoxine are collectively known as vitamin B_6. All three compounds are efficiently converted to the biologically active form of vitamin B_6, pyridoxal phosphate. This conversion is catalysed by the ATP requiring enzyme pyridoxal kinase. Pyridoxal phosphate functions as a cofactor in transamination reactions required for the synthesis and catabolism of the amino acids and glycogenolysis (Leklem, 1990) and hence supplementation may reflect protein intake and requirement (Baker *et al.*, 1986). Pyridoxal phosphate may also bind to steroid hormone receptors and may regulate steroid hormone action. Vitamin B_6 deficiency has not been identified in horses and there is insufficient evidence to establish a maximum tolerable limit (NRC, 1989). However, deficiencies have been observed as alterations in the function of the nervous system, dermatitis, glossitis and anaemia (Krinke *et al.*, 1980; NRC, 1987).

Biotin

Biotin (vitamin H or coenzyme R; hexahydro-2-oxo-1H-thienal [3,4-d]-imidazole-4-pentatonic acid) is the cofactor required for carboxylation reactions in animal cells for instance acetyl-CoA carboxylase and pyruvate carboxylase. Biotin is found primarily in liver, kidney and muscle of horses. The function of the vitamin is as a cofactor for four carboxylases that catalyses the incorporation of cellular bicarbonate into carbon metabolism. Acetyl-CoA carboxylase is located in the cytosol of the cell where it catalyse the formation of malonyl-CoA which in turn serves as a substrate for fatty acid elongation. The other carboxylases are located in the mitochondria. Pyruvate carboxylase catalyses the incorporation of bicarbonate into pyruvate to form oxaloacetate (an intermediate in the Krebs cycle) and methylcrotonyl-CoA carboxylase catalyses the incorporation of bicarbonate into propionyl-CoA to form methylmalonyl-CoA which is metabolised to intermediates that are processed in the Krebs cycle (Mock, 1996).

Biotin occurs in the diet and is synthesised by intestinal bacteria (Carroll *et al.*, 1949). Deficiencies of the vitamin are rare in horses and there is no unequivocal evidence of deficiency (NRC, 1989). Deficiency has however been observed in other mammals, leading to cracking of the plantar surface of the foot (pigs; Cunha *et al.*, 1946), decreased growth rate, non pruritic dermatosis, hyperkeratosis, decreased reproductive performance, anaemia, anorexia and hypercholesterolaemia (Lewis, 1995). The effects of excessive supply of biotin have not been reported in horses, but foetal reabsorption has occurred in rats injected with up to 100 mg/kg BW (NRC, 1987).

Cobalamin

Cobalamin is known as vitamin B_{12} and is the generic term for corrinoids that have qualitative biological activity of cyanocobalamin. Vitamin B_{12} is composed of a complex tetrapyrrole ring structure and a cobalt ion and is synthesised exclusively by microorganisms (Alexander and Davies, 1969; Davies, 1971; Salminen, 1975). It is found in the liver of animals bound to protein as methycobalamin or 5'-deoxyadenosylcobalamin. The vitamin must be hydrolysed from protein in order to be active. There are several reactions that require vitamin B_{12} as a cofactor; the catabolism of fatty acids with an odd number of carbon atoms, valine, isoleucine and threonine with the resultant production of propionyl-CoA and as a cofactor for methylmalonyl-CoA mutase in the conversion of methylmalonyl-CoA to succinyl-CoA. The 5'-deoxyadenosine derivative of cobalamin is required for this reaction. The conversion of homocysteine to methionine is catalysed by methionine synthase which requires vitamin B_{12} (Herbert, 1996). The reaction results in the transfer of the methyl group from N^5-methyltetrahydrofolate to hydroxycobalamin generating tetrahydrofolate and methylcobalamin. Vitamin B_{12} deficiency has not been observed in horses and there are no definitive studies demonstrating toxicity of the vitamin in equine metabolism (NRC, 1989).

Folic acid

Folic acid is a conjugated pteridine ring structure linked to para-aminobenzoic acid. Folic acid is then synthesised through the conjugation of glutamic acid residues to pteroic acid (Bailey, 1990). When stored in the liver or ingested, folic acid occurs in the polyglutamate form and some of the glutamate residues are cleaved in the intestinal mucosa through the action of conjugase. The removal of glutamate confers a lower negative charge and therefore increases the passage through the basal lamenal membrane of the epithelial cells of the intestine. The reduced form of folic acid, tetrahydrofolate (THF, also H_4folate) and the functions of THF derivatives are many as acceptors and donors of

Vitamins

one-carbon units in a variety of reactions involved in amino acid and nucleotide metabolism (Selhub and Rosenberg, 1996). Folate deficiency has not been observed in horses as dietary intake and microbial synthesis are likely to ensure sufficiency. In other species of animal, folate deficiency has been associated with megaloblastic anaemia but this form of deficiency may not be clearly distinguished from vitamin B_{12} deficiency (NRC, 1989; Bailey and Gregory, 1999).

Ascorbic acid

Ascorbic acid (vitamin C) is derived from glucose via the uronic acid pathway. The enzyme L-gulonolactone oxidase responsible for the conversion of gulonolactone to ascorbic acid is absent in primates, guinea pigs and the red winged bulbul making ascorbic acid a requirement of the diet. Horses do not need vitamin C in their diets (Lewis, 1995). The active form of vitamin C is ascorbic acid however ascorbate is a reducing agent for a number of different reactions. The most important reaction requiring ascorbate as a cofactor is the hydroxylation of proline (prolyl hydroxylase) and lysine (lysyl oxidase) residues in collagen and it is therefore required for the maintenance of normal connective tissue and in wound healing. Vitamin C is also necessary for bone remodelling, catabolism of tyrosine, synthesis of epinephrine and bile acids (NRC, 1989).

Deficiency in vitamin C leads to scurvy, as the vitamin has a role in the post-translational modification of collagen. Scurvy is characterised by easily bruised skin, muscle fatigue, soft swollen gums, decreased wound healing and haemorrhages, osteoporosis and anaemia. Symptoms of toxicity have not been observed in horses (NRC, 1989; Lewis, 1995).

Choline

Choline is a dietary component of many foods and is a component of several major phospholipids (including phosphatidylcholine and sphingomyelin) that are critical for normal membrane structure and function (Zeisel, 1997). The metabolism of choline, methionine, and methyl-folate are closely interrelated; the metabolic pathways intersect at the formation of methionine from homocysteine. Some choline can be formed from methionine (through the methylation of phosphatidylethanolamine by phosphatidylethanolamine Nmethyltransferase using S-adenosylmethionine as the methyl donor). The outer leaflet of plasma membrane is rich in these choline-phospholipids whereas the inner leaflet is dominated by phosphatidylethanolamine, phosphatidylserine and phosphatidylinositol. Phosphatidylcholine is the predominant phospholipid (>50%) in most mammalian membranes. It not only contributes to the structure of the membrane bilayer, but products of receptor-mediated lecithin hydrolysis also serve as important second messengers in signal cascades that control cell growth and gene expression. Disaturated phosphatidylcholine is the primary active component of surfactant in the lung and deficiency of the surfactant in the neonate leads to respiratory distress syndrome. No studies have been conducted to establish the requirements of the horse for choline.

10

Feeding practice in relation to health and welfare

This chapter provides an overview of the interaction of nutrition, health and welfare. Health problems related to poor nutrition have become a major topic of discussion and research for horse owners, the feed industry and veterinarians. Malnutrition can affect health by causing acute or chronic digestive or metabolic disturbances which can lead to injury and disease. Furthermore, these disturbances can also lead to stress related problems which elicit a behavioural or physiological response. It is not the purpose of this chapter to 're-invent the wheel'. Many of the factors associated with malnutrition have been highlighted throughout this book and are described in detail elsewhere (in particular: ENESAD, 2002; Watson, 1998; Harris *et al.*, 1999; Nadau *et al.*, 1998; Murray *et al.*, 1996; Lewis, 1996; Frape, 1996). What has become clear from reviewing the published research is that feeding practice is one of the greatest factors which influence the welfare of the horse and therefore this chapter aims to provide a "checklist" for optimal nutritional management.

Feeding in practice

There is no single correct way of feeding a horse in practice and a range of criteria (some good and some bad) have been developed and are currently applied when formulating rations. The selected criteria may include the 'traditional' approach according to the maxim "I have always done it this way and my horses look well", or they may involve detailed ration calculation according to the requirement tables and feed composition analysis. Other current texts on animal nutrition have discussed the mathematical processes of ration calculation and balancing of energy and protein in detail (Frape, 1998, McDonald *et al.*, 1995) but what should be stressed is that 'an average horse' does not exist and that ration calculations done without the necessary background knowledge relating to feed types, composition and individual animal requirements can lead to great mistakes. This approach is different to that taken for farm livestock as horses generally are managed as individuals and not in production groups. Before attempting to balance the nutrient requirements and supply from the ration the following key steps should be taken (Ellis, 2004):

1 Assess the body condition and live weight of the horse

2 Assess temperament of the horse

3 Calculate the dry matter requirements of the horse (approximately 1.6 to 2.2 % of body weight)

4 Assess the nutrient requirements of the horse in relation to work done and adjust for condition, body weight and temperament as required. To assess work done include not only level of work but duration per session and repetition per week. For feeds offered identify the chemical composition of the feed – e.g. starch, sugar, fibre, protein, mineral and vitamin profile)

5 **Assess structural fibre requirements of the horse (start with *ad libitum* feeding systems and reduce down to 2% of body weight (avoiding going below a minimum of 1% of body weight in structural/fibre). These calculations are to determine the bulk of feed (structural fibre ≠ crude fibre; it is roughage in its original form presented in the diet). (Ellis, 2004)**

6 Construct a ration according to 3, 4 and 5

7 Carry out a ration calculation to check main requirements are met

8 Adjust energy requirements according to 1 and 2

One important issue for any rationing exercise is the assessment of body weight. Recent work by Stanier *et al.* (2004) has provided a practical method of evaluating the body weight of growing Thoroughbred horses using linear measurements. The approach has modified the 'girth' and 'body length' only measurement (commonly implemented using weigh tapes; Carroll and Huntington, 1988) and has incorporated length of body, carpus circumference and forelimb length. This has improved

Health and Welfare

the estimation of body weight and will in the future provide a more accurate method of management of rations for growing and exercising horses.

The key point within ration formulation for the horse is the balancing of requirements for work we demand from the animal with the needs and requirements of the animal. The physiological and behavioural requirements of the equine (points 1-5) are therefore assessed before beginning a ration calculation – with point 5 being the central and most important factor. This is paramount in order to prevent nutrition-related health and behaviour problems – i.e. ensure good welfare of the animal.

Welfare and health

It is commonly accepted that animals should be kept in management systems which allow them to carry out the main species-specific behaviours, systems within which they 'feel comfortable' and certainly systems which do not cause unnecessary suffering or stress (Anon, 2001). Thus 'feelings' and 'emotions' are central to assessing welfare. These are not directly measurable but can be measured through related parameters such as observation of natural behaviour, measuring or recording of primary emotions (fear, aggression, pain), using choice tests and operant conditioning tests, measuring physiological changes in relation to stress (stress-hormones, heart rates), pathologies (skin conditions, immune reactivity, diseases, intestinal disturbances) as well as vitality of the animal (growth rates, reproduction, performance) (Beerda *et al.*, 2003).

Cognitive, emotional and motivational capacities have evolved in every species in order to cope with different environmental conditions. They regulate how an animal reacts to different situations. Domestication of the horse has led to a change in reaction to certain situations partially through habituation within a lifetime. Previous experience plays an important role as gradual habituation reduces the risk of welfare problems (Mills, 1999). Genetic factors as well as individual horse temperament affect the speed and extent of adaptation of the individual animal (Vecciiotti and Galanti, 1986). For the domesticated animal, the motivation and response to stimuli is very much the same as those of its ancestors. If the animal is returned to its natural environment it will quickly return to all these behaviours such as foraging for food and water, resting and social behaviour, which were not performed to a great extent in the stable (Beerda *et al.*, 2003). If these motivational behaviour patterns cannot be performed in any environmental condition the animal will try to adapt. For instance, feeding a horse with high energy density diets will not reduce voluntary feed intake, as the motivation to forage and eat seems to be greater than the physiological regulation of energy intake. When feeding a diet low in structural fibre (>1% of DM intake) to 18 horses for 3 months Ellis *et al.* (2003) observed a significant increase in coprophagy and woodshaving eating. Motivations which cannot be satisfied in any way will lead to frustration and stress. This is when the welfare of an animal is reduced. Inability to 'escape' from pain due to injury or disease is an important aspect of this which automatically links factors affecting health into the definition of good welfare.

As described earlier, the horse can be characterised as a 'herd', 'nomadic' and 'flight-animal', which spends about 60% of its daily behaviour on voluntary food intake (Duncan, 1980; Vulink *et al.*, 2001; Davidson, 1999). All these characteristics conflict with individual stabling and restriction of feed-bulk of this species (Figure 10.1).

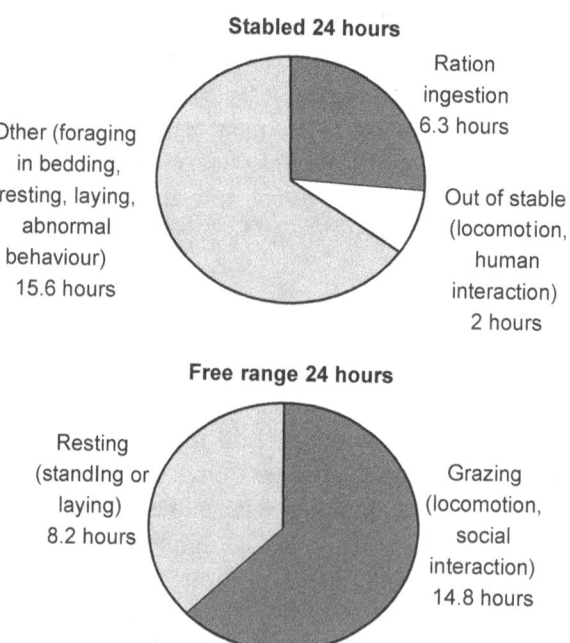

Figure 10.1. Mean time budgets of horses which are stabled 24 hours (diet: 8 kg hay, 3 kg concentrate feed) and horses allowed free range

Compromised welfare as a result of domestication can be listed as loss

Health and Welfare

of locomotion, loss of 'visual horizon' and 'flight' opportunity, alteration of natural environment, loss of social contact, loss of 'continuous browsing/feeding' activity and increased threat from disease. The strong instinct or 'need' to forage and search for food has been demonstrated. A need for shelter from weather conditions rarely overruled the needs of 'locomotion' and 'foraging' in previously stabled horses, which chose to spend only an average of 4.5 hours of cold, wet and windy nights inside a dry shelter provided with hay (Michanek and Bentorp, 1996). However, the need for a dry lying place was seen as the prime motivation for short-term shelter seeking.

'Measurable' consequences of impaired welfare may be perceived as 'behavioural problems', such as stereotypic behaviour, resistance, anxiety, nervosity or apathy. Any type of abnormal behaviour may be derived from a different frustration of a particular motivational system (feeding, locomotion, social contact, avoiding pain; Nicol, 1999). In a survey of 99 Thoroughbred racing yards the risk of horses performing stereotypic behaviour (weaving, box-walking, wood-chewing and windsucking) increased considerably with box designs that minimised social contact between animals, with non-edible bedding in stables and with low fibre feeding practices (McGreevy, 1995). The extent to which certain 'restrictions of natural behaviour' may inhibit welfare of the domesticated animal are therefore influenced by:

- Previous experience and adaptability of the animal
- Housing system (size of housing, type of housing, time spent inside, opening spaces and orientation of housing, ventilation, light, temperature, flooring and bedding)
- Training (duration, intensity, training aids used)
- Social contact with other animals
- Human-horse interaction
- Nutrition (foraging possibilities, amount and composition of feed, time of feeding, body condition)

This book has highlighted the role of nutrition in physiological processes and therefore health and welfare. What has become clear is that feeding practice can cause or influence many conditions which impair the welfare of the horse, the majority of which are summarised below (Table 10.1).

Table 10.1 Overview of various nutritional factors and their relationship to health problems in horses.

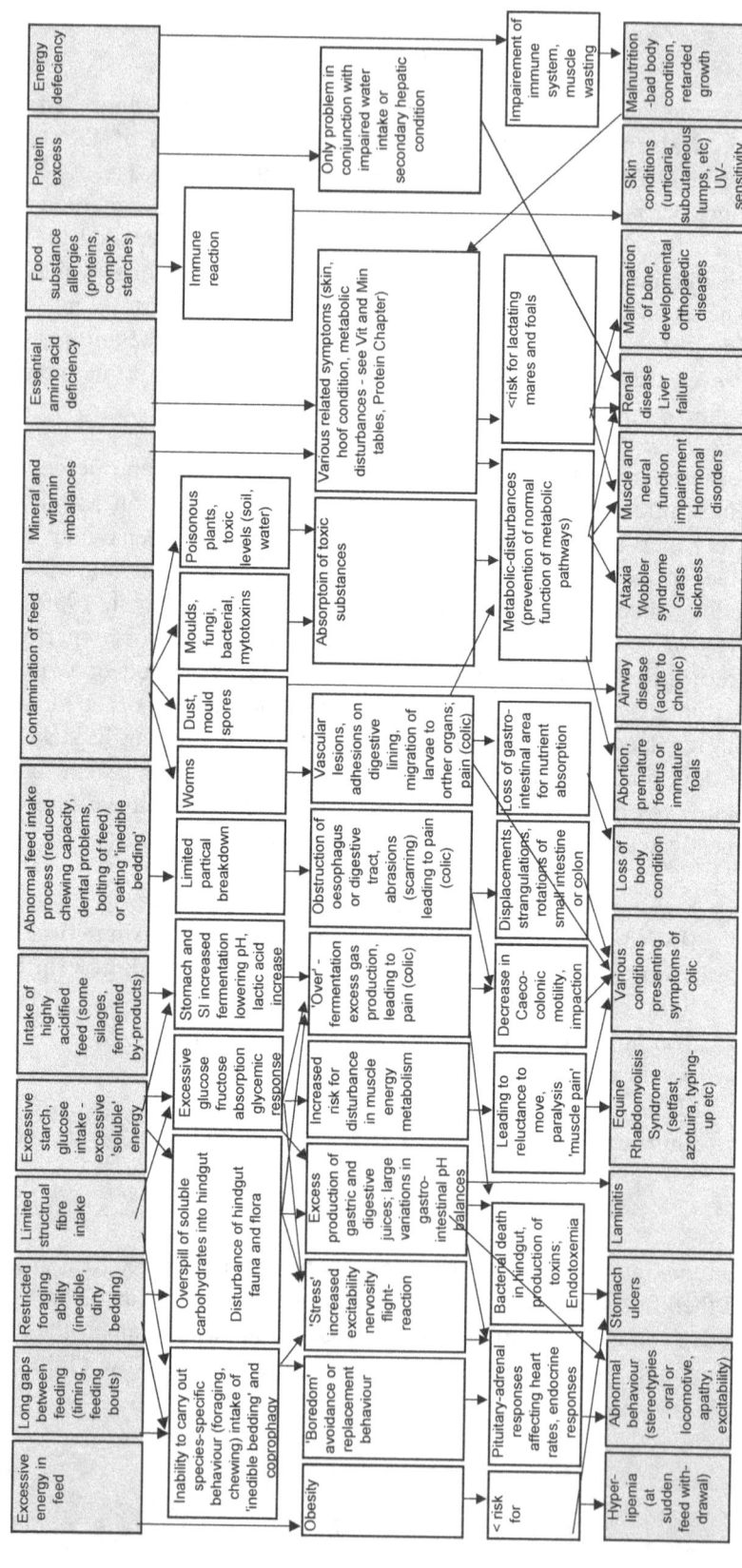

References

A

Adam, J.T. 1951. The quantity and distribution of the ciliate protozoa in the large intestine of the horse. *Parasitology* **41:** 301-311.

ADAS 1994. Role of near infrared reflectance spectroscopy (NIRS) in the analysis of undried forages. Drayton Research Centre, Stratford on Avon, Warwickshire, UK.

ADAS 1993. NIR Spectroscopy, Developments in Agriculture and Food, Drayton Research Centre, Stratford on Avon, Warwickshire, UK.

Aellini, L., Chiaradia E. and Gaiti, A. 1999. Effect of exercise training, selenium and vitamin E on some free radical scavengers in horses (Equus caballus). *Comparative Biochemistry and Physiology, Biochemistry and Molecular Biology* **123:**147-154.

Afzalzadeh, A, Hovell, F D DeB and Kyle, D J. 1997. Role of the omasum in the control of digesta flow from the reticulo-rumen. 117. *Proceedings of the British Society of Animal Science* Scarborough, UK

Agabriel, J., Martin-Rosset, W. and Robelin, J. 1984. Croissance et besoins du poulain. 370-384. In, *Le Cheval.* R. Jarrige and W. Martin-Rosset (eds) – INRA Editions – 78000 Versailles, France.

Agricultural Research Council 1980. The nutrient requirements of ruminant livestock. CAB International, Wallingford, UK.

Aharoni, Y., Brosh, A. and Holzer, Z. 1999. Comparison of models estimating digesta kinetics and fecal output in cattle from fecal conentrations of single-dosed markers of particles and solutes. *Journal of Animal Science* **77:** 2291-2304.

Ahlswede, L. and Konermann, H. 1980. Erfahrungen mit der Oralen und Parenteralen Applikation von Beta-Carotin beim Pferd. *Prakt.Tiererzt.* **61:** 47-53.

Aihara, K. Y., Nishi, Y., Hatano, S., Kihara, M., Okla, M., Sakoda, K., Uozumi, T. and Usui, T. 1985. Zinc, copper, managanese and selenium in patients with human growth hormone deficiency or acromegaly. *Journal of Pediatric Gastroenterology and Nutrition* **4:** 610.

Aitken, F.C. and Hankin, R.G. 1970. Vitamins in feeds for livestock. Techn. Comm, No. 25, Commonwealth Bureau of Animal Nutrition, Bucksburn, Aberdeen, Scotland

Aiken, G.E., Potter, G.D., Conrad, B.E. and Evans, J.W. 1989. Voluntary intake and digestion of coastal bermuda grass hay by yearling and mature horses. *Equine Veterinary Science* **9**: 262-264.

Akin, D.E. 1989. Histological and physical factors affecting digestibility of forages. *Agronomy Journal* **81**: 17-25.

Alberghina D., Medica P., Cusumano F., Fazio E. and Ferlazzo A., 2000. Effects of transportation stress and influence of different distance and age on beta-endorphin, ACTH and cortisol levels of horses. 108. Proceedings of 34th International Congress ISAE (Ramos A., Pinheiro Machado Filho and Hotzel M.J., eds.), Florianopolis, Brazil.

Alexander, F. and Davies, M.E. 1969. Studies on vitamin B_{12} in the horse. *British Veterinary Journal* **125**: 169.

Alexander, F. and Hickson, J.C. 1970. The salivary and pancreatic secretions of the horse. In: Phillipson, A. T. (ed) Physiology of digestion and metabolism in the ruminant. Oriel Press Ltd., Newcastle, UK. pp. 375-389.

Alexander, F., Lowe, J.E., Pickard, D.W. and Stevens, C.E. 1974. Digesta passage and water exchange in the equine large intestine. *American Journal of Physiology* **226**: 1035-1042.

Alini, M., Matsui, Y., Dodge, G.R. and Poole, A.R. 1992. The extracellular matrix of cartilage in the growth plate before and during calcification, changes in composition and degradation of type II collagen. *Calcified Tissue International* **50**: 327-335.

Allen, W.R. and Cooper, M.J. 1975. The use of synthetic analogues of prostaglandines for inducing luteolysis in mares. *Annals Bioanim. Biochimi. Biophys.* **15**: 461-469.

Allen, W.R. 1980. Hormonal Control of early pregnancy. *Veterinary Clinics of North America: Large Animal Practice* **2**: 291-302.

Alvarado, A. F., Marcou, M. and Breton, L. 1989. The incidence of osteochondrosis in a Standardbred breeding farm in Quebec. *Proceedings of the American Association Equine Practitioners* **35**: 295-307.

Amari, M. and Abe A. 1997. Application of near infrared reflectance spectroscopy to forage analysis and prediction of TDN cvontent. *Japan Agricultural Research Quarterly* **31**: 55-63.

Amici, A., Bartocci, Terramoccia, S. and Martilotti, F. 1997. Passage rate of solids and fluids in the digestive tract of buffaloes, cattle and sheep: Selection of non-linear model. *Journal of Animal Science* **64**: 63-69.

Amizuka, N., Kwan-Mei, Y., Goltzman, D., Ozawa, H., White, J. H. and Kwan, M.Y. 1999. Vitamin D3 differentially regulates parathyroid hormone/parathyroid hormone-related peptide receptor expression in bone and cartilage. *Journal of Clinical Investigation* **103**: 373-381.

References

Anderson, C.C., Cook, J.L., Kreeger, J.M., Tomlinson, J.L. and Wagner-Mann, C.C. 1999. In vitro effects of glucosamine and acetylsalicylate on canine chondrocytes in three-dimensional culture. *American Journal of Veterinary Research* **60**: 1546-1551

Anderson, C.E. Potter, G.D. Kreider, J.L. and Courtney, C.C. 1983. Digestible energy requirements for exercising horses. *Journal of Animal Science* **56**: 91.

Anderson, H.C. 1990. The role of cells versus matrix in bone induction. *Connective Tissue Research* **24**: 1-3.

Anderson, M.G. 1975a. The effect of exercise on blood metabolite levels in the horse. *Equine Veterinary Journal* **7**: 27-33.

Anderson, M.G. 1975b. The influence of exercise on serum enzyme levels in the horse. *Equine Veterinary Journal* **7**: 160-165.

Anderson N. V., DeBowes R. M., Nyrop K. A. and Dayton A. D., 1995. Mononuclear phagocytes of transport-stressed horses with viral respiratory tract infection. *American Journal Veterinary Research* **46**: 2272.

Anderson, R.A., Noella, A., Bryden, C., Evock-Clover, M. and Steele, N.C. 1997. Beneficial effects of Chromium on glucose and lipid variable in control and somatotropin-treated pigs are associated with increased tissue chromium and altered tissue copper, iron and zinc. *Journal of Animal Science* **75**: 657-661.

Anderson, R.R. 1992. Composition of trace elements in milk of four species. *Journal of Dairy Science* **74**: 3050-3055.

Anderson-Ecklund, L., Uhlhorn, H., Lundheim, N., Dalin, G. and Andersson, L. 2000. Mapping quantitative trait loci for principal components of bone measurements and osteochondrosis scores in a wild boar X Large White intercross. *Genetics Research* **75**: 223-230.

Andrieu, J. and Martin-Rosset, W. (1995) Chemical, Biological and Physical Methods of Predicting Organic Matter Digestibility of Forages in Horses. Fourteenth Equine Nutrition and Physiology Symposium, Ontario, California.

Andrieu, J., Jestin, M. and Martin-Rosset, W. 1996. Prediction of the organic matter digestibility of forages in horses by near infra-red spectrophotometry (NIRS). 229. *Proceedings of the 47th European Association of Animal Production*, Lillehammer, Norway.

Anonymous. 2001. Scientists' assessment of the impact of housing and mangement on animal welfare. *Journal of Applied Animal Welfare Science* **4**: 3-52.

Annous, K. F. and Song, W. O. 1995. Pantothenic acid uptake and metabolism by the red blood cell. *Journal of Nutrition* **125**: 2586-2593.

Anwandter, Q.C.G. 1974. Progesteron- und b-Carotin-Gehalt des Bovinen Corpus Luteum wahrend der verschiedenen Phasen des Sexualzyklus in Abhangigkeit von der Jahreszeit. Dissertation, Tierarztl. Hochschule, Hannover

Applegate, C.S. and Hershberger, T.V. 1969. Evaluation of in vitro and in vivo cecal fermentation techniques for estimating the nutritive value of forages for equine. *Journal of Animal Science* **28**: 18-22.

Apter, R.C. and Householder, D.D. 1996. Weaning and Weaning Management of Foals: a Review and Some Recommendations. *Journal of Equine Veterinary Science* **16**: 428-435.

Araba, B.D. and Crowelldavis S.L., 1994. Dominance relationships and aggression of foals (Equus caballus). *Applied Animal Behaviour Science* **41**: 1-25.

Arana, M., Rodiek, A. and Stull, C. 1989. Blood glucose and insulin responses to four different grains and four different forms of alfalfa hay fed to horses. *Proceedings of the 11th Equine Nutrition and Physiology Symposium,* Stillwater Oklahoma, USA. p. 160.

Argenzio, R.A. 1990. Physiology of digestive, secretary and absorptive processes. In: White, N.A. (ed.) *The Equine Acute Abdomen.* Philadelphia University Press, Philadelphia, USA. pp. 24-35.

Argenzio, R. A. 1993. Digestion and absorption of carbohydrate, fat and protein. In: *Duke's Physiology of Domestic Animals*, Eleventh Edition, CRC Press, USA. pp. 349-361.

Argenzio, R.A. and Hintz, H.F. 1971. Energy Utilization in the Horse, Waltham Reference Index, E0309.

Argenzio, R.A. and Stevens, C.E. 1975. Cyclic changes in ionic composition of digesta in the equine intestinal tract. *American Journal of Physiology* **228**: 1224-1230.

Argenzio, R.A., Southworth, M. and Stevens, C.E. 1974. Sites of organic acid production and absorption in the equine gastrointestinal tract. *American Journal of Physiology* **226**: 1043-1050.

Argenzio, R.A., Southworth, M., Lowe, J.E. and Stevens, C.E. 1977. Interrelationships of Na, HCO_3 and volatile fatty acid transport by equine large intestine. *American Journal of Physiology* **233**: 469 – 478.

Armsby, H. P. 1903. *The Principles of Animal Nutrition*, Chapman and Hall, London, UK.

Armstrong, R.B., Essen-Gustavson, B., Hoppeler, H., Jones, J.H., Jayar, S.R., Laughlin, M.H., Lindholm, A., Longworth, K.E., Taylor, C.R. and Weibel, E.R. 1992. O_2 delivery at VO_2max and oxidative capacity in muscles of Standardbred horses. *Equine Veterinary Journal* **25**: 532-536.

References

Arnold, F.F., Potter, G.D., Kreider, J.L., Schelling, G.T. and Jenkins, W.L. 1981. Carbohydrate digestion in the small intestine of the equine. *Proceedings of the 7th Equine Nutrition and Physiology Symposium*, Warrenton, Virginia, USA. pp. 19-22.

Arnold, G.W. 1985. Comparison of the time budgets and circadian patterns of maintenance activities in sheep, cattle and horses grouped together. *Applied Animal Behaviour Science* **13:** 19-30.

Arnbjerg, J. 1981. Poisoning in animals due to oral application of iron with description of a case in a horse. *Nord. Veterinaermed.* **33:** 71.

Arsenos, G., Tolkamp, B.J. and Kyriazakis, I. 2000. Conditioned feeding responses of sheep towards food flavours associated with administration of ruminally degradable and/or undegradable protein sources. 85. *Proceedings of the British Society of Animal Science*, Scarborough, UK.

Arthur, G.H. 1958. An analysis of reproductive performance of mares based on postmortem examination. *Veterinary Record* **70:** 682-686.

Arthur, G.H. 1970. The induction of oestrus in the mares by uterine infusion of saline. *Veterinary Record* **86:** 584-586.

Ashton, I.K. and Francis, M.J.O. 1978. Response of chondrocytes isolated from human foetal cartilage to plasma somatomedin activity. *Journal of Endocrinology* **76:** 473-477.

Aspinall, G.O. 1980. Chemistry of cell wall polysaccharides. In: J. Preiss (ed) *The biochemistry of plants* Vol. 3. Academic Press, New York, USA. pp. 473-500.

Atock, M.A. and Williams R.B. 1994. Welfare of competition horses. *Rev. Sci. Tech. Off. Int. Epiz.* **13:** 217-232.

Aucott, L.S. and Garthwaite, P.H. 1988. Transformations to reduce the effect of particle size in near infra-red spectra. *The Analyst* **113:** 1849-1854.

Austbo, D. 1996. Energy and protein evaluation systems and nutrient recommendations for horses in the Nordic countries. *Proceedings of the 47th European Associations of Animal Production,* Lillehammer, Norway. p. 293.

Austbo, D. 2002. Evaluating the protein requirements of performance horses. A comparison of practical application of different systems, First European Workshop on Equine Nutrition, ENESAD, France.

Avellini, L, Chiaradia E, and Gaiti A. 1999. Effect of exercise training, selenium and vitamin E on some free radical scavengers in horses. *Comparative Biochemistry Physiology and Molecular Biology* **123:**147-154.

Axelsson, J. 1949. Standard for nutritional requirement of domestic animals in the Scandinavian countries. *Vème Congrès International Zootechnie.* Paris Vol. 2, Rapports particuliers. Pp. 123-144.

B

Bach-Knudsen, K.E. 2001. The nutritional significance of "dietary fibre" analysis. *Animal Feed Science and Technology* **90**: 3-20.

Bacon, J.S.D. 1988. Feed Science. In Orskov, E. R. (ed) World Animal Science, Series B, A disciplinary approach No. 4, Elsevier Science Publishers, Oxford, UK

Back W. Smit L.D. Schamhardt H.C. and Barnveld A. 1999. The influence of different exercise regimes on the development of locomotion in the foal. *Equine Veterinary Journal* **31**: 106-111

Baecke M., Houweling M., Jharap S., Schravemade D. and Tobias M. 1999. Onderzoek naar de huisvesting van manegepaarden op maneges in Nederland. Rapport Hogeschool Delft in opdracht van de Nederlandse Vereniging tot Bescherming van Dieren.

Bagshaw C. S., Ralston S. L. and Fisher H., 1994. Behavioural and physiological effect of orally-administered tryptophan on horses subjected to acute isolation stress. *Applied Animal Behaviour Science* 40: 1-12

Bailey, C.B. 1958. The rate of secretion of mixed saliva in the cow. *Proceedings of the Nutrition Society* **18**: 13.

Bailey, L.B. 1990. Folate status assessment. *Journal of Nutrition* **120**: 1508-1515.

Bailey, L.B. and Gregory, J. F. 1999. Folate metabolism and requirements. *Journal of Nutrition* **129**: 779-782.

Bailey, S.R., Rycroft, A. and Elliott, J. 2002. Production of amines in equine cecal contents in an in vitro model of carbohydrate overload. *Journal of Animal Science* 80: 2656-2662.

Bailey, S.R., Baillon, M.L., Rycroft, A.N., Harris, P.A. and Elliott, J. 2003. Identification of equine cecal bacteria producing amines in an in vitro model of carbohydrate overload. *Applied and Environmental Microbiology* **69**: 2087-2093.

Baker, C.W. and Barnes, R. 1990. The application of near infra-red spectrometry to forage evalutation in the agricultural development and advisory service. 337-352. In, Wiseman, J. and Cole, D.J A. (eds.) *Feedstuff Evaluation*. Butterworths, London.

Baker, G.J. 1998. Dental physical examination. *Veterinary Clinics of North America, Equine Practice* **14**: 247-330.

Baker, H., Schor, S.M. and Murphy, B.D. 1986. Blood vitamin and choline concentrations in healthy domestic cats, dogs and horses. *American Journal of Veterinary Research* **47**: 1468-1471.

Baker, L.A., Topliff, D.R., Freeman, D.W., Telter, R.G. and Breazile, J.W.

References

1992. Effect of dietary cation-anion balance on acid-base status in horses. *Journal of Equine Veterinary Science* **12**: 160-163.

Baker, L.A. 2000. Nutritional and Management Effects on Developmental Orthopaedic Disease in Horses. 3rd Annual Equine School, Alltech, Fort Worth, Texas, USA.

Balch, C.C. 1950. Factors affecting the utilization of food by dairy cows: The rate of passage of food through the digestive tract. *British Journal of Nutrition* 4: 361.

Banach, M. and Evans, J.W. 1981. Effect of inadequate energy during gestation and lactation on the estrous cycle and the conception rates of mares and on their foal weights. 97. Proceedings of the 7th Equine Nutrition Physiology Symposium, USA.

Banach, M.A. and Evans, J.W. 1981. The effects of energy intake during gestation and lactation on reproductive performances in mares. 264-267. *Proceedings of the Western Section of the American Society of Animal Sciences,* Vancouver, British Columbia, Canada.

Barlet, J.P. 1984. Metabolisme mineral : besoins et apports. In, Jarrige, R. and Martin-Rosset, W. (eds.) Le Cheval, Reproduction, Selection, Alimentation, Exploitation, Instituut National de la Recherche Argronomique, Paris, France..

Barnes, R.J. 1988. Near infrared spectra of ammonia-treated straw and of isolated cell walls. *Animal Feed Science and Technology* **21**: 209-218.

Barneveld A. and Van Weeren P.R. 1999. The effect of exercise on the distribution and manifestation of osteochondritic lesions in the warmblood foal. Equine Veterinary Journal **31**: 16-25.

Barone G.W. and Rodgers B.M. 1989. Pediatric equestrian injuries: a 14-year review. *Journal of Trauma* **29**: 245-247.

Barth, K.M., Williams, J.W. and Brown, D.G. 1997. Digestible energy requirements of working and non-working ponies. *Journal of Animal Science* **44**: 585-589.

Barton, F.E., Wolsink, J.H. and Vedder, H.M. 1986. Near infrared reflectance spectroscopy of untreated and ammonia treated barley straw. *Animal Feed Science and Technology* **15**: 189-196.

Bathe, A.P., Humphrey, D.J. and Henson, F.M.D. 2000. The oral bioavailability of chondroitin sulphate in horses – a pilot study. In Lindner, A. (ed.) *The Elite Show Jumper.* Conference on Equine Sports Medicine and Science, Lensing Druck, Dortmund, FRG.

Baucus, K.L., Ralston, S.L.Rich, V.A. and Squires, E.L. 1987. The effect of dietary copper and zinc supplementation on composition of mares milk. 179-189. Proceeding of 10th Equine Nutrition and Physiology

Symposium, Fort Collins, Colorado, USA.
Bauman, D.E., Davis, C.L. and Buchholtz, H.F. 1971. Propionate production in the rumen of cows fed either a control or high-grain, low fiber diet. *Journal of Dairy Science* **54**: 1282-1287.
Bayly W.M., Liggit H.D., Huston L.J. and Laegreid W.W. 1986. Stress and its effects on equine pulmonary defences. 253-262. *Proceedings of 32nd Annual AAEP Convention..*
Beerda, B., Ellis, A.D., Blokhuis, H.J. and Meijering, A. 2003. Mogelijke dierwelzijnproblemen in de paardenhouderij (Animal Welfare Issues in relation to the horse husbandry in The Netherlands), ID-Lelystad, Report for the Advisory Group on Animal Affairs.
Behrendt C.Y., Adams M.H., Daniel K.S. and McDowell K.J. 1997. Oxytocin expression by equine endometrium. *Biological Reproduction* 56: 134.
Belko, A.Z., Barbieri, T.F. and Wong, E.C. 1986. Effect of energy and protein intake and exercise intensity of the thermic effect of food. *American Journal of Clinical Nutrition* **43**: 863-869.
Bell R.A., Nielsen B.D., Waite K., Rosenstein D. and Orth M. 2001. Daily access to pasture turnout prevents loss of mineral in the third metacarpus of Arabian weanlings. *Journal of Animal Science* **79**: 1142-1150
Belonje, P.C. and van Niekerk, C.H. 1975. A review of the influence of nutrition upon the oestrus cycle and early pregnancy in the mare. *Journal of Reproduction and Fertility* **23**: 167-169.
Benedict, F. G. 1938. Vital energetics: a study on comparative basal metabolism, Canegie Inst., Washington, 503, 175-176.
Bennett, D.K. 1980. Stripes do not a zebra make. Part 1: a cladistic analysis. *Systematic Zoology* **47**: 272-287.
Berger J., 1986. Wild Horses of the Great Basin. The University of Chicago Press, Chicago
Berhang, A.M. and Winslett, G., 1983. Equestrian injuries. *Physician Sports Medicine* 11: 90-97.
Beyers, F.M. and Schelling G.T. 1988. Lipids in Ruminant Nutrition. In Church, D.C. (ed.) (1988) *The Ruminant Animal*. Prentice-Hall, Inc., Englewood Cliffs, USA.
Beynen, A.C. 2000. Vragen omtrent de eiwitvoorziening van paarden, Open dagen, Praktijkonderzoek Veehouderij.
Beynen, A.C. and Hallebeek, J.M. 2002. High fat diets for horses. *Proceedings of the First European Equine Health and Nutrition Congress*, Scientec Matrix, Antwerp, Belgium.
British Horse Society 2002. Approved Riding Establishment, Riding Schools and Recreational Riding, The British Horse Society, Stoneleigh, UK.

References

Biesik, L.M. and Glade, M.J. 1986. Changes in serum hormone concentrations in weanling horses following gastric infusion of sucrose or casein. *Nutrition Reports International* **33**: 651-659.

Bigot, G., Trillaud-Geyl, C., Jussiaux, M. and Martin-Rosset, W. 1987. Elevage du cheval de selle du sevrage au débourrage : Alimentation hivernale, croissance et développement. Bul. Tech. Theix INRA **69**: 45-53.

Bille, N. 1970. Hypervitaminosis D og calciphylaxis hos husbyr. *Nord Veterinaermed.* **22**: 218-223.

Binder, H. J. 1970. Amino acid absorption in the mammalian colon. *Biochemica Biophysica Acta* **219**: 503-506.

Binnerts, W.T. 1986. The copper status of cattle in The Netherlands. *Tijdschrift voor Diergeneeskunde* **111**: 321-324.

Binnerts, W.T., Das, H.D. and Viets, T.C. 1993. Liver selenium analysis in cows with a fast method of neutron activation reveals deficiency areas in the Netherlands. *Netherlands Journal of Agricultural Science* **41**: 47-57.

Bixby-Hammett D.M. 1987. Accidents in equestrian sports. *American Farm Practice* **36**: 209-214.

Bixby-Hammett D.M. 1992. USPC completes ten-year accident study. USPC News 1992; Summer. Bloomfield: USPC 1992

Bizeray, D., Leterrier, C. and Faure, J.M. 2000. Using a classification of activity bouts to simplify observations in meat-type chickens. Measuring Behaviour *3rd International Conference on Methods and Techniques in Behavioural Research*, Noldus Information Technology, The Netherlands.

Björnhag, G., Sperber, I. and Holtenius, K. 1984. A separation mechanism in the large intestine of equines. *Canadian Journal of Animal Science* **64**: 89-90.

Blackmore, D.J. and Elton, D. 1975. Enzyme activity in the serum of Thoroughbred horses in the United Kingdom. *Equine Veterinary Journal* **7**: 34-39.

Blakley, B.R. 1985. Moldy sweet clover (dicoumarol) poisoning in Saskatchewan cattle. *Canadian Veterinary Journal* 26: 357-360.

Blanco, M., Coello, J., Iturriaga, H., Maspoch, S. and Pages, J 1999. Calibration in non-linear near infrared reflectance spectroscopy: a comparison of several methods. *Analytica Chimica Acta* **384**: 207-214.

Blokhuis H.J., 1995. Welzijnsproblematiek in een aantal veehouderijsectoren. NRLO-rapport nr 95/2.

Blumenthal, N.C., Posner, A.S., Silvermand, L.D. and Rosenberg, L.C. 1979.

Effect of proteoglycans on in vitro hydroxyapatite formation. *Calcified Tissue International* **27**: 75-82.

Blummel, M. and Becker, K.1997. The degradability characteristics of fifty-four roughages and roughage neutral-detergent fibres as described by in vitro gas production and their relationship to voluntary feed intake. *British Journal of Nutrition* **77**: 757-768.

Bochröder, B., Schubert, R. and Bödeker, D. 1994. Studies on the transport in vitro of lysine, histidine, arginine and ammonia across the mucosa of the equine colon. *Equine Veterinary Journal* **26**: 131-133.

Bondi, A and Skan, D. 1984. Vitamin A and carotene in animal nutrition. *Progress in Food and Nutrition Science* **8**: 165-191.

Bonucci, E. 1970. Fine structure and histochemistry of "calcifying globules" in epiphyseal cartilage. *Zeitschrift fur Zellforschung und Mikroskopische Anatomie* **103**: 192-217.

Boonstoppel M.E. and Schilder M.B.H. 1996. Stereotypieen bij het Nederlandse paard, UniversiteitUtrecht, Projectgroup Ethologie en Socio-ecologie.

Booth, M.E., Pearson, R.A., Cuddeford, D. 1998. Thermoregulation in wet Shetland ponies. 126. *Proceedings of the British Society of Animal Science*, Scarborough, UK.

Booth, S.L. and Suttie, J.W. (1998) Dietary Intake and Adequacy of Vitamin K. *Journal of Nutrition* **128**: 785-788.

Borchers, A. 2002. Die Körpergewichts- und Körpergrößenentwicklung des Warmblutfohlens während des ersten Lebenshalbjahres in Bezug zur Energie- und Proteinzufuhr sowie zum Auftreten der Osteochondrose. Dissertation, Institut für Tierernährung der Tierärztlichen Hochschule Hannover.

Boren, S.R., Topliff, D.R., Freeman, D.W., Bahr, R.J., Wagner, D.G. and Maxwell, C.V. 1987. Growth of weanling Quarter horses fed varying energy and protein levels. 43-48. Proceedings of the 10th Equine Nutrition and Physiology Society, Colorado State University, Fort Collins, 11-13 June 1987.

Borroni A. and Canali E., 1993. Behavioural problems in thoroughbred horses reared in Italy. 43-46. In, Nichelmann M., Wierenga H.K. and Braun S. (eds.) *Proceedings of International Congress on Applied Ethology*, Berlin, FRG.

Borton, A., Anderson, D.L. and Lyford, S. 1973. Studies of protein quality and quantity in the early weaned foal. 19-22. *Proceedings of 3rd Equine Nutrition Physiology Symposium*. University of Florida, Gainesville, USA.

Bouwman H. 1988. Paardevoeding in de praktijk. Uitgeverij Terra, The Netherlands.

References

Boyan, B. D., Swain, L. D., Luna, M. and Schwartz Z. (1992) Vitamin D-dependent regulation of extracellular matrix vesicles includes nongenomic mechanisms, In: Slavkin, H. and Price, P., Eds. (1992) Chemistry and biology of mineralized tissues, Elsevier Science, Amsterdam

Boyd, L. and Houpt, K.A. 1993. Przewalski's Horse: the History and Biology of an Endangered species. State University of New York Press, Albany, USA.

Boyd L. E., 1986. Behaviour problems of Equids in zoos. *Veterinary Clinic North America: Equine Practice* 2: 653-663.

Boyd L. 1998. The 24-h time budget of a Takhi harem stallion (*Equus ferus przewalskii*) pre- and post- reintroduction. *Applied Animal Behaviour Science* 60: 291-299.

Brama, P.A.J. 1999. Dynamics of equine articular cartilage, Phd Thesis, University of Utrecht.

Brama, P.A.J., TeKoppele, J.M., Beekman, Van El., B., Barneveld, A. and Van Weeren, P.R. 1998. Matrix metalloproteinase activity in equine synovial fluid: influence of age, osteoarthritis and osteochondrosis. *Annals of the Rheumatic Diseases* 57: 697-699.

Brama, P.A.J., TeKoppele, J.M., Beekman, Van El, B., Barneveld, A. and Van Weeren, P.R. 2000. Influence of development and joint pathology on stromelysin enzyme activity in equine synovial fluid. *Annals of the Rheumatic Diseases* 59: 155-157.

Brama P.A.J, TeKoppele J.M., Bank R.A,, Barnveld A. and van Weeren P.R. 2002. Development of biochemical heterogeneity of articular cartilage : influence of age and exercise. *Equine Veterinary Journal* 34: 265-269

Brandao-Neto, J., Stefan, V., Mendoca, B.B., Bloise, W. and Castro, A.V.B. 1998. The essential role of zinc in growth. *Nutrition Research* 15: 3.

Bremner, I and Mills, C.F. 1979. Effects of diet on toxicity of heavy metals. In CEP Consultants (eds.) Management and control of heavy metals in the environment. Edinburgh, UK.

Breuer, L.H. and Golden, D.L., 1971. Lysine requirement of the immature equine. *Journal of Animal Science* **33**:227.

Breuer. L.H. 1975. Effects of mare diet during late gestation and lactatation, supplemental feeding of foal, and early weaning on foal development. Proc. 4th Equ. Nutr. Physiol. Symp., Univ. California, Davis, 85-86

Breuer, L.H., Kasten, L.H. and Word, J.D. 1970. Protein and amino acid utilization in the young horse. 16. *Proceedings of 2nd Equine Nutrition Physiology Society Symposium*. Cornell University, Ithaca, USA.

Breukink, H.J. 2000. Gezondheid en ziekte bij paarden: van ademhaling tot zenuwstelsel, Forte Uitgevers BV.

Breznak, J.A. and Kane, M.D. 1990. Microbial H_2/CO_2 acetogenesis in animal guts: nature and nutritional significance. *FEMS Microbiology Reviews* **87**: 309-314.

Bridges C.H. and Moffitt P.G. 1990. Influence of variable content of dietary zinc on copper metabolism of weanling foals. *American Journal of Veterinary Research* **51**: 275–280.

Bridges C.H. and Harris E.D. 1988. Experimentally induced cartilaginous fractures (osteochondritis dissecans) in foals fed low copper diets. *Journal of the American Veterinary medical Association* **193**: 215–221.

Bridges C.H., Womack J.E., Harris E.D. and Scrutchfield, W.L 1984. Consideration of copper metabolism in osteochondrosis of suckling foals *Journal of the American Veterinary medical Association* **185**: 173 -178.

Britton, G. 1995. Structure and properties of carotenoids in relation to function. *FASEB Journal* 9: 1551-1558.

Broderick, G.A. and Cochran, R.C. 2000. In vivo and in situ methods for estimating digestibility with reference to protein degradability. 53–85. In, Theodorou, M.K. and France, J. (eds.) *Feeding systems and feed evaluation methods.* CAB International, Wallingford, UK.

Brody, S. 1945. Bioenergetics and Growth, Reinhold Publishing Corporation, New York, USA.

Bromiley M., 1993. Equine Injury, Therapy and Rehabilitation. Blackwell Scientific Publications, London

Broom D.M. and Johnson K.G. 1993. Stress and animal welfare. Chapman and Hall, London, UK.

Broom D.M. 1986. Indicators of poor welfare. *British Veterinary Journal* **142**: 524-526.

Broom D.M., 2000. Welfare assessment and problem areas during handling and transport. 43-61. In Grandin, T. (ed) Livestock Handling and Transport. CAB International, Wallingford, UK.

Broom D.M. and Johnson K.G. 1993. Stress and Animal Welfare. Chapman Hall, London, UK.

Brown, E.M. 2000. The extracellular Ca2+ Sensing Receptor, Central mediator of systemic calcium homeostasis. *Annual Reviews in Nutrition* **20**: 507-533.

Brown-Grant, K. 1957. The iodine concentrating mechanism of the mammary gland. *Journal of Physiology* **135**: 644.

Bruin, G. and Creemers, J. (1994) Het voorkomen van osteochondrose, Praktijkonderzoek Veehouderij

References

Bruining, M., Bakker, R., Bruchem van, J. and Tamminga, S. 1998. Rumen digesta kinetics in dairy cows fed grass, maize and alfalfa silage, 1.Comparison of conventional, steady-state and dynamic methods to estimate microbial degradation, communition and passage of particles. *Animal Feed Science and Technology* **73**: 37-78.

Buckwalter, J.A., Rosenberg, L.C. and Ungar, R. 1987. Changes in proteoglycan aggregates during cartilage mineralization. *Calcified Tissue International* **36**: 285-290.

Budiansky S., 1998. The nature of horses. Weidenfeld and Nicolson, London, UK.

Burk, R., Staniar, W.B., Kronfeld, D.S., Akers, R.M. and Harris, P.A. 2003. Insulin-like growth factor binding proteins fluctuate with age in growing Thoroughbred foals.84. *Proceedings of Equine Nutrition Physiology Society Symposium,* East Lansing, Michigan, USA.

Burns, H.D., Gibbs, P.G. and Potter, G.D. 1992. Milk-energy production by lactating mares. *Equine Veterinary Science* **12**: 118-120.

Bush, J.A., Freeman, D.E., Merchen, N.R. and Fahey, G.C. 2001. Dietary fat supplementation effects on in vitro nutrient disappearance and in vivo nutrient intake and total tract digestibility in horses. *Journal of Animal Science* **79**: 232-239.

Butler, W.R. 2000. Nutritional interactions with reproductive performance in dairy cattle. *Animal Reproduction Science* **60/61**: 449-457.

C

Cabrera, L. Leclere, L. and Tisserand, J.L. 1997. Effet de la nature de la source azotee alimentaire sur l'aminoacidemie chez le poney. *Annales Zootechnique* **46**: 93-103

Calson, G.P. and Jones, J.H. 1994. A mathematical model of energy costs for correlation with filed studies. In, Clarke, A.F. and Jeffcott, L.B. (eds.) *On to Atlanta.* The Equine Research Centre, Guelph, Canada.

Campbell-Beggs, C.L., Johnson, P.J., Messer, N.T., Lattimerm J.C., Johnson. G. and Casteel, S.W. 1994. Osteochiondritis dissecans in an Appaloosa foal associated with zinc toxicosis. *Journal of Equine Veterinary Science* **14**: 546-550.

Canali E. and Borroni A., 1994. Behavioural problems in thoroughbred horses reared in Italy, In: Proceedings of the International Congress on Applied Ethology, Berlin, Germany, Applied Animal Behaviour Science **40**: 74

Canali E., Ferrante V., Mattiello S., Sacerdote P., Panerai A.E., Lebelt D. and Zanella A., 1996. Plasma levels of ß-endorphin and in vitro lymphocyte proliferation as indicators of welfare in horses in normal or restrained conditions. Pferdeheilkunde **12:** 415-418

Caple, I.W., Edwards, S.J.A., Forsyth, W.M., Whiteley, P., Selth, R.H. and Fulton, L.J. 1978. Blood glutathione peroxidase activity in horses in relation to muscular dystrophy and selenium nutrition. *Australian Veterinary Journal* **54:** 57.

Carbo, A. 1973. Elektrostimulation in der Cervix uteri zur Zyklussteuerung beim Pferd. Ein Beitrag zur klinischen Behandlung von Stoerungen der Eierstockfunktionen. Hannover, Tieraerztl. Hochschule, Diss.

Carlson, C.S., Cullins, L.D. and Meuten, J.D. 1995. Osteochondrosis of the articular-epiphyseal cartilage complex in young horses: evidence for a defect in cartilage canal blood supply. *Veterinary Pathology* **32:** 641-647.

Carlson, C.S., Hilley, H.D. and Meuten, D.J. 1989. Degeneration of cartilage canal vessels associated with lesions of osteochondrosis in swine. *Veterinary Pathology* **26:** 47-57.

Carlson, G.P. and Mansmann, R.A. 1974. Serum electrolyte and plasma protein alterations in horses used in endurance rides. *Journal of the American Veterinary Medical Association* **165:** 262-264.

Carlstrom, B. and Hjarre, A. 1939. Durch B-avitaminose verursachte Mangelkrankheiten bei Militarpferden. *Tierernaehrung* **11:** 121.

Carre, B. and Brillouet, J.M. 1986. Yield and composition of cell wall residues isolated from various feedstuffs used for non ruminant farm animals. *Journal of the Science of Food and Agriculture* **37:** 341-351.

Carroll, C.L. and Huntington, P.J. 1988. Body condition scoring and weight estimation of horses. *Equine Veterinary Journal* **20:** 41-45.

Carroll, F.D., Goss, H. and Howell, C.E. 1949. The synthesis of B-vitamins in the horse. *Journal of Animal Science* **8:** 290.

Carroll, F.D. 1950. B vitamin content in skeletal muscle of the horse fed a B vitamin low diet. *Journal of Animal Science* **9:** 139.

Carson, G.P. 1996. Fluid and electrolyte balance in horses under hot/humid conditions. In, Clarke, A.F, and Jeffcot, L.B. (eds) *On to Atlanta*. Equine Research Centre, Guelph, Canada.

Carter, R.R. and Grovum, W.L. 1990. A review of the physiological significance of hypertonic body fluids on feed intake and ruminal function: Salivation, motility and microbes. *Journal of Animal Science* **68:** 2811-2832.

Casey, A. and Greenhaff, L. 2000. Does dietary creatine supplementaion play a role in skeletal muscle metabolsim and performance. *The American Journal of Clinical Nutrition* **72:** 607S-617S.

Casey, I.A. Brereton, A.J. Laidlaw, S. and McGilloway, D. 1997. Assessment of methodology for the study of short term grazing behaviour of

References

cattle. *British Grassland Society Fifth Research Conference*, University of Plymouth, Newton Abbot, Devon, UK

Casini, L., Gatta, D., Magni, L., Colombani, B. 2000. Effect of prolonged branched-chain amino acid supplementation on metabolic response to anaerobic exercise in Standardbreds. *Journal of Equine Veterinary Science* **20**: 120-123.

Caure, S., Tourtoulou, G., Valette, J.P., Cosnier, A. and Lebreton, P. 1998. Prevention de l'osteochondrose chez le trotteur au sevrage: edude experimentale. *Pratique Veterinaire Equine* **30**: 185-195.

Chakraborty, P.K., Steward, A.P. and Seager, S.W. 1983. Relationship of growth and serum growth hormone concentration in the prepubertal bitch. *Laboratory Animal Science* **33**: 51-55.

Chambers, A.R.M., Hodgson, J. and Milne, J.A. 1981. The development and use of equipment for the automatic recording of ingestive behaviour in sheep and cattle. *Grass and Forage Science* **36**: 97-105.

Cheeke, P. R. 1987. Rabbit Feeding and Nutrition, Academic Press Inc., London, UK

Chenost, M. 1986. Aspects methodologiques de la prevision de la digestibilite de l'herbe paturee par le mouten, les bovins et le cheval a partir de bols de l'osophage et de diverses caracteristiques fecale. *Annales des Zootechnie* **35**: 1-20.

Chenost, M. and Demarquilly, C. 1985. Measurement of Herbage Intake by Housed Animals. In Leaver, J.D. (ed) Herbage Intake Handbook, 2nd edition, British Grassland Society, Berkshire, UK.

Chenost, M. and Martin-Rosset, W. 1985. Comparaison entre especes (mouton, cheval, bovin) de la digestibilite et des quantites ingerees des fourrages verts. *Annales de Zootechnie* **34**: 291-312.

Christensen J.W., Ladewig J., Sondergaard E. and Malmkvist J., 2002. Effects of individual versus group stabling on social behaviour in domestic stallions. *Applied Animal Behaviour Science* **75**: 233-248.

Christensen J.W., Zharkikh T., Ladewig J. and Yasinetskaya N., 2002. Social behaviour in stallion groups (Equus przewaskii and Equus caballus) kept under natural and domestic conditions. *Applied Animal Behaviour Science* **76**: 11-20.

Church, D.C. 1988. The Ruminant Animal. Prentice-Hall, Inc., Englewood Cliffs, NJ, USA.

Church, J.S. and Hudson, R.J. 1999. Comparison of the stress of abrupt and interval weaning of farmed wapiti calves (Cervus elaphus). *Small Ruminant Research* **32**: 119-124.

Chapil, M. and Misiorowski, R. 1980. In vivo inhibition of lysyl oxidase by high dose of zinc. *Proceedings of the Society of Experimental Biology and Medicine* **164**: 137-141.

Clark D.K., Dellmeier G. and Friend T.H., 1988. Effect of the orientation of horses during transportation on behaviour and physiology. *Journal of Animal Science* **66**: 239.

Clark D.K., Friend T.H., and Dellmeier G., 1993. The effect of orientation during trailer transport on hearth rate, cortisol and balance in horses. *Applied Animal Behaviour Science* **68**: 345-351.

Clark, R.G. and Millar, K.R. 1983. Cobalt (Co). 27-37. In N. D. Grace (ed) The mineral requirements of grazing ruminants. New Zealand Society of Animal Production, Occasional Symposium 9.

Clarke, L.L., Roberts, M.C., Argenzio, R. 1990. Feeding and Digestive Problems in Horses. *Equine Practice* **6**: 433-447.

Clarke, T., Flinn, P.C. and McGowan, A.A. 1982. Low cost pepsin-cellulase assays for prediction of digestibility of herbage. *Grass and Forage Science* **37**: 147- 150.

Clegg, P.D., Coughlan, A.R. and Carter, S.D. 1998. Equine Timp-1 and Timp-2: Identification, activity and cellular sources. *Equine Veterinary Journal* **30**: 416-423.

Clutton-Brock T.H., Greenwood P.J. and Powell R.P., 1976. Ranks and relationships in Highland ponies and Highland cows. *Zeitschrift für Tierpsychologie* **41**: 202-216

Codazza, D., Maffeo, G. and Redaelli, G. 1974. Serum enzyme changes and haemato-chemical levels in Thoroughbreds after transport and exercise. *Journal of the South African Veterinary Association* **45**: 331-334.

Coenen, M 1986. Verdaulichkeit und praecaecale Passage einer suspendierfahigen Diat in Abhangigkeit von der Applikationsform. *Zeitschrift der Tierphysiologie Tierernahrung und Futter-mittelkunde* **56**: 104-117.

Coenen, M. 1986. Feeding during late pregnancy and the importance for health of mare and foal. 299. *Proceedings of the 37thAnnual meeting of the European Association for Animal Production.* Budapest, Hungary.

Coenen, M. 1992. Cl-Haushalt und Cl-Bedarf des Pferdes, Habilschrift, Tierarztliche Hochschule Hannover. In, GEH Empfehlungen zur Energie und Nahrstoffversorgung der Pferde, Gesellschaft der Ernahrungsphysiologie der Haustiere, DLG Verlag, Frankfurt.

Coenen, M., Landes, E. and Assmann, G. 1998. Selenium toxicosis in the horse – case report, *Journal of Animal Nutrition* **80**: 153-157.

Coenen, M and Vervuert, I. 2003. Wasser und Elektrolythaushalt arbeitender

References

Pferde. *Ubersicht der Tierernahrung* **31**: 29-73.
Cohen, N.D. 2003. Review Article: The John Hickman Memorial Lecture: Colic by numbers. *Equine Veterinary Journal* **35**: 343-349.
Cohen, N.D., Gibbs, P.G. and Woods, A.M. 1999. Dietary and other management factors associated with Colic in Texas. *Journal of the American Veterinary Medical Association* **215**: 53-60.
Cohen, N.D., Matejka, P.L., Honnas, C.M., Hooper, R.N. 1995. Case control study of the association between various management factors and development of colic in horses. *Journal of the American Veterinary Medical Association* **206**: 667-673.
Coleman, R.J., Mathison, G.W., Burwash, L., Milligan, J.D. 1997. The effect of protein supplementation of alfalfa cube diets on the growth of weanling horses. 59-64. Proceedings of the 15th Equine Nutrition and Physiology Symposium, Fort Worth, Texas, USA, 28-31 May 1997.
Coleman, R.J., Mathison, G.W. and Burwash, L. 1999. Growth and condition at weaning of extensively managed creep-fed foals. *Journal of Equine Veterinary Science* **19**: 45-50.
Coleman, R.J., Mathison, G.W., Burwash, L., Milligan, J.D. 1997. The effect of protein supplementation of alfalfa cube diets on the growth of weanling horses. 59-64. *Proceedings of the 15th Equine Nutrition and Physiology Symposium.* Fort Worth, Texas, USA, 28-31 May, 1997.
Coleman, S.W. and Murray, I. 1993. The use of near-infrared reflectance spectroscopy to define nutrient digestion of hay by cattle. *Animal Feed Science and Technology* **44**: 237-249.
Collins M.N., Friend T.H., Jousan F.D. and Chen S.C., 2000. Effects of density and displacement, falls, injuries, and orientation during horse transportation. *Applied Animal Behaviour Science* **67**: 169-179.
Cook, C.J. 1999. Patterns of weaning and adult response to stress. *Physiology and Behavior* **67**: 803-808.
Cook W.R.A. 2000. Solution to respiratory and other problems of the horse caused by the bit. *Pferdeheilkunde* **16**: 333-51
Cooke, B.C. and Comben, N. 1978. A study of the relationship between ß-carotene and fertility problems in dairy cows. *Animal Production* **26**: 356-357.
Cooke, P.S. and Nicoll, C.S. 1983. Hormonal control of fetal growth. *The Physiologis,* **26**: 317-323.
Cooper J.J. and Mason G.J. 1998. The identification of abnormal behaviour and behavioural problems in stabled horses and their relationship to horse welfare: a comparative review. *Equine Veterinary Journal* **27**: 5-9

Cooper J.J. 1998. Comparative learning theory and its application in the training of horses. *Equine Veterinary Journal* **27:** 39-43

Cooper J.J., McDonald, L. and Mills D.S., 1999. Increasing visual horizons reduces stereotypic patterns of weaving in the stabled horse, In: Harris, P.A., Gomarsall, G.M., Davidson, H.P.B. and Green, R.E. (eds.) *Proceedings of the BEVA specialist days on Behaviour and Nutrition*, Equine Veterinary Journal Ltd., UK.

Cooper J.J., McDonald, L. and Mills D.S. 2000. The effect of increasing visual horizons on stereotypic weaving: implications for the social housing of stabled horses. *Applied Animal Behaviour Science* **69:** 67-83

Costill, D.L., Sherman, W.M., Fink, W.J., Maresh, C., Witten, M. and Miller, J.M. 1981. The role of dietary carbohydrates in muscle glycogen resynthesis after strenuous running. *American Journal of Clinical Nutrition* **34:** 1831-1836.

Coughlan, A.R., Roberston, D.H.L., Burke, R., Beynon, R.J., Carter, S.D. 1998. Isolation and identification of canine matrix metalloproteinase-2 (MMP-2). *Veterinary Journal* **155:** 231-237.

Corrigan, J.J. 1979. Coagulation problems relating to vitamin E. *American Journal of Pediatrics, Haematology and Oncology* **1:** 169.

Cowgill, U.M., States, S.J. and Marburger, J.E. 1980. Smelter smoke syndrome in farm animals and manganese deficiency in northern Oklahoma, USA. *Environmental Pollution Series A* **22:** 259.

Crampton, E. 1923. Rate of growth of draft horses. Journal of Agriculture and Horticulture **26:** 172.

Crandell, K.G., Pagan, J.D., Harris, P.A. and Duren, S.E. 1998. A comparison of grain, vegetable oil and beet pulp as energy sources for the exercised horse Proceedings of the 5th International Conference on Equine Exercise Physiology, Utsumomiya, Japan.

Cross, D.L. Redmond, L.M. Strickland, J.R. 1994. Equine Fescue Toxicosis: signs and solutions. *Journal of Animal Science* **73:** 988-908.

Crowell-Davis S.L., 1986. Developmental behaviour. *Veterinary Clinics of North America: Equine Practice* **2:** 557-571.

Crowell-Davis S.L., Houpt K.A. and Carnevale J. 1985. Feeding and drinking behavior of mares and foals with free access to pasture and water. *Journal of Animal Science* **60:** 883-889.

Crozier, J.A., Allen, V.G., Jack, N.E., Fontenot, J.P. and Cochran, M.A. 1997. Digestibility, apparent mineral absorption and voluntary intake by horses fed alfalfa, tall fescue and caucasian bluestem. *Journal of Animal Science* **75:** 1651-1658.

Csapo J., Stefler, J., Martin, T.G., Makray, S. and Csapo-Kiss. Z. 1994.

References

Composition of mares' colostrum and milk. Fat content, fatty acid composition and vitamin content. *International Dairy Journal* **5**: 393-402.

Csapo, J., Stefler, J., Martin T.G., Makray, S. and Csapo-Kiss, Z. 1994. Fat content, fatty acid composition and vitamin content of mare's milk. *Acta Alimentaria* **23**: 169-178.

Csapo-Kiss, Z., Stefler, J., Martin, T.G., Makray, S. and Csapo, J. 1995. Composition of mares' colostrum and milk. Protein content, amino acid composition and contents of macro- and micro-elements. *International Dairy Journal* **5**: 403-415.

Cuddeford, D. 1986. Alternative feedstuffs for horses. In Practice, March Issue

Cuddeford, D. 1994. Artificially Dehydrated Lucerne for Horses. The Veterinary Record

Cuddeford, D. 1997. Mouthy matters, Dodson and Horrell, 2nd International Conference on Feeding.

Cuddeford, D. 1999. Why feed fibre to the performance horse today. *Proceedings of the British Equine Veterinary Association*, September 1999.

Cuddeford, D. 2000. The significance of pH in the hindgut, In 3rd International Conference on Feeding Horses, Dodson and Horrell Ltd, UK.

Cuddeford, D. 2002. Advantages and disadvantages of different systems. 59. In First European Workshop on Equine Nutrition: Which systems shall we choose in Europe, ENESAD, Dijon France.

Cuddeford, D. 2002. Voluntary food intake by horses. First European Workshop on Equine Nutrition, ENESAD, France.

Cuddeford, D. and Hughes, D. 1990. A comparison between chromium-mordanted hay and acid-insoluble ash to determine apparent digestibility of a chaffed, molassed hay/straw mixture. *Equine Veterinary Journal* **22**: 122-125.

Cuddeford, D. and Hyslop, J.J. 1996. Intake and digestibility of a high fibre concentrate offered ad libitum to ponies and donkeys. 296. Proceedings of the 47th Annual Meeting of the EAAP, Lillehammer, Norway.

Cuddeford, D., Pearson R. E., Archibald, R. F. and Muirhead, R. H. 1995. Digestibility and gastrointestinal transit time of diets containing different proportions of alfalfa and oat straw given to Thoroughbreds, Shetland ponies, Highland ponies and Donkeys. *Journal of Animal Science* **61**: 407-417.

Cuddeford, D., Woodhead, A. and Muirhead, R. 1992. A comparison

between the nutritive value of short-cutting cycle, high temperature-dried alfalfa and timothy hay for horses. *Equine Veterinary Journal* **24:** 84-89.
Cunha, T.J., Lindley, D.C. and Ensminger, M.E. 1946. Biotin deficiency syndrome in pigs fed desiccated egg white. *Journal of Animal Science* **5:** 219.
Cunha, T.J. 1991. Vitamin requirements. Horse Feeding and Nutrition. Academic Press, New York, USA.
Cunningham K. and Fowler, S. 1961. A study of growth and development in the Quarter Horse. Louisiana State University, Bulletin 546.
Cupps, P.J. and Howell, C.E. 1949. The effects of feeding supplemental copper to growing foals. *Journal of Animal Science* **8:** 286-289.
CVB. 1996. Documentatierrapport nr 15, Het definitieve VEP- en VREp-systeem, centraal veevoederbureau, Lelystad, The Netherlands.
CVB. 1996 Handleiding mineralonderzoek bij rundvee and praktijk, Commissie Onderzoek Minerale Voeding, Centraal Veevoederbureau, Lelystad, The Netherlands.
CVB. 2000. Veevoedertabel 2000, Centraal veevoederbureau, Lelystad, The Netherlands.
CVB. 2003. Tabellenboek Veevoeding 2003, Centraal veevoederbureau, Lelystad, The Netherlands.
Cymbaluk, N.F. 1990. Comparison of forage digestion by cattle and horses. *Canadian Journal of Animal Science* **70:** 601-609.
Cymbaluk, N.F. and Christison, G.I. 1990. Environmental effects on thermoregulation and nutrition of horses. *Veterinary Clinics of North America: Equine Practice* **6:** 355-372.
Cymbaluk, N.F. and Smart, M.E. 1993. A review of possible metabolic relationships of copper to equine bone disease. *Equine Veterinary Journal* **16:** 19-26.
Cymbaluk, N.F., Christison, G.I. and Leach, D.H. 1990. Longitudinal growth analysis of horses following limited and ad libitum feeding. *Equine Veterinary Journal* **22:** 198-204.
Cymbaluk, N.F., Fretz, P.B. and Loew, F.M. 1978. Amprolinium-induced thiamine deficiency in horses: Clinical features. *American Journal of Veterinary Research* **39:** 255-262.
Cymbaluk, N.F., Schreyver, H.F. and Hintz, H.F. 1981. Copper metabolism and requirements in mature ponies. *Journal of Nutrition* **111:** 87-93.
Cymbaluk, N.F., Schyver, H.F., Hintz, H.F., Smith, D.F. and Lowe, J.E. 1981. Influence of dietary molybdenum on copper metabolism in ponies. *Journal of Nutrition* **111:** 96-102.

References

D

DAFF. 2002. Farm Development Service, Minimum specifications for horse facilities and fencing, S 156. Department of Agriculture, Food and Rural Development, Republic of Ireland.

Dalley, D.E. and Sykes, A.R. 1989. Magnesium absorption from the large intestine of sheep. *Proceedings of the NZ Society of Animal Production* **49**: 229.

Dalley, D.E., Isherwood, P., Sykes, A.R. and Robson, A. 1992. Magnesium solubility in the caecum in response to pH changes. *Proceedings of the NZ Society of Animal Production* **52**: 103.

Danforth, E., Horton, E.S., O'Connell, M., Sims, E.A.H., Burger, A.G., Ingbar, S.H., Braverman, L. and Vagenakis, A.G. 1979. Dietary-induced alterations in thyroid hormone metabolism during over nutrition. *Journal of Clinical Investigations* **64**: 1336-1347.

Danforth, W. and Burger, A.G. 1989. The impact of nutrition on thyroid hormone physiology and actions. *Annual Review of Nutrition* **9**: 201-227.

Danks, D.M. 1980. Copper deficiency in humans 163-182. In Proceedings of the Ciba Foundation Symposium 79, Biological Roles of Copper, Amsterdam, The Netherlands.

Darenius, K. 1992. Early embryonic death in the mare. Histological, bacteriological and cytological findings in the endometrium. *Acta vet. Scand.* **33**: 147-160.

Darlington, J.M. and Hershberger, T.V. 1968. Effect of forage maturity on digestibility intake and nutritive value of alfalfa, timothy and orchardgrass by the equine. *Journal of Animal Science* **27**: 1572-1576.

Daughaday, W.H., Herington, A.C. and Phillips, L.S. 1975. The regulation of growth by the endocrines. *Annual Review of Physiology* **37**: 211-244.

Davidson H.P.B. 1999. Natural horse – unnatural behaviour: why understanding natural horse behaviour is important. In Harris, P.A., Gomarsall, G.M., Davidson, H.P.B. and Green, R.E. (eds) *Proceedings of the BEVA specialist days on Behaviour and Nutrition*. Equine Veterinary Journal Ltd., UK.

Davidson, N. and Harris, P. 2002. Nutrition and Welfare. 45-73. In Waran, N. (ed.) *The Welfare of Horses*. Dordrecht: Kluwer Academic Publishers, The Netherlands.

Davies-Morel, M.C.G. 1993. Equine reproductive physiology, breeding and stud management. Farming Press, Ipswich, UK

Davies, K.J.A., Quintanilha, G.A., Brooks, G.A. and Packer, L.1982. Free radicals and tissue damage produced by exercise. *Biochemicaal and Biophysical Research Communications* **107**: 1198-1201.

Davies, M.E. 1971. The production of B_{12} in the horse. *British Veterinary Journal* **127**: 34-40.

Davies, M.E., Pasqualicchio, M., Henson, F. and Hernandez-Vidal, G. 1996. Effects of copper and zinc on chondrocyte behaviour and matrix turnover. *Pferdeheilkunde* **3**: 367-370.

Day, F.T. 1939. Sterility in the mare associated with irregularities of the oestrus cycle. *Veterinary Record* **51**: 1113-1119.

De Bernard, B., Bianco, P., Bonucci, E., Constantini, M., Lunazzi, G.C., Marinuzzi, P., Modricky, C., Moro, L., Panfili, E., Pollesello, P. 1986. Biochemical and immunohistochemical evidence that in cartilage an alkaline phosphatase is a Ca2+-binding glycoprotein. *Journal of Cell Biology* **103**: 1615-1623.

De Bernard, B., Stagni, N., Colautti, I., Vitture, F. and Bonucci, E. 1977. Glycosaminoglycans and endochondral calcification. *Clinical Orthopaedic and Related Research* **126**: 285-291

De Boever, J.L., Andries, J.I., De Brabander, D.L., Cottyn, B.G. and Buysse, F.X. 1990. Chewing activity of ruminants as a measure of physical structure: a review of factors affecting it. *Animal Feed Science and Technology* **27**: 281-291.

De Boever, J.L., Cottyn, B.G., Buysse, F.X., Wainman, F.W. and Vanacker, J.M. 1986. The use of an enzymatic technique to predict digestibility, metabolizable and net energy of compound feedstuffs for ruminants. *Animal Feed Science and Technology* **14**: 203-214.

De Boever, J.L., Cottyn, B.G., Vanacker, J.M. and Boucque, Ch. V. 1993. Recent developments in the use of Near Infrared Spectroscopy for evaluating compound feeds and raw materials for ruminants. ADAS (1993) NIRS, Developments in Agriculture and Food, Drayton Research Centre, Stratford on Avon, UK.

De La Corte, F.D., Valberg, S.J., MacLeay, J.M., Williamson, S.E. and Mickelson, J.R. 1999. Glucose uptake in horses with polysaccharide storage myopathy. *American Journal of Veterinary Research* **60**: 458.

DeLuca, H.F. 1988. The vitamin D story: a collaborative effort of basic science and clinical medicine. *FASEB Journal* **2**: 224-236.

Deaville, E.R. and Baker, C.W. 1993. Spectral Interpretations in Relation to Feed Characterisation, In: ADAS (1993) NIR Spectroscopy, Developments in Agriculture and Food, Drayton Research Centre, Stratford on Avon, UK.

Deaville, E.R., Givens, D.I. and Baker, C.W. 1992. Use of normalised near

References

infra-red difference spectra to identify regions related to digestion of cell walls in straws. 219-222. In, Hildrum, K. L., Isaksson, T., Naes, T. and Tandberg, A. (eds.) *Near Infra-Red Spectroscopy*. Ellis Harwood Ltd., Chichester, UK.

DEFRA 2002. Equine industry welfare guidelines compendium for horses, ponies and donkeys. (A compendium produced by a number of al organizations including the Department for Environment, Food and Rural Affairs) ADAS consulting Ltd Wolverhampton, UK.

Dhanoa, M.S., Siddons, R.C., France, J. and Gale, D.L. 1985. A multicompartmental model to describe marker excretion patterns in ruminant faeces. *British Journal of Nutrition* **53**: 663-671.

Dik, K.J., Enzerink, E. and Van Weeren, P.R. 1999. Study design to evaluate the influence of exercise on the development of the musculoskeletal system of foals up to aged 11 months. *Equine Veterinary Journal* **31**: 9-15.

Dimock A.N. and Ralston S.L. 1999. Changes in indices of stress and immune function in transported horses. 4-5. *Proceedings of 18th Annual Meeting of AESM*, Reno, Nevada, USA.

Dixon, P.M. 2000. Removal of dental overgrowths. *Equine Veterinary Education* **12**: 68-81.

DLG. 1995. Futterwerttabellen fuer Pferde, 3.Aufl. 1995, DLG-Verlag, Frankfurt/Main, Germany.

Dodman N.H., Normille J.A., Shuster L. and Rand W. 1994. Equine self mutilation syndrome (57 cases). *American Journal of the Veterinary Medicine Association* **204**: 1219-1223.

Doherty, A.S., Mann, R.W., Temblay, K.D., Bartolomei, M.S. and Schultz, R.M. 2000. Differential Effects on Culture on Imprinted H19 Expression in the Preimplantation Mouse Embryo. *Biology of Reproduction* **62**: 1526-1535.

Dohms, T. 2002. Einfluss von genetischen und umweltbedingten Faktoren auf die Fruchtbarkeit von Stuten und Hengsten. Wissenschaftliche Publikation 25. FN-Verlag der Dt. Reiterlichen Vereinigung, Warendorf.

Doige, C.E., Owen, B.D. and Mills, J.H.L 1975. Influence of calcium and phosphorus on growth and skeletal development of growing swine. *Canadian Journal of Animal Science* **55**: 147.

Domingue, B.M.F., Dellow, D.W. and Barry, T.N. 1991. The efficiency of chewing during eating and ruminating in goats and sheep. *British Journal of Nutrition* **65**: 355-363.

Donoghue, S., Kronfeld, D.S., Berkowitz, S.J. and Copp, R.L. 1981. Vitamin A nutrition of the equine. *Journal of Nutrition* **111**: 365-374.

Doreau, M., Boulot, S. and Chilliard, Y. 1993. Yield and composition of milk from lactating mares: effect of body condition at foaling. *Journal of Dairy Research* **60**: 457-466

Doreau, M., Martin-Rosset, W. and Boulot, S. 1988. Energy requirements and the feeding of mares during lactation: a review. *Livestock Production Science* **20**: 53-68.

Douglas, J. 1994. Equine Osteochondrosis. The Equine Research Centre, University of Guelph, Ontario, Canada.

Dove, H. and Mayes, R.W. 1991. The use of plant wax alkanes as marker substances in studies of the nutrition of herbivores: A review. *Australian Journal for Agricultural Research* **42**: 913-952.

Dowman, M.G. and Collins, F.C. 1982. The use of enzymes to predict the digestibility of animal feeds. *Journal of Science Food and Agriculture* **33**: 689-696.

Driscoll, J., Hintz, H. F. and Schryver, H. F. 1978. Goiter in foals caused by excessive iodine. *Journal of American Veterinary Medical Association* **173**: 858-859.

Drogoul, C., Faurie, F. and Tisserand, J.L. 1996. Effects of forage granulation on the caecum and the colon metabolisms in ponies. Proceedings of the 47th European Association of Animal Porduction, Lillehammer, Norway.

Drogoul, C., Poncet, C. and Tisserand, J.L. 2000b. Feeding ground and pelleted hay rather than chopped hay to ponies: 1. Consequences for in vivo digestibility and rate of passage of digesta. *Animal Feed Science and Technology* **87**: 117-130.

Drogoul, C., Tisserand, J.L. and Poncet, C. 2000a. Feeding ground and pelleted hay rather than chopped hay to ponies: 2. Consequences on fibre degradation in the cecum and the colon. *Animal Feed Science and Technology* **87**: 131-145.

Dulphy, J.P., Martin-Rosset, W., Dubroeucq, H. and Jailler, M. 1997b. Evaluation of voluntary intake of forage trough-fed to light horses. Comparison with sheep, factors of variation and prediction. *Livestock Production Science* **52**: 97-104.

Dulphy. J.P., Martin-Rosset, W., Dubroeucq, H., Ballet, J.M., Detour, A. and Jailler, M. 1997a. Compared feeding patterns in ad libitum intake of dry forages by horses and sheep. *Livestock Production Science* **52**: 49-56.

Duncan, P. 1980. Time-budgets of Camargue horses. *Behaviour* **72**: 26-48.

Duncan, P. 1992. Horses and grasses - The nutritional ecology of equids and their impact on the Camargue. Springer Verlag, New York, USA.

Duncan, P., Foose, T.J., Gordon, I.J., Gakahu, C.G. and Lloyd, M. 1990. Comparative nutrient extraction from forages by grazing bovids and equids: a test of the nutritional model of equid/bovid competition and coexistence. *Oecologia* **84**: 411-418.

Dunnet, M. and Harris, R.C. 1999. Influence of oral ß-alanine and L-histidine supplementation on the carnosine content of the gluteus medius. *Equine Veterinary Journal* **30**: 499-504.

Dusek, J. and Richter, L. 1972. Aenderungen der Körpermasse von Stuten im Verlauf der Gravidität. *Arch. Tierzucht* **15**: 361-366.

Dutton, M.F. 1996. Fumonisins, mycotoxins of increasing importance: Their nature and their effects. *Pharmacological Therapy* **70**: 137-161.

Dyson, S.J. 1994. Training the Event Horse. In Hodgson, D.R. and Rose J.R. (eds) The Athletic Horse: The Principles and Practice of Equine Sports Medicine. WB Saunders Company, London, UK.

Dziewiatkowski, D.D. 1987. Binding of calcium by proteoglycans in vitro. *Calcified Tissue International* **40**: 265-269.

Dziewiatkowski, D.D. and Majznerski, L.L. 1985. Role of proteoglycans in endochondral ossification: inhibition of calcification. *Calcified Tissue International* **37**: 560-564.

Dyce, K.M. Sack, W.O. and Wensing, C.J.G. 1996. Textbook of Veterinary Anatomy. W.B. Saunders Co. Philadelphia, USA.

E

Eamens, G.J., Macadam, J.F. and Laing, E.A. 1984. Skeletal abnormalities in young horses associated with zinc toxicity and hypocuprosis. *Australian Veterinary Journal* **61**: 205-207.

Easley, J. 1997. Equine dentistry – The benefits of proper care. *World Equine Veterinary Review* **2**: 3.

Easley, J. 1998. Dental Corrective Procedures. *Veterinary Clinics of North America: Equine Practice* **14**: 114-158.

Eck, Van. G. 1987. Intake of fresh grass by horses. Paardenhouderij, Praktijkonderzoek Rundvee, Schapen en Paarden, Publikatie 49, Lelystad, The Netherlands.

Egan, D.A. and Murrin, M.P. 1973. Copper concentration and distribution in the livers of equine fetuses, neonates and foals. *Research in Veterinary Science* **15**: 147-148.

Eigenmann, J.E. 1986. Wachstumshormon und insulinahnlicher Wachstumsfaktor beim Hund: klinische und experimentelle Untersuchungen. *Schweiz Arch Tierheilkunde* **128**: 57-78.

Eigenmann, J.E., Patterson, D.F. and Froesch, E.R. 1984. Body size parallels insulin-like growth factor I but not growth hormone secretory capacity. *Acta Endocrinologica* **106**: 448-453.

Eitzer, O. and Rapp, H.J. 1985. Oral use of synthetic ß-carotene in breeding mares. *Praktische Tierarzt.* **66**: 123-126.

Ekmann, L. 1970. Klinisch chemische Diagnostik von Schilddrusenstorungen un der Veterinarmedizin. Wien. *Tierarztl. Wschr.* **57**: 286-292.

El Shaer, H.M., Omed, H.M., Chamberlain, A.G. and Axford, R.F.E. 1987. Use of faecal organisms from sheep for the in vitro determination of digestibility. *Journal of Agricultural Science, Cambridge* **109**: 257-259.

El Shorafa, W.M. 1978. Effect of Vitamin D and sunlight on growth and bone development of young ponies. *Journal of Animal Science* **48**: 882-886.

Ellis, A.D. 2003. Merries voeren veulens. Voeding in relatie tot osteochondrose. (The Mare feeds the foal, Feeding in relation to osteochondrosis). Praktijkonderzoek Veehouderij, Animal Sciences Group, WUR, The Netherlands

Ellis, A.D. 2001. Nutrition and the Development of Osteochondrosis in Foals. Internal rapport VPA-01-11. Research Institute for Animal Husbandry, ASG, WUR, The Netherlands.

Ellis, A.D. 2002a. Energy Assessment and Standards in Horses, Praktijkonderzoek Veehouderij, Animal Sciences Group, Wageningen UR, VPA-02-02-29, The Netherlands.

Ellis, A.D. 2002b. Energy sources and requirements for work, Internal report VPA-02-03, Praktijkonderzoek Veehouderij, Lelystad, The Netherlands.

Ellis, A.D. 2002c. Protein and essential amino acid requirements in the horse. Intern rapport VPA-02-31. Research Institute for Animal Husbandry, ASG, WUR, The Netherlands.

Ellis, A.D., Visser, E.K. and Reenen, C.G. 2003. Effects of high concentrate versus high fibre diets on performance parameters, behaviour and welfare of the horse. Proceedings of the 54th European Association, Rome, Italy.

Ellis, A.D. 2003a. Ingestive and digestive processes in equines. PhD thesis, Writtle College, Essex University, UK.

Ellis, A.D. 2004. Raar en Voer. Horse and Feed, Roodbank, NL.

Ellis, A.D. and Boekhoff, M. (2003) Mineral requirements for horses. Research Institute for Animal Husbandry. ASG, WUR, NL.

Ellis, A. D. and Hill J. 2000. Intake Behaviour of Horses when offered short chopped high temperature dried lucerne and short chopped lucerne silage. Measuring Behaviour *3rd International Conference on*

References

Methods and Techniques in Behavioural Research, Noldus Information Technology, The Netherlands.

Ellis, A.D. and Hill, J. 2002. Feed factors affecting intake behaviour and water intake in horses. *Proceedings of 52nd European Association of Animal Production*, Cairo, Egypt.

Ellis, A.D. and van Tilburg G.M. 2002. Assessment of growth rates in Dutch Warmblood horses in relation to osteochondrosis. *Proceedings of the 52nd European Association of Animal Production*, Cairo, Egypt.

Ellis, A.D., Hill, J., Fagence, K. and Warr, E.M. 2000. Effect of dental condition on short-term intake rates of hay and faecal particle size in adult horses. *Proceedings of the 51st European Association of Animal Production*, The Hague, The Netherlands.

Ellis J.M. 2002. Effect of forage intake on bodyweight and performance. *Equine Veterinary Journal* **34**: 66-70.

Ellis, J.,M., Hollands, T. and Allen, D.E. 2002. Effect of forage intake on bodyweight and performance. *Equine Veterinary Journal* **34**: 66-70.

Ellis, R.N.W and Lawrence, T.L.J. 1978. Energy under-nutrition in the weanling filly foal, - II Effects on body condition and epiphyseal plate closure in the fore-limb. *British Veterinary Journal* **134**: 322-332.

Ellis, R.N.W. and Lawrence, T.L.J. 1980. The energy and protein requirements of the light horse. *British Veterinary Journal* **136**: 116-21.

Ellis, W.C., Matis, J.H., and Lascano, C. 1979. Quantitating ruminal turnover. *Federation Proceedings* **38**: 2702-2706.

ENESAD 2002. 2nd European Workshop on Equine Nutrition. The growing horse: nutrition and prevention of growth disorders. Dijon, France.

Essen-Gustavsson, B., Blomsrand, E., Karlstrom, K., Lindholm, A. and Persson, S.G.B. 1991. Influence of diet on substrate metabolism during exercise. *Equine Exercise Physiology* **3**: 288-298.

Evans, J.W. 1971. Effect of fasting, gestation, lactation and exercise on glucose turnover in horses. *Journal of Animal Science* **33**: 1001-1004.

Evans, J.W. 1975. Relationship between luteal function and metabolic clearance and production rates of progesterone in the mare. *Journal of Reproduction and Fertility* **23**: 177-182.

Evans, J.W., Hughes, J.P., Neely, D.P., Stabenfeldt, G.H. and Winget, C.M. 1979. Episodic LH secretion patterns in the mare during the estrous cycle. *Journal of Reproduction and Fertility* **79**: 485.

F

Fagen R.M. 1981. Animal play behaviour. Oxford University Press, New York, USA.

Fahey, G.C. and Jung, H.G. 1983. Lignin as a marker in digestion studies: A review. *Journal of Animal Science* **48**: 941.

Faichney, G.J. 1975. The use of markers to partition digestion within the gastro-intestinal tract of ruminants. In, McDonald, I.W. and Warner, A.C.I. (eds.) Digestion and Metabolism in the Ruminant. University of New England Publishing Unit, Australia.

Faichney, G.J. 1993. Digesta Flow. In, Forbes, J.M. and France, J. (eds.) Quantitative aspects of Ruminant digestion and metabolism. Cambridge University Press, Cambridge, UK.

Farley, E.B., Potter, G.D., Gibbs, P.G., Schumacher, J. and Murracy-Gerzik, M. 1995. Digestion of soybean meal protein in the equine small and large intestine. 24-26. *Proceedings of the 14th Equine Nutrition Physiology Society*, Ontario, California.

Fazio E., Medica P. and Ferlazzo A., 1995. Effetto delle procedure pre-trasporto e del trasporto sulle funzionalità surrenalica e tiroidea nel Cavallo. *Atti Soc. It. Sci Vet.* **49**: 265-266.

Fazio E., Medica P., Campo G. M., Grasso L. and Ferlazzo A., 1996. Livelli circolanti di _-endorfina, ACTH e cortisolo in cavalli prima e dopo trasporto di differente lunghezza. *Atti Soc. It. Sci Vet.* **57**: 81-82.

Febbraio, M.A., Chiu, A., Angus, D.J., Arkinstall, M.J. and Hawley, J.A. 2000. Effects of carbohydrate ingestion before and during exercise on glucose kinetics and performance. *Journal of Applied Physiology* **89**: 2220-2226.

Feh C. 1988. Social behaviour and relationships of Przewalski horses in Dutch semi-reserves. *Applied Animal Behaviour Science* **21**: 71-87.

Feh C. 1999. Alliances and reproductive success in Camargue stallions. *Animal Behaviour* **57**: 705-713.

Feh C. and Mazières de J. 1993. Grooming at a preferred site reduces heart rate in horses. *Animal Behaviour* **46**: 1191-1194.

FEI 1999. World wide survey. FEI, Switzerland.

Feige, K., Furst, A., Eser, M.W. 2002. Effects of housing, feeding and use on equine health with emphasis on respiratory and gastrointestinal diseases. *Schweizer Archiv fur Tierheilkunde* **144**: 348-355.

Fenton, J.I. 1999. The effects of glucosamine on equine articular cartilage degradation. Michigan State University, PhD Thesis, USA.

Ferguson D.L. and Rosales-Ruiz, J. 2001. Loading the problem loader: the effects of target training and shaping on trailer-loading behavior of

References

horses. *Journal of Applied Behavioural Analysis* **34**: 409-423

Ferlazzo A., Fazio E., Murania C. and Piccione G. 1993. Physiological responses of stallions to transport stress. 544. *Proceedings of International Congress of Applied Ethology*, Humboldt University, Berlin, FRG.

Ferlazzo A., Medica P., Campo G.M., Grasso L. and Aronica V. 1997. Circulating levels of catecholamines, ß-endorphin, ACTH, cortisol, total and free iodothyronines in horses after transport on roads of different lengths. 53. *Proceedings of 5th World Equine Veterinary Association*.

Fernandez-Diaz M.D.P. 1990. Effects of the L-tryptophan on the stress response of Thoroughbred yearlings. MSc Thesis, University of Florida, USA.

Ferraro, J. and Cote, J.F. 1984. Broodmare management techniques improve conception rates. *Standardbred* **12**: 56-58

Feskanich, D., Weber, P., Willett, W.C, Rockett, H., Booth, S.L. and Colditz, G.A 1999. Vitamin K intake and hip fractures in women: a prospective study. *American Journal of Clinical Nutrition* **69**: 74-79.

Fadok, V.A. and Wild, S. 1983. Suspected cutaneous iodinism in a horse. *Journal of American Veterinary Medical Association* **183**: 1104.

Farley, E.B., Potter, G.D., Gibbs, P.G., Schumacher, J. and Murracy-Gerzik, M. 1995. Digestion of soybean meal protein in the equine small and large intestine. 24-26. *Proceedings of the 14th Equine Nutrition Physiology Society*, Ontario, California, USA.

Filmer, J.F. 1933. Enzootic marasmus of cattle and sheep. *Australian Veterinary Journal* **9**: 163 – 166.

Finkler-Schade, C. 1997. Felduntersuchung während der Weideperiode zur Ernährung von Fohlenstuten und Saugfohlen sowie zum Wachstumsverlauf der Fohlen, Dissertation, Rheinischen Friedrich-Wilhelms-Universitat, Bonn, FN Verlag

Finkler-Schade, C. 2000. So wird-bzw bleibt ihre Stute tragend. *Der Hannoveraner* **6**: 74-77.

Firth, E.C., Van Weeren, P.R., Pfeiffer, D.U., Delahunt, J. and Barneveld, A. 1999. Effect of age, exercise and growth rate on bone mineral density in third carpal bone and distal radius of Dutch Warmblood foals with osteochondrosis. *Equine Veterinary Journal* **31**: 74-78.

Fisher, P.W.F., Giroux, A. and L'Abbee, M.R. 1983. Effect of zinc on mucosal copper binding and on kinetics of copper absorption. *Journal of Nutrition* **113**: 462-469.

Flade, J. 1957. Wachstum und Entwicklung beim Pferd. *Tierzucht* **11**: 162-170.

Fleurence, G. and Duncan, P. 2001. Voluntary Intake of grass by horses at pasture. *Proceedings of 52nd European Association of Animal Production*, Budapest, Hungary.

Fonnesbeck, P.V., Lydman, R.K, Vander Nodt, G.W, Symonds, L.D. 1967. Digestibility of the proximate nutrients of forage by horses. *Journal of Animal Science* **26**: 1039-1045.

Fonnesbeck, P.V. 1968a. Consumption and excretion of water by horses receiving an all hay and hay-grain diet. *Journal of Animal Science* **27**: 1350-1356.

Fonnesbeck, P.V. 1968. Digestion of Soluble and Fibrous Carbohydrate of Forage by Horses, 1336 – 1344. New Jersey Agricultural Experiment Station, Department of Animal Sciences, New Brunswick, USA.

Fonnesbeck, P.V. 1981. Estimating digestible energy and TDN for horses with chemical analysis of feeds. *Journal of Animal Science* **53**: 241-242.

Fonnesbeck, P.V. and Symons, L.D. 1967. Utilisation of carotene of hay by horses. *Journal of Animal Science* **26**: 1030-1037.

Forbes, J.M. 1988. Metabolic aspects of the regulation of voluntary food intake and appetite. *Nutrition Research Review* **1**:

Forbes, J.M. 1995. Voluntary Food Intake and Diet Selection in Farm Animals, CAB International, Wallingford, UK.

Forbes, J.M. and France, J. 1993. Quantitative aspects of Ruminant digestion and metabolism. Cambridge University Press, Cambridge, UK

Foreman, J.H. 1996. Thermoregulation in the horse exercising under hot and humid conditions. *Pferdeheilkunde* **12**: 405-408.

Foss M.A. 1999. Myositis occurrence in endurance horses following air transport. 6-7. *Proceedings of 18th Annual Meeting of AESM*, Reno, Nevada, USA.

Fox, E. L. (1986) Sports Physiology, Saunders College Publishing, New York

Francis, D., Diorio, J., Laplante, P., Weaver, S., Seckl, J.R., and Meaney, M.J. 1996. The Role of Early Environmental Events in Regulating Neuroendocrine Development - Moms, Pups, Stress, and Glucocorticoid Receptors. Annals of the New York Academy of Sciences.

Frank, N.B., Meachyam, T.N., Easely, K.J. and Fontenot, J.P. 1983. The effect of by-passing the small intestine on nutrient digestibility and absorption in the pony. 243-248. *Proceedings of the 8th Equine Nutrition Physiology Society*, Lexington, USA.

Frape, D.L. 1981. Digestibility studies in horses and ponies. *Proceedings of the 32nd Annual Meeting of the European Association of Animal*

Production, Zagreb, Yugoslavia,

Frape, D.L. 1987. Calcium balance and dietary protein content. *Equine Veterinary Journal* **19**: 265-270.

Frape, D.L. 1998. Equine Nutrition and Feeding, Blackwell Science Ltd., London, UK.

Frape, D.L. 1988. Nutrition of the Leisure Horse. 205-219. In Recent Advances in Animal Nutrition (Haresign, W. and Cole D.J.A. eds). Butterworths, Kent.

Frape, D.L. 1989. Nutrition and the growth and racing performance of thoroughbred horses. *Proceedings of the Nutrition Society* **48**: 141-152.

Frape, D.L., Tuck, M.G., Sutcliffe, N.H. and Jones, D.B. 1982. The use of inert markers in the measurement of the digestibility of cubed concentrate and of hay given in several proportions to the pony, horse and white rhinoceros (*Diceros simus*). *Comparative Biochemistry and Physiology A* **72**: 77-83.

Fraser A.F. and Broom D.M. 1998. Farm Animal Behaviour and Welfare, 3rd ed., CAB International, Wallingford, UK.

Fraser A.F. 1992. The behaviour of the horse. CAB International Wallingford, UK

Frean, S.P., Abraham, L.A. and Lees, P. 1999. In vitro stimulation of equine cartilage proteoglycan synthesis by hyaluronan and carprofen. *Research in Veterinary Science* **67**: 183-190.

Freedman, L.J., Garcia, M.C. and Ginther, O.J. 1979. Influence of ovaries and photoperiod on reproductive function in the mare. *Journal of Reproduction and Fertility* **27**: 79-86.

Freeman D.A., Hinchcliff K.W. and Schott, H.C. 2001. Effect of water restriction on equine behaviour and physiology. *Equine Veterinary Journal* **33**: 97-98

Freeman, D.W., Potter, G.D., Schelling, G.T. and Kreider, J.L. 1988. Nitrogen metabolism in mature horses at varying levels of work. *Journal of Animal Science* **66**: 407-412.

Freetly, H.C., Ferrel, C.L. and Jenkins, F. 2000. Timing of realimantation of mature cows that were feed-restricted during pregnancy influences calf birth weight and growth rates. *Journal of Animal Science* **78**: 2790-2796.

Freinkel, N., Phelps, R.L. and Metzger, B.E. 1979. Intermediary metabolism during normal pregnancy. 1-31. In H.N. Sutherland and J.M. Stowers (eds.) Carbohydrate metabolism in pregnancy and the newborn. Springer, Berlin, FRG.

Friend, M.A. and Nash, D. 2000. Pasture intake by grazing horses. RIRDC

Publication No. 00/. Project No. UCS-22A. Rural Industries Research and development Corporation, Australia.

Frey L.P., Kline K.H., Foreman J.H. and Lyman, J.T. 2001 Technical note: using calcium carbonate as an osmolar control treatment for acid-base studies in horses. *Journal of Animal Science* **79**: 1858-1862.

Friedrich, W. 1979 Pelletieren von Mischfutter, Technischer Prozeß und Wirkung auf Inhalts und Zusatzstoffe. *Dtsch. Tierärztl. Wschr.* **86**: 399-405.

Froesch, E.R., Schmid, C., Schwander, J. and Zapf, J. 1985. Actions of insulin-like growth factors. *Annual Review of Physiology* **47**: 443-467.

Fubini, S.L, Erb, H.N., Freeman, K.P. and Todhunder, R.J. 1999. Prognostic factors affecting survival of 507 horses with joint disease (1983-1990). *Canadian Journal of Veterinary Research* **63**: 253-260.

G

Gabel, A.A. 1985. Correlation of dietary mineral to incidence and severity of metabolic bone disease in Ohio and Kentucky. *Proceedings of the American Association of Equine Practitioners* **31**: 445-464.

Gabel, A.A., Knight, D.A., Reed, S.M., Pultz, J.A., Powers, J.D., Bramlage, L.R. and Tyznik, W.J. 1987. Comparison of incidence and severity of developmental orthopedic disease on 17 farms before and after adjustment of ration. *Proceedings of the American Association Equine Practitioners* **33**: 163-169.

Gallagher, J.R. and McMeniman, N.P. 1988. The nutritional status of pregnant mares and non-pregnant mares grazing South East Queensland pastures. *Equine Veterinary Journal* **20**: 414-416.

Gallagher, K. and Stowe, H.D. 1980. Influence of exercise on serum selenium and peroxide reduction system of racing Standardbreds. *American Journal of Veterinary Research* **41**: 1333-1337.

Gallagher, J.R., Hintz, H., and Schryver, H.F. 1984. A nutritional evaluation of chopped hay for equines. *Animal Production in Australia* **15**: 349-352.

Gallagher, K., Leech, J. and Stowe, H. 1992b. Protein energy and dry matter consumption by racing Thoroughbreds: a field survey. *Journal of Equine Veterinary Science* **12**: 43-48.

Garcia, M.C., Freedman, L.H. and Ginther, O.J. 1979. Interaction of seasonal and ovarian factors in the regulation of LH and FSH secretion in the mare. *Journal of Reproduction and Fertility* **27**: 103.

References

Garner, H.E., Coffmann, J.R., Hahn, A.W., Hutcheson, D. and Tumbleson, M.E. 1975. Equine laminitis of alimentary origin: an experimental model. *American Journal of Veterinary Research* **36**: 441-449.

Garrido-Varo, A. 1999. Current and future applications of NIRS technology, *Feed Technology* **3**: 19–21.

Gaustad, G., Kjaersgaad, P. and Dolvik., N.I. 1995. Lameness in three-year old standardbred trotters - influence of parameters determined during the first year of life. *Journal of Equine Veterinary Science* **15**: 233-239.

Geelen, N.J., Sloet van Oldruitenborgh-Oosterbaan, M.M. and Beynen, A.C. 2001. Extra vet in de voeding van sportpaarden – een voordeel ? *Tijdschrift voor Diergeneeskunde* **126**: 310-316.

Geelen, N.J., Blazquez, C, Geelen, J.H., Sloet van Oldruitenborgh-Oosterbaan, M.M. and Beynen, A.C. 2001. High fat intake lowers hepatic fatty acid synthesis and raises fatty acid oxidation in aerobic muscle in Shetland ponies. *British Journal of Nutrition* **86**: 31-36.

Geelen, N.J., Jansen, W.L., Sloet van Oldruitenborgh-Oosterbaan, M.M., Breukirk, H.C. and Beynen, A.C. 2001. Fat feeding increases equine –released lipoprotein lipase activity. *Journal of Veterinary Internal Medicine* **15**: 478-481.

GEH (1994) Empfehlungen zur Energie und Nahrstoffversorgung der Pferde, Gesellschaft der Ernahrungsphysiologie der Haustiere, DLG Verlag, Frankfurt, Germany.

GEH, 1995. (Deutsch. Langerwirtschafts Gesellschaft). Futterwerttabellen. Pferde. 3. Erweiterte und neugestaltete Auflage. DLG. Verlage Frankfurt/Main, Germany.

George, M. and Ryder, O.A. 1986. Mitochondrial DNA evolution in the genus Equus. *Molecular Biology and Evolution* **3**: 535-546.

Georgievskii, V.I. 1982. The physiological role of microelements. 171-224. In Georgievskii, V.I (ed) Mineral Nutrition of Animals. Butterworths, London.

Gibbs A.E. and Friend T.H., 2000. Effect of animal density and trough placement on drinking behavior and dehydration in slaughter horses. *Journal of Equine Veterinary Science* **20**: 643-650.

Gibbs, P.G., Sigler, D.H. and Goehring, T.B. 1987. Influence of diet on growth and development of yearling horses. 37. *Proceedings of 10th Equine Nutrition Physiology Society* Fort Collins, Colorado, USA.

Gibbs, P.G., Potter, G.D., Schelling, G.T., Kreider, J.L. and Boyd, C.L. 1988. Digestion of hay protein in different segments of the equine digestive tract. *Journal of Animal Science* **66**: 400-406.

Gibbs, P.J., Potter, G.D., Schelling, G.T., Kreider, J.L. and Boyd, C.L. 1996.

The significance of small vs. large intestinal digestion of cereal grain and oilseed protein in the equine. *Journal of the Equine Veterinary Science* **16**: 60-65.

Gibbs, P.G. and Cohen, N.D. 2001. Early management of race-bred weanlings and yearlings on farms. *Journal of Equine Veterinary Science* **21**: 279-283.

Gierup J., Larrson M. and Lennquist S., 1976. Incidence and nature of horse-riding injuries. *Acta Chir. Scand.* **142**: 57-61.

Giger-Reverdin, S. 2000. Characterisation of feedstuffs for ruminants using some physical parameters. *Animal Feed Science and Technology* **86**: 53-69.

Gilder, H. and Boskey, A.L. 1990. Dietary lipids and the calcifying tissue. 244-265. In, Simmons, D.J. (ed) Nutrition and Bone Development, Oxford University Press, Oxford, UK.

Gill, M.S. and Lawrence, L.M. 1997. Effects of feeding frequency on digestion in ponies, Equine Nutrition Conference 1997, Kentucky Equine Research, Kentucky, USA.

Gillham S.B., Dodman N.H., Shuster L., Kream, R. and Rand, W. 1994. The effect of diet on cribbing behavior and plasma ß-endorphin in horses. *Applied Animal Behaviour Science* **41**: 147–153.

Givens, D.I., Baker, C.W. and Zamime, B. 1992. Regions of normalised near infrared reflectance difference spectra related to the rumen digestion of straws. *Animal Feed Science and Technology* **36**: 1-12.

Givens, D.I., Moss, A.R. and Adamson, A.H. 1993. Influence of growth stage and season on the energy value of fresh herbage. 1. Changes in metabolizable energy content. *Grass and Forage Science* **48**: 166-174.

Glade, M.J. 1983. Nutrition and performance of racing thoroughbreds. *Journal of Equine Veterinary Science* **15**: 31-36.

Glade, M J. 1984. The influence of dietary fiber digestibility on the nitrogen requirements of mature horses. *Journal of Animal Science* **58**: 638-645.

Glade, M.J., Krook, L., Schryver, H.F. and Hintz, H.F. 1981. Growth inhibition by chronic dexamethasone treatment of foals. *Journal of Equine Veterinary Science* **1**: 198-201.

Glade, M.J. and Belling, T.H. 1984. Growth plate cartilage metabolism, morphology and biochemical composition in over and underfed horses. *Growth* **48**: 473-482.

Glade, M.J. and Belling, T.H. 1986. A dietary aetiology for osteochondroitic cartilage. *Journal of Equine Veterinary Science* **6**: 175-187.

Glade, M.J. and Luba, N.K. 1987. Benefits to foals of feeding soybean

References

meal to lactating broodmares. 593-594. Proceedings of the 10th Equine Nutrition and Physiology Society, Colorado State University, Fort Collins, USA.

Glade, M.J., Beller, D., Bergen, J., Berry, D., Blonder, E., Bradley, J., Cupelo, M. and Dallas, J. 1985. Dietary protein in excess of requirements inhibits renal calcium and phosphorous reabsorption in young horses. *Nutrition Reports International* **31**: 649-659.

Glade, M.J., Drook, L., Schryver, H.F. and Hintz, H.F. 1983. Effects of dietary energy supply on serum thyroxine, triidothyronine and insulin concentrations in young horses. *Journal of Endocrinology* **104**: 93-98.

Glinsky, M.J., Smith, R.M., Spires, H.R. and Davis, C.L. 1976. Measurement of volatile fatty acid production in the cecum of the pony. *Journal of Animal Science* **42**: 1465-1470.

Godbee, R.G., and Slade, L.M. 1981. The effect of urea or soybean meal on the growth and protein status of young horses. *Journal of Animal Science* **53**: 670-676.

Goering, H.K. and van Soest, P.J. 1970. Forage fiber analysis. USDA Handbook No.379, Washington DC, USA.

Goedegebuure, S.A. and Hazewinkel, H.A.W. 1981. Voeding in bostofwisseling. *Tijdschrijft voor Diergeneeskunde* **106**: 234-243.

Goedegebuure, S.A., Hani, H.J., Van der Valk, P.C. and Van der Wal, P.G. 1980. Osteochondrosis in six breeds of slaughter pigs, I. A morphological investigation of the status of osteochondrosis in relation to breed and level of feeding. *Veterinary Quarterly* **2**: 28-41.

Goedhart, P.W. 1990. Comparison of multivariate calibration methods for prediction of feeding value by near infrared reflectance spectroscopy. *Netherlands Journal of Agricultural Science* **38**: 449-460.

Goodwin, D. 2002. Foraging enrichment for stabled horses: effects on behaviour and selection. *Equine Veterinary Journal* **34**: 686-691.

Goodwin, D., Davidson, H.P.B. and Harris, P. 2002. Foraging enrichment for stabled horses, Effects on behaviour and selection. *Equine Veterinary Journal* **34**: 686-691.

Gough M.R., 1999. A note on the use of behavioural modification to aid clipping ponies. *Applied Animal Behaviour Science* **63**: 171-175.

Goodson, J., Tyznik, W.J., Cline, J.H. and Dehority, B.A. 1988. Effects of an abrupt diet change from hay to concentrate on microbial numbers and physical environment in the cecum of the pony. *Applied and Environmental Microbiology* **54**: 1946-1950.

Grace, N.D., Gee, E.K., Firth, E.C. and Shaw, H.L.2002. Digestible energy intake, dry matter digestibility and mineral status of grazing New

Zealand thoroughbred yearlings. *New Zealand Veterinary Journal* **50:** 63-69.

Grace N.D., Pearce S.G., Firth E.C., and Hennessy P.F. 1999. Concentrations of macro- and micro-elements in the milk of pasture-fed thoroughbred mares. *Australian Veterinary Journal* **77:** 177-180.

Grace, N.D. 1983. Manganese (Mn). 80-83. In N. D. Grace (ed) The mineral requirements of grazing ruminants. New Zealand Society of Animal Production, Occasional Symposium 9.

Graham, P.M., Ott, E.A., Brendermuhl, J.H. and Ten Broeck, S.H. 1994. The effect of supplemental lysine and threonine on growth and development of yearling horses. *Journal of Animal Science* **72:** 380-386.

Graham, R., Sampson, J. and Hester, H.R. 1940. Results of feeding zinc to pregnant mares and to mares nursing foals. *Journal of the American Veterinary Medical Association* **97:** 41-47.

Graham, T.E., Turcotte, L.P., Kiens, B. and Richter, E.A. 1997. Effect of endurance training on ammonia and amino acid metabolism in humans. *Medicinal Science and Sports Exercise* **29:** 646-653.

Grandin T., 1987. Animal handling. *Veterinary Clinics of North America: Food Animal Practice* **3:** 323-338

Grandin T., 1999. Safe handling of large animals. *Occupational Medicine* **14:** 195-212.

Grandin T., McGee, K. and Lanier J.L. 1999. Prevalence of severe welfare problems in horses that arrive at slaughter plants. *Journal of American Veterinary Medicine Association* **214:** 1531-1533

Gray, P. 1998. Diseases of the digestive system. J.A. Allen and Company United, London, UK.

Green, E.M. and Green, S.L. 1986. Vitamin K_3 : Toxicosis and therapeutic considerations for use in horses. *Modern Veterinary Practice* 625-628.

Green, A.L., Simpson, E.J., Littlewood, J.J., Macdonald, I.A., Greenhaff, P.L. 1996. Carbohydrate ingestion augments creatine retention during creatine feeding in man. *Acta Physiol Scand.* **158:** 195–202.

Green, H.J., Jones, L.L., Hughson, R.L., Painter, D.C. and Farrance, B.W. 1987. Training-induced hypervolemia: lack of an effect on oxygen utilization during exercise. *Medical Science and Sports Exercise* **19:** 202-206.

Green, W.T. and Banks, H.H. 1953. Osteochondritis dissecans in children. *Journal of Bone Joint Surgery* **35A:** 26-47.

Greenhaff, P.L., Harris, R.C., Snow, D.H., Sewell, D.A. and Dunnett, M. 1991. The influence of metabolic alkalosis upon exercise metabolism

References

of the Thoroughbred horse. *European Journal of Applied Physiology and Occupational Physiology* **63**: 129-134.

Grenet, E., Martin-Rosset, W. and Chenost, M. 1984. Compared size and structure of plant particle in the horse and the sheep feces. *Canadian Journal of Animal Science* **64**: 345-346.

Greppi, G.F., Casini, L., Gatta, D., Orlandi, M. and Pasquini, M. 1996. Daily fluctuations of haematology and blood biochemistry in horses fed varying levels of protein. *Equine Veterinary Journal,* **28**: 350-353.

Groves, C.P. and Mazák, V. 1967. On some taxonomic problems of Asiatic wild asses with a description of a new subspecies (Perissodactyla, Equidae). *Zeitschrift für Säugetierkunde* **32**: 321-355.

Groves, C.P. and Ryder, O.A. 2000. Systematics and Phylogeny of the horse. 1 –24. In A.T. Bowling and A. Ruvinsky (eds) The Genetics of the Horse. CABI Publications, Wallingford, UK.

Grondahl, A.M. and Dolvik, N.J. 1993. Heritability estimation of osteochondrosis in the tibiotarsal joint and of bony fragments in the palmar/plantar portion of metacarpo- and metatarsophalangeal joints of horses. *Journal of the American Veterinary Medical Association* **216**: 1013-1017.

Grovum, W.L. and Williams, V.J. 1973. Rate of passage of digesta in sheep. 5. Theoretical considerations based on a physical model and computer simulation. *British Journal of Nutrition* **30**: 377-389.

Guise J., 1991. Humane animal management – the benefits of improved systems for pig production, transport and slaughter. 50-58. In, Carruthers, S.P. (ed). Farm Animals: It pays to be Humane. CAS Paper 22, Centre for Agricultural Strategy, Reading, UK.

Gunson, D.E., Kowalcyk, D.F., Shoop, C.R. and Ramberg, C.F. 1982. Environmental zinc and cadmium pollution associated with generalized osteochondrosis, osteoporosis, and nephrocalcinosis in horses. *Journal of the American Veterinary Medical Association* **180**: 255-299.

Gütte, J.O. 1972. Energiebedarf laktierender Stuten. In: Handbuch der Tierernährung, Bd. II (Hrsg.: Lenkeit, W., ind Breirem, K.). Paul Parey, Hamburg and Berlin, FRG.

H

Habener, J.F. and Potts, J.T. 1976. Relative effectiveness of magnesium and calcium on the secretion and biosynthesis of parathyroid hormone in vitro. *Endocrinology* **98**: 197-202.

Hachten, W. 1995. Cribbing treatment. *The Equine Athlete* **8**: 20-21.

Haenlein, G.F.W., Holdren R.D., Yoon Y.M. 1966. Comparative response of horses and sheep to different physical forms of alfalfa hay. *Journal of Animal Science* **25**: 740-743.

Haenlein, G.F.W., Smith, R.C. and Yoon, Y.M. 1966. Determination of the faecal excretion rate of horses with chromic oxide. *Journal of Animal Science* **25**: 1091-1095.

Haigh, J.C., Stookey, J.M., Bowman, P. and Waltz, C. 1997. A comparison of weaning techniques in farmed Wapiti (Cervus elaphus). *Animal Welfare* **6**: 255-264.

Hall S.J.G. and Bradshaw R.H. 1998. Welfare aspects of transport by road of sheep and pigs. *Journal of Applied Animal Welfare Science* **1**: 235-254.

Hale, C.E. and Moore-Colyer, M.J.S. 2001. Voluntary food intake and apparent digestibility of hay, big bale grass silage and red clover silage by ponies. 468-469. Proceedings of 17th Equine Nutrition and Physiology Symposium, Kentucky, USA.

Hallebeek J.M., van 't Klooster A.T. and Beynen A.C. 1999. Nutrition of horses: ration calculation and assessment. *Tijdschr Diergeneeskunde* **124**: 406-411

Hama H., Yogo M. and Matsuyama Y. 1996. Effects of stroking horses on both humans' and horses' heart rate responses. *Japanese Psychological Research* **38**: 66-73.

Hannah H.W. 2001. Liability for horse injury—extending the assumption of risk doctrine. *Journal of American Veterinary Medicine Association* **219**: 922-923

Hanson, R.R., Smalley, L.R., Huff, G.K., White, S. and Hammad, T.A. 1997. Oral treatment with glucosamine-chondroitin sulfate compound for degenerative joint disease in horses. *Equine Practice* **19**: 16.

Harbers, L.H., McNally, L.K and Smith, W.H. 1981. Digestibility of three grass hays by the horse and scanning electron microscopy of indigested leaf remnants. *Journal of Animal Science* **53**: 1671-1677.

Harman A.M, Moore S., Hoskins, R. and Keller, P., 1999. Horse vision and an explanation for the visual behaviour originally explained by the 'ramp retina'. *Equine Veterinary Journal* **31**: 384-390.

Harman J. 1999. Tack and saddle fit. *Veterinary Clinics of North America: Equine Practice* **15**: 247-261.

Harper, O.F., and Noot, G.W.V. 1974. Protein requirement of mature maintenance horses. *Journal of Animal Science* **39**: 183.

Harrington, D.D. 1974. Pathologic features of magnesium deficiency in young horses fed purified rations. *American Journal of Veterinary Research* **35**: 503.

References

Harrington, D.D., Walsh, J. and White, V. 1973. Clinical and pathological findings in horses fed zinc deficient diets. 51. Proceedings of 3rd Equine Nutrition and Physiology Symposium, Gainesville, Florida, USA.

Harrington, D.D. 1982. Acute vitamin D_2 (ergocalciferol) toxicosis in horses: Case report and experimental studies. *Journal of the American Veterinary Medical Association* **180**: 867-873.

Harris, P.A. 1997. Energy sources and requirements of the exercising horse. *Annual Review of Nutrition* **17**: 185-210.

Harris, P.A. and Harris, R.C. 1998. Nutritional ergogenic aids in the horse – uses and abuses, In, Lindner, A (ed.) Conference on equine sports medicine and science, Cordoba, Spain.

Harris, P.A., Gomarsall, G.M., Davidson, H.P.B., Green, R.E. 2003. *Proceedings of the BEVA Specialist Days on Behaviour and Nutrition.* Equine Veterinary Journal, Newmarket, UK, 11–14.

Hatfield, R.D., Jung, H.G., Ralph, J., Buxton, D.R. and Weimer, P.J. 1994. Comparison of the insoluble residues produced by the Klason lignin and acid detergent lignin procedure. *Journal of the Science of Food and Agriculture* **65**: 51-58.

Hausberger M. and Muller C. 2002. A brief note on some possible factors involved in the reactions of horses to humans. *Applied Animal Behaviour Science* **76**: 339-344.

Hawkes, J., Hedges, M., Daniluk, P., Hintz, H.F. and Schryver, H.F. (1985) Feed preferences of ponies. *Equine Veterinary Journal* **17**: 20-22.

Hayes, M.H. 1994. Veterinary Notes for Horse Owners. Stanley Paul, London, UK.

Hazewinkel., H.A.W., Van den Brom, W.E., Van 't Klooster, A.Th., Voorhout, G. and Van Wees, A. 1991. Calcium metabolism of Great Dane dogs fed diets with various calcium and phosphorus levels. *Journal of Nutrition* **121**: S99-S106.

Hedhammer, A., Wu, F., Krook, L. Schryver, H., DeLahunta, A., Whalen, J.P., Kallfelz, F., Nunex, E., Hintz, H.F., Sheffy, B.E. and Ryan, A.D. 1974. Overnutrition and skeletal disease, An experimental study in growing Great Dane dogs. *Cornell Veterinarian* **64**: 1-16.

Heffner H.E. and Heffner R.S., 1983. The hearing ability of horses. *Equine Practice* **5**: 27-32.

Heffner R.S. and Heffner H.E. 1983. Hearing in large animals: horses (Equus Caballus) and cattle (Bos Taurus). *Behaviour and Neurological Science* **97**: 289-309

Heleski, C.R., Shelle, A.C., Nielsen, B.D. and Zanella, A.J. 2002. Influence of housing on weanling horse behavior and subsequent welfare. *Applied Animal Behaviour Science* **78**: 291-302.

Henderson J.V. and Waran N.K., 2001. Reducing equine stereotypies using an Equiball (Tm). *Animal Welfare* **10**: 73-80

Henderson J.V., Waran N.K. and Young R.J. 1996. The effect of an operant foraging device (The modified "Edinburgh Foodball") on the performance of stereotypic behaviour in the stabled horse. *Proceedings of the 30th International Congress of the International Society for Applied Ethology* 14-17 August, 1996, Guelph, Ontario, Canada.

Henderson J.V., Waran N.K. and Young R.J., 1997. Behavioural enrichment for horses: the effect of foraging device The Equiball on the performance of stereotypic behaviour in stabled horses. In, Mills, D.S., Heath, S.E. and Harrington, L.J. (eds). *Proceedings of the First International Conference on Veterinary Behavioural Medicine.* UFAW, Potters Bar, UK.

Henneke, D., Potter, D. and Kreider, J. 1984. Body condition during pregnancy and lactation and reproductive efficiency of mares. *Theriogenology* **21**: 897-909.

Henson, F.M., Davenport, C., Butler, L., Moran, I., Shingleton, W.D., Jeffcott, L.B. and Schofield, P.N. 1997. Effects of insulin and insulin-related peptides on the growth of fetal equine chondrocytes. *Equine Veterinary Journal* **29**: 441-447.

Henson, F.M., Davies, M.E. and Jeffcott, L.B. 1997. Equine dyschondroplasia (osteochondrosis) - histological findings and type VI Collagen localisation. *Veterinary Journal* **154**: 53-62.

Henson, F.M.D., Davies, M.E., Schofield, P.N. and Jeffcott, L.B. 1996. Expression of types II, VI and X collagen in equine growth cartilage during development. *Equine Veterinary Journal* **28**: 189-199.

Henson, F.M.D., Davies, M.E., Skepper, J.N. and Jeffcott, L.B. 1995. Localisation of alkaline phosphatase in equine growth cartilage. *Journal of Anatomy* **187**: 151-159

Henson, F.M.D., Schofield, P.N. and Jeffcott, L.B. 1997. Transforming growth factor-b expression and localisation in normal and dyschondroplastic equine growth cartilage. *Equine Veterinary Journal* **29**: 267-273.

Herbert, V. 1996. Vitamin B-12. In Ziegler, E. E. and Filer, L.J. (eds.) Present Knowledge in Nutrition. International Life Sciences Institute Press, Washington, DC.

Herrera-Saldana, R.E., Huber, J.T. and Poore, M.H. 1990. Dry matter, crude protein and starch digestibility of five cereal grains. *Journal of Dairy Science* **73**: 2386-2393.

Hertel, J., Altmann, H.J. and Drepper, K. 1970. Ernahrungphysiologische Unetrsuchungen beim Pferd. II. Rohnahrstoffuntersuchungen im

Magen-Darm-Trakt von Schlachtpferden. *Z. Tierphysiol.* **26:** 169-174.

Hetzel, B.S. and Maberly, G.F. 1986. Iodine. In W. Mertz (ed) Trace elements in human and animal nutrition. Academic Press, London, UK.

Hernandez-Vidal, G., Jeffcott, L.B. and Davies, M.E. 1998. Immunolcalisation of cathepsin B in equine dyschondroplastic articular cartilage. *Veterinary Journal* **156:** 193-201.

Herrler, A., Pell, J.M., Allen, W.R., Beier, H.M. and Stewart, F. 2000. Horse conceptuses secrete insulin-like growth factor-binding protein 3. *Biology of Reproduction* **62:** 1804-1811.

Hertsch, B. 1980. Die Ossifikationsvorgange am Kniegelenk beim jungen Pferd. *Zentralblatt für Veterinärmedizin* A. **27:** 279-289

Hesse H. 1957. Entwicklung und Wachstumsverlauf bei Kleinpferden. *Z. Tierzüchtg. u. Züchtungsbiol.* **70:** 175-181.

Hickman J. 1987. Horse management. Academic Press, New York, USA.

Hidiroglou, M., Ivan, M., Bryan, M.K., Ribble, C.S., Janzen, E.D., Proulx, J.G. and Elliot, J.I. 1990. Assessment of the role of manganese in congenital joint laxity and dwarfism in calves. *Annales de Recherches Veterinnaires* **21:** 281-284

Hill, G.M., Ku, P.K., Miller, E.R., Ullrey, D.E., Stowe, H.D., Losty, T.A. and O'Dell, B.L. 1982. Zinc-induced copper deficiency in swine. 564-567. In, Gawthorne, J.M., Howell, J.M., White, C.L. (eds.) *Trace element metabolism in man and animals.* Springer Verlag, New York, USA.

Hill, J. 2002. Effect of level of inclusion and method of presentation of a single distillery by-product on the processes of ingestion of concentrate feeds by horses. *Livestock Production Science* **75:** 209-218.

Hill, J and Gutsell, S. 1998. Effect of supplementation of a hay and concentrate diet with live yeast culture on the digestibility of nutrients in horses. *Proceedings of the British Society of Animal Science,* Scarborough, UK. 128.

Hill, J. and Braithwaite, A.R. 1999. Ingestive behaviour of horses offered distillery by-products.144. *Proceedings of the British Society of Animal Science,* Scarborough, UK.

Hill, J., Davidson, E.V. and Kennedy, M.J. 2000. Short-term ingestion rate and ingestive behaviour of horses given dry concentrate feed. 365. *European Association of Animal Production, 51st Annual Meeting,* The Hague, The Netherlands.

Hill, J., Tracey, S.V., Willis, M., Jones, L. and Ellis, A.D. 2001 Yeast culture in equine nutrition and physiology. 97-114. Proceedings of Alltech 17th Annual Symposium, Nottingham University Press, UK.

Hinchcliff, K.W. 1998. Fluids and Electrolytes in Athletic Horses. *The*

Veterinary Clinics of North America, Equine Practice. W. B. Saunders Company, London

Hinds, G., Bell N.P., McMaster D. and McCluskey D.R. 1994. Normal red cell magnesium concentrations and magnesium loading tests in patients with chronic fatigue syndrome. *Annals of Clinical Biochemistry* **31**: 459-461.

Hintz H.F., Hogue D.E., Walker E.F., Lowe, J.E. and Schreyver, H.F. 1971. Apparent digestion in various segments of the digestive tract of ponies fed diets with varying roughage-grain ratios. *Journal of Animal Science* **32**: 245-248.

Hintz, H.F. 1990. Digestion in ponies and horses. *Equine Practice* **12**: 5-6.

Hintz, H.F. 1990. The use of crude protein and digestible protein to evaluate feedstuffs. *Equine Practice* **12**: 14-16.

Hintz, H.F. 1996. Round bales. *Equine Practice* **18**: 7-8.

Hintz, H.F., White, K.K., Short, C.E., Lowe, J.E. and Ross, M. 1980. Effects of protein levels on endurance horses. *Journal of Animal Science* **51**: 202-203.

Hintz, H.F. 1999. The many phases of selenium. *World Equine Veterinary Review* **4**: 19-22.

Hintz, H.F. and Loy, R.G. 1966. Effects of pelleting on the nutritive value of horse rations, *Journal of Animal Science* **25**: 1059-1062.

Hintz, H.F., Lowe, J.E. and Schryver, H.F. 1969. Protein sources for horses. 65-68. Proceedings of the Cornell Nutrition Conference for Feed Manufacturers, Cornell University, Ithaca, New York, USA.

Hintz, H.F., Schryver, H.F., Doty, J., Lakin, C. and Zimmerman, R.A. 1984. Oxalic acid content of alfalfa hays and its influence on the availability of calcium, phosphorus and magnesium in ponies. *Journal of Animal Science* **58**: 939.

Hintz, H.F., White, K., Short, C., Lowe, J. and Ross, M. 1980. Effects of protein levels on endurance horses. *Journal of Animal Science* **51**: 202-203.

Hobbs G.D, Yealy, D.M. and Rivas, J. 1994. Equestrian injuries: a five-year review. *Journal of Emergency Medicine* **12**: 143-145.

Hobo, S., Kuwano, A. and Oikawa, M. 1995. Respiratory changes in horses during automobile transportation. *Journal of Equine Science* **6**: 135-139.

Hochberg, Z., Maor, G., Lewinson, D. and Silbermann, M. 1989. The direct effects of growth hormone on chondrogenesis and osteogenesis. 123-128. In, Heap, R.B., Prosser, C.G., Lamming, G.E. (eds) Biotechnology in Growth Regulation. Butterworths, London, UK.

Hodgson, D.R. and Rose J.R. 1994. The Athletic Horse: The Principles and

References

Practice of Equine Sports Medicine. WB Saunders Company, London

Hodgson, D.R., Rose, J.R., Allen, J.R. and DiMauro, J. 1984. Glycogen depletion patterns in horses competing in day 2 of a three day event. *Cornell Veterinarian* **75**: 366-374.

Hodgson, J. 1985. Ingestive Behaviour, In, Leaver, J.D. (1985) Herbage Intake Handbook, British Grassland Society, Berkshire, UK.

Hoffman, R.R. 1989. Evolutionary steps of ecophysiological adaptation and diversification of ruminants: a comparative view of their digestive system. *Oecologia* **78**: 443-457.

Hoffmann, L., Schiemann, W., and Klippel, R. 1967. Untersuchungen über den Energieumsatz beim Pferd unter besonderer Berücksichtigung der horizontal Bewegung. *Archive Tierernährung* **17**: 441-449.

Hoffman, R.M., Lawrence, L.A., Kronfeld, D.S., Cooper, W.L., Sklan, D.J., Dascanio, J.J. and Harris, P.A. 1999. Dietary carbohydrates and fat influence radiographic bone mineral content of growing foals. *Journal of Animal Science* **77**: 3330-3338.

Hogan, J.P. and Phillipson, A.T. 1960. The rate of flow of digesta and their removal along the digestive tract of the sheep. *British Journal of Nutrition* **14**: 147.

Holland, J.L., Kronfeld, D.S. and Meacham, T.N. 1996. Behaviour of horses is affected by soy lecithin and corn oil in the diet. *Journal of Animal Science* **74**: 1252-1255.

Holland, J.L., Kronfeld, D.S., Sklan, D., Harris, P.A. 1998. Calculation of fecal kinetics in horses fed hay or hay and concentrate. *Journal of Animal Science* **76**: 1937-1944.

Holick, M.F. 1994. Vitamin D: new horizons for the 21st century. *American Journal of Clinical Nutrition* **60**: 619-630.

Hoppe, F. and Philipsson, J. 1985. A genetic study of osteochondrosis in Swedish horses. *Equine Practice* **7**: 7-15

Hörnicke, H., Meixner, R. and Pollmann, R. 1983. Respiration in exercising horses. 7-16. In, D.H. Snow, S.G.B. Persson, and R.J. Rose (eds.) Equine Exercise Physiology. Granta Edition, Cambridge, UK.

Hoskins, W.E. and Asling, C.W. 1977. Influence of growth hormone and thyroxine on endochondral osteogenesis in themandibular condyle and proximal tibial epiphyses. *Journal of Dental Research* **56**: 509-517.

Hospes, R., Herfen K. and Bostedt, H. 1996. Die Korrelationen zwischen Stute und Fohlen bezuglich der Selen- und Vitamin E-Versorgung im perinatalen Zeitraum. *Pferdeheilkunde* **12**: 194-196.

Houbiers, H.J.Ph.L. and Smolders, E.A.A. 1990. Opname van vers gras van verschillende opbrengsten, In: Praktijkonderzoek, Proefstation

voor de Rundveehouderij, Schapenhouderij en Paardenhouderij, Lelystad, The Netherlands.
Houghton Brown J. and Powell-Smith V. 1986. Horse and Stable Management. Collins, London, UK.
Houpt K.A. 1983. Self-directed aggression: a stallion behavior problem. *Equine Practice* **5**: 6-8.
Houpt, K.A. 1989. Investigating equine ingestive, maternal and sexual behaviour in the field and in the laboratory. *Journal of Animal Science* **68**: 4161-4166.
Houpt, K.A. 1990. Ingestive Behaviour. *Veterinary Clinics of North America: Equine Practice* **6**: 319-337
Houpt K. A. 1995. New perspectives on equine stereotypic behaviour. *Equine Veterinary Journal* **27**: 82-83.
Houpt K.A. 1998. Domestic Animal Behavior for Veterinarians and Animal Scientists. Ames: Iowa State University Press, USA.
Houpt K.A. and Houpt T.R. 1988. Social and illumination preferences of mares. *Journal of Animal Science* **66**: 2159-2164.
Houpt K.A. and Lieb S., 1993. Horse handling and transport. 233-252. In, Grandin, T. (ed) Livestock handling and transport. CAB International, Wallingford, UK.
Houpt K.A., Eggleston A., Kunkle K. and Houpt T.R. 2000. Effect of water restriction on equine behaviour and physiology. *Equine Veterinary Journal* **32**: 341-344.
Houpt K.A., Houpt T.R., Johnson J.L., Erb H.N. and Yeon S.C., 2001. The effect of exercise deprivation on the behaviour and physiology of straight stall confined pregnant mares. *Animal Welfare* **10**: 257-267
Houpt, T.R. and Houpt, K.A. 1971. Nitrogen conservation by ponies fed a low protein ration. *American Journal of Veterinary Research* **32**: 579-588.
Householder, P.D., Potter, G.D., Lichenwalnes, R.E. 1977. Digestible energy and protein requirements of yearling horses. 126. *Proceedings of the 5th Equine Nutrition Physiology Society Symposium.* St. Louis, USA.
Hudson J.M., Cohen N.D., Gibbs P.G., and Thompson J.A., 2001. Feeding practices associated with colic in horses. *Journal of the American Veterinary Medical Association* **219**: 1419-1425.
Huijser, M.P. 1996. Begrazing in de Oostvaardersplassen : effecten op de vegetatie-structuur en het terreingebruik van grote herbivoren en ganzen, Lelystad : Rijkswaterstaat, Directie IJsselmeergebied
Hunter, G.K. and Weinert, C.A. 1996. Inhibition of proteoglycan biosynthesis decreases the calcifiction of chondrocyte cultures. *Connective Tissue Research* **35**: 379-384.

References

Hunter, L. and Houpt K.A. 1989. Bedding material preferences of ponies. *Journal of Animal Science* **67**: 1986-1991.

Hurst, D., Romney, D.L. and Murray, A. H. 1999. Evaluation of the potential of short term intake rate (STIR) to predict effects of chop length on in vivo parameters in sheep. 105. Proceedings of the British Society of Animal Science, Scarborough, UK.

Hurtig, M.B. and Pool, R.R. 1996. Pathogenesis of equine osteochondrosis. 362-383. In, McIlwraith, C. W. and Trotter, G.W, (eds.) Joint Disease in the Horse. W.B. Saunders, Philadelphia, USA.

Hurtig, M.B., Green, S.L., Dobson, H., Mikuni-Taaki, Y and Choi, J. 1993. Correlative study of defective cartilage and bone growth in foals fed a low copper diet. *Equine Veterinary Journal* **16**: 66-73.

Hyslop, J.J. and Calder, S. 2001. Voluntary intake and apparent digestibility in ponies offered alfalfa based forages ad libitum. 90. *Proceedings of the British Society of Animal Science*, Scarborough, UK.

Hyslop, J.J. and Cuddeford, D. 1996. Investigations on the use of the mobile bag technique in ponies. *Proceedings of British Society of Animal Science,* Scarborough, UK.

Hyslop, J.J, Jessop, N.S., Stefansdottir, G.J. and Cuddeford, D. 1997. Comparative protein and fibre degradation measured in situ in the caecum of ponies and in the rumen of sheep *Proceedings of British Society of Animal Science*, Scarborough, UK.

Hyslop, J.J. 1998. Use of techniques adapted from ruminant research to evaluate the digestion of feedstuffs in horses. 131. *Proceedings of the British Society of Animal Science,* Scarborough, UK.

I

Ike, K., Nuruki, R., Imai, S and Ishii, T. 1983. Composition of intestinal ciliates and bacteria excreted in feces of the race horse. *Japanese Journal of Veterinary Science* **45**: 157-163.

Ilancic, D. 1959. Einfluß des Stutenalters auf die Trächtigkeitsdeuer und das Fohlengewicht. *Zuchthygiene* **3**: 128-131

Ingram, D.L. and Evans, S.E. 1980. Dependence of thyroxine utilization rate on dietary composition. *British Journal of Nutrition* **43**: 525.

INRA, 1978. Alimentation des Ruminants. INRA Publications, Route de Saint-Cyr 78000 Versailles, France.

INRA 1984. Le Cheval. Instituut National de la Recherche Agronomique, Paris, France.

INRA 1990. L'alimentation des chevaux. Instituut National de la Recherche Agronomique, Paris, France.

Irvine, C.H.G. and Alexander. S.L. 1998. Managing the mare for optimal fertility. *Journal of Equine Science* **9**: 83-87.

Isaksson, O.G.P., Eden S., Albertsson-Vikland, F., Jansson, J.O., Friberg, U. and Madsen, K. 1984. Direct action of growth hormone on cartilage metabolism. Human Growth Hormone Symposium. Plenum New York, USA.

Isaksson, O.P.G., Lindahl, A., Nielsson, A. and Isgaard, J. 1987. Mechanisms of the stimulatory effect of growth hormone on longitudinal bone growth. *Endocrine Reviews* **8**: 426-434.

Istasse, L., Van Eanaeme, C., Hornick, J.L., Van Calster, P. and Huet, D. 1996. Composition, Intakes and apparent digestibility of three grass silages offered to horses. Animal Science **62**: 647.

Ivers, T. 1986. Osteochondrosis, undernutrition or overnutrition. *Equine Practice* **8**: 15-19.

Ivers, T. 2002. Carbohydrates in performance horses. *Proceedings of the First European Equine Health and Nutrition Congress*, Scientec Matrix, Antwerp, Belgium

J

Jackson, M.J., Jones, D.A. and Edwards, R.H.T. 1983. Vitamin E and skeletal muscle. 224-239. Biology of Vitamin E, CIBA Foundation Symposium 101. Pitman Books, London, UK.

Janis, C. 1976. The evolutionary strategy of Equidae and the origin of rumen and cecal digestion. *Evolution* **30**: 757-774.

Janis, C.M. and Ehrhardt, D. 1988. Correlation of relative muzzle width and relative insicor width with dietary preference in ungulates. *Zoological Journal of the Linnean Society* **92**: 267-284.

Janosi, S. Huszenica, G.; Kulcsar, M. and Krodi, P. 1998. Endocrine and reproductive consequences of certain endotoxin-mediated diseases in farm mammals: a review. *Acta-Vet-Hung.* **46**: 71-84.

Jansen, W. 2001. Fat intake and apparent diegestibility of fibre in horses and ponies, PhD Thesis, Utrecht University, The Netherlands.

Jansen, W.L., Van der Kuilen, J., Geelen, S.N.J. and Beynen, A.C. 2000. The effect of replacing nonstructural carbohydrates with soybean oil on the digestibility of fibre in trotting horses. *Equine Veterinary Journal* **32**: 27-30

Jansson, J.O., Eden, S. and Isaksson, O. 1983. Sites of action of testosterone and estradiol on longitudinal bone growth. *American Journal of Physiology* **244**: E135-E140.

Jansson, A. and Dahlborn, K. 1999. Effects of feeding frequency and

References

voluntary salt intake on fluid and electrolyte regulation in athletic horses. *Journal of Animal Physiology* **87:** 50.

Jarrett, S.H., Schurg, W.A. and Reid, B.L. 1987. Plasma fractions of vitamin A alcohol, palmitate and acetate in horses fed deficient and excess dietary vitamin A. 1-4. *Proceedings of 10th Equine Nutrition and Physiology Symposium,* Fort Collins, Colorado, USA.

Jarrige. R. and Tisserand J.L. 1984. Nutrition et alimentation azotees, In: R. Jarrige, W. Martin-Rosset (eds) Le Cheval. Reproduction, sélection, alimentation, exploitation, INRA, Paris.

Jeffcott, L.B. 1997. Osteochondrosis in horses. *In Practice* **19:** 64-71.

Jeffcott, L.B., Buckingham, S.H.W., McCartney, R.N., Cleeland, J.C. and Scotti, E. 1988. Non-invasive measurement of bone: A review of clinical and research applications in the horse. *Equine Veterinary Journal* **6:** 71-78.

Jeffcott, L.B. and Davies, M.E. 1999. Osteochondrosis into the New Millennium. *Equine Veterinary Education* **12:** 51-56.

Jeffcott, L.B. and Henson, F.M.D. 1998. Studies on growth cartilage in the horse and their application to aetiopathogenesis of dyschondroplasia (Osteochondrosis). *The Veterinary Journal* **156:** 177-192.

Jeffcott, L.B. and Savage, C.L. 1996. Nutrition and development of osteochondrosis (dyschondroplasia). *Pferdeheilkunde* **12:** 338-342.

Jefferson, L.S., and Korner, A. 1967. A direct effect of growth hormone on the incorporation of precursors into proteins and nucleic acids of perfused rat liver. *Biochemical Journal* **104:** 826.

Jespersen, J. 1949. Normes pour les bsoins des animaux: chevaux, porcs et poules. In Ve Congress International Zootechie, Paris. 33-43. In, INRA 1984. Jarrige, R. and Martin-Rosset, W. (eds.) Le Cheval, Reproduction, Selection, Alimentation, Exploitation, Instituut National de la Recherche Agronomique, Paris, France.

Johannessen, A., Hagen, C. and Galbo, H. 1981. Prolactin, growth hormone, thyrotropin, 3,53'triiodothyronine, and thyroxine responses to exercise after fat and carbohydrate enriched diet. *Journal of Clinical Metabolism* **52:** 56-61.

Johansen, S., Hakannsson, K. and Anderson, K. 1993. Effect on carcass traits of selection for increased lean tissue growth rate in swine on low or high dietary protein levels. *Acta Agriculturae Scandinavica* **43:** 207-213.

Johnson, A.L. 1987. Gonadotropin-releasing hormone treatment induces follicular growth and ovulation in seasonally anoestrus mares. *Biology of Reproduction* **36:** 1199-1206.

Jones, W.E. 1988. Equine Sports Medicine, Lea and Fabinger, UK

Jordan, R.M. and Myers, Y. 1972. Effect of protein levels on the growth of weanling and yearling ponies. *Journal of Animal Science* **34**: 578-581.

Jordan, R.M., Meyers, V.S., Yoho, B. and Spurrell, F.A. 1975. Effect of calcium and phosphorus levels on growth, reproduction, and bone development of ponies. *Journal of Animal Science* **40**: 78.

Jordan, R.M. 1982. Effect of weight loss of gestating mares in subsequent production. *Journal of Animal Science* **55**: 208S.

Julliand, V. 1992. Microbiology of the equine hindgut. *Pferdeheilkd. (Sonderheft)* 42-47.

Jung, H.G. and Allen, M.S. 1995. Characteristics of plant cell walls affecting intake and digestibility of forages by ruminants. *Journal of Animal Science* **73**: 2774-2790.

Junnila, M., Korkeala, H., Rahko, T., and Salmi, A. 1987. The interaction of cadmium and selenium in horse kidney cortex in relation to histopathological changes. *Acta Veterinaria Scandanavia* **28**: 201-208

K

Kalkhoff, R.J., Kissebah, A.H. and Kim, H.J. 1979. The influence of hormonal changes of pregnancy on maternal metabolism. 29-46. Pregnancy metabolism, diabetes and the fetus. Ciba Foundation Symposium no 63. Excepta Medica. Amsterdam, The Netherlands.

Kallela, K. 1973. Effect of prolonged plant oestrogen treatment in female rats. 3. Some histochemical, biochemical and histopathological changes. *Nordisk-Veterinaermedicin* **25**: 232-241.

Kaneene, J.B., Miller, R.A., Ross, W.A., Gallagher, K., Marteniuk, J., Rook, J. 1997. Risk factors for colic in the Michigan (USA) equine population. *Preventive Veterinary Medicine* **30**:.23-36.

Kaneene, J.B., Ross, W.A., Miller, R.A. 1997. The Michigan equine monitoring system. II.: Frequencies and impact of selected heath problem. *Preventive Veterinary Medicine* **29**: 277-292.

Kaseda Y., Khalil A.M. and Ogawa H. 1995. Harem stability and reproductive success of Misaki feral mares. *Equine Veterinary Journal* **27**: 368-372.

Kaseda Y., Ogawa H. and Khalil A.M. 1997. Causes of natal dispersal and emigration and their effects on harem formation in Misaki feral horses. *Equine Veterinary Journal* **29**: 262-266.

Kay, R.N.B. 1960. The rate of flow and composition of various salivary secretions in sheep and calves. *Journal of Physiology* **29**: 395-415.

References

Kealy, R.D., Lawler, D.F. and Monti, K.L. 1993. Effects of dietary electrolyte balance on subluxation of the femoral head in growing dogs. *American Journal of Veterinary Research* **54**: 555-562.

Keeling, L.J., Blomberg, A. and Ladewig, J. 1999. Horse-riding accidents: When the human-animal relationship goes wrong. 86. *Proceedings of International Socikety for Applied Ethology* Lillehammer, Norway.

Keiper R. R. and Keenan M. A. 1980. Nocturnal activity patterns of feral horses. *Journal of Mammalogy* **61**: 116-118.

Keiper R.R. 1986. Social structure. *Veterinary Clinics of North America: Equine Practice* **2**: 465-483.

Kellner. O. and Fingerling, G. 1924. Die Ernährung der landwirtschaftlichen Nutziere, 10th Editions. Paul Parey, Berlin, Germany.

Kelly, A.P., Jones, J.R., Gillick, J.C. and Sims, L.D. 1984. Outbreak of botulism in horses. *Equine Veterinary Journal* **16**: 519-521.

Kemme, P.A. 1998. Phytate and phytases in pig nutrition. Phd Thesis, University of Utrecht, The Netherlands.

Kennedy M. J. and Hill J., 2000 Equine welfare research in the 21st century. *51st Annual Meeting of the European Association of Animal Production*, The Hague, The Netherlands.

Kennedy M.J., Schwabe A.E. and Broom D.M. 1993. Crib-biting and wind-sucking stereotypies in the horse. *Equine Veterinary Education* **5**: 142-147.

Kennedy, L. and Little, L. 1966. VFA in equine cecal fluid and blood. *Journal of Animal Science* **31**: 207-208

Kennedy, L.G. and Hershberger, T.V. 1974. Protein quality for the non-ruminant herbivore. *Journal of Animal Science* **39**: 506-511.

Kennedy, P.M. 1985. Effect of rumination on reduction of particle size of rumen digesta by cattle. *Australian Journal of Agricultural Research* **36**: 819-828.

Kern, D.L. and Bond, J. 1972. Eating patterns of ponies fed diets ad libitum. *Journal of Animal Science* **35**: 285.

Kern, D.L., Slyter, L.L., Leffel, Weaver, J.M. and Oltjen, R.R. 1974. Ponies versus Steers: Microbial and chemical characteristics of intestinal microflora. *Journal of Animal Science* **38**: 559.

Kesel, G.A., Knight, J.W., Kornegay, E.T., Veit, H.P. and Notter, D.R. 1983 Restricted energy and elevated calcium and phosphorus intake for boars during growth, 1. Feedlot performance and bone characteristics. *Journal of Animal Science* **57**: 82.

Khalil, A. M. and Murakami, N. 1999. Effect of natal dispersal on the reproductive strategies of the young Misaki feral stallions. *Applied Animal Behaviour Science* **62**: 281-291.

Kienzle, E. 1994. Small intestinal digestion of starch in the horse. *Medecine Veterinaire* **145**: 199-204.

Kienzle, E., Fehrle, S. and Opitz, B. 2002. Interactions between the apparent energy and nutrient digestibilities of a concentrate mixture and roughages in horses. *American Journal of Nutrition* **132**: 1778s-1780s.

Kienzle, E., Pohlenz, J. and Radicke, S. 1998. Microscopy of starch digestion in the horse. *Journal of Animal Physiology and Nutrition* **80**: 213-216.

Kienzle, E., Radicke, S., Wilke, S., Landes, E. and Meyer, H. 1992. Praeileale Starkeverdauung in Abhangigheit von Starke und zubereitung, Erste Europaische Konferenz uber die Ernahrung des Pferdes, Institut fur Tierernahrung, Tierarztliche Hochschule, Hannover.

Kiley M. 1972. The vocalisations of ungulates, their causation and function. *Z.Tierpsychology* **31**:171-182.

Kiley-Worthington M., 1987. The Behaviour of Horses in Relation to Management and Training. J. E. Allen, London.

Kiley-Worthington M., 1997. Equine welfare. J.A. Allen and Company Ltd. London, UK

Kiley-Worthington, M. 1984. Time-budgets and social interactions in horses: the effect of different environments. *Applied Animal Behaviour Science* **13**: 181.

Kilmer, DN., Sharp, D.C., Berghund, L.A., Grubaugh, W., McDowell, K.J. and Peck. L.S. 1982. Melatonin rythms in pony mares and foals. *Journal of Reproduction and Fertility* **32**: 303.

Kimura R. 1998. Mutual grooming and preferred associate relationships in a band of free-ranging horses. *Applied Animal Behaviour Science* **59**: 265-276

Kincaid, S.A., Allhands, R.V. and Pijanowski, G.J. 1985. Chondrolysis associated with cartilage canals of the epiphyseal cartilage of the distal humerus of growing pigs. *American Journal of Veterinary Research* **46**: 726-732.

Kirsch, T., Nah, H.D., Demuth, D.R., Harrison, G., Golub, E.E., Adams, S.L. and Pacifici, M. 1997. Annexin V-mediated calcium flux across membranes is dependent on the lipid composition: implications for cartilage mineralization. *Biochemistry* **36**: 3359-3367.

Klein, G.L. and Coburn, J.W. 1991. Parenteral Nutrition: Effect on bone and mineral homeostasis. *Annual Reviews in Nutrition* **11**: 93-119.

Klemt, O.W. 1986. The effect of supplementation with synthetic b-carotene on postpartum fertility of thoroughbred mares studied by progesterone estimation in milk. PhD Thesis, Hannover Veterinary School, Germany.

Klooster, van 't Hallebeek, J.M. and Beynen, A.C. 1999. Voeding van

References

Paarden: Vertering, Energie- en Eiwitwaardering en Voedernormen. *Tijdschr. Diergneeskd.* **124:** 401-405.

Klug, E., Merkt, H., and Guenzel, A.R. 1977. Klinische Erfahrungen mit Prostaglandin F2a. Ueber den Einsatz von ICI 81008 Fluprostenol (Equimate) zur Zyklussteuerung beim Pferd. *Tieraerztl. Praxis* **5:** 474-480.

Knaap, J., Van Weeren, P.R. and Firth, E.C. 2000. Influence of copper status at birth on the development of osteochondrotic lesions. *51st Annual Meeting of the European Association of Animal Production,* The Hague, The Netherlands.

Knight, D.A., Gabel, A.A., Reed S.M., Bramlage, L.R., Tyznik, W.I. and Embertson, R.M. 1985. Correlation of dietary mineral to incidence and severity of metabolic bone disease in Ohio and Kentucky. *Proceedings of the American Association of Equine Practitioners* **31:** 445-461.

Knight, D.A., Weisbrode, S.E., Schmall, L.M., Reed, S.M., Gabel, A.A., Bramlage, L.R. and Tyznik, W.I. 1990. The effects of copper supplementation on the prevalence of cartilage lesions in foals. *Equine Veterinary Journal* **22:** 426-432.

Knox, K.L., Crownover, J.C., Wooden, G.R. 1970. Maintenance energy requirements for mature idle horse. 186-194. *Proceedings of the 7th Equine Nutrition and Physiology Symposium,* Warenton, Virginia, USA.

Knudsen, O. and Velle, W. 1964. Ovarian oestrogen levels in the non pregnant mare. Relationship to histological appearance of the uterus and its clinical status. *Journal of Reproduction and Fertility* **2:** 130.

Koenen, E.P.C., Dik, K.J., Knaap, J.H., Kuil, R.J.G. and Van Weeren, P.R. 2000. Evaluatie van de efficiëntie van selectiestrategieën tegen osteochondrose binnen de KWPN-rijpaardpopulatie, Koniklijk Warmbloed Paardenstamboek in Nederland.

Kold, S. E., Hickman, J. and Melson, F. 1986. An experimental study of the healing process of equine chondral and osteochondral defects. *Equine Veterinary Journal* **18:** 18-24.

Kollarczek, B., Enders, C., Friedrich, M. and Gedek, B. 1992. Auswirkungen der Rationszusammensetzung auf das Keimspektrum im Jejunum von Pferden. *Pferdeheilkunde, Sonderheft,* 49-54.

Kohlmeier, M., Salomon, A., Saupe, J. and Shearer, M.J. 1996. Transport of vitamin K to bone in humans. *Journal of Nutrition* **126:** 1192-1196.

Koller, B.L. Hintz, H.F. Robertson, J.B. and Van Soest, P.J. 1978. Comparative cell wall and dry matter digestion in cecum of the pony and the rumen of the cow using in vitro and nylon bag techniques. *Journal of Animal*

Science **47**: 1

Kolter L., 1984. Social relationship between horses and its influence on feeding activity in loose housing. In, Unshelm J., Putten van G. and Zeeb K. (eds.) *Proceedings of the International Congress of Applied Ethology in Farm Animals.* KTBL Darmstadt, Kiel, pp 151-155

Kornegay, E.T., Wang, Z., Wood, C.M. and Lindemann, M.D. 1997. Supplemental chromium picolinate influences nitrogen balance, dry matter digestibility and carcass traits in growing finishing pigs. *Journal of Animal Science* **75**: 1319-1323.

Kotb, A.R. and Luckey, T.D. 1972, Markers in Nutrition. *Nutrition Abstracts and Reviews* **42**: 812-845.

Krawielitzki, K., Schadereit, R., Wünsche, J., Völker, T. and Bock, H.D. 1983. Untersuchungen über Resorption und Verwertung von ins Zäkum wachsender Schweine infundierten Aminosäuren. *Arch. Tierernährung* **33**: 731-742.

Krinsky, N.I. 1993. Actions of carotenoids in biological systems. *Annual Review in Nutrition* **13**: 561-587.

Kristnamoorthy, U., Muscato, T.V., Sniffen, C.J. and van Soest, P.J. 1982. Nitrogen fractions of selected feedstuffs. *Journal of Dairy Science* **65**: 217-225.

Kromann, R.P. 1967. A mathematical determination of energy values of ration ingredients. *Journal of Animal Science* **26**: 1131.

Kroneman, J. and Goedegebuure, S.A. 1980. Zinc poisoning in a foal Intra-articular damage. *Tijdschrijft voor Diergeneeskunde* **105**: 1049-1053.

Kruger, M.C., Coetzer, H. and De Winter, R. 1995. Eicosapentaenoic acid and docosahexaenoic acid supplementation increase calcium balance. *Nutrition Research* **15**: 211-219.

Kruzhova, E. 1968. Mikroelementy I vosproizvodeitel'naja funkeija kobyl. *Tr. Vses. Inst. Konevodstvo.* **2**: 28.

Krzak W.E., Gonyou H.W. and Lawrence L.M., 1991. Wood chewing by stabled horses, diurnal pattern and effects of exercise. *Journal of Animal Science* **69**: 1053–1058.

Kusunose R. 1992. Diurnal pattern of cribbing in stabled horses. *Japanese Journal of Equine Science* **3**: 173-176

Kuusaari J. 1983. Acupuncture treatment of aerophagia in horses. *American Journal of Acupuncture* **11**: 363-370.

Kwong, W.Y., Wild, A.E., Roberts, P., Willis, C. and Fleming, T.P. 2000. Maternal undernutrition during preimplantation period of rat development causes blastocyst abnormalities and programming of postnatal hypertension. *Development* **127**: 4195-4202.

References

L

LaCasha, P.A., Brady, H.A., Allen, V.G., Richardson, C.R. and Pond, K.R. 1999. Voluntary intake, digestibility, and subsequent selection of matua bromegrass, coastal bermudagrass, and alfalfa hays by yearling horses. *Journal of Animal Science* **77**: 2766-2773

Ladefoged, O. and Sturup, S. 1995. Copper deficiency in cattle, sheep and horses caused by excess molybdenum from fly ash: a case report. *Veterinary and Human Toxicology* **37**: 63-65

Lane J. G. and Mair T. S. 1987. Observations on headshaking in the horse. *Equine Veterinary Journal* **19**: 331-336.

Langer, P. 1988. The mammalian herbivore stomach: comparative anatomy function and evolution. G. Fischer, Stuttgart, Germany.

Laut J.E., Houpt K.A., Hintz H.F. and Houpt T.R. 1985. The effects of caloric dilution on meal patterns and food intake of ponies. *Physiology and Behavior* **35**: 549-554

Lawrence, L.A., Ott, E.A., Asquith, R.L. and Miller, G.J. 1987. Influence of dietary iron on growth, tissue mineral composition, apparent phosphorus absorption, and chemical properties of bone. 563. *Proceedings of 10th Equine Nutrition and Physiology Symposium*, Fort Collins, Colorado, USA.

Lawrence, L.M. 1986. The use of non-invasive techniques to estimate bone mineral content and bone strength in the horse. PhD dissertation, University of Florida, USA.

Lawrence, L.M. 1990. Nutrition and fuel utilization in the athletic horse. *Veterinary Clinics of North America: Equine Practice* **6**: 393-418.

Lawrence, L. 1994. Nutrition and the Athletic Horse. In: Hodgsen, D. R. and Rose, R. (eds) The Athletic Horse, W. B. Saunders Company, London.

Lawrence, T.L.J. 1990. Influence of palatability on diet assimilation in non-ruminants. In, Wiseman, J. and Cole, D.J.A. Feedstuff Evaluation. Butterworths, London, UK.

Leadon D.P., 1989. A preliminary report on studies on equine transit stress. *Journal of Equine Veterinary Science* **9**: 200-202.

Lebowitz, H.F. and Eisenbarth, G.S. 1975. Hormonal regulation of cartilage growth and metabolism. *Vitamins and Hormones* **33**: 575-648.

Lee J., Floyd T. and Houpt K.A. 2001. Operant and two-choice preference applied to equine welfare. 110. *Proceedings of the 35th International Society of Applied Ethology International Congress.*

Lee J., Houpt K.A. and Doherty O. 2001. A Survey of Trailering Problems in Horses. *Journal of Equine Veterinary Science* **21**: 237-241.

Lee, E.R., Lamplugh, L., Shepard, N.L. and Mort, J.S. 1995. The septoclast, a cathepsin B-rich cell involved in the resorption of growth plate cartilage. *Journal of Histochemistry and Cytochemistry* **43**: 525-536.

Lee, J., McAllister, E.S. and Scholz, R.W. 1995. Assessment of selenium status in mares and foals under practical management conditions. *Journal of Equine Veterinary Science* **15**: 240-245.

Lee, J.A. and Pearce, G.R. 1984. The effectiveness of chewing during eating on particle size reduction of roughages by cattle. *Australian Journal of Agricultural Research* **35**: 609.

Lehner P.N. 1987. Design and execution of animal behavior research: an overview. *Journal of Animal Science* **65**: 1213-1219.

Lema, O. and Sandstead, H.H. 1970. Zinc deficiency, effect on collagen and glycoprotein synthesis and bone mineralization. *Federation Proceedings* **29**: 297.

Leklem, J. E. 1990. Vitamin B6. 341-392. In, Machlin, L.J. (ed) Handbook of Vitamins. Marcel Dekker, New York, USA.

Lewis, L.D. 1979. Nutrition of the broodmare and growing horse and its role in epiphysitis. *Proceedings of American Association of Equine Practitioners* **25**: 269-288.

Lewis, L.D. 1995. Equine clinical nutrition: Feeding care. Williams and Williams, USA

Lillich, J.D., Bertone, A.L., Malemud, C.J., Weisbrode, S.E., Ruggles, A.J. and Stevenson, S. 1997. Biochemical, histochemical and immunohistochemical characterization of distal tibial osteochondrosis in horses. *American Journal of Veterinary Research* **58**: 89-98.

Lindner, A. 1997. Biochemical variable of energy metabolism in blood and plasma. Performance Diagnosis of Horses, Wageningen Pers, The Netherlands.

Lindner, A., Haupt, M., von Wittke, P. and Sommer, H. 1993. Effect of Mg supplementation on fertility parameters of mares and vitality of newborn foals. *Equine Nutrition and Physiology Society* 305-306.

Lindsell, C.E., Hilbert, B.J., McGill, C.A. 1983. A retrospective clinical study of osteochondrosis dissecans in 21 horses. *Australian Veterinary Journal* **60**: 291-293.

Linerode, P.A. 1966. Studies on the synthesis and absorption of B-complex vitamins in the equine. PhD dissertation, Ohio State,University, Columbus, USA.

Linerode, P.A. 1967. Studies on the synthesis and absorption of B-complex vitamins in the horse. *American Association of Equine Practitioners* **13**: 283.

Linklater, W.L. 2000. Adaptive explanation in socio-ecology: Lessons from

References

the Equidae. *Biological Reviews of the Cambridge Philosophical Society* **75:** 1-20

Lippiello, L., Idouraine, A., McNamara, P.S., Barr, S.C. and McLaughlin, R.M. 1998. Cartilage stimulatory and antiproteolytic activity is present in sera of dogs treated with a chondroprotective agent. *Canine Practice* **23:** 10-12.

Liu, S.K., Dolensek, E.P., Adams, C.R. and Tappe, J.R. 1983. Myelopathy and vitamin E deficiency in six Mongolian wild horses. *Journal of the American Veterinary Medical Association* **183:** 1266.

Longland, A. and Cairns, A. 1998. Sugars in grass – an overview of sucrose and fructan accumulation in temperate grasses. Dodson and Horrell Ltd. 1st-International Conference on feeding horses.

Lowry, J.B., Conlon, L.L., Schlink, A.C. and McSweeney, C.S. 1994. Acid detergent dispersible lignin in tropical grasses. *Journal of the Science of Food and Agriculture* **65:** 41-49.

Lopez Rivero, J.L., Sporleder, H.P., Quiroz-Rothe, E., Vervuert, I., Coenen, M. and Harmeyer J. 2002. Oral L-Carnitine combined with training promotes changes in skeletal muscle. In, Lindner, A. (ed) The Elite Dressage and 3-day Event Horse. Lensing Druck, Dortmund, FRG.

Lothammer, K.H. and Ahlswede, L. 1977. Untersuchungen uber eine spezifische, Vitamin- A-unabhangige Wirkung des ß-Carotins auf die Fertalitat des Rindes. 3. Mitteilung: Blutserumuntersuchungen (ß-Carotin, Vitamin A, SGOT, Gesamtcholesterin, Glukose, anorganischer Phosphor). *Deutsche Tierarztl Wochenschr.* **84:** 220-226.

Lucas, P.W. and Pereira, B. 1990. Estimation of fracture toughness of leaves. *Functional Ecology* **4:** 819-822.

Lucke, J.N. and Hall, G.N. 1980. Further studies on the metabolic effects of long distance riding: Golden Horseshoe Ride 1979. *Equine Veterinary Journal* **12:** 189-192.

Luescher U.A., McKeown D.B. and Dean H. 1998. A cross-sectional study on compulsive behaviour (stable vices) in horses. *Equine Veterinary Journal* **27:** 14-18.

Luescher U.A., McKeown D.B. and Halip J., 1991. Reviewing the causes of obserssive-compulsive disorders in horses. *Veterinary Medicine* **86:** 527-530.

Luginbuhl, J.M., Pond, K.R., Burns, J.C. and Fisher, D.S. 2000. Intake and chewing behaviour of steers consuming switchgrass preserved as hay or silage. *Journal of Animal Science* **78:** 1983-1989.

Lukaski, H. C. 1999. Chromium as a supplement. *Annual Reviews in Nutrition* **19:** 279-330.

Luo, G., Ducy, P., McKee, M.D., Pinero, G.J., Loyer, E., Behringer, R.R.

and Karsenty G. 1997. Spontaneous calcification of arteries and cartilage in mice lacking matrix GLA protein. *Nature* **386:** 78-81.

Lyons, R.K., Stuth, J.W., Huston, J.E. and Angerer, J.P. 1993. Predictions of the nutrient composition of the diets of supplemented versus unsupplemented grazing beef cows based on NIRS of faeces. *Journal of Animal Science* **71:** 530-538.

M

Macheboeuf, D., Marangi M., Poncet, C. and Martin-Rosset, W. 1995. Study of nitrogen digestion from dfferent hays by the mobile nylon bag technique in horses. *Annales de Zootechnie* **44:** 219.

Macievicz, R.A., Wootton, S.F., Etherington, D.J. and Duance, V.C. 1991. Susceptibility of the cartilage collagens types II, IX and XI to the cysteine proteinases, catepsins B and L. *FEBS Letters* **269:** 189-192.

Mackay, A. 1961. Some effects of drugs "in the doping of" racehorses. *New Zealand Veterinary Journal* **9:** 129.

Mackie, R.I. and Wilkins C.A. 1988. Enumeration of anaerobic bacterial microflora of the equine gastrointestinal tract. *Applied and Environmental Microbiology* **54:** 2155-2160.

Madigan, J.E. and Bell S.A. 1998. Characterisation of headshaking syndrome – 31 cases. *Equine Veterinary Journal* **27:** 28-29.

Madigan, J. E. and Bell S. A. 2001. Owner survey of headshaking in horses. *Journal of American Veterinary Medicine Association* **219:** 334-337.

Madigan, J. E., Kortz G., Murphy C. and Rodger L., 1995. Photic headshaking in the horse: 7 cases. *Equine Veterinary Journal* **27:** 306-311.

Madsen, J., Stensig, T., Weisbjerg, M.R., and Hvelplund, T. 1994. Estimation of the physical fill of feedstuffs in the rumen by the in sacco degradation characteristics. *Livestock Production Science* **39:** 43-47.

MAFF 1992. Energy Allowances and Feeding Systems for Ruminants, ADAS Reference Book 433, HMSO, London, UK.

Mahan, D.C. 2000. Effect of organic and inorganic selenium sources and levels in sow colostrum and milk selenium content. *Journal of Animal Science* **78:** 100-105.

Mair, T., Love, S., Schumacher, J. and Watson, E. 2002. Equine medicine, surgery and reproduction. WB Saunders Company. Ltd, London, UK.

Mal, M.E., Friend T.H., Lay D.C., Vogelsang S.G. and Jenkins O.C. 1991. Behavioural responses of mares to short-term confinement and social isolation. *Applied Animal Behaviour Science* **30:** 203-221.

Mal, M.E., Friend T.H., Lay D.C., Vogelsang S.G. and Jenkins O.C. 1991. Physiological responses of mares to short term confinement and social

References

isolation. *Equine Veterinary Science* **11**: 96-102.
Mal, M.E. and McCall C.A. 1996. The influence of handling during different ages on a halter training test in foals. *Applied Animal Behaviour Science* **50**: 115-120.
Mal, M.E., McCall C.A., Cummins K.A. and Newland M.C. 1994. Influence of preweaning handling methods on post-weaning learning ability and manageability of foals. *Applied Animal Behaviour Science* **40**: 187-195.
Manteca, X. and Deag, J.M. 1993. Individual differences in temperament of domestic animals: a review of methodology. *Animal Welfare* **2**: 247-268.
Mariani, P., Martuzzi, F., Formaggioni, A., Sabbioni, A. and Summer, A. 2000 Nitrogen distribution in Haflinger mare milk throughout six lactation months. *51st Annual Meeting of the European Association of Animal Production*, The Hague, The Netherlands.
Marinier, S.L. and Alexander A.J. 1988. Flehmen behaviour in the domestic horse: discrimination of conspecific odours. *Applied Animals Behaviour Science* **19**: 227-237.
Mars, L.A., Kiesling H.A., Ross T.T., Armstrong J.B. and Murray L. 1992. Water acceptance and intake in horses under shipping stress. *Equine Veterinary Journal* **12**: 17-20.
Martin, R.G., McMeniman, N.P., Norton, B.W. and Dowsett, K.F. 1996. Utilisation of endogenous and dietary urea in the large intestine of the mature horse. *British Journal of Nutrition* **76**: 376-386.
Martin-Rosset, W. 2001. Croissance osseuse chez le cheval. *Proceedings 27th J. Rech. Eq. Paris* **27**: 73-100.
Martin-Rosset, W., Boccard, R., Jussiaux, M., Robelin, J. and Trillaud-Geyl. C. 1983. Croissance relative des différents tissus, organes et régions corporelles entre 12 et 30 mois chez le cheval de boucherie de différentes races lourdes. *Annales Zootechnie* **32**: 153-174.
Martin-Rosset, W. 2000. Feeding standards for energy and protein for horses in France. *Advances in Equine Nutrition*, Nottingham University Press, UK.
Martin-Rosset, W. and Dulphy, J.P. 1987. Digestibility Interactions between Forages and Concentrates in Horses: Influence of Feeding Level - Comparison with Sheep. *Livestock Production Science* **17**: 263-276.
Martin-Rosset, W., Vermorel, M., Doreau, M., Tisserand, J.L. and Andrieu, J. 1994. The French Horse Feed Evaluation System and Recommended Allowances for Energy and Protein. *Livestock Production Science* **40**: 37-57.
Martin-Rosset, W. and Tisserand, J.L. 2002. Evaluation and expression of

protein allowances and protein value of feeds in the MADC system for the performance horse, First European Workshop on Equine Nutrition, ENESAD, France.

Martin-Rosset, W. and Vermorel, M. 1991. Maintenance energy requirements determined by indirect calorimetry and feeding trials in light horses. *Equine Veterinary Science* **11**: 42-45.

Martin-Rosset, W., Doreau, M., Boulot, S. and Miraglia, N. 1990. Influence of level of feeding and physiological state on diet digestibility in light and heavy breed horses. *Livestock Production Science* **25**: 257-264.

Masters, R.G., 1991. Equestrian injuries: a review. *Clinical Journal of Sport Medicine* **1**: 123-126.

Masumitsu, H., Ueda, Y., Yoshida, K., Nagasawa, Y. and Fujii, Y. 1981. Radiographic findings in limbs of foals and young growing horses. *Bulletin of the Equine Research Institute (Japan)* **18**: 19-27.

Matsui, T., Murakami, H., Yano, H., Fujikawa, H., Ossava, T. and Asai, Y. 1999. Phytate and phosphorus movements in the digestive tract of horses. *Equine Veterinary Journal* **30**: 505-507.

Maylin, G.H., Rubin, D.S. and Lein, D.H. 1980. Selenium and vitamin E in horses. *Cornell Veterinarian* **70**: 272.

Mathews, D.K. and Fox, E.L. 1976. The physiological basis of physical education and athletics. W B Saunders Company, London, UK.

Matthews, J.L., Martin, J.H., Sampson, H.W., Kunin, A.S. and Roan, J.H. 1970. Mitochondrial granules in the normal and rachitic rat epiphysis. *Calcified Tissue Research* **5**: 91-99.

McAfee, L.M., Mills D.S. and Cooper J.J. 2002. The use of mirrors for the control of stereotypic weaving behaviour in the stabled horse. *Applied Animal Behaviour Science* **78**: 159-173.

McAllan, A.B. and Lewis, P.E. 1985. The removal of glucose, maltose and different starches from the small intestine of steers. *Arch Tierernahr.* **35**: 495-505.

McKenzie, R.A., Blaney, B.J. and Gartner, R.J.W. 1981. The effect of dietary oxalate on calcium, phosphorus and magnesium balances in horses. *Journal of Agricultural Science, Cambridge* **97**: 69.

McBane, S., 1994. Behaviour Problems in Horses. David and Charles, Birmingham, UK.

McBride, S.D. 1996. A comparison of physical and pharmacological treatments for stereotyped behaviour in the horse. 26. In, Duncan, I.J.H., Widowski, T.M. and Haley D.B. (eds.) *Proceedings 30th International Congress International Society Applied Ethology.* CSAW, Guelph, Canada.

McBride, S.D. and Cuddeford, D. 2001. The putative welfare-reducing

References

effects of preventing equine stereotypic behaviour. *Animal Welfare* **10:** 173-189.
McBride, S.D. and Long, L. 2001. Management of horses showing stereotypic behaviour, owner perception and the implications for welfare. *Veterinary Record* **148:** 799-802.
McCall, C.A., Potter G.D. and Krender J.L. 1985. Locomotor, vocal and other behavioural responses to varying methods of weaning foals. *Applied Animal Behaviour Science* **14:** 27-35.
McCall, C.A., Potter, G.D., Kreider, J.L. and Jenkins, W.L. 1987. Physiological responses in foals weaned by abrupt or gradual methods. *Journal of Equine Veterinary Science* **7:** 368-374.
McCutcheon, L.J., Geor, R.J. and Hinchcliff, K.W. 1999. Effects of prior exercise on muscle metabolism during sprint exercise in horses. *Journal of Applied Physiology* **87:** 192-194.
McDonald, P., Edwards, R.A., Greenhalgh, J.F.D. and Morgan, C.A. 1995. Animal Nutrition. Longman, London, UK.
McDonnell, S.M. 1992. Normal and abnormal sexual behavior. *Veterinary Clinics of North America: Equine Practice* **8:** 71-89.
McDonnell, S.M. 1993. More on self-mutilative behavior in horses. Journal of the American Veterinary Medicine Association **202:** 1545-1546.
McDowell, L.R. 2000. Vitamins in Animal and Human Nutrition. Blackwell Science Limited, London, UK.
McGilvery, R.W. and Goldstein, G.W. 1983. Biochemistry: A functional approach W. B. Saunders Company, Philadelphia, USA.
McGreevy, P.D., Cripps P.J., French N.D., Green, L.E. and Nicol C.J. 1995. Management factors associated with stereotypic and redirected behaviour in the Thoroughbred horse. *Equine Veterinary Journal* **27:** 86–91.
McGreevy, P.D., French, N.P. and Nicol, C.J. 1995. The prevalence of abnormal behaviours in dressage, eventing and endurance horses in relation to stabling. *Veterinary Record* **137:** 36-37.
McGreevy, P.D. and Nicol C.J. 1996. Behavioural and physiological consequences associated with prevention of crib-biting. 135-136. *Proceedings of the 29th International Congress of the International Society for Applied Ethology.* UFAW, London, UK.
McGreevy, P.D. and Nicol C.J. 1998. The effect of short term prevention on the subsequent rate of crib-biting in Thoroughbred horses. *Equine Veterinary Journal* **27:** 30–34
McGreevy, P.D. and Nicol C.J. 1998. Prevention of crib-biting: a review. *Equine Veterinary Journal* **27:** 35–38
McGreevy, P.D., Richardson, J.D., Nicol, C.J. and Lane, J.G. 1995.

Radiographic and endoscopic study of horses performing an oral based stereotypy. *Equine Veterinary Journal* **27**: 92-95.

McIlwraith, C.W. 1998. Subchondral bone cysts in the horse: aetiology, diagnosis and treatment options. *Equine Veterinary Education* **10**: 313-317.

McIlwraith, C.W. and Trotter, G.W. 1996. Joint Disease in the Horse. W.B. Saunders Company, London, UK.

McLaughlin, B.G. and Doige, C.E. 1982. A study of ossification of carpal and tarsal bones in normal and hypothyroid foals. *Canadian Veterinary Journal* **23**: 164-168.

McLean, A.N. 2004. Short-term spatial memory in the domestic horse. *Applied Animal Behaviour Science* **85**: 93-105.

McClean, B.M.L., Afzalzadeh, A., Bates, L., Mayes, R.W. and Hovell, F.D.DeB. 1995. Voluntary intake, digestibility and rate of passage of a hay and a silage fed to horses and to cattle. *Animal Science* **60**: 555.

McLean, B.M.L., Hyslop, J.J., Longland, A.C., Cuddeford, D. and Hollands, T. 1999. In vivo apparent digestibility in ponies given rolled, micronised or extruded barley. 133. *Proceedings of the British Society of Animal Science,* Scarborough, UK.

McLean, B.M.L., Hyslop, J.J., Longland, A.C., Cuddeford, D. and Hollands, T. 1999. Gas production in vitro from purified starches using equine faeces as the source of inocula. 132. *Proceedings of the British Society of Animal Science*, Scarborough, UK.

McLean, B.M.L., Hyslop, J.J., Longland, A.C., Cuddeford, D. and Hollands, T. 1999. Effect of physical processing on in situ degradation of maize and peas in the caecum of ponies. 134. *Proceedings of the British Society of Animal Science*, Scarborough, UK.

McLean, B.M.L., Hyslop, J.J., Longland, A.C., Cuddeford, D. and Hollands, T. 1999. In situ degradation of crude protein in physically processed barley, maize and peas in the caecum of ponies. 135. *Proceedings of the British Society of Animal Science*, Scarborough, UK.

McLean, B.M.L., Hyslop, J.J., Longland, A.C., Cuddeford, D. and Hollands, T. 1999. Effect of screen diameter on particle size and water holding capacity of 15 starch based equine feedstuffs ground through a 1.00 mm or 0.5 mm screen. 136. *Proceedings of the British Society of Animal Science*, Scarborough, UK.

McLean, B.M.L., Hyslop, J.J., Longland, A.C., Cuddeford, D. and Hollands, T. 1999. Gas production in vitro from either unprocessed, micronised or extruded maize, peas, wheat, naked oats and barley using equine faeces as the source of inocula. 137. *Proceedings of the British Society of Animal Science*, Scarborough, UK.

References

McLean, B.M.L., Hyslop, J.J., Longland, A.C., Cuddeford, D. and Hollands, T. 1999. Development of the mobile bag technique to determine the degradation kinetics of purified starch sources in the pre-caecal segment of the equine digestive tract. 138. *Proceedings of the British Society of Animal Science*, Scarborough, UK.

McLean, B.M., Mayes, R.W. and Hovell, F.D. 1996. The use of n-alkanes for estimating intake and passage rate in horses. *Animal Science* **62**: 646.

McLean, F.M., Keller, P.J., Genge, B.R., Walters, S.A. and Wuthier, R.E. 1987. Disposition of preformed mineral in matrix vesicle: Internals localization and association with alkaline phosphatase. *Journal of Biological Chemistry* **262**: 10481-10488

McLeod, M.N. and Minson, D.J. 1982. Accuracy of predicting digestibility by the cellulase technique: The effect of pretreatment of forage samples with neutral detergent or acid pepsin. *Animal Feed Science and Technology* **7**: 83-92.

McMiken, D.F. 1983. An energetic basis of equine performance. *Equine Veterinary Journal* **15**: 123-125.

McMeniman, N.P. 2000. Nutrition of grazing broodmares, their foals and young horses. RIRDC Publication No 00/28. Project No. UQ-45A. Rural Industries Research and Development Corporation, Australia.

Meakin, D.W. 1979. Bone mineral content determination of the equine third metacarpal via radiographic photometry and the effect of dietary lysine and methionine supplementation on growth and bone development in the weanling foal. M.S. thesis, University of Florida, Gainesville, Florida, USA.

Merkt, H. and Günzel, A. 1979. A survey of early pregnancy losses in West German Thoroughbred mares. *Equine Veterinary Journal* **11**: 256-258.

Meadow, R.H. and Uerpmann, H.P. 1986. Equids in the Ancient World. Ludwig Riechart Verlag, Wiebaden, FRG.

Meadows, D.G. 1979. Utilization of dietary protein or non-protein nitrogen by lactating mares fed soybean meal or urea. *Dissertation Abstracts International B* **40**: 999.

Medina, B., Girard, I.D., Jacotot, E. and Julliand, V. 2002. Effect of a preparation of *Saccharomyces cerevisiae* on microbial profiles and fermentation patterns in the large intestine of horses fed a high fiber or a high starch diet. *Journal of Animal Science* **80**: 2600-2609.

Merrit, J.B. and Pearson, R.A. 1989. Voluntary food intake and digestion of hay and straw diets by donkeys and ponies. *Proceedings of the Nutrition Society* **48**: 169A.

Mertens, D.R. 1993. Rate and extent of digestion. In, Forbes, J.M. and France, J.(eds.) Quantitative aspects of Ruminant digestion and metabolism. Cambridge University Press, Cambridge, UK.

Mesini, A. 1998. L'Osteocondrosi, una questione aperta. *Rivista di Suinicoltura* **39** : 46-48.

Mesochina, P., Martin-Rosset, W., Peyraud, J.L., Duncan, P., Mico, D. and Boulot, S. 1998. Prediction of the digestibility of the diet of horses: evaluation of faecal indices. *Grass and Forage Science* **53**: 189-196.

Metzler, D.E. 1977. Biochemistry: The Chemical Reactions of Living Cells, Academic Press Inc., London.

Meyer, H. 1980. Neuere Erkenntnisse zur Dickdarmverdauung des Pferdes. *Übersicht Tierernährung,* **8:** 123-150.

Meyer, H. 1980. Ein Beitrag zur Regulation der Futteraufnahme beim Pferd. *Deutsche Tierärztliche Wochenschrift* **87**: 404-408.

Meyer, H. 1983. Protein metabolism and protein requirement in horses. 4th International Symposium on Protein Metabolism and Nutrition, Clermont-Ferrand, France, INRA.

Meyer, H. 1984. Intestinaler N-Stoffwechsel, endogener N-Verlust und N-Bedarf ausgewachsener Pferde. *Übersichten Tierernährung* **12**: 251-271.

Meyer, H. 1987. Nutrition of the Equine Athlete. In, Gillespie J. (ed.) Equine Physiology II, Davis ICCEP Publication, USA.

Meyer, H. 1992. Intestinaler Wasser und Elektrolytstoffwechsel des Pferdes. *Übers. Tierernährung,* **20:** 135-166.

Meyer, H. 1995. Pferdefütterung, 3. Auflage, Blackwell Wissenschafts-Verlag, Berlin, Germany.

Meyer, H. and Ahlswede, L. 1977. Untersuchungen zum Mg-Stoffwechsel des Pferdes. *Zentrabk. Veterinacrmed.* **24:** 128.

Meyer, H. and Landes, E. 1994. Beobachtungen über den Gehalt an organischen Säuren und den pH-Wert im Jejunal- und Ileumchymus bei Pferden. *Pferdeheilkunde* **10:** 381-392.

Meyer, H. and Pferdekamp, M. 1980. Auswirkungen uberhohter Proteingaben beim Pferd. *Zeitblatt der Veterinar Medizin* **A27:** 756-757.

Meyer, H. and Tiegs, W. 1995. Cu-Gehalte in der Leber von Foten und neugeborenen Fohlen. *Pferdeheilkunde* **11:** 5-11.

Meyer, H., Ahlswede, L. and Reinhard, H. 1975. Untersuchungen uber Fressdauer, Kaufrequenz und Futtterzerkleinerung beim Pferd. *Dtsch. Tierarztl. Wschr.* **82:** 54-58

Meyer, H., Ahlswede, L. and Pferdekamp, M. 1980. Untersuchungen uber die Magenentleerung und Zusammensetzung des Mageninhaltes beim Pferd *Deutsche Tierärztliche Wochenschrift* **87:** 43-47.

References

Meyer, H., Coenen, M. and Gurer, C. 1985. Investigations of saliva productin and chewing in horses fed various feeds. 38-41. *Proceedings of the 9th Equine Nutrition and Physiology Society*, East Lansing, Michigan, USA.

Meyer, H. Radicke, S., Kiengle, E., Wilke, S. and Kleffken, D. 1993. Investigations on preileal digestion of oats, corn and barley starch in relation to grain processing. 92-97. *Proceedings of the 13th Equine Nutrition and Physiology Society,* Gainesville, Florida, USA.

Meyer, H. Schmidt, H. and Lindemann, G., 1983. Prececal and postileal lactose and starch metabolism and their influence on the digestibility of NH_3 treated straw in horses, Tierarztliche Hochschule Hannover, West Germany.

Meyer, H., Flothow, C., Radicke, S. 1997. Preileal digestibility of coconut fat and soybean oil in horses and their influence on metabolites of microbial origin of the proximal digestive tract. *Archives of Animal Nutrition* **50**: 63-74.

Meyer, H., Pferdekamp, M. and Huskamp, B. 1979. Untersuchungen uber die Verdaulichkeit und Verträglichkeit verschiedener Futtermittel bei typhlectomierten Ponies. *Deutsche Tierärztliche Wochenschrift,* **86**: 384-390.

Meyer, H., Schmidt, M. and Güldenhaupt, V. 1981. Untersuchungen über Mischfutter für Pferde. *Deutsche Tierärztliche Wochenschrift* **88**: 2-5.

Meyer, H., Zentek, J., Heikens, A. and Struck, S. 1995. Untersuchungen zure Selen-Versorgung von Pferden in Norddeutschland. *Pferdeheilkunde* **11**: 313-321.

Meyer, H., Schmidt, M. and Güldenhaupt, V. 1981. Untersuchungen über Mischfutter für Pferde. *Deutsche Tierärztliche Wochenschrift* **88**: 2-5.

Meyer, H., Stadermann, B. 1991. Energie- und Nährstoffbedarf hochtragender Stuten. *Pferdeheilkunde* **7**: 11-20

Meyer, H., Zentek, J., Heikens, A. and Struck, S. 1995. Untersuchungen zure Selen-Versorgung von Pferden in Norddeutschland. *Pferdeheilkunde* **11**: 313-321.

Michalet-Doreau, B., Fernandez, I and Fonty, G. 2002. A comparison of enzymatic and molecular approaches to characterise the cellulolytic microbial ecosystems of the rumen and cecum. *Journal of Animal Science* **80**: 790-796.

Michanek, P. and Bentorp M. 1996. Time spent in shelter in relation to weather by two free-ranging thoroughbred yearlings during winter. *Applied Animal Behaviour Science* **49**: 104.

Micol, D. and Martin-Rosset, W. 1995. Feeding systems for horses on high forage diets in the temperate zones. 569-584. *Proceedings IVth International Symposium Nutrition Herbivores.* Clermont-Ferrand, France.

Microsteed 1998. Horse feed rationing system. Kentucky Equine Research, USA

Miller, R.D. and Hayes, K.C. 1982. Vitamin excess and toxicity. 81-133. In, Hathcock, J.N. (ed) Nutritional Toxicology. Academic Press, New York, USA.

Miliani, A., Bergero, D. and Salomoni, M. 1994. Osteochondrosis and nutrition: The effect of various dietary strategies in jumper foals bred in Italy. *Ippoloia* **5**: 51-62.

Miller, W.H., Scott, D.W. and Wellingon, J.R. 1992. Treatment of dogs with hip arthritis with a fatty acid supplement. *Canine Practice* **17**: 6-8.

Miller-Graber, P.A. and Lawrence, L.M. 1988. The effect of the dietary protein level on exercising horses. *Journal of Animal Science* **66**: 2185-2192

Milligan, J.D., Coleman, R.J. and Burwash, L. 1985. Relationship of energy intake weight gain in yearling horses. 8. *Proceedings of 9th Equine Nutrition Physiology Society Symposium.* East Lansing, Michigan, USA.

Mills, D.S. and Davenport, K. 2002. The effect of a neighbouring conspecific versus the use of a mirror for the control of stereotypic weaving behaviour in the stabled horse. *Animal Science* **74**: 95-101.

Mills, D.S. 1998. Applying learning theory to the management of the horse: the difference between getting it right and getting it wrong. *Equine Veterinary Journal* **27**: 44-48

Mills, D.S. 1998. Personality and individual differences in the horse, their significance, use and measurement. *Equine Veterinary Journal* **27**: 10-13

Mills, D.S., Cook S., Taylor K. and Jones B. 2002. Analysis of the variations in clinical signs shown by 254 cases of equine headshaking. *Veterinary Record* **150**: 236-240

Mills, D.S., Eckley, S. and Cooper J.J. 2000. Thoroughbred bedding preferences, associated behaviour differences and their implications for equine welfare. *Journal of Animal Science* **70**: 95-106.

Mills, D.S. and Nankervis, K.J. 1999. Equine Behaviour: principles and practice. Blackwell Science, Oxford, UK.

Minero, M., Canali E., Ferrante V., Verga M. and Odberg F.O., 1999. Heart rate and behavioural responses of crib-biting horses to two acute stressors. *Veterinary Record* **145**: 430-433.

Minson, D J. 1982. Effect of Chemical Composition of Feed Digestibility and Metabolizable Energy. *Nutrition Abstracts and Reviews, Series B* **52**: 591-615.

Minson, D.J. 1990. Forage in ruminant nutrition. Academic Press, New York, USA.

Mock, D.M. 1996. Biotin. 220-235. In, Ziegler, E.E. and Filer, L.J. (eds) Present Knowledge in Nutrition. International Life Sciences Institute Press, Washington DC, USA.

Moore, B.E and Dehorty, B.A. 1993. Effects of Diet and Hindgut Defaunation on Diet Digestibility and Microbial Concentrations in the Cecum and Colon of the Horse. *Journal of Animal Science* **71**: 3350-3358.

Moore-Coyler, M., Hyslop, J.J., Longland, A.C. and Cuddeford, D. 1997. The degradation of organic matter and crude protein of four botanically diverse feedstuffs in the foregut of ponies as measured by the mobile bag technique. 120. *Proceedings of the British Society of Animal Science*, Scarborough, UK.

Moore-Colyer, M.J.S. and Longland, A.C. 2000. Intake and in vivo apparent digestibilities of four types of conserved grass forage by ponies. *Animal Science* **71**: 527-534.

Moore-Colyer, M.J.S., Morrow, H.J. and Longland, A.C. 2003. Mathematical modelling of digesta passage rate, mean retention time and in vivo apparent digestibility of two different lengths of hay and big-bale silage in ponies. *British Journal of Nutrition* **90**: 109-118.

Morrison, F. B. 1950. Feeds and Feeding. 20th edition, The Morrison Pub. Co, USA.

Morris, F.H., Makowski, E.L., Meschia, G. and Battaglia, F.C. 1975. The glucose oxygen quotient of the term human fetus. *Biol. Neonate* **25**: 44-52.

Morris, R.P., Rich, G., Ralston, S., Squires, E. and Pickett, B. 1987. Follicular activity in transitional mares as affected by body condition and dietary energy. 93. *Proceedings of 10th Equine Nutrition Physiology Symposium*, Colorado State University, USA.

Morrow, H.J., Moore-Colyer, M.J.S. and Longland, A.C. 1999. The apparent digestibilities and rates of passage of two chop lengths of big bale silage and hay in ponies. 142. *Proceeding of the British Society of Animal Science*, Scarborough, UK.

Mort, J.S., Recklies, A.D. and Poole, A.R. 1984. Extracellular presence of the lysosomal proteinase cathepsin B in rheumatoid synovium and its activity at neutral pH. *Arthritis and Rheumatism* **27**: 509-515.

Moseley, G. and Manendez, A.A. 1998. Factors affecting the eating rate of forage feeds. 789-790. *Proceedings of the XVI International Grassland Congress*, Nice, France.

Mubarak, S.J. and Caroll, N.C. 1982. Juvenile osteochondritis dissecans of the knee: etiology. *Clinical Orthopaedic Research* **157**: 200-211.

Mueller, P.J. and Houpt K.A., 1991. A comparison of the responses of donkeys (Equus asinus) and ponies (Equus caballus) to 36 hours of water deprivation. 86-95. In, Fielding, D. and Pearson, R.A. (eds.) Donkeys, Mules and Horses in Tropical Agricultural Development University of Edingburgh, Scotland.

Mullaney, T. and Brown, C. 1988. Iron toxicity in neonatal foals. *Equine Veterinary Journal* **20**: 119.

Mungall, B.A., Kyaw-Tanner, M. and Pollitt, C.C. 2001. In vitro evidence for a bacterial pathogenesis of equine laminitis. *Veterinary Microbiology* **79**: 209-223.

Murphy, M. R. and Kennedy, P. M. (1990) Particle dynamics, In: J. M. Forbes and J. France (eds) Quantative aspects of ruminant digestion and metabolism, 92, 105, CAB International, UK.

Murray, M.J., Schusser, G.G., Pipers, F.S. and Gross, S.J. 1996. Factors associated with gastric lesions in Thoroughbred racehorses. *Equine Veterinary Journal* **28**: 368-347.

Murray, R.C. 2000. Equine carpal articular cartilage fibronectin distribution associated with training, joint location and cartilage deterioration. *Equine Veterinary Journal* **32**: 47- 51.

N

Nadau, J.A., Andrews, F.M., Mathew, A.G., Argenzio, R.A. and Blackford, J.T. 1998. The effect of diet on severity of gastric ulcers in horses. *Gastroenterology* **114**: A238

Nadeau, J.A., Andrews F.M., Patton C.S., Argenzio R.A., Mathew A.G. and Saxton A.M. 2003. Effects of hydrochloric, valeric, and other volatile fatty acids on pathogenesis of ulcers in the nonglandular portion of the stomach of horses. *American Journal of Veterinary Research* **64**: 413-417.

Nakano, T. and Aherne, F.X. 1994. The pathogenesis of osteochondrosis - a hypothesis, *Medical Hypotheses* **43**: 1-5.

Nap, R.C. 1993. Nutritional Influences on Growth and Skeletal Development in the Dog, Thesis, Utrecht University, The Netherlands.

Nash-Holmes, L., Song G.K. and Price E.O. 1987. Head partitions facilitate feeding by subordinate horses in the presence of dominant pen-mates. *Applied Animal Behaviour Science* **19**: 179-182.

Nash, D.G., Avery, A., Dempsey, W and Nash, G. 2000. Improved pastures more than just grass for horses to exercise on: Intake of Young Horses

References

on Pasture. 3rd Annual Equine School, Fort Worth, Texas, USA.
National Research Council 1989. Nutrient requirements of horses. 5th edition, National Academy of Sciences, Washington DC, USA
National Research Council 1987. Predicting Feed Intake - Feed Intake Control Mechanisms, Producing Animals. National Academy of Sciences, Washington DC, USA
National Research Council, 1987. Vitamin tolerance of animals. National Academy of Science, Washington DC, USA.
National Research Council 1978. Nutrient Requirements of Horses, 4th ed. Revised. National Academy of Sciences Washington DC, USA
Naujeck, A., Hill, J. and Gibb, N.J. 2005. Influence of sward height on diet selection by horses. *Appl. Animal Behaviour Science* **90(1)**, 49-63.
Newton, S.A., Knottenbelt D.C. and Eldridge P.R. 2000. Headshaking in horses-possible aetiopathogenesis suggested by the results of diagnostic tests and several treatment regimes used in 20 cases. *Equine Veterinary Journal* **32**: 208-216.
Nicol, C.J., 1999. Stereotypies and their relation to management, In, Harris, P.A., Gomarsall, G.M., Davidson, H.P.B. and Green, R.E. (eds.) *Proceedings of the BEVA specialist days on Behaviour and Nutrition*, Equine Veterinary Journal Ltd., UK.
Nicol, C. J. 1999. Understanding equine stereotypies. *Equine Veterinary Journal* **28**: 20-25.
Nicol, C.J., Davidson, H.P.B., Harris, P.A., Waters, A.J. and Wilson, A.D. 2002. Study of crib-biting and gastric inflammation and ulceration in young horses. *Veterinary Record* **151**: 658-662.
Nijland, N., Hertog den P.C. and Ommeren van P. 1997. Hoe veilig is de ruitersport; Een studie naar omvang, ernst en aard van ongevallen met paarden. Stichting Consument en Veiligheid, Rapport nr. 196, Amsterdam, The Netherlands.
Nixon, A.J. and Cummings, J.F. 1994. Substance P immunohistochemical study of the sensory innervation of normal subchondral bone in the equine metacarpophalangeal joint. *American Journal of Veterinary Research* **55**: 28-34.
Norbury, G.L. and Sanson, G.D. 1992. Problems with measuring diet selection of terrestrial, mammalian herbivores. *Australian Journal of Ecology* **17**: 1-7.
Norris, K. H., Barnes, R. F., Moore, J.E. and Shank, J. S. (1976) Predicting Forage Quality by Infrared Reflectance Spectroscopy, Journal of Animal Science, **43**: 4, 889-897
Nieberle, R. and Chors, S. 1954. Lehrbuch der Speziellen Pathologischer Anatomia der Holasterire. Gustav Fischer, Jena, Germany.

O

Ödberg, F.O. and Bouissou M.F., 1999. The development of equestrianism from the baroque period to the present day andits consequences for the welfare of horses. *Equine Veterinary Journal* **28**: 26-30.

Ödberg, F.O. 1978. A study of the hearing ability of horses. *Equine Veterinary Journal* **10**: 82-84.

Ödberg, F.O. 1987. Chronic stress in riding horses. *Equine Veterinary Journal* **19**: 268-269.

O'Donohue, D.D., Smith, F.H. and Strickland, K.L. 1992. The incidence of abnormal limb development in the Irish Thoroughbred from birth to 18 mths. *Equine Veterinary Journal* **24**: 305-309.

Oeudraogo, T. and Tisserand, J.L. 1996. Etude comparative de la valorisation des fourrages pauvres chez l'abe et le mouton. Ingestibilite et digestibilite. *Annales Zootechnie* **45** : 437-444.

Oikawa, M. and Kusunose, R. 1995. Some epidemiological aspects of equine respiratory disease asociated with transport. *Journal of Equine Science* **6**: 25-29.

Olson, N. and Ruudevere, A. 1955.The nutrition of the horse. *Nutrition Abstracts and Reviews* **25**: 1-18.

Olsson, S.E. and Reiland, S. 1978. The nature of osteochondrosis in animals. *Acta Radiologica* **358**: 299-306.

Omed, H.M. Axford, R.F.E. Chamberlain, A.G. and Givens, D.I. 1989. A comparison of three laboratory techniques for the estimation of the digestibility of feedstuffs for ruminants. *Journal of Agricultural Science, Cambridge* **113**: 35-39.

Ordakowski, A.L., Kronfeld, D.S., Holland, J.L., Hargreaves, B.J., Gay, L.S., Harris, P.A., Dove, H. and Sklan, D. 2001. Alkanes as internal markers to estimate digestibility of hay or hay plus concentrate diets in horses. *Journal of Animal Science* **79**: 1516-1522.

Oldham, J.D., Buttery, P.J., Swan, H. and Lewis, D. 1977. Interactions between dietary carbohydrates and nitrogen and digestion in sheep. *Journal of Agricultural Science, Cambridge* **89**: 467-479.

Orme, C.E., Harris, R.C., Marlin, D. and Hurley, J. 1997. Metabolic Adaptation to a Fat-Supplemented diet by the Thoroughbred Horse. *British Journal of Nutrition* **78**: 443-458.

Orme, C.E., Harris, R.C. and Marlin, D. 1994. The effect of elevated plasma free fatty acids on fat and carbohydrate utilisation during low intensity exercise in the horse. *4th International Conference on Equine Exercise Physiology*, Queensland Australia

Ornehult, L., Eriksson, A. and Bjornstig, U., 1989. Fatalities caused by

References

nonvenomous animals: a ten-year summary from Sweden. *Accid. Anal. Prev.* **21:** 377-381.

Orskov, E.R. 1988. Feed Science, World Animal Science: A disciplinary approach Volume 4. Elsevier Science Publishers B.V., Oxford, UK.

Orskov, E.R. 1991. Manipulation of Fibre Digestion in the Rumen. *Proceedings of the Nutrition Society* **50:** 187-196.

Orskov, E.R., Reid G.W. and Kay, M. 1988. Prediction of intake by cattle from degradation characteristics of roughages. *Animal Production* **46:** 29-34.

Orth, M.W (1999) The regulation of growth plate cartilage turnover, Journal of Animal Science, 77, **Supplement 2,** 183-189

Orton, R.K., Hume, I.D. and Leng, R.A. 1985. Effects of exercise and level of dietary protein on digestive function in horses. *Equine Veterinary Journal* **17:** 386-390.

Orton, R.K., Hume, I.D. and Leng, R.A. 1985. Effects of level of dietary protein and exercise on growth rates of horses. *Equine Veterinary Journal* **17:** 381-385.

Osbourne, B.G. and Fearn, T. 1986. Near infrared spectroscopy in food analysis. Longman Group, Harlow, UK.

Osman, N.H.I. and Sykes, A.R. 1989. Comparative effects of dietary molybdenum concentration on distribution of copper in plasma in sheep and red deer. *Proceedings of the New Zealand Society of Animal Production* **49:** 15-20.

Ott, E.A. and Asquith R.L. 1995. Trace mineral supplementation of yearling horses. *Journal of Animal Science* **73:** 466-471.

Ott, E.A. 1981. Influence of level of feeding on digestion efficiency of the horse. 37-43. *Proceedings of the 7th Equine Nutrition and Physiology Symposium,* Virginia, USA.

Ott, E.A. and Johnson E.L. 2001. Effect of trace mineral proteinates on growth and skeletal and hoof development in yearling horses. *Journal of Equine Veterinary Science* **21:** 287-292.

Ott, E.A. and Asquith, R.L. 1983. Influence of protein and mineral intake on growth and bone development of weanling horses. 39. *Proceedings of the 8th Equine Nutrition and Physiology Symposium,* Lexington, USA.

Ott, E.A. and Asquith, R.L. 1986. Influence of level of feeding and nutrient content of the concentrate on growth and development of yearling horses. *Journal of Animal Science* **62:**290.

Ott, E.A., Asquith, R.L. and Feaster, J.P. 1981. Lysine supplementation of diets for yearling horses. *Journal of Animal Science* **53:**1496.

Ott, E.A., Asquith, R.L. and Feaster, J.P. and Martin, F.G. 1979. Influence of protein level and quality on the growth and development of yearling foals. *Journal of Animal Science* **49**:620.

Ott, E.A. and Asquith, R.L. 1995. Trace mineral supplementation of yearling horses. *Journal of Animal Science* **73**: 466-471.

Ott, E.A. and Asquith, R.L. 1989. The influence of mineral supplementation on growth and skeletal development of yearling horses. *Journal of Animal Science* **67**: 2831-2840.

Ott, E.A. and Asquith, R.L. 1994. Trace mineral supplementation of brood mares. *Journal of Equine Veterinary Science* **14**: 93-101.

Ott, E.A. and Kivipelto, J. 1999. Influence of chromium tripicolinate on growth and glucose metabolism in yearling horses. *Journal of Animal Science* **77**: 3022-3030.

Otte, K., Rozell, B., Gessbo, A. and Engstrom, W. 1996. Cloning and sequencing of an equine insulin-like growth factor I cDNA and its expression in fetal and adult tissues. *General and Comparative Endocrinology* **102**: 11-15

Owen, R.A., Fullerton J. and Barnum D.A., 1983. Effect of transportation, surgery, and antibiotic therapy in ponies infected with salmonella. *American Journal of Veterinary Research* **44**: 46-50.

P

Pagan, J.D. 1988. An Evaluation of Feeding Fat to Racehorses. *Equine Sports Medicine* **7**: 51-54.

Pagan, J.D. 1995. Nutrient Digestibility in Horses. *International Conference on Feeding Horses*, Dodson and Horrell Ltd., UK. pp. 1-4.

Pagan, J.D., Rotmensen, T. and Jackson, S.G. 1995. The effect of chromium supplementation on metabolic response to exercise in Thoroughbred horses. *Proceedings of the 14th Equine Nutrition and Physiology Symposium*, Ontario, Canada. Pp. 96-101.

Pagan, J.D. 1994. Nutrient Digestibility in Horses. Kentucky Equine Research, Conference Proceedings.

Pagan, J.D. 1996 Energy and the Performance Horse. In: Clarke, A.F. and Jeffcott, L.B. (eds) *On to Atlanta*. The Equine Research Centre, Guelph, Canada.

Pagan, J.D. 1999. Time of feeding critical for performance, In: *Advances in Equine Nutrition*, Proceedings of the 1999 Equine Nutrition Conference for Feed Manufacturers, KER, Kentucky, USA. pp. 117-125.

Pagan, J.D. 2000. Time of feeding critical to performance, *3rd International Conference on Feeding Horses*, Dodson and Horrell Ltd, UK.

References

Pagan, J.D. 1988. An evaluation of feeding fat to racehorses. *Equine Sports Medicine* **7**: 51-54.

Pagan, J.D. 1997. Gastric ulcers in horses: A widespread but manageable disease. *World Equine Veterinary Review* **2**: 28-30.

Pagan, J.D., Harris, P.A., Brewster-Barnes, T., Duren, S.E. and Jackson, S.G. 1998. Exercise affects digestibility and rate of passage of all-forage and mixed diets in Thoroughbred horses. *Journal of Nutrition* **128**: 2704-2707.

Pagan, J.D. and Hintz, H. F. 1986. Equine Energetics. I: Relationship between body weight and energy requirements in horses. *Journal of Animal Science* **63**: 815-821.

Palmer, J. L. and Bertone, A. L. 1994. Joint Structure, biochemistry and biochemical disequilibrium in synovitis and equine disease, Eqine Veterinary Journal, **26**: 263-277.

Palmgren Karlsson, C.P., Lindberg, J.E. and Rundgren, M. 2000. Associative effects on total tract digestibility in horses fed different ratios of grass hay and whole oats. *Livestock Production Science* **65**: 143-153.

Palmquist, D.L., Jenkins, T.C. and Joyner, A.E. 1986. Effect of dietary fat and calcium sources on insoluble soap formation in the rumen. *Journal of Dairy Science* **69**: 1020-1025.

Pantke, P., Hyland, J., Galloway, D.B., Maclean, A.A. and Hoppen, H.O. 1991. Changes in Luteinising hormone bioactivity associated with gonadotrophin pulses in the cycling mare. *Journal of Reproduction and Fertility* **44**: 13.

Papendorp, D.H., Coetzer, H. and Kruger, M.C. 1995. Biochemical profile of osteoporotic patients on essential fatty acid supplementation. *Nutrition Research* **15**: 325-334.

Patterson, P.H., Coon, C.N. and Hughes, I.M. 1985. Protein requiremetns of mature working horses. *Journal of Animal Science* **61**: 187-196.

Pan, J., Koike, S., Susuki, T., Ueda, K. Kobayashi, Y., Tanaka, K. and Okubo, M. 2003. Effect of mastication on degradation of orchardgrass hay stem by rumn microbes: fibrolytic enzyme activities and microbial attachment. *Animal Feed Science and Technology* **106**: 69-79.

Pattison, M.L., Chen, C.L. and King, S.L. 1972. Determination of LH and oestradiol-17b surge with reference to the time of ovulation in mares. *Biology of Reproduction* **7**: 136.

Pearce, S.G., Firth, E.C., Grace, N.D. and Fennessey, P.F. 1997. Liver biopsy techniques for adult horses and neonatal foals to assess copper status. *Australian Veterinary Journal* **75**: 194-197.

Pearce, S.G., Grace, N.D., Firth, E.C., Wichtel, J.J., Holle, S.A. and Fennessey, P.F. 1998. Effect of copper supplementation on the copper status of pasture-fed young Thoroughbreds. *Equine Veterinary Journal* **30**: 204-210.

Pearce, S.G., Grace, N.D., Wichtel, J.J., Firth, E.C. and Fennessey, P.F. 1998. Effect of copper supplementation on copper status of pregnant mares and foals. *Equine Veterinary Journal* **30**: 200-203.

Pearce, S.G., Firth, E.C. Grace, N.D. and Fennessy, P.F. 1998. Effect of copper supplementation on the evidence of developmental orthopaedic disease in pasture-fed New Zealand Thoroughbreds. *Equine Veterinary Journal* **30**: 211-218.

Pearce, S.G., Firth, E.C., Grace, N.D. and Fennessy, P.F. 1999. The effect of high pasture molybdenum concentrations on the copper status of grazing horses in New Zealand. *New Zealand Journal of Agricultural Research* **42**: 93-99.

Pearson, P.B. and Schmidt, H. 1948. Pantothenic acid studies with the horse. *Journal of Animal Science* **7**: 78.

Pearson, R.A., Archibald R.F., and Muirhead R.H. 2001. The effect of forage quality and level of feeding on digestibility and gastrointestinal transit time of oat straw and alfalfa given to ponies and donkeys. *British Journal of Nutrition* **85**: 599-606.

Pearson, R.A. and Merritt, J.B. 1991. Intake, digestion and gastrointestinal transit time in resting donkeys and ponies and exercised donkeys given ad libitum hay and straw diets. *Equine Veterinary Journal* **23**: 339-343.

Peek, S.F., Divers, T.J. and Jackson, C.J. 1997. Hyperammonaemia associated with encephalopathy and abdominal pain without evidence of liver disease in four mature horses. *Equine Veterinary Journal* **29**: 70-74.

Pell, S.M., McGreevy P.D. 1999. A study of cortisol and beta-endorphin levels in stereotypic and normal thoroughbreds. *Applied Animal Behaviour Science* **64**: 81-90.

Persson, S.G.B. 1983. Analyses of fitness and state of training. *Proceeding of the 1st Equine Physiology Symposium*. Snow D.H., Persson S.G.B., Rose R.J. (eds) Granta Editions, Cambridge, UK.

Petazzi F., Zarrilli A. and Ceci L. 1983. Comportamento del T3, T4 e del cortisolo in Cavalli adulti sottoposti a stress da trasporto. *Obiettivi e documenti veterinari* **4**: 55-56.

Petito, S.L. and Evans, J.L. 1984. Calcium status of growing rat as affected by diet acidity from ammonium chloride, phosphate and protein. *Journal of Nutrition* **114**: 1049-1059.

Phillips, H.O. and Grubb, S.A. 1985. Familial multiple osteochondritis dissecans. *Journal of Bone and Joint Surgery* **67A**: 155-156.

References

Phillips, L.S., Belosky, D.C., Young, H.S. and Reichard, L.A. 1979. Nutrition and somatomedin. VI. Somatomedin activity and somatomedin inhibitory activity in serum from normal and diabetic rats. *Endocrinology* **104**: 1519-1524.

Phillips, L.S., Herington, A.C. and Daughaday, W.H. 1974. Hormone effects on somatomedin action and somatomedin generation. In: Rati S. (ed.) *Advances in Human Growth Hormone Research.* DHEW Publication No. (NIH) 74-612, Washington, DC, USA. pp. 50-67.

Pick, D.F., Lovell G., Brown S. and Dail D. 1994. Equine color perception revisited. *Applied Animal Behaviour Science* **42**: 61-65.

Pickersgill, C.H. and Marr, C.M. 1998. Carbohydrate overload with secondary endotoxaemia in a pony. *Equine Veterinary Education* **10**: 294-299.

Pilliner, S. 1999. *Horse Nutrition and Feeding*, Blackwell Science, London, UK.

Pitt, M., Fraser, J. and Thurley, D.C. 1980. Molybdenum toxicity in sheep, Epiphysiolysis, exostoses and biochemical changes. *Journal of Comparative Pathology* **90**: 567-576.

Platt, H. 1984. Growth of the equine foetus. *Equine Veterinary Journal* **16**: 247-252.

Podoll, K.L., Bernard, J.B., Ullrey, D.E., DeBar, S.R., Ku, P.K. and Magee, W.T. 1992. Dietary selenate versus selenite for cattle, sheep and horses. *Journal of Animal Science* **70**: 1965-1970.

Pollitt, C. 2002. Aetiology of fructan-induced laminitis; mechansim of fructan involvement, alteration of hindgut microflora and quantities required. Dodson and Horrell Ltd. 4th-International Conference on feeding horses.

Pollitt, C.C. and Davies, C.L. 1998. Equine laminitis: its development post alimentary carbohydrate overload coincides with increased sublamellar blood flow. *The Equine Hoof: Equine Veterinary Journal Supplement* **27**: 125-132.

Pollitt, C.C., Pass, M.A. and Pollitt, S. 1998. Batimastat (BB-94) inhibits matrix metalloproteinases of equine laminitis. *The Equine Hoof: Equine Veterinary Journal Supplement* **27**: 119-124.

Pollock, J. 1987. Welfare lessons of equine social behaviour. *Equine Veterinary Journal* **19**: 86-90.

Pond, K.R., Ellis W.C. and Akin D.E. 1984. Ingestive mastication and fragmentation of forages. *Journal of Animal Science* **58**: 1567-1574.

Pond, K.R., Ellis, W.C. Matis, J.H. Ferreiro, H.M. and Sutton, J.D. 1988. Compartment models for estimating attributes of digesta flow in cattle. *British Journal of Nutrition* **60**: 571-595.

Pond, W.C., Church, D.C., Pond, K.R. 1995. *Basic Animal Nutrition and Feeding*. J Wiley, New York, USA.

Popesko, P. 1971. *Topographical Atlas of Domestic Animals*. WB Saunders Company, Philadelphia, USA.

Poppi, D.P., France, J. and McLennan, S.R. 2000. Intake, passage and digestibility. In: M.K. Theodorou and J. France (eds) *Feeding Systems and Feed Evaluation Models*. CAB International, Wallingford, UK. pp. 35-52.

Potter, G.D. 1981. Use of cottonseed meal in rations for young horses. *Feedstuffs* (December 28): 29.

Potter, G.D. and Huchton J.D. 1975. Growth of yearling horses fed different sources of protein with supplemental lysine. *Proceedings of the 4th Equine Nutrition Physiology Society Symposium*. Pomona, California, USA. p. 19.

Potter, G.D., Arnold, F.F., Householder, D.D., Hansen, D.H. and Brown, K.M. 1992. Digestion of starch in the small or large intestine of the equine. *Pferdeheilkunde* 107-111.

Potter, G.D., Evans, J.W., Webb, G.W. and Webb, S.P. 1987. Digestible energy requirements of Belgian and Percheron horses. *Proceedings of the 10th Equine Nutrition and Physiology Society Symposium*, Fort Collins, Colorado, USA.

Potter, G.D., Gibbs, P.F., Haley, R.F. and Klendshoj, C. 1992. Digestion of protein in the smalland largeintestines of equines fed mixed diets. Erste Europäische Konferenz über die Ernährung des Pferdes, Institut für Tierernährung, Tierärztliche Hochschule, Hannover, 3-4 September 1992. pp. 140-143.

Potter, G.D., Webb, S.P., Evans, J.W. and Webb, G.W. 1990. Digestible energy requirements for work and maintenance of horses fed conventional and fat-supplemented diets. *Journal of Equine Veterinary Science* **10**: 214-218.

Prins, R.A. and Lankhorst, A. 1977. Synthesis of acetate from CO_2 in the cecum of some rodents. *FEMS Microbiology Letters* **1**: 255-258.

Prior, R.L., Hintz, H.F., Lowe, J.E. and Visek, W.J. 1974. Urea recycling and metabolism of ponies. *Journal of Animal Science* **8**: 565.

Prothero, D.R. and Schoch, R.M. 1989. *The Evolution of Perissodactyls*. Oxford University Press, UK.

Price, E.O. and Wallach S.J.R. 1990. Physical isolation of herd reared Hereford bulls increases aggressiveness towards humans. *Applied Animal Behaviour Science* **27**: 263-267.

Price, E.O., Harris, J.E., Borgwardt, R.E., Sween, M.L. and Connor, J.M. 2003. Fenceline contact of beef calves with their dams at weaning

reduces the negative effects of separation on behavior and growth rate. *Journal of Animal Science* **81**: 116-121.
Prince D., 1987. Stable vices. In: *Behaviour problems in horses*. David and Charles, Newton Abbot, UK. pp. 115-122.
Prior, R.L., Hintz, H.F., Lowe, J.E. and Visek, W.J. 1974. Urea recycling and metabolism of ponies. *Journal of Animal Science* **8**: 565.
Proudman, C.J. 1991. A two year, prospective survey of equine colic in general practice. *Equine Veterinary Journal* **24**: 90-93.
Provenza, F.D. and Balph, D.F. 1987. Diet learning by domestic ruminants: Theory, evidence and practical implications. *Applied Animal Behaviour Science* 18: 211-232.

R

Rackyleft, D.J. and Love D.N., 1989. Influence of head posture on the respiratory tract health of horses. *Australian Equine Veterinarian* **8**: 123.
Raidal, S.L., Love D.N. and Bailey D.G. 1996. Effects of posture and accuymulated airway secretions on tracheal mucociliary transport in the horse. *AustralianVeterinary Journal* **73**: 45-49.
Raidal, S.L., Love D.N.and Bailey D.G. 1995. Inflammation and increased numbers of bacteria in the lower respiratory tract of horses within 6 to 12 h of confinement with the head elevated. *Australian Veterinary Journal* **72**: 45-50.
Ralston, S.L. 1987. Nutritional management of horses competing in 160 km races. *Cornell Veterinarian* **78**: 53-61.
Ralston, S.L. 1991. Dietary influence on serum copper and zinc concentrations in horses. Erste Europäische Konferenz über die Ernährung des Pferdes, Hannover, Germany.
Ralston, S.L. 1992. Regulation of feed intake in the horse in relation to gastrointestinal disease. *Pferdeheilkunde* **8**: 15-18.
Ralston, S.L. 1996. Hyperglycemia/hyperinsulinemia after feeding a meal of grain to young horses with osteochondritis dissecans lesions. *Pferdeheilkunde* **12**: 320-322.
Ralston, S.L. Puzio, C. and Cuddeford, D. 1993. Dietary Carbohydrate Acid/ Base Status and Urinary Calcium and Phosphorus Excretion in Horses. *Proceedings of 13th Equine Physiology and Nutrition Symposium*, University of Florida, Gainesville, USA.
Ralston, S.L., Foster, D.L., Divers, T. and Hintz, H.F. 2001. Effect of dental correction on feed digestibility in horses. *Equine Veterinary Journal* **3**: 390-393.

Ralston, S.L., Freeman, D.E. and Baile, C.A. 1983. Volatile fatty acids and the role of the large intestine in the control of feed intake in ponies. *Journal of Animal Science* **57**: 815-820.

Ralston, S.L. and Baile, C.A. 1982a. Plasma glucose and insulin concentrations and feeding behaviour in ponies. *Journal of Animal Science* **54**: 1132-1137.

Ralston, S.L. and Baile, C.A. 1982b. Gastrointestinal stimuli in the control of feed intake in ponies. *Journal of Animal Science* **55**: 243-253.

Ralston, S.L., Jackson, S.A., Rich, V.A. and Squires, E.L. 1985. Effect of vitamin A supplementation on the seminal characteristics and sexual behaviour of stallions. 74. Proceedings of the 9th Equine Nutrition and Physiology Society Symposium, East Lansing, Michigan, USA.

Ralston, S.L. 1984. Controls of Feeding in Horses. *Journal of Animal Science* **59**: 1354-1361.

Ralston, S.L. 1992. Regulation of feed intake in the horse in relation to gastrointestinal disease. *Pferdeheilkunde* 15-18.

Randall, R.P., Schurg, D.C. and Church, D.C. 1978. Responses of horses to sweet, salty, sour and bitter solutions. *Journal of Animal Science* **47**: 51-55.

Raphel C.F. and Beech J. 1982. Pleurisy secondary to pneumonia or lung abscessation in 90 horses. *Journal of the American Veterinary Medicine Association* **181**: 808-810.

Raub, R.H., Jackson, S.G. and Baker, J.P. 1989. The effect of exercise on bone growth and development in weanling horses. *Journal of Animal Science* **67**: 2508-2514.

Raut, B., Ranjhan, S.K., and Pathak, N.N. 1982. Nutrient utilization by broodmares fed all-rouhage ration during advanca pregnancy. *Indian Journal of Animal Science* **52**: 1169-1173.

Redbo I., Redbo-Torstensson P., Odberg P.O., Hedendahl, A. and Holm J. 1998. Factors affecting behavioural disturbances in race-horses. *Animal Science* **66**: 475-481.

Reece, V. P., Friend T.H., Stull C.H., Grandin T. and Cordes T. 2000. Equine slaughter transport update on research and regulations. *Journal of the American Veterinary Medicine Association* **216**: 1253-1258.

Reed, S.M. and Bayly, W.M. 1998. *Equine internal medicine*. WB Saunders, Philadelphia, USA.

Reeves, M.J., Salman, M. D. and Smith, G. 1996. Risk factors for equine acute abdominal disease (colic): Results from a multi-center case-control study. *Preventive Veterinary Medicine* **26**: 285-301.

Rebhun, W.C., Tennant, B.C. and Dill, S.G. 1984. Vitamin K_3 induced renal toxicosis in the horse. *Journal of American Veterinary Medical*

References

Association **184**: 1237-1239.
Reeds, P.J. and Fuller, M.F. 1983. Protein intake and turnover. *Proceedings of the Nutrition Society* **42**: 463-471.
Reitnour, C.M. 1982. Protein utilization in response to caecal corn starch in ponies. *Equine Veterinary Journal* **14**: 149-152.
Reitnour, C.M. and Salsbury, R.L. 1972. Digestion and utilization of cecally infused protein by the equine. *Journal of Animal Science* **35**: 1190-1193.
Reitnour, C.M. and Salsbury, R.L. 1976. Utilization of proteins by the equine species. *American Journal of Veterinary Research* **37**: 1065-1067.
Reitnour, C.M. and Salsbury, R.L. 1975. Effect of oral or caecal administration of protein supplements on equine plasma amino acids. *British Veterinary Journal* **131**: 466-471.
Rey, F., Hallebeek, J.M. and Beynen, A.C. 2001. Apparent digestibility of crude fibre in ponies fed either a low or high-protein diet. *Journal of Animal Physiology and Nutrition* **85**: 251- 254.
Rhoads, R.P, Greenwood, P.L., Bell, A.W. and Boisclair, Y.R. 2000. Organization and regulation of the gene encoding the sheep acid-labile subunit of the 150-kilodalton insulin-like growth factor-binding protein complex. *Endocrinology* **141**: 1425-143.
Rice, O., Geor, R., Harris, P., Hoekstra, K., Gardner, S. and Pagan, J. 2001. Effects of restricted hay intake on body weight and metabolic responses to high-intensity exercise in Throroughbred horses. *Proceedings 17th Equine Nutrition and Physiology Symposium*, pp. 273-279.
Richardson, D.C. and Zentek, J. 1998. Nutrition and osteochondrosis. *Veterinary Clinics of North America* **28**: 115.
Richardson, D.W. and Dodge, G.R. 1998. Molecular characteristics of equie stromelysin and the tissue inhibitor of metalloproteinase 1. *American Journal of Veterinary Research* **59**: 1557-1562.
Ricketts, S.W., Greet, T.R.C., Glyn, P.J., Ginnet, C.D.R., McAllister, E.P., McCraig, J., Skinner, P.H., Webbon, P.M., Frape, D.L., Smith, G.R. and Murray, L.G. 1984. Thirteen cases of botulism in horses fed big bale silage. *Equine Veterinary Journal* **16**: 515-518.
Rieger, R.J. and Hakola, S.E. 2000. *Illustrated Atlas of Clinical Equine Atonomy and Common Disorders of the Horse: Volume 2: Reproduction, Internal Medicine and Skin*, second edition, Equistar Publications Limited, USA.
Riley, C.B., Scott, W.M., Caron, J.P., Fretz, P.B., Bailey, J.W. and Barber, S.M. 1998. Ostochondritis dissecans and subchondral cystic lesions in draft horses, a retrospective study. *Canadian Veterinary Journal* **39**: 627-633.

Robb, J., Harper, R.B., Hintz, H.F., Lowe, J.E., Reid, J.T., and Schryver, H.F. 1972. Body composition of the horse: Interrelationships among proximate components, energy content, liver and kidney size, and body size and energy value of protein and fat. *Animal Production* **14**: 25.

Robelin, J. and Daenicke, J. 1980. Variation of net requirements for cattle growth with live weight, gain, breed and sexes. *Annales Zootechnie* **29**: 99-118.

Robelin, J. and Geay, Y. 1978. Estimation de la composition chimique du corps entier des bovins à partir du poids des dépôts adipeux totaux. *Annales Zootechnie* **27**: 159-167.

Rodenwold, B.W. and Simms, B.T. 1935. Iodine for brood mares. *Proceedings of the American Society of Animal Production* **34**: 89.

Rodgers, A.R. 1988. Evaluating preferences in laboratory studies of diet selection. *Canadian Journal of Zoology* **68**: 188-190.

Rojas, E., Arispe, N., Haigler, H.T., Burns, H.L. and Pollard, H.B. 1992. Identification of annexins as calcium channels in biological membranes. *Bone Mineralisation* **13**: 214-218.

Ronca, F., Palmieri, L., Panicucci, P. and Ronca, G. 1998. Anti-inflammatory activity of chondroitin sulphate. *Osteoarthritis and Cartilage* **6A**: 14-21.

Roneus, B.O. and Lindholm, B. 1983. Glutathione peroxidase activity in blood of healthy horses given different selenium supplementation. *Nordisk Veterinaer Medicin* **35**: 337.

Roneus, B.O., Hakkarianen, R.V.J., Lindholm, C.A. and Tyopponen, 1986. Vitamin E requirements of adult Standardbred horses evaluated by tissue depletion and repletion. *Equine Veterinary Journal* **18**: 50.

Rose, R.J., Knight, P.K. and Bryden, W.L. 1991. Energy use and cardirespiratory responses to prolonged submaximal exercise. In: Persson S.G.B., Lindholm, A. and Jeffcott, L.B. (eds) *Equine Exercise Physiology 3*. ICEEP Publications, UC Davis, California, USA. pp 281.

Ross, C.A. 1999. Vitamin A and retinoids. In: Shils, M.E., Olson, J.A., Shike, M. and Ross, C.A. (eds.) *Modern Nutrition in Health and Disease*. Williams and Wilkins, Baltimore, USA. pp. 305-328.

Roughan, P.G. and Holland, R. 1977. Predicting in-vivo digestibilities of herbages by exhaustive enzymatic hydrolysis of cell walls. *Journal of the Science of Food and Agriculture* **38**: 1057-1064.

Rubenstein, D.I. and Hack, M.A. 1992. Horse signals: the sounds and scents of fury. *Evolutionary Ecology* **6**: 254-260.

Ruckebusch, Y. 1972. The relevance of drowsiness in the circadian cycle of farm animals. *Animal Behaviour* **20**: 637-643.

Rushen, J., Passillé de A. M., Munksgaard L. and Tanida H., 2001. People as social actors in the world of farm animals. In: Keeling, L.J. and Gonyou, H.W. (eds) *Social behaviour in farm animals*. CAB International, Wallingford, UK. pp. 353-372.

Russel, J.D., Murray, I. and Frazer, A.R. 1989. Near and mid-infrared studies of the cell wall structure of cereal straw in relation to its rumen degradability. In: Chesson, A. and Orskov, E. (eds.) *Physico-Chemical Characterisation of Plant Residues for Industrial and Feed Use*, Elsevier Applied Science, London, UK. pp 13-24.

Russell, R.W. and Gahr, S.A. 2000. Glucose availability and associated metabolism. In: D'Mello, J.P.F. (ed.) *Farm Animal Metabolism and Nutrition*, CAB International, Wallingford, UK.

Rutberg, A.T. 1990. Inter-group transfer in Assateague pony mares. *Animal Behaviour* **40**: 945-952.

Rutter, S.M. 2000. Graze: A program to analyze recordings of the jaw movements of ruminants. *Behaviour Research Methods, Instruments and Computers* **32**: 86 –92.

Ryan, M.F. 1991. The role of magnesium in clinical biochemistry: an overview. *Annals of Clinical Biochemistry* **28**: 19-26.

S

Saastamoinen, M. T., Koskinen, E. 1993. Influence of quality of dietary protein supplement and anabolic steroids on muscular and skeletal growth of foals. *Animal Production* **56**: 135-144.

Saastamoinen, M.T. 1990. Heritabilities for body size and growth rate in young horses. *Acta Agriculturae Scandinavica* **46**: 377-386.

Saastamoinen, M.T. 1996. Protein, amino acid and energy requirements of weanling foals and yearlings. *Pferdeheilkunde* **12**: 297-302.

Saastamoinen, M.T. and Koskinen, E. 1993. Influence of quality of dietary protein supplement and anabolic steroids on muscular and skeletal growth of foals. *Animal Production* **56**: 135-144.

Sainsbury, D.W.B. 1987. Housing the Horse. In: Hickman, J. *Horse Management*. Academic Press, London, UK.

Salter, R.E. and Hudson R.J. 1979. Feeding ecology of feral horses in western Alberta. *Journal of Range Management* **32**: 221-225.

Sambraus, H.H. and Rappold D. 1991. Crib-biting and wind-sucking in horses. *Pferdeheilkunde* **7**: 211-216.

Sandgren, B., Dalin, G., Carlsten, J. and Lundeheim, N. 1993. Development of osteochondrosis in the tarsocrural joint and osteochondral fragments in the fetlock joints in Standardbred trotters, II, body measurements and clinical findings. *Equine Veterinary Journal* **16**: 38–41.

Saslow, C.A. 2002. Understanding the perceptual world of horses. *Applied Animal Behaviour Science* **78**: 209-224.

Sauer, G.R., Adkisson, H.D., Genge, B.R. and Wuthier, R.E. 1989. Regulatory effect of endogenous zinc and inhibitory action of toxic metal ions on calcium accumultion by matrix vesicles in vitro. *Bone Mineralisation* **7**: 233-244.

Salminine, K. 1975. Cobalt metabolism in horses. Serum level and biosynthesis of vitamin B_{12}. *Acta Veterinaria Scandanavia* **16**: 84.

Salomonsson, A.C., Theander, O. and Westerland, E. 1984. Chemical characterisation of some Swedish cereal whole meal and bran fractions. *Swedish Journal of Agricultural Research* **14**: 111-118.

Sarkijarvi, S. and Saastamoinen, M. 2001. Silage digestibility in equine diets. In: NJF Seminar No 326 *Production and utilisation of silage with emphasis on new techniques*. Nordic Association of Agricultural Scientists (NJF) Lillehammer, Norway.

Sauvant, D, Baumont R. and Faverdin, P. 1996. Development of a mechanistic model of intake and chewing activities of sheep. *Journal of Animal Science* **74**: 2785-2802.

Sauvant, D. 1996. Methods in modelling herbivore nutrition, use of mathematics and statistics in nutrition modelling, methods in modelling feeding behaviour intake in herbivores, growth functions and their application in animal science, A comparative evaluation of models of whole rumen function, growth in ruminants: A comparison of some mechanistic models *Annales de Zootechnique* **45**: 141-193.

Savage, C.J., MacCarthy, R.N. and Jeffcott, L.B. 1993. Effects of dietary energy and protein on induction of dyschondroplasia in foals. *Equine Veterinary Journal* **16**: 74-79.

Schams, D., Hoffman, B., Lotthammer, K.H. and Ahlswede, L. 1977. Untersuchungen uber eine spezifische Vitamin A unabhangige Wirkung des ß-Carotins auf die Fertalitat des Rindes 4. Mittailung: Auswirkung auf hormonale Parameter wahrend des Zyklus. *Deutsche Tierarztl Wochenschrift* **84**: 307-310.

Scharrer, E. and Geary, N. 1977. Regulation der Futteraufnahme bei Monogastriden. *Übers. Tierernährun* **5**: 103-122.

Scherft, J.P. and Moskalewski, S. 1984. The amount of proteoglycans in cartilage matrix and the onset of mineralization. *Metabolic Bone Disease and Related Research* **5**: 195-203.

Schilder, M.B.H., Vanhooff, J.A.R.A.M., vanGeer-Plesman C.J. and Wensing J.B. 1984. A quantitative analysis of facial expressions in the plains

References

zebra. *Zeitschrift fur Tierpsychologie (Journal of Comparative Ethology)* **66**: 11-32.

Schmitz, M., Ahrens, F., Schon, J. and Hagemeister, H. 1991. Beitrag der Absorption von Aminosauren im Dickdarm zur Proteinversorgung von Rind. *Advances in Animal Physiology and Animal Nutrition* **22**: 67-71.

Schneider, B.H. and Flatt, W.P. 1975. *The evaluation of feeds through digestibility experiments.* University of Georgia Press, Athens, USA.

Schoenmakers, I., Hazewinkel, H.A.W., Voorhout, G., Carlson, C.S. and Richardson, D. 2000. Effect of diets with different calcium and phosphorus contents on the skeletal development and blood chemistry of growing great danes. *Veterinary Record* **147**: 652-660.

Schöntaler, S. 1998. Intersuchungen zur Selenversorgung von Vollblutstuten und deren Fohlen während Trächtigkeit, Laktation und Aufzucht. *J. Insti. Tierernähtung des Fachbereichs Veterinärmedizin der Freien Univ. Berlin*, 2170.

Schougaard, H., Basse, A., Gissel-Nielsen, G. and Simesen, M.G. 1972. Nutritional muscular dystrophy (NMD) in foals. *Nord Veterinaermed.* **24**: 67.

Schryver, H.F., Parker, M.T., Daniluk, P.D., Pagan, K.I., Williams, J., Soderholm, L.V. and Hintz, H.F. 1987. Salt consumption and the effect of salt on mineral metabolism in horses. *Cornell Veterinarian* **77**: 122-131.

Schryver, H.F. 1990. Mineral and Vitamin Intoxication in Horses. *Veterinary Clinics of North America, Equine Practice.* **6**: 295-315.

Schryver, H.F., Hintz, H.F., Lowe, J.E., Hintz, R.L., Harper, R.B. and Reid, J.T. 1974. Mineral composition of the whole body, liver and bone of young horses. *Journal of Nutrition* **104**: 126-132.

Schryver, H.F. and Hintz, H.F. 1972. Calcium and phosphorus requirements of the horse, *Feedstuffs* **44**: 35-38.

Schryver, H.F., Hintz, H.F. and Craig, P.H. 1971a. Calcium metabolism in ponies fed high phosphorus diets. *Journal of Nutrition* **101**: 259.

Schryver, H.F., Meakim, D.W., Lowe, J.E., Williams, J., Soderholm, L.V. and Hintz, H.F. 1987. Growth and calcium metabolism in horses fed varying levels of protein. *Equine Veterinary Journal* **19**: 280-287.

Schryver, H.F., Oftedal, O.T., Williams, J., Sodeholm, L.V. and Hintz, H.F. 1986. Lactation in the horse: The mineral composition of mare's milk. *Journal of Nutrition* **116**: 2142.

Schryver, H.F., Parker, M.T., Daniluk, P.D., Pagan, K.I., Williams, J., Soderholm, L.V. and Hintz, H.F. 1987. Salt consumption and the effect of salt on mineral metabolism in horses. *Cornell Veterinarian*

77: 122-31.
Schryver, H.F., Craig, P. H. and Hintz, H. F. 1971. Phosphorus metabolism in horses fed varying levels of phosphorus. *Journal of Nutrition* **101**: 1257-1264.
Schumacher, J. and Schumacher, S. 1995. Diseases of the salivary glands and ducts of the horse. *Equine Veterinary Education* **7**: 313-319.
Schurg, W.A., Frei, D.L., Cheeke, P.R., and Holan, D.W. 1977. Utilization of whole corn plant pellets by horses and rabbits. *Journal of Animal Science* **45**: 1317-1321.
Schwartzmann, J.A., Hintz, H.F and Schryver, H.F. 1978. Inhibition of calcium absorption in ponies fed diets containing oxalic acid. *Journal of Veterinary Research* **3**: 1621.
Schwarz, F.J.M. and Kirchgessner H. 1979. Spurenelementbedarf und versorgung in der Pferdefutterung. *Ubersicht Tierernahrung* **6**: 257-278.
Scoggins, R.D. 1998. A practitioners viewpoint: Dentistry for the equine patient. *Equine Practice* **20**: 10-12.
Scott, C.A., Gibbs, H.A., Thomson, G. 1996. Osteochondrosis as a cause of lameness in purebred Suffolk lambs. *Veterinary Record* **139**: 165-167.
Seigel, R.C., Pinnell, S.R. and Martin, G.R. 1970. Crosslinking of collagen and elastin, Properties of lysyl oxidase. *Biochemical Journal* **9**: 4486-4492.
Sellers, A.F., Lowe, J.E., Drost, C.J., Randano, W.T., Georgi, J.R. and Roberts, M.C. 1982. Retropropulsion in the equine large colon. *American Journal of Veterinary Research* **43**: 390-396.
Selhub, J. and Rosenberg, J.H. 1996. Folic acid. In: Ziegler, E.E. and Filer, L.J. (eds) *Present Knowledge in Nutrition*. International Life Sciences Institute Press, Washington, DC, USA. pp. 206-219.
Sevinga, M., Barkema, H.W. and Hesselink, J.W. 2002. Serum calcium and magnesium concentrations and the use of a calcium-magnesium-borogluconate solution in the treatment of Friesian mares with retained placenta. *Theriogenology* **57**: 941-947.
Sgoifo, A., de Boer, S.F., Westenbroek, C., Maes, F.W., Beldhuis, H., Suzuki, T. and Koolhaas, J.M. 1997. Incidence of arrhythmias and heart rate variability in wild-type rats exposed to social stress. *American Journal of Physiology* **273**: H1754-1760.
Sgoifo, A., Pozzato, C., Costoli, T., Manghi, M., Stilli, M., Ferrari, P.F., Ceresini, G. and Musso, E. 2001. Cardiac autonomic responses to intermittent social conflict in rats. *Physiology and Behaviour* **73**: 343-349.

References

Shapiro, I. M., Golub, E.E., May, M., and Rabinowitz, J.L. 1983. Studies of nucleotides of growth-plate cartilage: evidence linking changes in cellular metabolism with cartilage calcification. *Bioscience Reports* **3**: 345-351.

Shingleton, W.D, Mackie, E.J., Cawston, T.E. and Jeffcott, L.B. 1997. Cartilage canals in equine articular epiphyseal cartilage and a possible association with dyschondroplasia. *Equine Veterinary Journal* **29**: 360-364.

Shipley, L.A., Gross, J.E., Spalinger, D.E., Thompson Hobbs, N. and Wunder, B.A. 1994. The scaling of intake rate in mammalian herbivores. *The American Naturalist* **143**: 1055-1082.

Shoshan, S. and Finkelstein, S. 1976. Lysyl oxidase: a pitutuitary dependent enzyme. *Biochemisty and Biophysiology Acta* **439**: 358-362.

Shearer, M.J., McBurney, A. and Barkhan, P. 1974. Studies on the absorption and metabolism of phylloquinone (vitamin K_1) on mares. *Vitamins and Hormones* **32**: 513.

Shupe, J.L. and Olson, A.E. 1971. Clinical aspects of fluorosis in horses. *Journal of American Veterinary Medical Association* **158**: 167-171.

Simpson, A.M., Mills, C.F. and McDonald, I. 1982. Tissue copper retention or loss in young growing cattle. 133-136. In: J.M. Gawthorne, J. McC. Howell and C. L. White (eds) *Trace element metabolism in man and animals*. Springer-Verlag, New York, USA.

Sibbald, A.M. 1996. A comparison of the effects of body condition and short-term food restriction on the feeding behaviour of sheep. *Proceedings of British Society of Animal Science*, Scarborough, UK. pp. 174.

Siciliano, P.D. 2002. Nutrition and feeding of the geriatric horse. *Veterinary Clinics in North. America: Equine Practice* **18**: 491-508.

Silver, M. and Comline, R.S. 1975. Transfer of gases and metabolites in the equine: a comparison with other species. *Journal of Reproduction and Fertility* **23**: 589-594.

Silver, M. and Fowden, A.L. 1982. Uterine prostaglandin F metabolite production in relation to availabity in late pregnancy and a possible influence of diet on time of delivery in the mare. *Journal of Reproduction and Fertility* **32**: 511-519.

Simpson, B.S. 2002. Neonatal foal handling. *Applied Animal Behaviour Science* **78**: 303-331.

Singer, E.R. 1998. Gastric reflux: what does it mean? *Equine Veterinary Education* **10**: 191-197.

Sires, U.I., Schmid, T.M., Fliszar, C.J., Wang, Z.Q., Gluck, S.L. and Welgus, H.G. 1995. Complete degradation of type X collagen requires the combined action of interstitial collagenase and osteoclast-derived cathepsin-B. *Journal of Clinical Investigation* **95**: 2089-2095.

Slade, L.M. and Hintz, H.F. 1969. Comparison of digestion in horses, ponies, rabbits and guinea pigs. *Journal of Animal Science* **28**: 842-843.

Slade, L.M., Bishop, R., Morris, J.G. and Robinson, D.W. 1971. Digestion and the absorption of N-labelled microbial protein in the large intestine of the horse. *British Veterinary Journal* **127**: 11-13.

Slater, M.R. and Hood D.M. 1997. A cross-sectional epidemiological study of equine hoof wall problems and associated factors. *Equine Veterinary Journal* **29**: 67-69.

Sloet van Oldruitenborgh-Oosterbaan M. and Knottenbelt D.C. 2001. *The practitioners guide to equine dermatology.* Libre, UK.

Sloet van Oldruitenborgh-Oosterbaan, M.M., Mol, J.A. and Barneveld, A. 1999. Hormones, growth factors and other plasma variables in relation to osteochondrosis. *Equine Veterinary Journal* **31**: 45-54.

Smith, B.L., Jones, J.H., Carlson, G.P. and Pascoe, J.R. 1994. Body position and direction preferences in horses during road transport. *Equine Veterinary Journal* **26**: 346-347.

Smith, B.L., Jones, J.H., Carlson, G.P. and Pascoe, J.R. 1994. Effects of body direction on heart rate in trailered horses. *American Journal of Veterinary Research* **55**: 1007-1011.

Smith, S. and Goldman L. 1999. Color discrimination in horses. *Applied Animal Behaviour Science* **62**: 13-25.

Slavkin, H. and Price, P. 1992. *Chemistry and biology of mineralised tissues.* Elsevier Science, Amsterdam, The Netherlands.

Smith, D. 1981. Removing and analysing total non structural carbohydrates from plant tissues. Wisconsin Agricultural Experimental Station Report No. R2107, Madison, USA.

Smith, J.E., Moore, K., Cipriano, J.E. and Morris, P.G. 1984. Serum ferritin as a measure of stored iron in horses. *Journal of Nutrition* **114**: 677-684.

Smolders, E. A. A. and Liefbroer P., 1984. Gebruik van diverse strooisels in de Paardenhouderij, Intern Rapport Nr. 144. Praktijkonderzoek Veehouderij.

Smolders, E.A.A, Steg, A. and Hindle, V.A. 1990. Organic matter digestibility in horses and its prediction. *Netherlands Journal of Agricultural Science* **38**: 435-447.

Smolders, E.A.A. 1990. Praktijkonderzoek, Proefstation voor de Rundveehouderij, Schapenhouderij en Paardenhouderij, Lelystad, The Netherlands.

Snow, D.H, Baxter, P. and Rose, R.J. 1981. Muscle fiber composition and

References

glycogen depletion in horses competing in an endurance ride. *Veterinary Record* **108**: 374.

Snow, D.H. and Harris, R.C. 1985. Thoroughbreds and greyhounds: biochemical adaptations in creatures of nature and man. 227-239. In: Giles, R. (ed.) *Circulation, Respiration and Metabolism*, Springer Verlag, Berlin, Germany.

Soeta, S., Mori, R., Kodaka, T., Naito, Y. and Taniguchi, K. 1999. Immunohistochemical observations on the initial disorders of the epiphyseal growth plate in rats induced by high dose of vitamin A. *Journal of Veterinary Medical Science* **61**: 233-238.

Solaroli, G., Pagliarnini, E. and Peri, C. 1993. Composition and nutritional quality of mare's milk. *Italian Journal of Food Science* **1**: 3-10.

Sondergaard, E. and Halekoh, U. 2003. Young horses' reaction to humans in relation to handling and social environment. *Applied Animal Behaviour Science* **84**: 265-280.

Sondergaard, E. and Jago J.G. 2001. The effect of early handling of young foals on their subsequent reaction to humans, novelty and foal-mare relationship. *Proceedings 35th ISAE Conference* Universiity of Carlifornia, Davis, USA.

Soodan, J.S., Randhawa, S.S. and Roy, K.S. 2000. Histoenzymological studies on molybdenum induced hypocuprosis in buffalo calves. *Buffalo Journal* **16**: 115-121.

Song, W.O. 1990. Pantothenic acid - How much do we know about this B-vitamin? *Nutrition Today* **25**: 19-26.

Spais, A.G., Papasteriadis, A., Roubies, N., Agiannidis, A., Yantzis, N. and Argyroudis, S. 1977. Studies on iron, manganese, zinc, copper and selenium retention and interaction in horses. 501-505. *Proceedings of the 3rd International Symposium on Trace Element Metabolism in Man and Animals*, Greece.

Spencer, H., Kramer, L. and Osis, D. 1988. Do protein and phospherus cause calcium loss?, *Journal of Nutrition* **118**: 657-660.

Spencer, J.D., Allee, G.L. and Sauber, T.E. 2000. Phosphorus, bio-availability and digestibility of normal and genetically modified low-phytate corn for pigs. *Journal of Animal Science* **78**: 675-681.

Sperber, I., Bjoirnhag, G. and Holtenius, K. 1992. A separation mechanism and fluid flow in the large intestine of the equine, Erste Europäische Konferenz über die Ernährung des Pferdes, Hannover, pp. 29-32.

Spiers, S., May, S.A., Bennett, D. and Edwards, G.B. 1994. Cellular sources of proteolytic enzymes in equine joints. *Equine Veterinary Journal* **26**: 43-47.

Sporn, M.B., Roberts, A.B. and Goodman, D.S. 1994. *The Retinoids*. Raven

Press, New York, USA.
Spring, P. 2000. The Role of Probiotics in Equine Nutrition. *Proceedings of the 3rd International Conference on Feeding Horses*, Dodson and Horrell Ltd, UK.
Stabenfeldt, G.H., Hughes, J.P. and Evans, J.W. 1972. Ovarian activity during the oestrus cycle of the mare. *Journal of Endocrinology* **90**: 1397.
Stanback, R. 1997. Equine Dentistry – The Benefits of Proper Care. *World Equine Veterinary Review* **2**: 24-26.
Stanier, W.B., Kronfeld, D.S., Hoffman, R.M., Wilson, J.A. and Harris, P.A. 2004. Weight prediction from linear measures of growing Thoroughbreds. *Equine Veterinary Journal* **36**: 149-154.
Stark, B.A. 1988. Effects of grazing animals of ingestion of inorganic and organic materials contained in sewage sludge. PRU-1691-M, Water Research Centre, Medmenham, UK.
Stensig, T., Weisbjerg, M.R., Madsen, J. and Hvelplund, T. 1994. Estimation of voluntary feed intake from in sacco degration and rate of passage DM and NDF. *Livestock Production Science* **39**: 49-52.
Stevens, C.E. 1988. *Comparative Physiology of the Vertebrate Digestive System*, Cambridge University Press, Cambridge, UK.
Stewart, G.A. 1972. Drugs, performance and response to exercise in the racehorse. 2. Observations on amphetamine, promazine and thiamine. *Australian Veterinary Journal* **48**: 544.
Sticker, L.S., Thompson, D.L., Bunting, L.D., Fernandez, J.M. and DePew, C.L. 1995. Dietary protein and (or) energy restriction in mares. *Journal of Animal Science* **73**: 136-144.
Sticker, L.S., Thompson. D.L., Fernandez, J.M., Bunting, L.D. and DePew, C.L. 1995. Dietary protein and (or) energy restriction in mares: plasma growth hormone, IGF-I, prolactin, cortisol, and thyroid hormone responses to feeding, glucose, and epinephrine. *Journal of Animal Science* **73**: 1424-1432.
Strickland, K., Smith, F., Woods, M. and Mason, J. 1987. Dietary molybdenum as a putative copper antagonist in the horse. *Equine Veterinary Journal* **19**: 50-54.
Stull C.L. and Rodiek A.V., 2000. Physiological responses of horses to 24 hours of tansportation using a commercial van during summer conditions. *Journal of Animal Science* **78**: 1458-1466.
Stull C.L. 1999. Responses of horses to trailer design duration and floor area during commercial transportation to slaughter. *Journal of Animal Science* **77**: 2925-2933.
Stull, C. and Rodiek, A. 1995. Effect of prost-prandial interval and feed type on substrate availability during exercise. *Equine Veterinary Journal* **18**: 362-366.

References

Stowe, H.D. 1968a. Alpha-tocopherol requirements for equine erythrocyte stability. *American Journal of Clinical Nutrition* **21**: 135.

Stowe, H.D. 1968b. Expermental equine avitaminosis A and E. *Proceedings of 1st Equine Nutrition and Physiology Symposium*, Lexington, Kentucky, USA. pp. 27.

Suttie, J.W. 1992. Vitamin K and human nutrition. *Journal of the American Dietetic Association* **92**: 585-590.

Suttle, N.F. 1974a. Effects of organic and inorganic sulphur on the availability of dietary copper to sheep. *British Journal of Nutrition* **32**: 559-568.

Suttle, N.F. 1974b. Effects of molybdenum and sulphur at concentrations commonly found in ruminant diets on the availability of copper to sheep. In: W.G. Hoekstra, J.W.Suttie, J.E. Ganther and W Mertz (eds) *Trace element metabolism in animals*, Volume 2. University Park Press, Baltimore, USA. pp. 612-614.

Sufit E., Houpt K.A. and Sweeting M. 1985. Physiological stimuli of thirst and drinking patterns in ponies. *Equine Veterinary Journal* **17**: 12-16.

Suggett R.H.G. 1999. Horses and the rural economy in the United Kingdom. *Equine Veterinary Journal* **28**: 31-37.

Suttle, N.F., Small J.N.W., Collins, E.A., Mason, D.K. and Watkins, K.L. 1996. Serum and hepatic copper concentrations used to define normal, marginal and deficient copper status in horses. *Equine Veterinary Journal* **28**: 497-499.

Sutton, E., Bowland, J. and Ratcliff, W. 1977. Influence of level of energy and nutrient intake by mares on reproductive performance and on bloodserum of the mares and foals. *Canadian Journal of Animal Science* **58**: 551-558.

Sweeting, M.P., Houpt, C.E. and Houpt, K.A. 1985. Social facilitation of feeding and time budgets in stabled ponies. *Journal of Animal Science* **60**: 369-374.

T

Teare, J. A., Krook, L., Kallfelz, F.A. and Hintz, H.F. 1979. Ascorbic acid deficiency and hypertrophic osteodystrophy in the dog: a rebuttal. *Cornell Veterinarian* **69**: 384-401.

Thissen, J.P., Ketelslegers, J.M. and Underwood, L.E. 1994. Nutritional regulation of insulin-like growth factors. *Endocrinology Review* **15**: 80-101.

Thompson, J.M. and Von Hollen B. 1996. Causes of horse-related injuries in a rural western community. *Canadian Family Physician* **42**: 1103-1109.

Thompson, K.N., Baker, J.P. and Jackson, S.G. 1988. The influence of supplemental feed on growth and bone development of nursing foals. *Journal of Animal Science* **66**: 1692.

Thompson, K.N., Baker, J.P., Lew, J.P. and Baruc, C.J. 1981. Digestion of hay and grain fed in varying ratios to mature horses. *Proceedings of the 7th Equine Nutrition and Physiology Symposium*, Virginia, USA. pp. 3-7.

Thompson, K.N., Jackson, S.G. and Baker, J.P. 1984. Apparent digestion coefficients and associative effects of varying hay:grain ratio fed to horses. *Nutrition Reports International* **30**: 189-197.

Thompson, K.N., Jackson, S.G. and Baker, J.P. 1988. The influence of high planes of nutrition on skeletal growth and development of weanling horses. *Journal of Animal Science* **66**: 2459-2467.

Thorp, B.H., Erman, S., Jakowlew, C. and Goddard, C. 1995. Porcine osteochondrosis: deficiencies in transforming growth factor-b and insulin-like growth factor-I. *Calcified Tissue International* **56**: 376-381.

Timney B. and Macuda T. 2001. Vision and hearing in horses. *Journal of the American Veterinary Medicine Association* **218**: 1567-1574.

Tinker, M.K., White, N.A., Lessard, P., Thatcher, C.D., Pelzer, K.D., Davis, B. and Carmel, D.K. 1997. Prospective study of equine colic risk factors. *Equine Veterinary Journal* **29**: 454-458.

Todd, L.K., Sauer, W.C., Christopherson, R.J., Coleman, R.J. and Caine, W.R. 1995. The effect of level of feed intake on nutrient and energy digestibilities and rate of feed passage in horses. *Journal of Animal Physiology and Animal Nutrition* **73**: 140-148.

Todd, L., Sauer, W.C. and Coleman, R.J. 1983. Voluntary intake and nutrient digestibility in cubes, pellets, chopped or loose alfalfa for mature horses. *Journal of Animal Science* **57**: 273.

Todhunter, R.J., Wootton, J.A.M., Lust, G. and Minor, R.R. 1994. Structure of equine type I and II collagens. *American Journal of Veterinary Research* **55**: 425-431.

Topliff, D.R., Potter, G.D., Krieder, J.L., Dutson, T.R. and Jessup, G.T. 1985. Diet manipulation, muscle glycogen metabolism and anaerobic work performance in the equine. *Proceedings of the 5th Equine Nutrition and Physiology Society*, Gainesville, Florida, USA.

Topliff, D.R., Potter, G.D., Kreider, J.L. and Creagor, C.R. 1981. Thiamin supplementation for exercising horses. *Proceedings of 7th Equine Nutrition and Physiology Symposium*, Warrenton, Virginia, USA. pp 167-172.

References

Traub-Dargatz, J.L., Kopral, C. A., Hillberg Seitzinger, A., Garber, L. P., Forde, K., White, N. A. 2001. Estimate of the national incidence of and operation-level risk factors for colic among horses in the United States, Spring 1998 to Spring 1999. *Journal of the American Veterinary Medical Association* **219**: 67-71.

Tucker, K.E., Henderson, K.A. and Duby, R.T. 1991. In vitro steroidogenesis by granulosa cells from equine preovulatory follicles. *Journal of Reproduction and Fertility* **44**: 45.

U

Uauy, R., Castillo-Duran, C., Fisberg, M. Fernandez, N., Valenzueal, A. 1985. Red cell superoxyde dismutase activity as an index of human copper nutrition. *American Institute of Nutrition* 1650-1655.

Uden, P. and Van Soest, P.J. 1982. The determination of digesta particle size in some herbivores. *Animal Feed Science and Technology* **7**: 35-44.

Uden, P., Colucci, P.E. and Van Soest, P J. 1980. Investigation of Chromium, Cerium and Cobalt as markers in Digesta Rate of Passage Studies. *Journal of Science of Food and Agriculture* **31**: 625-632.

Ullrey, D.E., Ely, W.T. and Covert, R.L. 1974. Iron, zinc and copper in mare's milk. *Journal of Animal Science* **38**: 1276.

Ullrey, D.E. 1992. Basis for regulation of Selenium supplements in animal diets. *Journal of Animal Science* **70**: 3922-3927.

Uden, P., Rounsaville, J.R., Wiggans, G.R., Van Soest, P.J. 1982. The measurements of liquid and solid digesta retention in ruminants, equines and rabbits given timothy hay. *British Journal of Nutrition* **48**: 329-339.

Uhlinger, C. 1990. Effects of three anthelmintic schedules on the incidence of colic in horses. *Equine Veterinary Journal* **22**: 251-254.

Ulyatt, M.J., Dellow, D.W., John, A., Reid, C.S.W. and Waghorn, G.C. 1984. Contribution of chewing during eating and rumination to the clearance of digesta from the reticulorumen. In: Milligan, L.P, Grovum, W.L. and Dobson, A. (eds.) *The Control of Digestion and Metabolism in Ruminants*, Proceeding of the Forth International Symposium on Ruminant Physiology, pp. 488-514.

Undersander, D., Mertens, D.R. and Thiex, N. 1993. Forage analyses procedures. National Forage Testing Association Proceedings. Omaha, New England, USA. pp. 95-103.

Underwood, E.J. 1977. *Trace elements in human and animal nutrition.* Academic Press, New York, USA.

Underwood, E.J. 1981. *The mineral nutrition of livestock.* CAB International,

Unna, K. and Greslin, J.S. 1941. Studies of the toxicity and pharmacology of pantothenic acid. *Journal of Pharmacology and Experimental Therapy* **73**: 126.

V

Valberg, S. 2000. Recent advances into the cause and managemnt of chronic tying-up. 3rd International Conference on Feeding Horses, Dodson and Horrell Ltd, UK.

Valberg, S.J. 1986. Glycogen depletion patterns in the muscle of standardbred trotters after exercise of varying intensities and durations. *Equine Veterinary Journal* **18**: 479-484.

Valberg, S.J. 1999. Skeletal muscle metabolic response to exercise in horses with 'tying-up' due to polysccharide storage myopathy. *Equine Veterinary Journal* **31**: 43-47.

Van de Lest, C.H.A., Van den Hoogen, B.M., Van Weeren, P.R., Brouwers, J.F.H.M, Van Golde, L.M.G. and Barneveld, A. 1999. The influence of birth weight, rate of weight gain and final achieved height and sex on the development of osteochondrotic lesions in a population of genetically predisposed Warmblood foals. *Equine Veterinary Journal* **31**: 26.

Van de Lest, C.H.A., Van den Hoogen, B.M., Van Weeren, P.R., Brouwers, J.F.H.M, Van Golde, L.M.G. and Barneveld, A. 1999. Changes in bone morphogenic enzymes and lipid composition of equine osteochondrotic subchondral bone. *Equine Veterinary Journal* **31**: 31.

Van den Hoogen, B.M., Van de Lest, C.H.A., Van Weeren, P.R., Van Golde, L.M.G. and Barneveld, A. 1999. Changes in proteoglycan metabolism inosteochondroitic articular cartilage of growing foals. *Equine Veterinary Journal* **31**: 38-44.

Van den Hoogen, B.M., Van den Lest, C.H.A., Van Weeren, P.R., Van Golde, L.M.G. and Barneveld, A. 1999. Effect of exercise on the proteoglycan metabolism of articular cartilage in growing foals. *Equine Veterinary Journal* **31**: 62-66.

Van Doorn, D. 2003. Equine Phosphorus absorption and excretion. PhD Thesis, Utrecht University, The Netherlands.

Van Niekerk, C.H. 1965. Early embryonic resorption in mares. *Journal of the South African Veterinary Medical Association* **36**: 61-69.

Van Niekerk, C.H., van Heerden, J.S. 1972. Nutrition and ovarian activity of mares early in the breeding season. *Journal of the South African*

References

Veterinary Medical Association **43**: 351-360.

Van Niekerk, F.E. and Van Niekerk, C.H. 1997. The effect of dietary protein on reproduction in the mare I. The composition and evaluation of digestability of dietary protein from different sources. *Journal of the South African Veterinary Medical Association* **68**: 78-80.

Van Niekerk, F.E. and Van Niekerk, C.H. 1997. The effect of dietary protein on reproduction in the mare II. Growth of foals, body mass of mares and serum protein concentration of mares during the anovulatory, transitional and pregnant periods. *Journal of the South African Veterinary Medical Association* **68**: 81-85.

Van Niekerk, F.E. and Van Niekerk, C.H. 1997. The effect of dietary protein on reproduction in the mare III. Ovarian and uterine changes during the anovulatory, transitional and ovulatory periods in the non-pregnant mare. *Journal of the South African Veterinary Medical Association* **68**: 86-92.

Van Niekerk, F.E. and Van Niekerk, C.H. 1997. The effect of dietary protein on reproduction in the mare IV. Serum progestagen, FSH, LH and melatonin concentrations during the anovulatory, transitional and ovulatory periods in the non-pregnant mare. *Journal of the South African Veterinary Medical Association* **68**: 114-120.

Van Niekerk, F.E. and Van Niekerk, C.H. 1998. The effect of dietary protein on reproduction in the mare V. Endocrine changes and conception during the early postpartum period. *Journal of the South African Veterinary Medical Association* **69**: 81-88.

Van Niekerk, F.E. and Van Niekerk, C.H. 1998. The effect of dietary protein on reproduction in the mare VI. Serum progestagen concentrations during pregnancy. *Journal of the South African Veterinary Medical Association* **69**: 143-149.

Van Niekerk, F.E. and Van Niekerk, C.H. 1998. The effect of dietary protein on reproduction in the mare VII. Embryonic development, early embryonic death, foetal losses and their relationship with serum progestagen. *Journal of the South African Veterinary Medical Association* **69**: 150-155.

Van Pappendorf, D.H., Coetzer, H. and Gruger, M.C. 1995. Biomedical profile of osteoporotic patients on essential fatty acid supplementation. *Nutrition Research* **15**: 325-334.

Van Saun, R.J. 1997. Assessing the nutritional status of the horse. *World Equine Veterinary Review* **2**: 4.

Van Soest, P.J. 1994. Nutritional Ecology of the Ruminant, Cornell University Press, Ithaca, USA.

Van Soest, P.J. and Robertson, J.B. 1977. What is fibre and fibre in food.

Nutrition Reviews **35**: 12-22.

Van Soest, P.J. 1965a. Use of detergents in analyses of fibrous feeds. II. A rapid method for the determination of fiber and lignin. *Journal of the Association of Official Agricultural Chemists* **46**: 829-835.

Van Soest, P.J. 1965b. Use of detergents in analyses of fibrous feeds. III. Study of effects of heating and drying on yields of fiber and lignin in feeds. *Journal of the Association of Official Agricultural Chemists* **48**: 785-791.

Van Soest, P.J. and Mason, V.C. 1991. The influence of the Maillard reaction upon the nutritive value of fibrous feeds. *Animal Feed Science and Technology* **32**: 45-53.

Van Soest, P.J. and Wine, R.H. 1967. Use of detergents in analysis of fibrous feeds. IV. *Journal of the Association of Official Agricultural Chemists* **50**: 50-55.

Van Soest, P.J., Robertson, J.B. and Lewis, B.A. 1991. Methods for dietary fibre; neutral detergent fibre, and non starch polysaccharides in relation to animal nutrition. *Journal of Dairy Science* **74**: 3583-3597.

Van Weeren, P.R. and Barneveld, A. 1999. Study design to evaluate the influence of exercise on the development of the musculoskeletal system of foals up to age 11 months. *Equine Veterinary Journal* **31**: 4-8.

Van Weeren, P.R. and Barneveld, A. 1999. The effect of exercise on the distribution and manifestation of osteochondrotic lesions in the Warmblood foal. *Equine Veterinary Journal* **31**: 16-25.

Van Weeren, P.R., Sloet Van Oldruitenborgh-Oosterbaan, M.M. and Barneveld, A. 1999. The influence of birth weight, rate of weight gain and final achieved height and sex on the development of osteochondrotic lesions in a population of genetically predisposed Warmblood foals. *Equine Veterinary Journal* **31**: 26-30.

Van Weeren, P.R., Knaap, J. and Firth, E.C. 2003. Influence of liver copper status of mare and newborn foal on the development of osteochondrotic lesions. *Equine Veterinary Journal* **35**: 67-71.

Vandenput, S., Istasse, L., Nicks, B., Lekeux, P. 1997. Airborne dust and aeroallergen concentrations in different sources of feed and bedding for horses. *Veterinary Quarterly* **19**: 154-158.

Vander Noot, G.W., Symons, L.D., Lydman, R.K. and Fonnesbeck, P.V. 1967. Rate of passage of various feedstuffs through the digestive tract of horses. *Journal of Animal Science* **26**: 1309-1311.

Vander Noot, G.W. and Trout, J.R. 1971. Prediction of digestible components of forages by equines. *Journal of Animal Science* **33**: 38-41.

VanDierendonck M.C., Devries H. and Schilder M.B.H. 1995. An analysis of dominance, its behavioural parameters and possible determinants in a herd of Icelandic horses in captivity. *Netherlands Journal of Zoology* **45**: 362-385.

VanDierendonck M.C., Bandi N., Batdorj D., Dugerlham S. and Munkhtsog B., 1996. Behavioural observations of reintroduced Takhi or Przewalski horses (Equus Ferus Przewalskii) in Mongolia. *Applied Animal Behaviour Science* **50**: 95-114.

Vecchioti, G. and Galanti, R., 1986. Evidence of heredity of cribbing, weaving and stall-walking in Thoroughbred horses. *Livestock Production Science* **14**: 91-95.

Vermeer C., Jie, K.S.G. and Knapen, M.H.J. 1995. Role of vitamin K in bone metabolism. *Annual Reviews in Nutrition* **15**: 1-22

Vincent, J.F.V. 1990. Fracture properties of plants. *Advances in Botanical Research* **17**: 235-287.

Visser E.K., Reenen van C.G., Hopster H., Schilder M.B.H., Knaap J.H., Barneveld A. and Blokhuis H.J., 2001. Quantifying aspects of young horses' temperament: consistency of behavioural variables. *Applied Animal Behaviour Science* **74**: 241-258.

Voss, J.L. and B.W. Picket. 1974. Effect of a nutritional supplement on pregnancy rate in nonlactating mares. *Journal of the American Veterinary Medicine Association* **165**:702.

Vusse van der, G., and Groot, de M.J. 1992. Interrelationsship between lactate and cardiac fatty acid metabolism. *Molecular and Cellular Biochemistry* **116**: 11-17.

Van 't Klooster AT, Hallebeek JM, Beynen AC. 1999. Nutrition of horses: digestion, energy and protein evaluation and nutritional standards. *Tijdschr Diergeneeskd* **124**: 401-405.

Vermorel, M. and Martin-Rosset, W. 1997c Concepts, scientific basis, structure and validation of the French horse net energy system (UFC). *Livestock Production Science* **47**: 261-275.

Vermorel, M., Martin-Rosset, W. and Vernet, J. 1997a Energy utilisation of twelve forages or mixed diets for maintenance by sport horses. *Livestock Production Sciences* **47**: 157-167.

Vermeer, C. and Ulrich, M. 1992. Vitamin K-dependent carboxylase in horse liver, spleen and kidney. *Thrombosis Research* **28**: 71.

Vermorel, M., Vernet, J. and Martin-Rosset, W. 1997b. Digestive and energy utilisation of two diets by ponies and horses. *Livestock Production Science* **51**: 13-19.

Vernet, J., Vermorel, M. and Martin-Rosset, W. 1995. Energy cost of eating long hay, straw and pelleted food in sport horses. *Animal Science* **61**: 581-588.

Voit, E. 1901. Uber die Grosse des Energiebedarfs der Tiere im Hungerzustande. *Zeitschrift der Biologie* 41: 113.

W

Waldo, D.R. 1984. Effect of forage quality on intake and forage-concentrate interactions, *Journal of Dairy Science* **69**: 617-631.

Waldo, D.R., Smith, L.W., Cox, E.L., Weinland, B.T., and Lucal, H.L. 1971. Logarithmic normal description of sieved forage materials. *Journal of Dairy Science* **54**: 1465-1469.

Waran N.K. and Cuddeford D. 1995. Effects of loading and transport on the heart rate and behaviour of horses. *Applied Animal Behaviour Science* **43**: 71-81.

Waran N.K., Robertson V., Cuddeford D., Kokoszko A. and Marlin D.J. 1996. Effects of transporting horses facing either forwards or backwards on their behaviour and heart rate. *Veterinary Record* **139**: 7-11.

Waring G.H. 2002. Horse Behavior. The behavioral traits and adaptations of domestic and wild horses, including ponies. Noyes, New Jersey, USA.

Warren, L.K., Lawrence, L.M., Parker, A.L., Barnes, T. and Griffin, A.S. 1998. The effect of weaning age on foal growth and radiographic bone density. *Journal of Equine Veterinary Science* **18**: 335-339.

Waters, A.J., Nicol, C.J. and French, N.P. 2002. Factors influencing the development of stereotypic and redirected behaviours in young horses: Findings of a four year prospective epidemiological study. *Equine Veterinary Journal* **34**: 572-579.

Watson, T. 1998. Metabolic and Endocrine Problems of the Horse. Harcourt Brace and Company Ltd, London.

Webb, S.P., Potter, G.D., Evans, J.W. and Webb, G.W. 1991. Influence of body fat content on digestible energy requirements of exercising horses in temperate and hot environments. *Equine Veterinary Science* **10**: 116-120.

Webster, A.J.F., Clarke, A.F., Madelin, T.M. and Wathes, C.M. 1987. Air hygiene in stables 1. Design, ventilation and management on the concentration of respirable dust. *Equine Veterinary Journal* **19**: 448-453.

Wehr, U., Englschalk, B., Kienzle, E. and Rambeck, W.A. 2002. Iodine balance in relation to iodine intake in ponies. *Journal of Nutrition* **132**: 1767-1768.

Weiss, D.J., Evanson, O.A., MacLeay, J. and Brown, D. 1998. Transient alteration in intestinal permeability to technecium Tc99m diethylene triaminopentaacetate during the prodromal stages of alimentary laminitis in horses. *American Journal of Veterinary Research* **59**: 1431-1433.

Weisweiler, B., Twehues, R., Kucza, A., Meyer, H. and Harmeyer, J. 1993. Einfluss hoher Vitamin-D-Dosierungen auf Ca-, Mg- und P-Stoffwechsel von Pferden. *Pferdeheilkunde* **9**: 343-352.

Welch, J.G. and Smith, A.M. 1978. Particle sizes passed from the rumen. *Journal of Animal Science* **46**: 1.

Wentik, G.H., Duivelshof, J.A.M. and Counotte, G.H.M. 1988 Selenium deficiency as a cause of retained placentae. *Tijdschrift voor Diergeneeskunde* **113**: 624-626.

Wichert, B., Frank, T. and Kienzle, E. 2002. Zinc, Copper and Selenium Intake and Status of Horses in Bavaria. *Journal of Nutrition* **132**: 1776-1777.

Whitten W.K. 1985. Vomeronasal organ and the accessory olfactory system. *Applied Animal Behaviour Science* **14**: 105-109.

Willard, J.G., Willard, J.C. Wolfram, S.A. and Baker, J.P. 1977. Effect of diet on caecal pH and feeding behaviour of horses. *Journal of Animal Science* **45**: 87-93.

Williams, C.H., David, D.J. and Iismaa, O. 1962. The determination of chromic oxide in faeces samples by atomic absorption spectrophotometry. *Journal of Agricultural Science* **59**: 381-385.

Willoughby, R.A, McDonald E., McSherry, B.J. and Brown, G. 1972 Lead and zinc poisoning and the interaction between Pb and Zn poisoning in the foal. *Canadian Journal of Comparative Medicine* **36**: 348-359.

Wilson, J.R., Akin, D.E., McCleod, M.N. and Minson, D.J. 1989a. Particle size reduction of leaves of a tropical and a temporate grass by cattle. II. Relation of anatomical structure to the process of leaf breakdown through chewing and digestion. *Grass and Forage Science* **44**: 65-75.

Wilson, J.R., McCleod, M.N. and Minson, D.J. 1989b. Particle size reduction of leaves of a tropical and a temporate grass by cattle. I. Effect of chewing during eating and varying times of digestion. *Grass and Forage Science* **44**: 55-63.

Winchester, C.F. 1943. The energy cost of standing. *Science* **97**: 24.

Witte, S.T., Will, L.A., Olsen, C.R., Kinker, J.A., Miller-Graber, P. 1993. Chronic selenosis in horses fed locally produced alfalfa hay. *Journal of American Veterinary Medical Association* **202**: 406-409.

Wolfe, R.R. 2000. Protein supplements and exercise. *American Journal of*

Clinical Nutrition **72**: 551S-557.
Wolter, R. 1984. La digestion chez le cheval. In: *Le Cheval*. R. Jarrige and W. Martin-Rosset (eds). INRA, Paris, France.
Wolter, R. and Chaarbouni, A. 1979. Etude de la digestion de l'amidon chez cheval par analyse du contenu digestif apres abattage. *Revue Medecine Veterinaire* **130**: 1345-1357.
Wolter, R. Durix, A. and Letourneau, J.C. 1974. Influence du mode de presentation due fourage sur la vitesse du transit digestif chez le poney, *Annale Zootechnique* **23**: 293-300.
Wolter, R. Gouy, D. Durix, A. Letourneau, J.C., Carcelen, M. and Landreau, J. 1978. Digestibilite et activite beiochimique intracaecale chel le poney recevant un meme aliment complet expansee ou semi-expansee. *Annale Zootechnique* **27**: 47-60.
Wolter, R., Nouwakpo, F., and Durix, A. 1980. Etude comparative de la digestion d'un aliment complet chez le poney et le lapin. *Reproduction.Nutrition and Development* **20**: 1723-1730.
Wolter, R. Durix, A. and Letourneau, J.C. 1975 Influence du mode de presentation du fourrage sur la digestibilite chez le poney. *Annale Zootechnique* **24**: 237-242.
Wolters, M.G.E., Diepenmaat, H.B., Hermus, R.J.J. and Voragen, A.G.J. 1993. Relation between in vitro avialability of minerals and food composition: A mathematical model. *Journal of Food Science* **58**: 1349-1355.
Woodbury, M.R., Fiest, M.S., Clark, E.G. and Haigh, J.C. 1999. Osteochondrosis and epiphyseal abnormalities associated with copper deficiency in bison calves. *Canadian Veterinary Journal* **40**: 878-880.
Wooden, G.R., Knox, K. and Wild, C.L. 1970. Energy metabolism of light horses. *Journal of Animal Science* **30**: 544-548.
Wright, W. and Illius, A.W. 1995. A comparative study of the fracture properties of five grasses. *Functional Ecology* **9**: 269-278.

X

Xu, T.S., Soares, J.H. and Xu, T.S. 1998. Molecular aspects of tibula dyschondroplasia in the chicken. *Nutrition Research* **18**: 809-822.

Y

Yamaguchi, M. and Takahashi, J. 1984. Role of zinc as an activator of bone metabolism in weanling rats. *Journal of Bone and Mineral Metabolism* **2**: 186-191.

References

Yang, P. and Klimis-Tavantzis, D.J. 1998. Manganese deficiency alters arterial glycosaminoglycan structure in the Sprague-Dawley rat. *Journal of Nutrition and Biochemistry* **9**: 324-331.

Yoakam, S.C., Kirkham, W.W. and Beeson W. M. 1978. Effect of protein level on growth in young ponies. *Journal of Animal Science* **46**: 983-991.

Younglove, G.A., Gibbs, P.G., Potter G.D., Murray-Gerzik, M. and Dorsett, D.J. 1994. Comparative feeding value of cubed alfalfa: Corn plant product as an exclusive diet for exercising horses. *Journal of Equine Veterinary Science* **14**: 598-602.

Yagi, K. 1994. Flavins and Flavoproteins. Walter de Gruyter, New York, USA.

Yang, M.G., Manoharan, K. And Mickelsen, O. 1970. Nutritional contribution of volatile fatty acids from the cecum of rats. *Journal of Nutrition* **100**: 545-550.

Yoakam, S.C., Kirkham, W.W. and Beeson W.M. 1978. Effect of protein level on growth in young ponies. *Journal of Animal Science* **46**: 983-991.

Z

Zeisel, S. 1997. Choline: essential for brain development and function. *Advances in. Pediatrics* **44**: 263-295.

Zeyner, A. 1995. Ermittlung des Gehalts an verdaulicher Energie im Pferdefutter über die Verdaulichkeitsschätzung. *Übers. Tierernährung* **23**: 55-104.

Zeyner, A., 1993. Untersuchungen zur Schatzung des Energiegehaltes in Rationen fur Pferde. *Proceedings of the Society of Nutrition and Physiology* **1**: 95.

Zeyner, A., Hoffmann, M. und Fuchs, R. 1992. Moglichkeiten zur Schatzung des Energiegehaltes in Rationen zur Sportpferdefutterung (Sonderausgabe) pp. 175-178.

Zuntz, N. and Hagemann, O. 1898. Untersuchungen über den Stoffwechsel des Pferdes bei Ruhe und Arbeit. *Land. Jahrb.* **27**: 3.

Zeeb K. and Schnitzer U., 1997. Housing and training of horses according to their species-specifiec behaviour, Elaboration from the German Ministry for Nutrition, Agriculture and Forestry – Guidelines 'Animal Protection concerning Horse Management and concerning Sport Horses', Livestock Production Science **49**: 181-189.

Zeitler-Feicht M.H. and Prantner V., 2000. Recumbence Resting Behaviour of Horses in Loose Housing Systems With Open Yards. Archiv Fur

Tierzucht - Archives of Animal Breeding **43** (4): 327-335.

Zemmelink, G., 1980, Effect of selective consumption on voluntary intake and digestibility of tropical forages, Department of Tropical Animal Production, 1980, Agricultural Research Reports, No 896.

Zuntz, N. and Hagemann, O. 1898. Untersuchungen über den Stoffwechsel des Pferdes bei Ruhe und Arbeit. *Land. Jahrb.* **27**: 3.

Index

A

acidosis 27,50,190
acid-base balance 184,190,198
acid detergent fibre (ADF) 31,53,79,99
amino acids
  absorption 36,170,171
  essential (EAA) 63,160,170,178
  in diet 7,61-63,159,160
  metabolism 139
  non-essential (NEAA) 63,160
  requirements 171,172,175
apparent digestibility determination 83,84,97

B

behaviour
  eating 22
  natural 255,256,258
  stereotypic 6,59,257

C

caecum 5,8,9,38
carbohydrate
  and performance 145,146
  digestion 7
  non-structural 44-52,78
  soluble 4,31,78
  structural 13,32,44,52-60
cellulose
  herbivore diet 3
  plant cell wall 66
  structure 53,54
  voluntary feed intake 29
colic 41,50
colon 5,8,9,41,42
concentrate feed 74,75
  and behaviour 59
  feed intake 29,60
  high levels in diet 4
  mastication 20
  stabled horses 69
crib-biting 6

D

diarrhoea 50
dietary fibre 16,35,169
  solubility 33,37
  utilisation 4,39
  varying levels in diet 3,33
digesta passage
  carbohydrate digestion 57-59
  comparison with rumen 55
  markers 89-92
  measurements 89-96
  retention times of digesta 89-96
  variability 97-99,168
digestive physiology
  in comparison to ruminants 2,4
digestive tract
  anatomy 7—42
dry matter (DM) 44
  acquisition 10
  intake 29
duodenum (*see also small intestine*) 7,34

E

electrolytes (*see also minerals*) 201,203
energy
  balance 37,56
  expenditure during work 146-155
  high levels in diet 65
  metabolic body weight 120
  metabolism
    and protein 139,140
    and fats 140-146

net energy (NE) 22,114-118,128,129
predicting energy values of feed 101-118
  gross, digestible energy (GE, DE) 105-110,151
  metabolisable energy (ME) 110-114
requirements
  comparing recommendations 156-158
  maintenance 119-129
  work 130-139
sources 55,64,65
enzymes
  and minerals 194,210,211,224
  carbohydrases 4,52
  exogenous, in the diet 52
  in the small intestine 35
  proteases 32,62
  protein metabolism 159-161
  salivary 16
  secretion 7
equine polysaccharide storage myopathy (EPSM) 143

F

fats 64-66
  characterisation 81,82
  digestion 32,65,66
  high levels in diet 141
fatty acids 7,64,141,142
feed
  characterisation 75-82
  classification 69,70
  evaluation 82-87
  ingestion process 12
  intake levels 12,66
  moisture levels 13,16
  pelleting 20
  physiochemical properties 66-68
  presentation 87-89
  raw materials 20,26,75
  retention time 40
  sensory perception 11

fermentation 5,7,33,169
  comparison with rumen 5
foal
  feed intake 12,13,177,178
  minerals 192,194,197,198,222
  saliva 15
forage
  acquisition 10
  digestibility trials 13
  particle size 24
  utilisation 4
  voluntary intake 13

G

gastrointestinal tract 4
glucosamine 207,208
glucose
  amylase 35,36,52
  non-structural polysaccharides 45-48,52
  muscles and exercise 140-144
  production from VFA 55
  starch digestion 35,36,41
  voluntary diet intake 29
glycogen 141-144
  glycogenolysis 180
grass 23,28,52,66,73
grazing 10

H

hay 70-73
  chopped 28,67
  digestion 59,66
  haylage 57,69
  mastication 20,23,25
  soaked 12
hind gut 27,63,166,170

I

ileum (see also small intestine) 7,9,36
  protein digestion 36
insulin 29,141,142

Index

J

jejunum *(see also small intestine)* 7,9,36

L

lameness
  mineral deficiency 181,219,224,234
laminitis 47,49,50,52,62
large intestine
  anatomy 9,37-41
  and dietary fibre 37
  fermentation 37
legumes 28,53,198
lignin 39,44,52-60,66

M

maintenance requirements*(see also minerals)*
  energy 119-129
  protein 172-175
mastication 66,67,127
micro organisms
  and fibre 4
  fermentation by 5,7,33,169
  mouth 16
  physiology 5
  stomach 15,31
minerals
  calcium
    absorption 183
    bone structure 182187-189,192
    deficiency/toxicity 183
    mineral interactions 183,188
    muscle function 180-182
    parathyroid hormone (PTH) 189-192
    requirements 185,186,192,193
    vitamin interactions 182,187,193
  chromium 238,239
  cobalt 237,238
  copper 210-216
  fluorine 233,234

iodine 231-233
iron 227-231
magnesium
  function 194-196
  requirements 196-198
manganese 224-226
molybdenum 226,227
of feeds 43,70
phosphorus 180-194
  acid-base balance 184
  parathyroid hormone 190,191
  phytate 184
  requirements 185-188,192,193
saliva 17,18
selenium 234,237
small intestine 35
sodium potassium and chlorine
  acid base balance 198,200,201
  function 199
  requirements 202,204
sulphur
  function 205
  glucosaminoglycans 206-208
  requirements 208,209
zinc 218-224
muscles
  and energy 130-133
  and protein 175-177
  biochemistry 134-139,180
  glycogen 141-144
  mineral deficiencies 180,181
  zinc 218

N

neutral detergent fibre (NDF) 53,79,99
  apparent digestibility 29,31,39
non-starch polysaccharide (NSP) 53

O

obesity 29
oesophagus 29

olfaction 10,11,26
osteochondrosis 214-216
osteoporosis 181

P

palatability 12
  choice tests 13
protein
  digestion 4,36,61-63,160-163,166-171
  high levels in diet 5
  nitrogen metabolism 159,160
  requirements 139,140
    growth 177,178
    maintenance 172-175
    work 175-177
  structure 163-165
  urea cycle 63
proteoglycan 188,206-208

R

rickets 181,182
roughage 3,51,60,69
  and saliva 14,44

S

saliva
  and digestion 31
  composition 16,18
  salivary glands 14,16
  stimulation of 16,21
  processes 16,17
silage 25,66,70-73
small intestine
  anatomy 7,8
  comparison to ruminants 27,30
  digestion 34-37,62,166,168
  fermentation 57
starch (*see also carbohydrates*)
  apparent digestibility 26,31
  digestion 35,36,41,46,48,49,51
  degradation, enzymes 36,46,47
  high levels in diet 6,33,49,59
  role in diet 3
stomach
  anatomy 4,7-10,30,35
  particle size 34
straw 20,73

T

taste 11
  and digestible energy 12
  choice tests 13
  specific flavours 12
taxonomy and evolution 1 3
teeth
  and age 19
  and forage 18
  and feed intake 22,23
  dentition 18,19
  incisors 10,19
  mastication 19-21
  molars 19
  problems with 20,22,23,234
thoroughbred 192
tongue 11

V

vitamins
  fat soluble
    vitamin A 64,187,241-243
    vitamin D 64,182,193,243,244
    vitamin E 64,244,245
    vitamin K 64,245,426
  pre-mixes 70
  water soluble 246-252
    choline 251,252
    vitamin B complex 246-251
    vitamin C (ascorbic acid) 251
volatile fatty acids (VFA)
  and feed intake 29

Index

and methane 41
production 31,33,39,41,53,55,57,65

W

water 5,42,179,203
weaving 6,257
welfare 6,253-258
wind-sucking 6,257

www.ingramcontent.com/pod-product-compliance
Lightning Source LLC
Chambersburg PA
CBHW070748230426
43665CB00017B/2296